GERHARD HERZBERG

An Illustrious Life in Science

Gerhard Herzberg

GERHARD HERZBERG

An Illustrious Life in Science

Boris Stoicheff

NRC·CNRC
NRC Press
Ottawa

McGill–Queen's University Press
Montreal & Kingston • London • Ithaca

Printed in Canada on acid-free paper.
ISSN 1701-1833
ISBN 0-660-18757-4
NRC No. 44462

National Library of Canada cataloguing in publication data
Stoicheff, B. (Boris), 1924–
Gerhard Herzberg: an illustrious life in science

(NRC Press biography series, No. 1, ISSN 1701-1833)
Co-published by McGill-Queen's University Press.
Includes bibliographical references.
Issued by the National Research Council of Canada.
ISBN-0-660-18757-4

1. Herzberg, Gerhard, 1904–1999. 2. Spectrum analysis — History.
3. Molecular spectroscopy — History. 4. Physicists — Canada — Biography.
5. Scientists — Canada — Biography.
I. National Research Council Canada. II. Title III. Series.

QC16.H47S86 2002 530′.092 C2002-980029-3

Inquiries: Monograph Publishing Program, NRC Press, National Research Council of Canada, Ottawa, Ontario K1A 0R6, Canada.
Web site: www.monographs.nrc.ca

Correct citation for this publication: Stoicheff, B. 2002. *Gerhard Herzberg: An Illustrious Life in Science*. NRC Press, Ottawa, Ontario, Canada. 468 pp.

Dedicated to my wife Joan

CONTENTS

FOREWORD

Gerhard Herzberg was a great scientist whose eventful life spanned most of the twentieth century. He began his research in Germany at a time when the new quantum mechanics was just beginning to unravel the mysteries of the microscopic world. He became one of the founders of modern spectroscopy, the study of spectra, the most accurate and intricate fingerprints of atoms and molecules. Spectroscopy played a central role in the development of modern science, and Herzberg dedicated his life to its development. He made many experimental and theoretical discoveries and was responsible for systematizing the field. His textbook *Atomic Spectra and Atomic Structure* and the three-volume monograph *Molecular Spectra and Molecular Structure* became the "bible" for spectroscopically oriented physicists, chemists, and astronomers. His laboratory in Ottawa, Canada, became the scientific mecca for a generation of spectroscopists, and he is aptly called the founding father of molecular spectroscopy. We benefited not only from Herzberg's dedication to science, but also from his commitment to humanity; his enthusiasm and sincerity inspired those of us who were lucky enough to be associated with him. I am thrilled that this biography will inform a wider audience about this great man, his work, and his humanity.

Boris Stoicheff, the author of this biography, belonged to Herzberg's research group at the National Research Council (NRC) in Ottawa from 1951 to 1964, first as a postdoctoral fellow and then as a staff member. He is 20 years younger than Herzberg and is famous in the field for his pioneering contributions to Raman spectroscopy and later to non-linear optics. He knew Herzberg closely in his early years, but he also worked with other great scientists, and this gives him both great insight and perspective. In fact, more than 30 years ago, the ever-prescient Herzberg himself "appointed" Stoicheff as his biographer. He knew of Stoicheff's love of reading biographies and histories of science, as well as his excellence as a writer and his scholarly accuracy to details. Herzberg must also have sensed Stoicheff's genuine admiration for him as a scientist and a person. Stoicheff's love and respect for Herzberg, his expertise in science, and his knowledge of people in the field, as well as his insights into Canadian science policy, make him Herzberg's ideal biographer. The knowledge of and love and respect for our predecessors is a pillar of our civilization, and this book is a great contribution to both science and humanity.

Professor T. Oka
The Enrico Fermi Institute
The University of Chicago

PROLOGUE

It was the afternoon of November 2nd, 1971, and Gerhard Herzberg, sitting on the Moscow Express, wondered about the delay in leaving the Leningrad Station. He had been brought to the train on this cold and damp day with much fanfare by scientific colleagues of Leningrad University. They carried his bags, saw him settled comfortably at a reserved window seat, and waved cheerfully as the "All Aboard" sounded. But the train remained motionless, as restless passengers continually checked their watches. Soon he became aware of some commotion on the platform as a burly figure was hurriedly guided by a conductor, gesturing to Herzberg's car and cabin. The next moment, Herzberg was being addressed by a breathless man who removed his fur hat and stood at attention. "Professor Herzberg, I am the Secretary of the Soviet Academy of Science, and I have the honour to report that you have been awarded the Nobel Prize in Physics." With these words, the Secretary shook hands with Herzberg and quickly stepped off the train as it began moving.

So it was that Gerhard Herzberg of the National Research Council of Canada first learned of the supreme scientific accolade, while far away from home and alone. He was on a train to Moscow, left with his own thoughts for six hours among strangers who knew little if any English, and he no Russian. They obviously did not understand the hurried message, and he could not share his pleasure, somewhat tinged with bewilderment, that the award, if true, was in physics. Of course, he was a physicist, yet one with many interests in chemical and astrophysical problems. All of his studies and university degrees were in physics. He had spent ten years at the Physics Institute of the Technische Hochschule in Darmstadt and another ten as a faculty member of the Physics Department at the University of Saskatchewan. He had been at the National Research Council (NRC) in Ottawa since 1948, where he served as Director of the Pure Physics Division for two decades. Yet he knew that his books on atomic and molecular spectra and structures, and his latest discoveries in free radicals, were of more immediate interest to chemists and to chemistry. So why, if true, the Prize in Physics?

Normally, while travelling by plane or train, with time on his hands, Herzberg would review his upcoming visit, recall the scientists he was most likely to meet, and then try to catch up on reading recent publications in his many areas of scientific interest. But none of this was possible at this moment, nor could he rest. Today's news upset his usual sense of discipline and overwhelmed his very being. Past events flooded his mind.

The untimely death of his wife Luise, barely six months before, was foremost in his thoughts, along with her support for almost forty-two years and especially her courage on their leaving Germany during the dark days of the Nazi regime. Over the years, they had collaborated in research and co-authored many papers on molecular spectra. From their earliest time together, with his concentration on science, Luise was his window to the world. But no more. Since her death he was isolated from the day's happenings and was as lonely as he now felt in this train compartment with strangers. As night quickly fell, the enveloping darkness added to this cheerless atmosphere and kindled his memories of family hardships during the tumultuous years of his youth.

Only as the train sped through the brightly lit city of Novgorod did this emptiness leave him to be replaced by more genial thoughts. He recalled that it was his good fortune to start scientific work just as the new quantum theory was developing, with rapid applications to atomic and molecular problems. He had matured as a scientist in the right place at the right time, namely in Germany in the 1920s, and he cherished the memory of his outstanding mentors. A year in Göttingen, the world centre of mathematics and physics, gave him the opportunity to meet and work with some of the greatest scientific minds of that era. Best of all, he met Luise there. He also enjoyed his year in Bristol, where he met many of the English physicists and chemists. Then came an exciting five-year period during which he developed his own research laboratory in Darmstadt with eager students and visitors from abroad. But conditions in Germany deteriorated rapidly with the Nazis in power, and in 1935 he finally found a safe haven in Saskatoon on the Canadian prairies, where he and Luise were warmly welcomed. They quickly fell in love with Canada and, having decided that Canada was to be their home, raised a son and daughter. He remembered that at the University of Saskatchewan, everything possible was done to enable him to pursue his beloved spectroscopy and to write two volumes of his trilogy *Molecular Spectra and Molecular Structure*. After ten happy years there, he had the good fortune to fulfill a boyhood dream of being an astronomer. He felt that his three years at Yerkes Observatory of The University of Chicago, working among the world's top astrophysicists, were most productive.

Then he was given the extraordinary opportunity to establish a major spectroscopy laboratory at the NRC in Ottawa with unstinting encouragement by two of its Presidents, C. Jack Mackenzie and E.W.R. (Ned) Steacie. He made the most of it. His laboratory became the "Mecca" for molecular studies and attracted aspiring young scientists from around the world as well as visits from the major players in the field. A succession of important results followed, and he felt that the pinnacle of his own research had been reached with the pioneering work on free radicals. But lately, with continual reviews by government committees and drastically reduced budgets for research, the atmosphere at the NRC was changing. He wondered what would be the final outcome of the new Senate Committee hearings on Science Policy. So far this committee had severely and unfairly criticized the operation of the NRC, whereas the NRC was acclaimed throughout the world as one of the major institutes of fundamental and applied science and engineering. He recalled a brief meeting a few months earlier, when Bill Schneider, President of the NRC, told him that the future for basic research in the laboratories looked bleak, but that an award of a Nobel Prize might save the NRC.

Herzberg's mood of foreboding immediately changed as the long expanse of bright lights signalled his arrival in Moscow. He was delighted to be greeted at the station by his friends S.L. Mandelstam and I.I. Sobel'man, who congratulated him on being awarded the Nobel Prize in Chemistry. The news that it was the prize in chemistry was confirmed by laudatory telegrams from NRC President Schneider and from the Nobel Foundation and by the bustling members of the U.S.S.R. radio and TV media. Now Herzberg could believe that the Nobel Prize was indeed his; it set his mind at rest as he was whisked to Mandelstam's apartment for a quiet celebratory evening.

PART ONE

THE EARLY YEARS (1904–1934)

The most beautiful thing we can experience is the mysterious.
It is the source of all true art and science.

Albert Einstein

1. FAMILY AND EARLY EDUCATION

Family and Childhood[1]

In later years, when Gerhard Herzberg was reminded that he shared a very famous birthday, he replied with his hearty laugh, "Yes, with Sir Isaac Newton." Gerhard was born on 25 December 1904 in Osdorf, Pinneberg, a northwestern suburb of the "Free City" of Hamburg, Germany. He was the younger son of Albin and Ella Herzberg, his brother Walter having been born in January of the same year. This was a middle-class family, with Albin Herzberg working as the assistant manager of a small manufacturing and exporting company in Hamburg. Nominally of Evangelist Lutheran denomination, Gerhard's parents rarely attended church and attached no special significance to the day of his birth. As a child, Gerhard quickly realized that being born on Christmas Day meant missing out on birthday parties and extra gifts.

Gerhard later learned from a cousin that the Herzberg genealogy could be traced back eleven generations to 1573 through the records of two Lutheran churches in the town of Langensalza where the Herzberg families had lived for almost four hundred years. Joachim Hertzbergk (eventually Herzberg) was first on the list. He had apparently changed his name from Hans Quatmer,[2] and although this change suggested a connection with the nearby city of Herzberg, according to the city archivist, none has been found. All of the Herzbergs had been born in Langensalza and lived there until Albin's move to Hamburg. Albin was born on 12 April 1872, the sixth child in a family of five sisters and two brothers. His father, Franz Otto Herzberg, and mother, Anna Sophia Christina Kürsten, were both born in Langensalza, where Franz Otto spent his life as a merchant. Albin was not a healthy youth, and friends convinced him to become a vegetarian for the good of his health. As luck would have it, he met Ella Biber at a social gathering of vegetarians in Hamburg and they soon married.

Ella was seventeen when she married Albin, thirteen years her senior, in Hamburg in November of 1902, and so she came into new family responsibilities at a young age. Ella was born in Hamburg on 7 July 1885

Gerhard and Walter, 1906

The Herzberg Family, 1910

and became accustomed to heavy responsibilities with the death of her mother when she was only seven years old. Henrietta Maria died at the age of thirty-five, leaving Ella and her sisters Marie, Henny, and Anni in the care of their father, Rudolf Alber Biber. Biber, a master glazier in Hamburg, was overtly religious and raised the girls as vegetarians. Soon after Ella's marriage, Biber emigrated to Canada and, after spending a few years in Vancouver, settled in Seattle, Washington.

At the turn of the century, Langensalza was a town of about 12,500 inhabitants, mainly Protestants. It was built along the Salza River near its juncture with the Unstrut River, in the plains of Thuringia, just east of a heavily forested region and south of the Hartz Mountains, near the larger cities of Eisenach, Erfurt, and Weimar. Langensalza was situated along north–south and east–west trade routes and prospered with the mining of travertine, weaving and cloth making, and the cultivation of woad, a plant from which blue pigment was extracted.

Young Gerhard spent several summers in Langensalza where he stayed with his aunts, the widow Ida and spinster Anna Marie (called Mimi by Gerhard), who lived in an apartment above his favourite bakery at 7 Kornmarkt Strasse. His grandparents, Franz Otto and Anna Sophia, lived nearby at 16 Marktkirche beside St. Bonifacii Church, but he didn't come to know them well as they had died by the time he was five. Gerhard explored the town's extensive medieval walls and watch towers and old Dryburg Castle, the home of Hermann von Salza, who was the grand master of the Teutonic Order in the early thirteenth century and under whom the order rose to prominence. Gerhard spent a summer accompanying Herr Griem, an artisan friend of his aunts, on long walks to several townships as he plied his trade and took orders for goods to be delivered on future trips. Among the nearby towns they visited was Eisenach, twenty-eight kilometres away, the birthplace of Johann Sebastian Bach in 1685 and the site of Wartburg Castle, where Martin Luther sought safety in 1521 and translated the New Testament into German. The castle was also noted for its *Sängerkrieg*, the contests of knights, poets, and singers of courtly love, later used by Richard Wagner in the opera *Tannhäuser*. Langensalza's medieval atmosphere attracted the romantic poets Klopstock, Novalis, and Brentano in the late eighteenth century, who together with Goethe and Schiller in nearby Weimar were the acknowledged cultural inspiration for Germany at that

"Even a Nobel Prize winner once wore a sailor's suit
and played [cowboys and] Indians", according to Walter Herzberg.

time. It was also Langensalza's historic fate to be the location of a major battle of the Austro-Prussian Wars in 1866, where King George V of Hannover lost his kingdom to Otto von Bismarck of Prussia, who then united Germany in 1871.

Gerhard was the sole Herzberg to be given that Christian name over the four centuries of the Herzberg family, with most having the name Heinrich, Friedrich, or Otto. Not surprisingly, he was christened Gerhard Heinrich Friedrich Otto Julius on 9 July 1905, with all four godfathers, who were friends and relatives, present at the ceremony. In view of his own failing health following heart problems, Albin chose this many godfathers for both of his sons to ensure that they would be looked after. The christening took place in St. Gertrudkirche along the Eilbekkanal where Gerhard was confirmed fifteen years later. Albin Herzberg was anxious that his two sons have the best education possible. Because they lived in the bustling city of Hamburg, Albin recognized the need for a much better education than he had or than was the custom of the Herzbergs living in Langensalza. In fact, there was no indication whatsoever of past academic pursuits or any university connections in the family. Gerhard's great-grandfather, Friedrich Wilhelm, was a wound-dresser, and Uncle Karl apprenticed in chemistry and became the resident chemist of a sugar factory in Austria. There seemed to be even less educational tradition in Ella Biber's family.

In his late teens, Albin left Langensalza to seek employment in Hamburg and remained there for the rest of his short life. In time, he earned a reasonable income, paid taxes, and owned real estate and was entitled as a Bürger to vote for members of the Hamburg Parliament. The Free and Hanseatic City of Hamburg, situated on the Elbe and Alster rivers about one hundred kilometres from the North Sea, was Germany's largest city and Europe's busiest port. It developed into a city of canals, with twin lakes at its centre, the Binnenalster (Inner Alster) and the Aussenalster (Outer Alster), ringed by parks and many old churches. Hamburg originated in the ninth century and became a member of the Hanseatic League of medieval German towns that together provided security for merchant trading with foreign lands at a time when Germany lacked a strong national government. The city grew rapidly to become an industrial and shipping centre of great wealth and remains so today. With its many shipping and import and export offices, Hamburg seemed to be an ideal location to find employment for anyone unsuited to heavy labour, as was Albin's lot. He was successful in finding a job in the central offices of Fred C. Jenkins, Hamburg, a fabri-

Downtown Hamburg, with the Inner and Outer Alster Lakes.

cator and distributor of specialty electrical products, and was quickly promoted to become its assistant manager at the age of twenty-two.

Since the Herzbergs were reasonably well-off, the family moved to an apartment on the elegant Isestrasse so that the boys could attend the highly recommended Vorschule (part of the Oberrealschule of Eppendorf) on Hegestrasse, just two blocks away from their apartment. The Vorschule of that period was equivalent to our elementary school, the difference being that the school year began in April and the program lasted four years. Children started school at age six, but a case of measles delayed the entry of Gerhard for a year, and he finally started school in 1911. Two years later, the family moved to a house in Langenhorn at the north end of the city, and the boys went to school on the new metro line, which had a station stop near their school. Because Ella was musically inclined, a piano was purchased, much to the enjoyment of Walter, who began serious study of the piano in what was to become his profession. Gerhard took up the violin.

Gerhard often visited his father at work downtown, on Lilienstrasse near the central railway station. His main interest was in the library on the corner, which was dedicated to Bürgemeister Mönckeburg (1839–1908). This was the library where he first borrowed books on astronomy. At that time, he could see the stars at night as he walked the streets of Hamburg and wondered "what does it all mean", kindling an interest which continued throughout his life. Gerhard also took a liking to the nearby seated statue of the poet Heinrich Heine, father of the song "Die Lorelei", depicting the poet reading a scroll, "What does the lonely tear want—it only spoils my view."[3] A special treat for the family on some Sundays was a boat cruise through the twin lakes and canals, ending with dinner at the Vegetarische Gaststätte above the Alster Arcade, a vegetarian restaurant owned and operated for many years by Herr Schubarth, a friend of Albin's. The family spent the summers at their cottage in Duvenstedt, near a forest and game preserve north of Hamburg.

Gerhard was an excellent student throughout his four years at the Vorschule, and on completing the program in 1915, he was awarded his first prize, a book on the Great Fire of 1842, which destroyed a quarter of the inner city of Hamburg leaving over twenty thousand people homeless. A century later, fire rained from the skies during the Second World War, destroying half the city and killing almost fifty-five thousand of its inhabitants.

Just before Gerhard's graduation, his father died. Albin was a small man, a hunchback, who was persistently ill. He suffered from "Wasser sucht", or dropsy, with the accumulation of water and swelling of the body, a problem originating from an earlier heart condition. He tried many remedies and, in the summer of 1914, even went south to Italy to recuperate, but this was not of much help. The Great War started later that year, but Albin was not called for military service. He died at home on 21 February 1915 at forty-three years of age, leaving a young widow and the boys aged ten and eleven. At Albin's funeral, his eldest sister Emma Eichelmann and her husband persuaded Ella to let Gerhard live with them in Frankfurt and attend secondary school there. Thus, on completion of the school year, Gerhard moved to Frankfurt and in April began attending the Liebig-Oberrealschule, a high school for training as a teacher. The ten year old youngster soon became homesick. He found his uncle, who tried to change his vegetarian ways, to be rather stern and Gerhard talked of returning home. After six unhappy months, he was sent home to his mother. In the meantime Ella Herzberg had given up her home, and to make ends meet, she and Frau Kind, a friend, opened a small confectionery store on Mühlendammstrasse. Ella and her sons lived in a few rooms behind the store. As the war continued and sugar became scarce, the two women changed the candy store into a sewing shop.

The Realgymnasium of the Johanneum

On the advice of his teachers from the Vorschule, Gerhard was persuaded to attend a Gymnasium, a school in preparation for entry into university. Originally, the Gymnasium in Germany existed for the study of the great German poets and thinkers, as well as the classics of antiquity in Latin and Greek. Only a small fraction of the youth attended such schools, mainly the well-to-do and upper middle class. As science and technology became important in the culture and economic well-being of the nation, the Gymnasium came to consist of two parts: the Humanistische Gymnasium with emphasis on the classics and languages and the Realgymnasium with science and mathematics being three-quarters of the curriculum. Gerhard enrolled in the Realgymnasium of the Johanneum in the fall semester. The Johanneum was one of the oldest secondary schools in Hamburg, dating

The Realgymnasium of the Johanneum in Hamburg.

back to 1550. It was a famous boys' school and "The School" in Hamburg. The Johanneum was a fee-school, but thanks to his excellent Vorschule record, Gerhard won a scholarship for his nine years at the Johanneum, beginning with the *sexta* in 1915 through to the *ober prima* in 1924. Student enrollment was six hundred at the time, with the majority completing programs in six years for the professions or mercantile trades. Only about ten students each year completed the *Abitur* or school-leaving certificate, the necessary qualification for university entrance. The school was situated on Armgartstrasse at the Eilbekkanal just across the street from St. Gertrudkirche, within walking distance from home. Another of Hamburg's famous schools was the Heinrich Hertz Gymnasium, named in honour of the scientist who first generated and detected electromagnetic waves, a field of research related to Gerhard's later studies.

During these early years, Gerhard immersed himself in his science studies and developed a particular love for astronomy. This led to the building of a small telescope with his friend Hans-Werner Döring and to his lasting fascination with the heavens. Along with his favourite subjects of mathematics, physics, and chemistry, the curriculum included Latin, French, Spanish, and English. He soon added the works of Goethe, Schiller, Klopstock, Kant, and others to his studies and developed a proficiency in shorthand, which helped him throughout his schooling. He and Hans-Werner formed a close friendship with Alfred Schulz, a classmate who joined the Johanneum somewhat later when the Schulz family moved from the Rhineland to Hamburg. These three were inseparable during the gymnasium years, completely imbued with German culture and constantly discussing science and philosophy and the present political scene. They maintained their close relationship up to the early 1930s by correspondence and brief visits, while continuing their studies and professions and living in different cities.

The Johanneum was close to the Aussenalster, the favourite swimming area for Gerhard and his friends. One day, after his swim, he saw someone doing exercises on the bank and engaged him in conversation on the value of exercising, what was a good technique, and how regularly it should be done. He learned that the method used by this man was based on the book *Mein System* by J.P. Müller, which promoted good health through fifteen minutes of exercising each day.[4] Gerhard was so enthused by this demonstration that he purchased the book and followed its illustrated routine faithfully until he reached the age of eighty-five. Swimming and this daily

Gerhard and Walter with their mother, 1918.

exercise activity helped to make up for his reluctance to participate in team sports or to join the new German pathfinder clubs (or boy scouts) that were springing up all over the country. Herzberg also became interested in the optimism of autosuggestion by the French psychotherapist Emil Coué. In vogue in the 1920s was the saying "Day by day, in every way, I am getting better and better", which Herzberg took up in a determined way.

In the early 1900s, less than 10 percent of all German students were studying science of any kind, a fact that was borne out by the small class in the Realgymnasium.[5] Nevertheless, the Johanneum had teachers of the highest calibre, one of which was Professor Wilhelm Hillers, a science teacher, and it was Gerhard's good fortune to study under him. Hillers had revised one of the best physics texts of that time and had edited a *Teacher's Journal of Physics* (the German equivalent of today's *American Journal of Physics*).[6] The text of two large volumes, *Lehrbuch der Physik*, was written by E. Grimsehl, a former teacher at the Johanneum who died in the Great War. These volumes were kept up-to-date by Hillers and H. Starke, a professor of the Technische Hochschule in Aachen, and the revised texts were in use by German universities until recent times. It was Hillers who first aroused Gerhard's interest in atomic physics and spectra of atoms.

At that time a major upheaval of classical physics was taking place with Albert Einstein's new ideas of relativity and Max Planck's quantum principle. Hillers gave a stimulating course in modern physics during special classes held from seven o'clock each morning until the regular school opening at eight o'clock. Along with his lectures, Hillers would carry out spectacular demonstrations for the class. What especially caught Gerhard's attention was the model of an atom, the emission of light, and the spectra of gases. When Hillers passed the light from an electric lamp through a glass prism, a vivid rainbow of colors was produced on a screen. This was what Isaac Newton had seen about 250 years before when he shone sunlight coming through a slit in a window shutter into a prism and then onto a wall. He called the spread of colour a spectrum. In the early 1800s, Joseph Fraunhofer of Munich examined the spectrum of sunlight in more detail by placing a telescope after the prism instead of a screen. He observed a greater spread of the spectrum of colours and noted that it was crossed with a large number of dark lines. He measured the positions of about seven hundred of them, which are now called the Fraunhofer spectrum. At that time it was not known what these spectral lines meant, but later they were found to be due to absorption of sunlight by the cooler gases in the sun's atmosphere. Fraunhofer also observed the spectra of stars and planets and came to be regarded as the father of the science of spectroscopy and astrophysics. Somewhat later, G.R. Kirchhoff and R. Bunsen at the University of Heidelberg studied the spectra of various salts in flames and discovered the principle of spectrum analysis—that emission and absorption spectra are characteristic of the atoms and molecules that produce them.

There followed an enormous number of studies of flame, arc and spark spectra, and solar and stellar spectra, and the spectra of distinctive wavelengths, which are unique for each element, became known. No satisfactory explanations were forthcoming for the production of spectra until 1913 when Niels Bohr, a young Danish physicist working in the Manchester laboratory of Ernest Rutherford, presented his epoch-making theory.[7] Bohr dealt with hydrogen, the simplest atom and element. He accepted Rutherford's planetary atomic model that hydrogen consisted of a positively charged, heavy nucleus at the centre and one negatively charged electron orbiting around it. Bohr then assumed that the electron could only occupy specific stable orbits, each of different energy, and that the electron did not lose energy while whirling around in any of these orbits. However, when the electron jumped from a higher more energetic orbit to a lower orbit of less energy, light would be emitted. Conversely, light was absorbed when the electron was raised from a lower to a higher orbit. The light energy emitted or absorbed was a quantum of energy, namely the difference in energy of the two orbits, given by $E = h\nu$, where according to Max Planck, h is a constant (now named after Planck) and ν is the frequency of the radiation. Bohr's theory was successful in accounting for the observed spectra of hydrogen and ionized helium (that is, helium possessing only a single electron after removal of the second electron) and, with further elaboration, predicted and explained many other features of atomic spectra.

The demonstrations of the spectra of different gases entranced the young Gerhard, and he was intrigued that light was produced by electrons in atoms jumping from higher orbits to lower ones. Moreover, the spectrum of each of the known elements was strikingly different and could be used to identify the gas producing it, whether observing light from the stars, planets, or laboratory sources. These results remained imbedded in his mind. Within a few years, Gerhard was to produce one of the finest and most complete spectra of atomic hydrogen in the visible region as his first independent piece of research.[8]

As the tide of the Great War turned against Germany, the economic situation worsened, with a shortage of food and only a few vegetables available. This culminated in the "turnip winter" of 1916–1917 when all soups, meals, jams, and desserts were limited to turnips.[9] The Herzberg fortunes, along with those of most Germans, reached a critical stage by the war's end in November 1918. Moreover, Ella fell prey to swindlers and sold the family cottage and a piece of land for a pittance. Inflation raised living costs to inconceivable levels: a litre of milk, which was 1.5 Marks (M) in June of 1920, jumped to 10 in June of 1922, to 1,000 in May of 1923, to 2 million in August, to 5 trillion the following month, and to 400 trillion in November. On 15 November 1923, the new Rentenmark (RM), equal to a trillion old Marks, was introduced, and some economic stability was achieved.

Under these severe postwar economic conditions, the sewing shop had very little work to do. Finally, in late 1922, as the devastating inflation continued to grow, Ella's partner, Frau Kind, convinced Ella to emigrate to America to marry her widowed son in Wyoming and to leave Gerhard and Walter, aged seventeen and eighteen, in her care. The boys were severely disappointed at this latest turn of events, realizing this would end any semblance of a family life, and they wondered when they would see their mother again. The family's financial situation was desperate and this seemed to be a reasonable solution. In Wyoming, Ella first worked as a housekeeper for the widower, and then finding she could not manage his five unruly children, she hastily moved to Seattle, Washington, where her father and a sister lived. Ella's monthly letters from America brought a few dollars to help with expenses and a little pocket money for Walter and Gerhard. To make ends meet, Gerhard began tutoring in mathematics and science. Walter completed the six year diploma program at the Johanneum and became an apprentice in a business firm. He played the piano in local restaurants in the evenings and gave lessons to children on weekends, while seriously practicing for the concert stage at every opportunity.

Thoughts of University

As the final school year came to a close and his friends began making plans to attend university, Gerhard wondered what lay in store for him. At Easter of 1924, Gerhard was one of nine students to obtain the "Abitur". Of course, he too wanted to go to university and was determined to do so. Moreover, being one of the top students in his graduating class, Gerhard was constantly encouraged by his teachers to continue his education. But how could he afford it? His family had no funds of any kind. And where should he go? Astronomy was at the top of his list. He sought the advice of a vocational guidance bureau (Berufsberatungsstelle) that existed at that time in Hamburg. The counsellor took Gerhard's interest in astronomy seriously and wrote on his behalf to Dr. Schorr, the Director of the Hamburg Observatory. The response was most discouraging: "There is no point in thinking of a career in astronomy unless one has private means of support." Obviously, astronomy was out of the question. Gerhard then turned his attention to mathematics and physics. On the advice of his counsellor, he considered another, more practical possibility such as enrolling in a new program of *technische physik*, or engineering physics, recently introduced in several universities, the closest being the Technische Hochschule in Darmstadt. Surprisingly, the University of Hamburg, in Germany's second most populated city, had only been incorporated in 1919 and was not yet strong in science or engineering. Gerhard sent away to several universities for information about their programs and applied to the technical schools in Munich, Danzig, Dresden, and Darmstadt.

Graduating class of 1924.
Top row: Alfred Schulz, – , – , Gerhard, Hans-Werner Döring.

The remaining and major problem, however, was financial. Gerhard had managed so far on the few dollars received from his mother and his earnings from tutoring. Where would he find the funds to register at a university, pay tuition fees, and live in another city? At best, it would mean finding a supplementary job, with only about half of his time devoted to school and studies. The financial problem was a constant concern. Matters were quickly coming to a head, since the university terms began in late April and it was already mid-March.

One day, at the home of his friend Alfred Schulz, Gerhard was discussing this worrisome problem with the family. Alfred's father was the Hamburg representative of the Aachen cloth firm "Tuchfabrik van Gülpen" and, as a merchant and trader in fine cloths, had become acquainted with the established families and businessmen of Hamburg. Herr Schulz suggested that Gerhard write to the wealthy industrialist Hugo Stinnes. Stinnes had started a shipping company in 1892 and developed it into a huge corporation and trust, controlling mines, shipbuilding and shipping, paper mills, and foundries, with vast holdings reaching as far as South America. He was also one of the founders of the conservative German People's Party and an elected member of the Reichstag since 1920.

At first the thought of asking for financial assistance from someone he didn't know seemed to be a brazen idea to the young Gerhard, but in desperation he finally wrote to Herr Stinnes on 22 March 1924, enquiring about the possibility of a loan:

> Dear Herr Stinnes,
>
> Please excuse me for writing to you today out of necessity in a personal matter. I am nineteen years old and my father who was an assistant manager with a local company died nine years ago. My mother emigrated to Seattle in America a year and a half ago so as to make a livelihood possible for me and my brother, and she lives there herself in very modest circumstances.
>
> I have attended the Realgymnasium of the Johanneum on Armgartstrasse and recently graduated with the Abitur according to the enclosed copy of my graduating certificate. I would now like to take up the study of engineering physics in Munich. According to information from the Technische Hochschule in Munich, I will need a minimum monthly amount of about 90 to 120 RM. Until recently my mother has been able to support my quite modest livelihood, and I have helped with some tutoring which I am doing at present. My most recent attempt to obtain support for my studies from an uncle has floundered since he does not have the means.
>
> I now take the liberty, dear Herr Stinnes, of enquiring of you whether you would possibly help me with a loan. The professors and teachers mentioned in the copy of my certificate would in every way oblige you with information about me.
>
> I look forward to your most kind answer, and sign
>
> With all respect, quite humbly,[10]
>
> Gerhard Herzberg.

He wrote a similar letter to the banker Max Warburg, who replied instantly that "in view of the difficult economic situation, only in the most serious emergencies can we consider helping".[11]

While visiting his aunts in Langensalza two weeks later, Gerhard was astounded to receive an acknowledgement from the Stinnes Company dated 8 April, requesting that he present himself to Herr Heinersdorff at the offices of the company on any afternoon, preferably between four and six o'clock, for further discussion on this matter.[12] Because the trip to Hamburg was beyond his means, Gerhard replied sending a photograph of himself and asking whether his friend Alfred Schulz could come in his place to provide more information on his future plans.[13] On second thought, however, and helped by a payment from his relative Otto Herzberg, who owned a dry-goods store in Langensalza, Gerhard appeared in person at the Stinnes Company on the elegant boulevard Jungfernstieg on 17 April, not knowing that Hugo Stinnes had died on 10 April. The interview with Herr Heinersdorff, now representing Hugo Stinnes, Jr., was brief and friendly but ended without any verbal commitment. In the meantime, Gerhard was still undecided as to whether to go to Munich or Darmstadt. Although the Technische Hochschule in Munich was considered to be the top school, Gerhard was frightened by what he had read of the political situation in Munich and of the "Beer Hall Putsch" the past November, with Adolf Hitler's attempt to overthrow the Weimar Republic.[14] Living costs were higher than in Darmstadt, and moreover, as late as 23 April, he still had not received a notice of acceptance. Understandably, his preference was for Darmstadt.

A few days after the Heinersdorff interview, he was pleasantly surprised to receive word (dated the same day as his visit) that he had been awarded a scholarship "for the next while" at 90 RM per month.[15] There were no conditions attached to the scholarship, such as having to repay it as in a loan, nor was it clear to Gerhard whether he was obliged to report about his studies and progress, or how often. With the major financial problem resolved in this beneficent way, Gerhard hurriedly prepared to move to Darmstadt and to enroll in the Technische Hochschule in time for lectures beginning in a few day's time on 29 April. There was little to pack and take with him, only a few clothes, his beloved Grimsehl texts, his violin, a typewriter, and bicycle. On the way to Darmstadt, he stopped in Frankfurt to spend a day with his cousins and aunt and uncle, the Eichelmanns.

To add spice to my life, I would wish for no other society than the one which Darmstadt has to offer.

18th Century French Traveller

2. UNIVERSITY YEARS

Darmstadt

Darmstadt, the capital of the Grand Duchy of Hesse-Darmstadt for centuries, was a city of the arts and learning and a treasure of the eighteenth and nineteenth centuries, the greatest age of German culture and architecture.[1] It was a prosperous provincial town, primarily a residential and small-business centre of approximately ninety thousand inhabitants. Situated twenty-five kilometres south of Frankfurt, it was nestled in rolling farmland, surrounded by forests, and in the neighbourhood of the larger cities of Mannheim, Mainz, and Wiesbaden. The inner core of Darmstadt was the old town, with quaint half-timbered houses in a maze of narrow cobbled streets radiating outwards from the seventeenth century Landgraf's Castle, the residence of the Grand Duke Ernst Ludwig. Its tall bell tower overlooked the Marktplatz, a central market square, itself a remnant of the early fourteenth century. Scattered among the gabled wooden houses stood lesser palaces and great houses that had been built in the days when Hesse was among the most notable independent German principalities. To the north of the Castle stood the Landestheater, an outstanding work of architecture that was completed in the early nineteenth century and was one of the largest theatres in its time. Beside it was the Landesmuseum, built almost a century later, that contained collections tracing the history of the ruling families of Hesse and of the art and culture of the region.

At the very centre of Darmstadt was the Luisenplatz with its landmark statue of the Grand Duke Ludwig I, which sat on a thirty-nine metre high column and was affectionately called *langer Ludwig* (long Louis) by the locals. A few hundred metres to the east of the Castle rose the *Mathildenhöhe*, a small hill with the five-fingered *Hochzeitstrum* (Wedding Tower) atop. This was the crowning piece of the celebrated *Künstlerkolonie* (artists colony), which established the *Jugendstil* or Art Nouveau movement at the turn of the century, leading to Darmstadt's reputation as a prominent centre of art. Several churches and two synagogues graced the city. The oldest church, dating from 1330, was the City Church, the burial place of the House of George I. Overlooking the Luisenplatz was the Church of St. Ludwigs (1827), a replica of the Pantheon in Rome built to

Darmstadt with Landgraf's Castle in centre, Landesmuseum and Landestheater on left, and Herrngarten Park with the Technische Hochschule in background.

one-fifth scale. A small, exquisite Russian Chapel on Mathildenhöhe was commissioned by Nikolas II, the last Romanov Czar, who married Princess Alixandra of Darmstadt and needed an Orthodox church for worship when visiting his wife's family.

Darmstadt's largest industry was chemical, with almost half of the workforce employed in the large factories of E. Merck and Rohm & Haas, located north of the railway station. About 10 percent of the workers were employed by the government. Others worked in printing houses and small factories making photographic paper, leather goods, and wood products, and shopkeepers and craftsmen plied their trades from stores and workshops beside their homes. Until the Great War, Darmstadt had been the garrison town of Hesse, but by 1920 the military units had disappeared and the barracks were converted into much-needed living quarters, schools, and offices. This loss of the military led to economic hardships and damage to

Typical Darmstadt houses in the old town near the THD.

the prestige of the city, resulting in questioning whether Darmstadt should remain as the capital of Hesse, a decision postponed for the time being.

The close of 1923, a year of crisis for Germany, marked the end of wild inflation, the threat of Bavarian separatism, and fighting against French occupation of the Ruhr. Along with the overthrow of the Hitler Putsch in Munich in November, some semblance of economic stability was finally achieved. In Darmstadt, a housing program was started, industrial buildings and sports and recreational facilities were being built, and a streetcar system was being developed. Moreover, the intellectual and cultural life in Darmstadt was improving, as efforts were made to lead the city back to being the cultural capital of Hesse once again.

The Technische Hochschule Darmstadt (THD)

The pride of Darmstadt was its Technische Hochschule, the only technical university among the five universities of the State of Hesse.[2] It had lowly beginnings in 1826 as the "Secondary and Technical School", a school for the training of tradesmen and craftsmen. Ten years later the technical part became the "Higher Trade School" and erected its own building bordering the old town. Over the years, as Germany became an industrial country, the trade school developed into the "Polytechnic School". Following the Franco-Prussian War and the union of the German states in 1871 to form the Second Reich, the school received its charter to become the Technische

Hochschule zu Darmstadt in 1877, with a commitment to teaching and research and with the Abiturum being the prerequisite for admission.[3] At that time, the enrollment was only about two hundred full- and part-time students in all five Departments (Schools of Construction, General Engineering, Mechanical Engineering, Mathematics and Natural Sciences, and the Chemical–Technical School) and dropped rapidly to a total of only ninety-eight students a few years later as a result of the economic crisis of the 1870s.

Enrollment at the THD recovered in 1882 with the creation by Erasmus Kittler of the first School of Electrical Engineering in a German technische hochschule. Kittler had joined the THD that year and became known as one of the fathers of electrical engineering in Germany. This program proved to be very popular and student numbers increased rapidly, with many students attracted from eastern Europe. Approval was given for a new building for the THD on land of Herrngarten Park donated by the Grand Duke Ernst Ludwig. By the time of the inauguration in 1895, the building was already too small for the increased enrollment, and further extensions including a large auditorium were approved. In the meantime, the THD was accorded

Mathildenhöhe with the Wedding Tower and Russian Chapel, Darmstadt.

Technische Hochschule Darmstadt, 1924.

the right to grant doctorate degrees. By the turn of the century, over 2,000 students were registered in its engineering departments, and in 1909–1910, four women were admitted for the first time, following the trend of the major universities in Germany. During the Great War, enrollment dropped drastically but increased rapidly at war's end from 1,180 in the winter of 1918–1919 to 2,131 a year later and to 3,011 in 1922–1923.[4] This increase added to the already serious housing shortage. In 1924 the General Faculty, which combined all non-technical subjects, was split into the Department of Cultural and Political Science and the Department of Mathematics and Natural Science. Two degree programs were developed in physics. One was based on the existing theory-oriented course with qualification in physics, introducing the students to research. The other was a practice-oriented course with qualification in engineering—the Technical Physics program. The latter was a major step in extending the curriculum beyond the purely technical and in preparing engineers, through liberal arts courses, for their leading role in society. At that time, total enrollment at the THD was 2,346, of which 69 were in the new Department of Mathematics and Natural Science.

The study of physics had been promoted as early as 1869 at the Polytechnic School with the establishment of the Institute of Physics. Dr. Friedrich Kohlrausch was a professor there from 1871 to 1875, carrying on research in electrolytes. *Practical Physics,* his textbook on the techniques of measurement, became an indispensable guide for generations of physicists. Dr. Paul Schering arrived at the THD in 1888 as Professor of Physics and served as Dean of the Institute of Physics at the time of the opening of the new building in 1905. The main research instruments were a synchronized clock and seismograph with a pendulum extending through four stories from the roof to the basement. After Professor Schering reached Emeritus status, Professor Hans Rau took over as Director of the Institute. Konrad Zeissig was an Assistant in 1893 and, on receiving his Doctorate in Göttingen in 1897, became a Professor of Physics at the THD. His survey of magnetic fields in Hesse served as a model for future surveys. When approval was granted for establishing an Institute for Technical Physics, he taught the physics course until his retirement in 1934.

Herzberg Enrolls in the THD

Herzberg arrived in Darmstadt on 26 April 1924 to register in the Technical Physics program of the Technische Hochschule. Darmstadt was to be his home until 1935, except for a two year interval spent as a postdoctoral fellow in Göttingen and Bristol. With only a few Rentenmarks in his pocket, savings from tutoring and his mother's allowance, and the promise of 90 RM per month from the Stinnes Company, he set out to find suitable quarters near the university. Housing was scarce, as most of the students had already arrived and registered, but after a day's search, he managed to find a simple attic room on Hobrechtstrasse in a nice residential district near the Odenwald. It was a large, airy room but had no gas or electric light or similar comforts, and so the rent was relatively cheap, 18 RM per month, and well within his limited budget. The THD was within walking distance through the interesting downtown region of the Marktplatz, Rathaus, and Castle. Herzberg was impressed with the huge campus of the THD and its extensive buildings, with the Institutes of Physics and Chemistry in separate buildings. He registered on 28 April for the summer semester from Easter to early August and was relieved to learn that he could pay the first year's fees of 157 RM in two instalments.

On that same day, he was pleasantly surprised to receive his first payment of 90 RM from the Stinnes Company and wrote a long letter to Alfred Schulz about his impressions and experiences in Darmstadt.[5] Herzberg attended the opening ceremonies presided by "His Magnificence", the Rector of the THD, and was informed of the heavy course load of at least forty hours per week, almost double the hours at a normal university.[6] His courses included mathematics, physics, chemistry, mechanics, engineering drawing, and philosophy. He also enrolled in a physics laboratory for an extra fee. All in all, Herzberg's schedule was close to fifty hours per week, Monday through Saturday. This was such a heavy load that he gave up further practice of the violin. He planned to keep Sundays free for exploring Darmstadt and for hiking in the surrounding forests. At home each night, he reviewed his lectures with the help of his shorthand notes and worked through the physics lecture material in his Grimsehl texts, leaving little time for other activities. Nevertheless, he was in constant touch with Walter and his friends Alfred and Hans-Werner by letter, a habit he developed early and continued throughout his university years. Moreover, since these letters were Gerhard's only connection with his roots and early life, he began to save those he received as well copies of his own.

Fraternity life on campus was in full bloom, a large number of the students belonged to these *Korps* societies. Many members were "colour-wearing", that is, often dressed in colourful uniforms, and participated in fencing classes. As Gerhard wrote to Alfred: "Of course, if I find a fraternity or an association which suits me very much, I shall join; but my conditions are rather difficult to meet." He obviously was not well informed about fraternities. In any case, he would not have fitted into their way of life very easily, since he was a vegetarian and teetotaller, while fraternity members seemed duty-bound to participate in rituals of beer drinking. Besides, he would not have been able to afford the obligatory costs of being a member. Nevertheless, he was hurt to learn that most of the newcomers were besieged with invitations to become members, but not a single fraternity approached him. Eventually he found out that Jews were not admitted to fraternities, and he surmised that the reason for this personal slight was his Jewish-sounding name.[7] Students did not understand that although Hertzberg was indeed a Jewish name, Herzberg (without the "t") was an Aryan name.

This was his first realization of the anti-Semitic atmosphere at the THD, a situation endemic in German universities at that time and one that was to grow much worse and change his life irrevocably ten years later. This first experience hurt deeply, as revealed by his noting many instances of misbehaviour of fraternity members in his letters to Alfred. During the first semester, he found that many fraternity members were not serious students and did not attend lectures or problems classes regularly. Moreover, in the physics laboratory where students worked in groups of four because of overcrowding, some in his group took little interest in the experiments or in the accuracy of their measurements. The students wanted to finish as quickly as possible and so copied from previous reports as well as from notes and exercises of their fraternity members. Only the exceptionally good philosophy course given by Professor Julius Goldstein seemed to attract the students' concentration. Professor Goldstein was such an extremely fine lecturer that even though he was Jewish, the *Korps* students attended his classes and paid attention. What particularly disturbed Gerhard was learning that for the past two years these students did not carry out the solstice celebrations on the usual date of 21 or 22 June but on the 24th, the day the Foreign Minister Walter Rathenau (1867–1922), a Jew, was assassinated by nationalists who opposed his attempts to fulfill the Versailles Treaty obligations.[8]

Money was also a constant worry, and Gerhard was in a terrible predicament during May and early June, waiting day in and day out for receipt of his next 90 RM from Stinnes, until it arrived in mid-June.[9] He had paid only half of the tuition fees (90 RM) and needed at least 45 RM (1.5 RM per day) for food, and his rent was 18 RM. His last 25 RM was spent on the necessary drawing instruments, leaving him no money to buy books. Moreover, he somehow had to put aside at least 30 RM per month to pay the tuition fees for the next semester. After only a month at the THD, he began to plan on how to spend August and September, the months between summer and winter semesters, most profitably. University students in Germany at that time used to move about, spending the summers in a small university town in order to enjoy nature and sport; Herzberg, however, could only think of the expenses of the next semester and how he might meet them. He applied to several industries for employment. He hoped to work in Stuttgart, where he had been invited to live with an uncle free of charge, and so could save money for his schooling. But the factories to which he applied answered in the negative.

Near the end of the first semester, Herzberg was offered a job in the instrument shop of the THD. This turned out to be a blessing, not only for the remuneration, but also because he was befriended by Heinrich Peters, a graduate student in physics, from whom he learned much about the Institute of Physics, its faculty, and what professor to study under and work for. Peters was working for his *Diplom Ingenieur*, the Engineering Diploma, under Professor Hans Rau, the Director of the Institute of Physics, and he encouraged Herzberg to enroll in Rau's physics course. That summer, Herzberg also set his sights on an academic career, as he wrote to Alfred:

> At the shop I also learned that an academic profession is not so expensive or hopeless. When one finishes the exams, one accepts an assistant position with a starting salary of 250 RM, then one can *Habilitate* as a *Privatdozent* and remain as an assistant with salary. One has most of all to strive to publish a lot of papers in order to become "known", thus having a good chance to "get a call". It is certain that I shall follow this path, if I can only find the necessary abilities in me.[10]

At that time, it was normal for a graduate in physics to be employed in industry or as a gymnasium teacher, with only the rare, brilliant, and usually affluent graduate able to continue studies to the Doctorate degree and proceed to an academic career. At this very early stage, in his first year of university, Herzberg had decided on his future path and he never lost sight of this ambitious goal.

Cultural activities were plentiful during the summer of 1924; there were performances of plays by Ernst Barlach and Henrik Ibsen and controversial works by Igor Stravinsky and George Bernard Shaw. With few resources at his disposal, Herzberg limited his attendance to the musical events celebrating the sixtieth anniversary of Richard Strauss and the one hundredth of Anton Bruckner. A different exciting event for Darmstadters was the flight over the city of Zeppelin LZ 126 in September to open an air show, a precursor to the building of an airport as a joint project of the THD, industry, the state, and the city.

A Lonely First Semester

The prevalent, lackadaisical, fraternity atmosphere resulted in a very lonely first semester for Herzberg, who did not develop any new close friendships and rarely participated in social activities. As for female companionship, this too seemed rare, because of his meagre means and his serious study habits. In fact he found sparse representation of women on campus, on average about 1 percent, with attendance mainly in chemistry classes and general lectures, and almost none in the technical courses. The few women in his classes were not given any special consideration, and most professors began their lectures with the words "Gentlemen …". As he wrote to Alfred "There is no ground here for your suspicion of my spending time with women."[11]

This was a difficult period for Gerhard, not only was he living by himself in a vastly different setting and constantly concerned about making ends meet, but above all, he missed his brother and friends Alfred and Hans-Werner. Even the regular writing and receipt of letters hardly made up for the lack of their daily companionship. While his news to Walter and Hans-Werner dealt mainly with his studies and Sunday hikes in the Odenwald and Neckar Valley, he carried on extensive and heated arguments on philosophy and politics with Alfred, who was immersed in his studies of history. Meanwhile, the four of them were making plans for a two week cycling trip in the Black Forest near Lake Constance at the end of September.

An argument that Gerhard and Alfred carried on for months by lengthy letters concerned Alfred's leaning towards nationalism and Gerhard's tendancy towards socialism and pacifism. It seemed that Alfred had earlier approved of the Hitler Putsch but suddenly had changed his mind, to Gerhard's relief. The Nazis fancied themselves to be nationalists, whereas Gerhard thought that a national person would want the best for his people and would call every war, even a victorious one, a national misfortune because all cultural and economic valuables are destroyed by war. As he wrote to Alfred:

> Having a pacifist and socialist Ramsay MacDonald as leader in Great Britain and an Édouard Herriot in France might have some influence in Germany.… Furthermore, to claim that a real culture is only possible with a strong feeling of national identity is disproved by the fact that Schiller, Goethe, Lessing, Herder, Kant, [and others of the *Sturm und Drang* Movement] thought much more cosmopolitan than national. Lessing wrote: "Patriotism, a heroic weakness." Goethe once said to Eckermann something like: "Nationalism is strongest at the lowest level of culture. The higher a culture stands, the more patriotism loses its meaning." … And quoting Schopenhauer: "Every poor soul who has nothing in the world to be proud of seizes as a last resort on being proud of the nation to which he belongs. In doing so he recovers and is now gratefully ready to defend all the shortcomings and blunders that are hers."[12]

Such correspondence continued back and forth, and heated discussions were then carried on during their vacation in the Black Forest. In the end, Gerhard and Alfred could not agree on any important points in politics and world view and, because of their longer hours of course work in the following semester, decided not to carry on such lengthy arguments by weekly letters. However, this did not stop them from keeping each other informed about their studies and well-being in the short term. Yet they could not resist their habitual discussions of politics and philosophy, and within a year, they resumed bimonthly correspondence on topics of the day.

Professor Dr. Hans Rau

The winter semester of October to February 1924–1925 provided Herzberg with the stimulus to decide on a career in basic physics rather than in engineering physics. This came about while attending the physics classes of Dr. Rau, who gave extraordinarily good lectures that were illustrated with clever demonstrations.[13] The lectures were in a very large hall with about five hundred students in attendance. But Rau could be heard, and he was exciting. His lectures were modelled after those of Professor Zenneck of the Technische Hochschule Braunschweig who was renowned in Germany for his outstanding lecturing style, as was Professor Pohl of the University of Göttingen.

Rau had studied mathematics and physics at the Universities of Munich and Würzburg. After his Doctorate in 1906, he was an assistant to Professor Zenneck, a specialist in wireless telegraphy, and so became familiar with his lecturing methods. Rau obtained the Habilitation at the TH Braunschweig in 1909, and in 1911, he returned to Würzburg as Privatdozent and assistant to Professor Wilhelm Wien, who was awarded the Nobel Prize that year for his discoveries regarding the laws governing the radiation of heat. In 1920, Dr. Rau became Assistant Professor in Munich and made a reputation for his research on positive or canal rays. When he joined the THD in 1922, he accepted so many university duties, first as Director of the Institute of Physics, then as Dean of Mathematics and the Natural Sciences from 1925 to 1927, and Rector in 1928, that he had no time for research and hardly published any more. In spite of his many responsibilities, Rau found time to supervise the research of several students, and Herzberg considered himself very lucky to be one of these. Thus began a lifelong association with Rau, his scientist father, who meant so much to Herzberg and whom he considered to be one of the finest people of his acquaintance.

During the tenure of the Stinnes award, Herzberg sent letters to Herr Heinersdorff every six months regarding his progress and plans for future studies. In the first semester, he was counselled that he was taking too many courses and that it would be better to take fewer and have the chance to study them better.[14] In June 1925, he was congratulated on his achievements in the first year and advised to take a one or two week vacation and come back refreshed for the next semester.[15] Only a month later Herzberg was shocked to learn that the scholarship would end.[16] Because of the sudden downturn in the economy at the time, and barely a year after the death of Hugo Stinnes, the Stinnes Corporation in Hamburg was bankrupt. Herzberg immediately wrote back about his difficulties with the sudden termination of this scholarship, and on 5 August, he received an additional, and final, two month payment to tide him over.[17,18] He immediately gave up his Sunday walks in the nearby forests and began tutoring in mathematics and physics, and he remained in Darmstadt during holidays in an effort to reduce expenses.

Darmstadt also experienced a serious economic setback as many companies closed, including G. Erhardt & Sons, which produced Art Nouveau (Jugendstil) furniture. Strikes at the chemical plants of Merck and Rohm & Haas were damaging, and unemployment in Darmstadt increased from 340 in July 1925 to 1,625 in the next six months and to 3,200 in the winter of 1926–1927, with about 18,000 inhabitants receiving benefits from the government.

With Herzberg's excellent record, the THD waived his tuition fee, and just at that time, the German government established a new bursary program, the *Studienstiftung des deutschen Volkes,* for the best students in the country. A very strong recommendation from Dr. Rau resulted in Herzberg being awarded one of the first bursaries, with payments continuing through to completion of his diploma and Doctorate degrees and including a postdoctorate year (1929) in Göttingen. When Herzberg learned that Alfred's family was suddenly in dire straits, he strongly recommended that Alfred apply for a bursary with strong support from his professors.

In spite of the growing economic uncertainties, Darmstadt continued its focus on musical and cultural events. During the summer of 1925, there were performances by the State Opera Orchestras of Dresden and of Berlin and by the Vienna Philharmonic Symphony directed by Bruno Walter.

Herzberg found the time and carefully saved, even skimping on meals and the purchase of books, in order to attend some of these special concerts.

The Engineering Diploma Program

Along with his full-time technical curriculum, Herzberg managed to participate in English classes and developed a fairly good facility with written and oral English. This capability was important for his future research since about half of the technical journals were published in English. He also began to attend the weekly colloquia in his second year at the THD in order to get acquainted with the visiting research scientists and engineers of Germany and their work. He found it exciting to be in the presence of such eminent visitors, even though much of the discussion was well beyond his comprehension. In 1925, he attended an International Conference on Physical Chemistry held in Darmstadt and was inspired by talks given by Svante Arrhenius, one of the earliest Nobel Prize winners in chemistry, and by Friedrich Paneth, one of the first to produce the methyl free radical (CH_3), whose spectrum and structure was to become Herzberg's legacy to chemistry four decades later.

With his switch to pure physics, Herzberg kept up with current research by reading the technical journals *Annalen der Physik* and *Zeitschrift für Physik* in the small library of the THD. In his third year (1926), he saw in a current issue of *Annalen der Physik* the first article in the series of four by Erwin Schrödinger titled "Quantization as an Eigenvalue Problem" and was intrigued.[19] He had just taken classes in partial differential equations from the mathematician Professor Jakob Horn and so was familiar with the term "eigenvalue". This, together with his knowledge of the Bohr theory of the atom and its concept of quantization, caused him to study the paper until he understood it. He became so engrossed in the subject that he reported on the Schrödinger paper at the weekly Physics Colloquium, his first presentation to a scientific audience of his peers and professors. He was then persuaded by William Prager, a young Privatdozent in mechanical engineering, to give this colloquium to the engineers. Subsequently, Rau learned that Schrödinger was to give a lecture in Freiburg and sent Herzberg to hear him along with a letter of introduction. There, he heard a fine lecture in a charming Viennese accent and had the opportunity to meet the creator of the new "Wave Mechanics", a heady experience for a young man just learning about atomic physics and quantum theory.

For the research requirement for the Engineering Diploma, Herzberg joined the small group of students working under the supervision of Rau. He found Kurt Lion to be a friendly and skilled experimenter from whom he learned much. Lion and Hermann Rodenstock, a member of the family that owned the Rodenstock optical firm in Munich, were carrying out experiments on canal rays. Heinrich Peters, whom he had met in the workshop, and Margarethe Blumenthal, related to the founders of Blumenthal & Co. in Darmstadt, were working on the spectra of hydrogen. Peters had joined the THD in 1921, and the others came in 1923, a year earlier than Herzberg. Rau had given Peters the difficult assignment of trying to find the spectrum of H_3. At that time, the existence of the hydrogen ions H^+, H_2^+, and H_3^+ in an electrical discharge was known from the mass spectrometer studies of J.J. Thompson (the English scientist who had discovered the electron).[20] Rau had asked Peters to excite hydrogen by canal rays, then to separate the H_3^+ by electric and magnetic fields, and to look for the spectrum of H_3 in emission. This turned out to be an exceedingly perplexing problem which Peters did not complete.[21] Herzberg would discover the spectrum of H_3 serendipitously about fifty years later using a different source.[22] For Herzberg's diploma research, Rau suggested that he work with Margarethe Blumenthal, who was experiencing experimental difficulties. The research problem was to excite the emission spectrum of hydrogen. So began Herzberg's work on hydrogen, leading to a lifetime of interest in atomic and molecular hydrogen.

For this research, Herzberg became adept at glassblowing and made a glass discharge tube that had the possibility of permitting hydrogen gas to flow through it at a controlled rate. He found, as others had observed before him, that in the visible region, the emission spectrum of the reddish-blue electrical discharge consisted of a few atomic lines superimposed on the many-line spectrum of molecular hydrogen. As he increased the voltage of the discharge, the atomic lines increased in intensity, and he noted that the molecular lines persisted at the walls of the tube, suggesting that hydrogen atoms combined more readily to form molecular hydrogen at the walls. When he cooled the walls of the tube with ice, the colour of the discharge changed to purple, and the spectrum consisted mainly of a progression of atomic lines with smaller and smaller spacing, ending in a series limit, the so-called ionization limit. This extended the known spectrum of atomic hydrogen in the visible region to about twenty lines of the Balmer series.

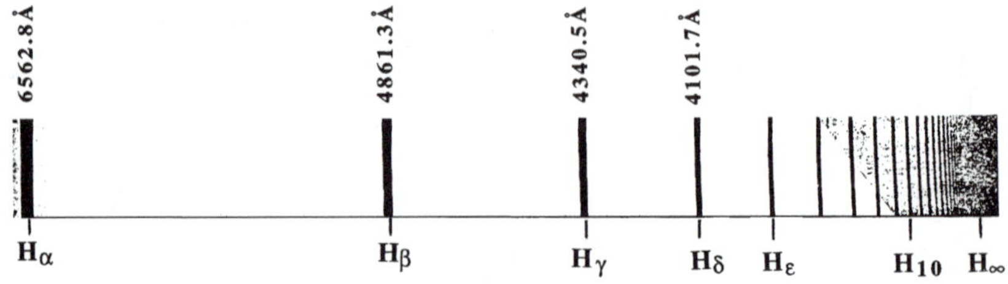

Herzberg's spectrum of the hydrogen atom, the Balmer series.

Wavelengths for this series of lines are represented by the simple formula first given by J.J. Balmer in 1885 and derived by Niels Bohr in 1913:

$$1/\lambda = R_H(1/2^2 - 1/n^2)$$

where λ is the wavelength, R_H is a constant now known as the Rydberg constant, and n is an integer greater than 2. It is not surprising that this simple line spectrum of hydrogen by Herzberg in 1927 is reproduced in hundreds of texts today as the prime example of our understanding of atomic spectroscopy.

By Easter of 1927, Herzberg had completed the course and research requirements for the *Diplom Ingenieur,* having received the highest possible ranking of *sehr gut* in all of his courses, except for a 2 in machine drawing.[23] He was awarded the Mueller–Alewyn–Plakette Medal as the outstanding THD graduand for this degree. On receiving the award, Herzberg made a point of thanking all of his professors in an acknowledgement included in his diploma dissertation.

Herzberg's brief experimental research project on the emission spectrum of atomic hydrogen resulted in his first three scientific papers and launched him on a distinguished career in spectroscopy.[24] His third paper, titled "On the Continuous Spectrum of Hydrogen", was the publication of his first oral presentation at a Physical Society Meeting.[25] This was held in Kissingen, near Würzburg, with Professor Wilhelm Wien as chairman of the session. The discussion that followed Herzberg's presentation, with questions from W. Wien and the spectroscopists W. Grotrian and L.S. Ornstein, was also included in the published proceedings.

Herzberg was the sole author of all three papers, with due acknowledgment that the work was based in part on joint experiments with M. Blumenthal. He also heartily thanked Rau, his highly respected teacher, for his constant stimulation and interest and for his generosity in making available the means to carry out this research. That Rau, his supervisor or *Doktor-Vater*, would not insist on his own name appearing on these papers was a rare practice in research institutes in Germany and elsewhere and remains so today. In this regard, Rau was a highly unusual mentor. At that time in Germany, the scientific society was stratified, with the professor having tremendous power: he determined everything, and it was very difficult for a young experimentalist, especially a student, who depended on the use of instruments provided by the professor, to work on his own or on his own ideas.[26] Rau, however, encouraged independent research and a high standard of thoroughness and accuracy. While he was a very busy teacher and administrator, he was always interested in the work of his students and had good suggestions to help overcome any difficulties in research. Student projects were never considered as joint work with this supervisor, and Rau did not add his name to their published papers. In fact, Herzberg was the sole author for his next nine publications, which formed the basis of his thesis for the "Doctor of Engineering" degree. This experience impressed Herzberg immensely, and he put it to good use during his later career as supervisor and director of research.

The Doctor of Engineering Degree

When Herzberg informed Professor Rau that he wanted to continue his studies with him in spectroscopy for the Doctorate degree, Rau consented immediately. At that time there were no qualifying examinations for the Doctorate in physics, and acceptance of a research student was entirely up to the Professor. For this research, Rau suggested that Herzberg read Arnold Sommerfeld's famous book *Atomic Structure and Spectral Lines* published in 1919, which contained all of the knowledge in the field at that time, and see whether he could come up with a good idea.[27] Herzberg's first idea seemed an obvious one, an extension of the work of Bohr on the spectrum of atomic hydrogen, namely an atomic system with a single electron orbiting a nucleus. Sommerfeld had already applied the theory to the spectrum of He^+, the helium ion. Helium, with a nucleus of charge two and two electrons, is next to hydrogen in the periodic table. When one electron is removed, forming He^+, its spectrum is similar to that of hydrogen except that the energy levels are increased by a factor of four (the square of the

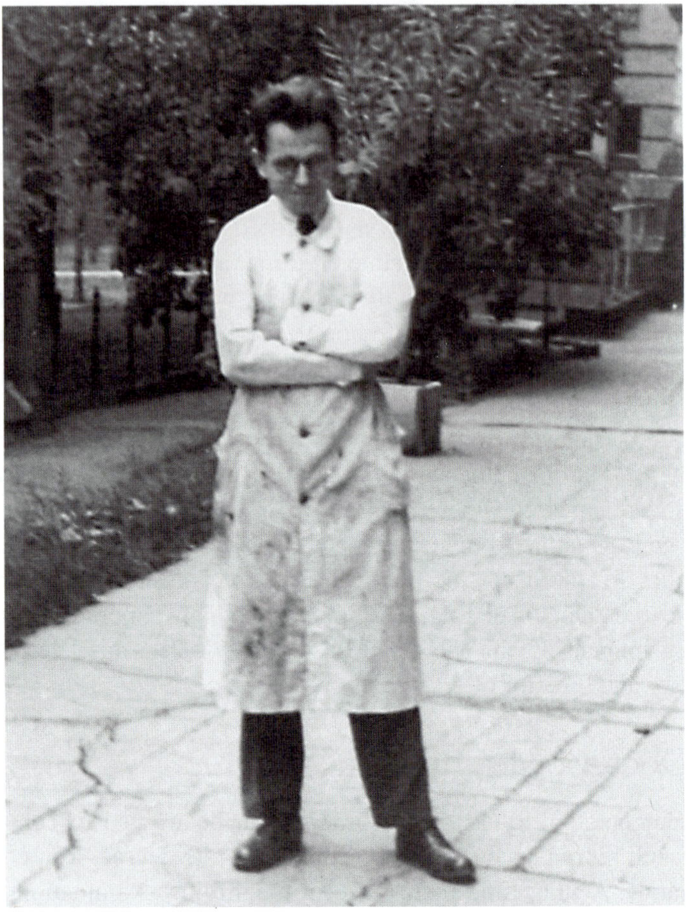

A hard-working researcher at the THD.

nuclear charge) and the wavelengths of the principal series of lines are reduced by the same factor. The next element is lithium with a nuclear charge of three and three orbiting electrons. When two electrons are removed, leaving Li^{++}, a system with one electron orbiting a nucleus, its spectrum would be expected to be similar to that of hydrogen but with wavelengths reduced by a factor of nine. Rau agreed that this would be a worthy problem.

In preparation for the spectroscopy of Li^{++}, Herzberg designed a discharge cell, and a glass shop near the THD made it for him. Having set up the apparatus, he began working with electrical discharges and soon was sidetracked onto a completely different investigation. As he recalled, he did not get a really good start on the Li problem, nor did he ever return to it.

The fortuitous observation that caught Herzberg's attention during these discharge experiments was the persistence of a brilliant yellow–golden glow many seconds after the electrical discharge was switched off. This was such a striking phenomenon that it aroused his curiosity about its source. He decided to study the spectrum of this afterglow, and it became the subject of his thesis for the Doctorate degree. Because vacuum pumps in those early days were inefficient, it was difficult to remove all traces of air in the cell, and he found the presence of nitrogen to be the explanation of the beautiful yellow afterglow. Thus, instead of working with an atomic spectrum, Herzberg realized he was now dealing with a more complex molecular spectrum, that of the nitrogen molecule N_2 and possibly its ion N_2^+. The analysis of such a spectrum would require the study of molecular spectroscopy of diatomic molecules.

He found that in general, the spectra of molecules show characteristics akin to the spectra of atoms. As in atoms, there are a number of electronic states as a result of different energies of electrons binding the atoms to form a molecule. The atoms in a molecule can vibrate against each other, and the structure as a whole can rotate, and these motions obey quantum rules. Thus, for each electronic state, there is a series of almost equally spaced vibrational levels having discrete energies of $E_v = h\nu_{osc}(v + 1/2)$. Here h is Planck's constant, ν_{osc} is the vibrational frequency of the molecule, and the vibrational quantum number v can take the values 0, 1, 2, 3, etc. In turn, each vibrational level consists of rotational levels with energies given by $E_r = BJ(J + 1)$, where B is known as the rotational constant and is related to the moment of inertia of the molecule and J is the rotational quantum number having values 0, 1, 2, 3, etc.[28]

Transitions take place between the various energy levels according to known selection rules, giving rise to three types of spectra. *Rotation spectra* occur by transitions from one rotational level to another in the same vibrational level and same electronic state and appear as nearly equidistant lines in the far infrared and microwave regions of the spectrum. *Rotation–vibration spectra* arise from transitions from rotational levels in one vibrational level to rotational levels of another vibrational level in the same electronic state, producing what are called "bands" in the infrared

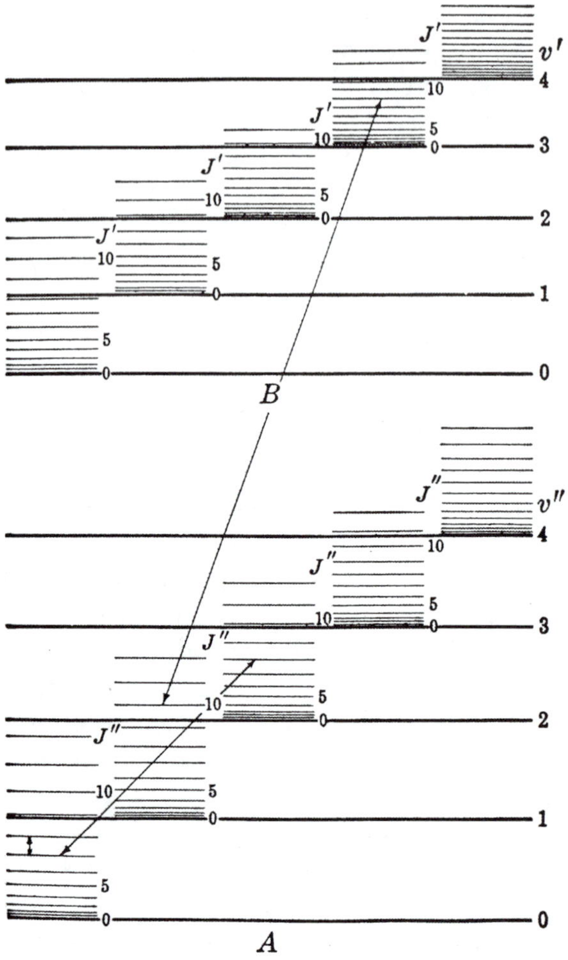

Vibrational and rotational levels of two electronic states A and B of a diatomic molecule, with transitions shown by the vertical arrows.

region. *Electronic spectra* are due to transitions from rotational levels of various vibrational levels of one electronic state to the rotational and vibrational levels of another electronic state, yielding a series of bands with rotational structure, which can be seen at high resolution. Such spectra occur in the visible and ultraviolet regions of the spectrum. These three types of spectra require vastly different experimental techniques for observation, including light sources and methods of excitation, spectrometers, and methods of detection.

Herzberg's investigation of the afterglow yielded electronic spectra of N_2 and of the ion N_2^+, with much vibrational and rotational structure. He observed the so-called "tail bands" of N_2^+ for the first time and recognized that the positions of a series of band heads can have a parabolic dependence as a function of vibrational quantum number and can show convergences within a series.[29] Similar results were reported simultaneously for the iso-electronic molecule CN by Francis A. Jenkins of New York University. Herzberg also found in the spectra of the afterglow that only certain rotational levels occurred in N_2, a result explained later as arising from perturbations in these levels.

All of the spectra in these studies were photographed with glass and quartz prism instruments built at the THD under the guidance of Herr Sting, a superb machinist. Rau had a close connection with the C.A. Steinheil–Söhne Company of Munich, makers of prism spectrographs, and was able to obtain blueprints for a three-prism spectrograph. Several of these instruments were built at the THD with long and short focal lengths and were used by Herzberg in this early work. Grating instruments with their higher resolution were few in Germany, and no source for gratings existed in Europe at that time.[30] Such spectrographs were only available at the THD after Herzberg's postdoctoral years in Göttingen and Bristol, when they were designed by him and built by Herr Sting at the THD with gratings from England and the United States of America.

In his paper on the afterglow in nitrogen, Herzberg disagreed with an explanation suggested in an earlier study.[31] Soon after, at a meeting in Göttingen, Herzberg met one of the authors, Karl-Friedrich Bonhoeffer, the eldest son of the large, distinguished Bonhoeffer family. He was considerably older than Herzberg, and at that time, Bonhoeffer was a section head at the Kaiser–Wilhelm Institute in Berlin-Dahlem. A few years later he became Professor of Chemistry and established the Institute of Physical Chemistry at the University of Frankfurt. Herzberg was enchanted by Bonhoeffer's personality and how he took this criticism from a young man. They quickly became close friends. Herzberg came to value this relationship throughout his life as Bonhoeffer was not only a first-rate scientist, who had helped separate ortho- and para-hydrogen, but also a very warm person and a most courageous one, as later events were to prove.

Doktor Ingenieur Herzberg, 1928.

The spectroscopic studies of the nitrogen afterglow were completed in a year of concentrated research, written up, and published. These early results, all obtained with a simple discharge tube with air and nitrogen, were small yet important contributions to this developing field and launched Herzberg on his life's work in molecular spectroscopy. This research was accepted for his Doctorate thesis, "On the Afterglow of Nitrogen and Oxygen and on the Structure of the Negative Bands of Nitrogen", which he submitted on 8 May 1928.[32] The readers of this brief dissertation, which consisted mainly of published papers, were the Rector Hans Rau and Hans Baerwald, a professor of theoretical physics. Herzberg passed his oral examination with a *sehr gut* on 26 May and was awarded the Doctor of Engineering degree.

After the Doctorate Degree

Having obtained his Doctorate degree, Herzberg took a week off to relax from this arduous year.[33] He accepted Rau's invitation to stay at his chalet in the picturesque Bavarian town of Garmisch-Partenkirchen and spent the week by himself, hiking in the Alps and mainly thinking about his future.

He was anxious to continue his studies at another institute, and luckily the Studienstiftung would continue for this additional year. Even before completing his Doctorate, Herzberg was invited to be an assistant by Professor Rudolf Ladenburg at the Kaiser-Wilhelm Institute in Berlin-Dahlem, on the recommendation of K.-F. Bonhoeffer. He was invited to carry out investigations of anomalous dispersion, with complete freedom to dwell on any theme in this field.[34] This would be an enviable opportunity to join the prestigious Berlin school with the giants of physics, Einstein, Planck, von Laue, and Schrödinger, and the extraordinary group of younger scientists, including Walther Nernst, Lise Meitner, Rudolf Ladenburg, and Friedrich Paschen. However, Herzberg was intent on improving his theoretical understanding of molecular physics, and what better place than the University of Göttingen, the birthplace of quantum mechanics in 1925 and the recognized centre of atomic and molecular physics. He had been invited to give a colloquium there in the summer of 1928 and was most impressed with the scientific atmosphere, the well-equipped laboratories, and particularly Professors James Franck and Max Born.[35] The lecture Herzberg gave, essentially a progress report on his thesis work, was in fact an informal test for his admission as a postdoctoral fellow, and he was accepted to join this famous centre for the year 1929. He hoped to learn much from the outstanding people there and from the many leading scientists who visited in a constant stream from the continent, Great Britain, and North America. He would not be disappointed. But first he had research to complete, papers to write, and much reading to do in order to catch up on the theoretical advances in molecular spectroscopy being reported from around the world.

The years 1926–1928 are remembered as vintage years for the development of many of the basic ideas of molecular spectroscopy and molecular structure, and Herzberg was immersed in this new field of science almost from its beginning. By this time the new theory of quantum mechanics had been used to obtain a full understanding of the electronic structure of atoms, and now it was being extended to the problems of molecular structure. In turn, the spectra of atoms and molecules proved to be a natural testing ground for the theory of quantum mechanics.

Rules for determining the types and number of electronic states for diatomic molecules that result from states of the separated atoms were developed in 1927 by E. Wigner and E.E. Witmer in Göttingen.[36] A major step that simplified the application of quantum theory for the analysis of molecular spectra was the recognition that because of the large difference in masses of nuclei and electrons (a factor of about two thousand), the lighter electrons move very much faster than the vibrating or rotating nuclei. One of the first applications of this idea was in 1925 by James Franck, who proposed that an electron jumps to a higher or lower energy level in a molecule so rapidly in comparison to the vibrational motion of the nuclei that immediately afterwards the nuclei still have essentially the same relative position and velocity as before the jump.[37] A year later, while in Göttingen, Edward U. Condon derived this idea quantum mechanically and it became known as the Franck–Condon Principle.[38] Another important result was derived by J. Robert Oppenheimer and Max Born in 1927, the Born–Oppenheimer Approximation.[39] They proposed that electrons complete many cycles of their motion, whereas the nuclei barely move, and that interactions between electrons and nuclei could be ignored. Thus the motions of electrons and nuclei are treated separately, and the total energy of a molecule is written as a sum of the electronic, vibrational, and rotational energies, namely $E = E_{\mathrm{e}} + E_{\mathrm{v}} + E_{\mathrm{r}}$.

The first quantum mechanical calculation of molecule formation was developed in Zurich in 1927 by Walter Heitler and Fritz London for hydrogen (H_2).[40] Their treatment, which led to the valence theory for chemical bonds, assumed that a molecule is composed of atoms bound together by electrons of the separated atoms. This method was subsequently extended and modified by John C. Slater and Linus Pauling. An alternative treatment, known as the molecular orbital theory, began from the premise that a molecule is a unit, with the outer electrons belonging to the molecule as a whole. Fundamental papers on the latter were published in 1926–1927 by Friedrich Hund and by Robert S. Mulliken a year later.[41,42] Herzberg studied these many basic contributions thoroughly in preparation for his year in Göttingen.

Added to these theoretical developments was the experimental discovery of the Raman effect in 1928 by C.V. Raman and R.S. Krishnan in India and, independently a few weeks later, by G. Landsberg and L. Mandelstam of the Soviet Union.[43,44] It was found that when monochromatic light traverses a transparent medium, the spectrum of scattered light consists of new weak radiation of shifted frequency, in addition to the strong unshifted "Rayleigh" line. The new lines in the spectrum, known as "Raman" lines, are characteristic of the medium and correspond to transitions between rotational and vibrational levels in the molecular medium. Raman spectra complement infrared spectra and provide valuable information on molecular symmetry, vibrational frequencies, rotational constants, and molecular structure.

Along with his concentrated studies of these various new theoretical and experimental developments, Herzberg managed to complete experiments on a new band system in carbon monoxide, CO, and to report his findings in two papers. He also completed papers on the dissociation energy of nitrogen, N_2, and on intensity distributions in band spectra. With twelve published papers to his credit, another accepted for publication, and his head full of the exciting new advances in molecular spectroscopy, Herzberg now felt that he was ready for the challenges he would face in Göttingen.

During these summer months, he had been so immersed in his research that he was completely oblivious to the changing political atmosphere on campus, which had become exceedingly National Socialist. Although the Rector did not permit political party groups to elect members to the Student Body at the THD, the National Socialist German Student Union agitated strongly for change. When renamed the "Peoples Students", this group managed to elect three student representatives in 1928. At the summer solstice celebrations of that year, the uniformed Nazi militia, the brown-shirted storm troopers or SA (*Sturmabteilung*), appeared for the first time in Darmstadt.[45]

Just before moving on to Göttingen, Herzberg participated in one of the large Conferences of German Scientists and Physicians, held in Hamburg in September of 1928, and had the opportunity to meet many physicists and chemists. As is customary at such popular general conferences, he found these personal meetings and discussions to be far more important than listening to the many short and detailed technical presentations. He chose this occasion to spend an extra few days in his hometown visiting Walter and friends Alfred and Hans-Werner, catching up on their news and activities.

It is not knowledge, but the act of learning, not possession but the act of getting there, which grants the greatest enjoyment.

Carl Friedrich Gauss

3. A YEAR IN GÖTTINGEN

The city of Göttingen was famous for its university, the George August University of Göttingen, founded in the 1730s by the Elector of Hannover, who was King George II of England.[1] In the 1920s the University of Göttingen was the acknowledged world centre of atomic physics and mathematics and was famous for the development of the new quantum theory. It had an enrollment of about thirty-five hundred students with almost a third taking mathematics and physics. Its international prestige was first established in mathematics by the famous mathematician, physicist, and astronomer Carl Friedrich Gauss (1777–1855) and enhanced in the 1900s by Felix Klein, David Hilbert, Hermann Minkowski, Richard Courant, Carl Runge, and Hermann Weyl, all of whom were also very much interested in physics. To this group of mathematicians were added the outstanding physicists Max Born, Robert Pohl, and James Franck. They directed the Institute of Theoretical Physics and the First and Second Institutes of Physics, respectively, with all three Institutes housed in the same building, along with the Institute of Mathematics under the direction of Richard Courant.

The Institute of Physics, University of Göttingen.

The strength of this formidable research centre lay in the interaction of mathematicians, theorists, and experimentalists with joint colloquia and the free movement of students and visitors among the Institutes. Thus, Göttingen attracted many famous visitors as well as some of the most brilliant students from all over the world.

Max Born and James Franck

Herzberg had chosen to spend the first half of his stay in the Institute of Theoretical Physics directed by Max Born, whose group had created quantum mechanics, and the other half with the Nobel Laureate James Franck at the Second Institute of Physics.[2] Born and Franck formed a powerful team, and joined by the mathematics faculty, they played an outstanding role in atomic and molecular physics in the twelve years of their tenure in Göttingen.[3,4] They first met as young students at the University of Heidelberg in 1901 and became lifelong friends. Both were born to well-established German Jewish families, Born's father having a Chair at the University of Breslau, and Franck's father being a banker in Hamburg. Although the early studies of Born and Franck were in humanistic gymnasiums with emphasis in the classics, each clearly had decided on a career in physics. Born continued his studies at the University of Göttingen, received his Doctorate in 1907, and stayed on as Privatdozent until 1914, when he was offered a Chair at the University of Berlin. Physically unfit for the army in World War I because of asthma, he first worked on a farm and then helped to improve communications systems and tested inventions for the artillery. In 1919, he accepted Max von Laue's proposal to exchange chairs and moved to the University of Frankfurt. Two years later, Born was offered the prestigious post of Professor and Director of one of the two Institutes of Physics in Göttingen, the other being under Professor Robert Pohl whose main interest was solid state physics. Born foresaw the need and opportunity to establish a centre for atomic physics in Göttingen and accepted the appointment on the condition that he serve as Director of a new Institute of Theoretical Physics and that his friend James Franck be appointed a Professor and Director of the Second Institute of Physics in order to supervise experimental research in atomic physics.[5] At that time in German universities, it was customary for each physics professor to have his own institute with a faculty, docents, assistants, and students, and this is what Born proposed. He knew that Franck and Pohl had been at the same

Professors Max Born, James Franck, and
Robert Pohl of the University of Göttingen.

school in Hamburg and were great friends, so there would be good relations between the two experimental institutes. This plan was accepted, leading to the University of Göttingen becoming a third strong centre for physics, in addition to Munich and Berlin.

James Franck had studied at the Wilhelm Gymnasium in Hamburg and, after a semester in Heidelberg, he enrolled in the University of Berlin, which was the centre of physics at that time, with the distinguished professors Max Planck and, later, Albert Einstein. The Physics Department was noted for its regular Wednesday Colloquia, which Franck considered to be the most important happening in his education, as some of the greatest minds in physics discussed the problems presented by the discoveries in atomic physics and Planck's quantum hypothesis. Franck obtained his Doctorate in 1906 for research in collisions of electrons and ions. In Berlin, he continued with studies of collisions of electrons and gaseous atoms, and in 1914 while experimenting with mercury, he and his younger colleague Gustav Hertz showed that energy was transferred from an energetic electron to an atom only in discrete quanta.[6] This result was correctly interpreted by them to mean that quantization applies to all atomic processes, not just to absorption and emission of radiation, and to all atomic systems, not only to hydrogen. The Great War interrupted this research. Both were called up and immediately left the university, eventually joining Pioneer Regiment No. 36, a special unit for chemical warfare organized by Fritz Haber, the Director of the Kaiser-Wilhelm Instituts für Physikalische Chemie. While on the Russian front in 1916, Franck contracted severe polyneuritis which affected his legs and was sent home to recuperate. He was awarded the Iron Cross first and second class and the Hanseatic Cross of Hamburg for bravery.[7] From 1917 to 1921 he served as a Section Head in Haber's Institute in Berlin-Dahlem.

James Franck agreed to join Max Born in Göttingen. At the same time, Richard Courant was appointed to the Institute of Mathematics. The addition of these three to the Science Faculty in 1921 led to mockery of "the Jewish University" by Göttingen students but did not dissuade them from enrolling in the courses of these distinguished professors.[8] Born's insistence that Franck be appointed in Göttingen was amply justified when Franck and Hertz were awarded the Nobel Prize for Physics in 1925 for their discovery of the laws governing the impact of an electron upon an atom. Franck's interest in collisions of electrons with atoms expanded to include collisions between atoms, the formation and dissociation of molecules, fluorescence emission, and chemical processes. His laboratory soon became recognized as the leading centre for molecular spectroscopy, and he was quickly surrounded by talented research students from the world over. There was great informality in the laboratory, and Professor and assistants would bicycle together at lunchtime for a swim and snack at the swimming pool by the Leine River. Franck was revered by all who knew him for his open friendliness and general approach to science and everyday life. One young scientist said of him, "His character was written on his face. The affection he inspired can be ascribed to two features which stood out in his character: his absolute, natural honesty, and his profound human warmth."[4] Another added, "He was the most immediately lovable man I have ever met."[9] Herzberg was also to come under his spell.

Herzberg arrived in Göttingen on 2 November 1928 and spent two days in search of an affordable room.[10] In the process he became familiar with this walled city and its narrow alleys with half-timbered houses, reminiscent of Darmstadt's old town. Many of the houses were student taverns, and others were small shops to serve the various needs of the university community. It was a city of 42,500 inhabitants, and its centre was teeming with students circling the legendary "Goose Girl" statue and fountain behind the thirteenth century Rathaus on whose wall he noted the Latin motto *Extra Göttingen non est vita*—Away from Göttingen there is no life. Beyond the old walls were a series of scientific industries and laboratories, a forerunner of today's research parks. To his surprise, Herzberg found that one of the main roads in Göttingen, named Herzberger Landstrasse, led to the small city of Herzberg about fifty kilometres to the northeast, which he later visited. He wondered whether there was any connection to his name, since Langensalza, the Herzberg family home for four centuries, was only about one hundred and fifty kilometres southeast of this city, but archival studies suggest that there is no relationship in the names of town and family.

Herzberg's search for lodgings revealed that rooms in Göttingen were not scarce, but many in the vicinity of the university were in poor condition and others were very costly. At the suggestion of James Franck he found a suitable and reasonably priced room (at 40 RM per month with breakfast and maid service) in the home of George Schlüter, a former mayor of Göttingen, at 5 Merkelstrasse, in the outskirts of the city.[10] Other residents included a professor, a dentist, and a widow. As Herzberg soon learned, the mathematician Hermann Weyl lived next door at No. 3, and James Franck lived just across the street at No. 4, a palatial home with a high tower overlooking the city. This region was adjacent to a park and extensive forest but a considerable distance east of the town centre and the main university buildings. The Institutes of Physics were housed in a large brick building at the southern end of town about a ten minute walk from the centre. Herzberg could obviously make use of a bicycle and would have to save for this added expense or borrow from his friends back home.

Member of the Institute of Theoretical Physics

Although Herzberg had no intention of becoming a theorist, he hoped to develop a deeper understanding of the new quantum theory and apply it to the analysis of molecular spectra. Quantum mechanics had been formulated by Werner Heisenberg, Max Born, and Pascual Jordan in Göttingen in 1925. Wave mechanics was introduced a year later by Erwin Schrödinger in Zurich, and a more general form of quantum mechanics was introduced by Paul Dirac in Cambridge. These new theories were quickly applied to the clarification of atomic spectra, and excitement ran high that quantum theory would be equally useful in the understanding of molecular spectra. Herzberg particularly wanted to study the wave mechanical treatment of the valency forces in molecular hydrogen recently presented by Walter Heitler and Fritz London. He was also intrigued by the molecular orbital theory being developed by Erich Hückel and Friedrich Hund in Germany, John E. Lennard-Jones in England, and Robert S. Mulliken in the United States.

At the University, Herzberg learned that Professor Born had suffered a nervous breakdown from the long hours and months of strenuous effort in supervising and keeping up with his group of brilliant young theorists. Among his group were Wolfgang Pauli, Werner Heisenberg, Friedrich Hund, Pascual Jordan, Walter Heitler, Lothar Nordheim, Eugene Wigner, J. Robert Oppenheimer, and E.U. Condon.[11] A tiring trip to Russia in 1928 as well as worries over the deteriorating political situation in Germany did not help matters, and Born was forced to interrupt teaching and research and relax for much of the year that Herzberg spent in Göttingen.[12] Although Born's frequent absences were a disappointment to Herzberg, Born was able to lecture from time to time and Herzberg made certain to attend these sessions.

Almost the first person he met on arrival at the Institute was Walter Heitler, already famous for his paper on valence theory, also twenty-four years old, and now assistant to Born. They immediately recognized their mutual interests in molecular problems and enjoyed discussions while

Walter Heitler.

Friedrich Hund.

walking in the nearby forests and hiking in the Alps. Thus began a lifetime friendship and scientific collaboration resulting in the publication of two papers while they were in Göttingen. Others in the theoretical group at that time were assistants Wigner and Hund, young students Maria Goeppert, Max Delbrück, and Victor F. Weisskopf from Vienna, and Professor John E. Lennard-Jones, a visitor from the University of Bristol.

As a matter of course, all members of the Institutes of Physics attended the famous weekly Physics Colloquia held jointly by the three Professors.[13] These were at a very high level and often given by visitors and foreign guests. At this time when theoretical physicists were inclined to be somewhat abstract and mathematical in their presentations, using the new tools of matrix, operator, and eigenvalue methods not yet generally familiar to physicists, Franck would intervene to ask the theorists to bring out the physics of their topics. His presence was a benefit to all, especially to the younger experimentalists and students.[9] At an early stage, Herzberg was asked to give a colloquium on his most recent work on a new band system in carbon monoxide, CO, and felt that the ensuing discussion came off well. With his continuing interest in astronomy, he attended the Astronomy Colloquia, as well as the more informal joint seminars on theoretical and experimental physics. Also much time was spent in study and discussion with the theorists. All in all, this was a most stimulating year and rewarding experience, although it took many long hours of constant work to try to keep up with the many new ideas and rapid developments in all of these fields. Herzberg also kept up with the current scientific literature and developed a system of index cards noting references and brief abstracts of the papers that interested him. This collection of references proved to be indispensable to his later writings. He was completely absorbed in his work, with little time for other activities, except for writing letters to his friends in Darmstadt and Hamburg and to the ever-widening circle of molecular spectroscopists around the world. He developed the habit of typing a number of letters each evening and kept copies, which he filed meticulously along with the letters he received.

Herzberg also had the opportunity to participate in several conferences. In December of 1928, he presented a paper on his work with Heitler titled "New theoretical and experimental results on homopolar binding" at a regional conference of Hessian physicists in Frankfurt. At this conference, he heard an introductory lecture by Schrödinger on the theoretical perception of the value of physical models which was particularly illuminating and clear. He then spent several days in Darmstadt, staying with his colleague Kurt Lion, and gave a colloquium at the THD on "Quantum theory and chemistry". In February, a Conference of the German Physical Society was held in Göttingen with a large attendance. Here, among other spectroscopists, he met his friend Karl-Friedrich Bonhoeffer, the physical chemist, and while discussing recent research, Herzberg learned that the Delbrück and Bonhoeffer families had been neighbours in the wealthy Grunewald suburb of Berlin and that Karl-Friedrich's brother Klaus had married Max Delbrück's sister Emmie.[14] Towards the end of June 1929, Herzberg presented his work on the dissociation energy of oxygen at a conference in Bad Nauheim near Frankfurt. Again, he took the opportunity to spend a few days at the THD for talks with Rau and colleagues and to give two colloquia, one on electron spin and the second on ortho- and para-hydrogen.

During the first part of his stay in Göttingen, Herzberg concentrated his attention on the electronic structure of molecules, and using the Wigner–-Witmer rules, he was able to show from a theoretical argument that the accepted value for the dissociation energy of oxygen was not correct. He was also able to establish an upper limit for the dissociation energy of nitrogen. As he wrote to his friend Hans-Werner, he was especially pleased that he had priority in determining this new value, confirmed three months later by R.T. Birge and R.S. Mulliken, two American leaders in spectroscopy.[15] Although these contributions were not of major significance, they were important steps in the development of molecular science and introduced Herzberg's name to the international community. The "build-up principles" of diatomic molecules occupied most of his time, and he applied the molecular orbital theory of Hund and Mulliken with modifications to distinguish between bonding and anti-bonding electrons in molecules. He wrote a long and detailed paper on this topic and presented his work in the Physics Colloquium. Because he could not assume that the audience was familiar with this new theory, he expanded his presentation with an introductory tutorial and gave two colloquia on the subject for a total time of three hours. There was much discussion and helpful comment, which caused him to make extensive changes to his manuscript before submission to *Zeitschrift für Physik.*[16] He also submitted a paper on this topic to the 1929 Conference of the German Physical Society, held in Prague in mid-September. This new work was deemed to be of such importance by many in the community that

Herzberg's name became linked with those of Hund and Mulliken in the early development of molecular orbital theory.

One of Herzberg's most important contributions in Göttingen was based on the observed rotational Raman spectrum of nitrogen (N_2) obtained by Franco Rasetti at that time.[17] On seeing the published spectrum, Herzberg immediately recognized the difference in intensity alternation of rotational lines in N_2 from that in H_2. He thought it significant that the even-numbered lines were stronger than the odd-numbered lines in N_2, while the reverse was true for H_2. He contacted Heitler, who also sensed its importance, and in a short time they analyzed the problem and submitted a brief paper to *Die Naturwissenschaften* with their explanation.[18] Intensity alternation of rotational lines in a molecular spectrum, that is, whether the even- or odd-numbered lines are stronger, is based on whether an atomic nucleus contains an even or odd number of particles (leading to the so-called Bose or Fermi statistics, respectively). At that time (1929), only two elementary particles were known, protons and electrons, both of which obey Fermi statistics, and the premise was made that protons and electrons were constituents of nuclei. Hydrogen nuclei have a mass of one atomic unit and a positive charge of one unit and consist of a single proton, that is, an odd number of particles, and therefore obey Fermi statistics. This is in keeping with the observation that the odd-numbered rotational lines in the spectra of H_2 are more intense than even-numbered lines. Nitrogen nuclei (mass of fourteen atomic units and a positive charge of seven units) were assumed to have fourteen protons and seven electrons, that is, an odd number of Fermi particles, and therefore the spectra of N_2 should exhibit odd-numbered lines that are more intense, just as in H_2. However, this was contrary to the spectrum observed by Rasetti, which showed that N nuclei do not obey Fermi statistics but rather Bose statistics. Heitler and Herzberg were the first to point out this remarkable result for N nuclei and its discrepancy with the then current theory. Although this result was the first indication that electrons are not present in nuclei, Heitler and Herzberg did not go that far in explaining the discrepancy: they suggested that electrons in the nucleus lose their spin and thus their influence on the statistics of the nucleus. Only after the discovery of the neutron (mass of one atomic unit and no charge), by James Chadwick in Cambridge three years later (1932), was it proposed by Heisenberg that nuclei consist of protons and neutrons, but not electrons. Thus nitrogen nuclei consist of seven protons and seven neutrons, an even number of particles in total, and so obey Bose statistics, as first demonstrated by molecular spectroscopy.[19] Although the paper by Heitler and Herzberg was essential to this result and to Heisenberg's assumption that neutrons are fermions, he made no mention of their work in his paper.

Member of the Second Institute of Physics

During the last half of his ten month stay in Göttingen, Herzberg carried out experimental research at the Second Institute of Physics directed by James Franck and also continued his close contact with the theorists. Two of Franck's assistants were Hertha Sponer and Heinrich G. Kuhn, both accomplished experimental scientists, completely immersed in investigations of electronic spectra of diatomic molecules, studies which were of great interest to Herzberg. At that time, few women were attending universities and only rarely were they employed as assistants or staff members. Sponer and the mathematician Emmy Noether were the only women faculty members at the University of Göttingen. Both were unpaid, *unbeamter ausserordentlicher* professors (unofficial extraordinary professors) among 235 male faculty members. In time, both were recognized as eminent contributors to their specialized fields of study. Sponer was known among the spectroscopy group as a methodical worker and a stickler for details, yet Herzberg found he could profitably work with her because of their interests in similar molecular problems. Later he was to collaborate with Sponer on a joint paper and to help her in providing data and checking tables of data for her book *Molecular Spectra and Applications in Chemical Problems.*

Each morning, Franck with his assistants and senior guests (the *Rundgang*) visited the graduate students to discuss progress and problems. In this way, Herzberg became familiar with the overall research program of the Institute. Herzberg collaborated in experimental research with Professor Günter Scheibe, a visitor from the University of Erlangen in Bavaria. He and Scheibe took up a suggestion by Franck and looked at the electronic spectra of the methyl halides, but all they found with eight different methyl compounds were continuous spectra in the wavelength region 2000–8000 angstroms (Å). These, of course, were not as interesting as discrete spectra and were difficult to understand. Herzberg and Scheibe expected to find vibrational structure at shorter wavelengths, and later, when a fluoride-prism, vacuum spectrograph was at their disposal, they observed a discrete spectrum of methyl iodide (CH_3I). Theirs was the first study of methyl halide spectra occurring in the vacuum ultraviolet region, and the results were submitted for presentation at the Discussions of the Faraday Society to be held in late September in Bristol and for publication.[20,21] This was Herzberg's first work on polyatomic spectra.

Herzberg also met with the group enrolled in the First Physical Institute directed by Robert Pohl, although their research on crystals, crystal spectra, and solid state problems was far removed from his own interests in atoms and molecules in the gas phase. To his surprise, he was asked by the younger students in the First Institute of Physics to give an overview of recent developments in gaseous spectroscopy, because they had difficulty following the talks on atomic and molecular physics in the Colloquia. While others in Göttingen with more experience could have given these lectures, Herzberg agreed and presented a series of informal lectures as an introduction to atomic and molecular spectroscopy. These were also attended by graduate students and researchers from the other Institutes, including some from Born's theoretical group. One of these was the recently arrived Victor Weisskopf, who recalled that at that time students had two choices of outstanding schools in atomic physics in Germany: they could go either to Göttingen or to Munich, where there was Arnold Sommerfeld and his great school:

> I went to Göttingen and there I met the great physicists who were the creators of quantum mechanics. The important thing, however, was not to meet the great ones, but the many young people who were on my level, or a little more advanced, all eager to learn, to discuss and to argue. There were young instructors like Heitler, Herzberg, Nordheim, and Wigner, and graduate students, people of my age or a little older, such as Delbrück and Teller and Maria Goeppert. We learned quantum mechanics together. It was a great experience and sensation. I will never forget G. Herzberg—he also remains in my memory as one of the outstanding teachers—he at that time taught for the first time the course "Introduction to Atomic Physics" which is now immortalized in his book which you all know, *Atomic Spectra and Atomic Structure*. It was an outstanding course at that time and still is, a fantastic achievement after forty years! Atomic quantum mechanics, the consequences of symmetry, the term spectra, the systematics of spectroscopy, the transition probabilities, all this was exciting because it was so beautiful, and only a few years old.[22]

Even at this early stage in his career Herzberg was demonstrating his abilities as a superb teacher, with the clear exposition and excitement of research that have characterized his lectures ever since. Another who attended these lectures was his colleague Scheibe, who immediately suggested that Herzberg should publish this work as a book. He offered to contact Theodor Steinkopff, a publisher in Dresden whom he knew very well, and to introduce Herzberg and the idea of the book to him. This he did, and before long, Herzberg was negotiating a book on atomic and molecular spectroscopy with the publisher. Thus began the writing of the series of books that became classics in physics and chemistry.

While Herzberg spent most of his time in the laboratory of Franck's Institute and in studying, writing, and in discussions with the groups and visitors, he wanted to sit in on one or two of Franck's courses. However, as he soon learned, Franck was not interested in giving the typical lecture course and had come to an agreement with Pohl, who consented to give the main lectures in physics, for which he became renowned throughout Germany. Franck much preferred to hold sessions of small informal seminars given by his students, visitors, and himself. In one of these seminars, Herzberg heard an account of recent spectroscopic research by Luise Hedwig Oettinger, one of Franck's students, and engaged her in discussions of the work. By chance, she lived only a block away from Herzberg, at 19 Dahlmannstrasse, and they often met on the way to or from the University. He enjoyed these encounters, and before long found they had similar views of their future careers and common intellectual interests. She was as determined as he to become a research scientist and to focus on molecular science. They became close friends, and together they attended Göttingen's cultural and musical events, as well as social activities in professors' homes, and hiked on Sundays in the nearby forests. They would marry by year-end.

While Göttingen was undoubtedly one of the main European centres of learning, Herzberg was disappointed with the quantity and quality of music and theatre, which could not compare with what he had enjoyed in Darmstadt. In Göttingen, too, the *Korps* societies seemed to play a dominant role in campus life, but of course, he took no interest in their activities. To make up for the lack of cultural occasions, professors and their wives regularly entertained friends and students in their homes. Many faculty members were talented musicians, and their favourite relaxation was the informal playing of the works of the German and Austrian composers. For the younger set, there were parties and dances at professors' homes. One of the most memorable locations was the huge entrance hall of the home of Professor and Mrs. Franck, where their two daughters hosted assistants, visitors, and students. A special treat was the view of Göttingen at night from the high tower of the Franck home.[23] During a Christmas party at the Institute of Physics, humorous stories were told, one being about an Egyptian king's daughter, whose face the storyteller thought looked very much like that of Luise, and from that time on, Luise was known as the Egyptian princess, much to the amusement of her friends.

Among the many visitors in Göttingen whom Herzberg met were J.G. Winans, a National Research Fellow at Princeton University, and E.C.G. Stueckelberg, a Swiss theorist, who had jointly written a paper titled "The origin of the continuous spectrum of the hydrogen molecule".[24] This topic had been the subject of Herzberg's first presentation at a Physical Society Meeting and his third paper, which he realized had given a far-out suggestion for the origin of this spectrum. He immediately understood that this latest work, based on quantum theory, gave the correct explanation for the spectrum as arising from transitions from a bound to an unbound or repulsive state. Another visitor was the Dutch physicist M.J. Druyvesteyn, who described a spectrum in a mixture of helium and neon but could not explain its origin.[25] Although Herzberg was not particularly interested in this work at the time, he made a note of it. To his surprise, about fifty years later while working on spectra of the noble gases, he obtained the same spectrum at much higher resolution and solved the riddle: the spectrum was due to the ion $HeNe^+$.[26]

Friedrich Hund, a former assistant of Max Born, already known for his important contributions in atomic physics, was a frequent visitor to Göttingen. Hund was applying his knowledge of atoms to molecules and had published his basic papers on molecular orbital theory in 1927. Herzberg was by now well versed in this concept, having thoroughly studied Hund's papers, and had several discussions with him about his own applications to molecular structure and spectra. From this initial acquaintance, a strong friendship developed through their scientific interests, and it continued for seven decades, with Hund reaching the age of one hundred. Another visitor interested in molecular orbital theory was John E. Lennard-Jones (later Sir John), Professor of Theoretical Physics at the University of Bristol. At a young age, he had made important contributions to the study of the forces between atoms and molecules and introduced the empirical form A/r^n –

B/r^m (where m and n are integers) for the potential energy of two molecules at a distance r from each other, a relationship known by his name. He spent six months in Göttingen and became familiar with Herzberg's ideas on molecular orbital theory expressed in his recent paper on the topic from an experimentalist's viewpoint.[16] Lennard-Jones found that his own theoretical thoughts were along similar lines and suggested they might continue discussions and collaboration if Herzberg would come to spend a year in Bristol. Herzberg welcomed the idea and thought that a year in England would be very worthwhile, giving him the opportunity to visit universities and meet English scientists, as well as a chance to become fluent in English. Little did he realize what an enormous benefit his facility in English would become in just a few years.

At that time the Department of Physics at Bristol was under the chairmanship of Arthur M. Tyndall, who was determined to build a first-rate research school in physics following those of Oxford and Cambridge, and he and his staff members were on the lookout for promising young physicists. His first priority was to bring together a group in molecular physics to be headed by Lennard-Jones, the Melville Wills Chair of Theoretical Physics, who personally invited Herzberg and Max Delbrück during his stay in Göttingen. With the knowledge that the young Herzberg was already being recognized as an authority in molecular spectroscopy, Professor Tyndall offered him a Research Studentship at £300 per annum in May of 1929, to begin sometime in September following his fellowship in Göttingen.[27] Although very little spectroscopic work was being done in Bristol at that time, Tyndall asked Herzberg to provide details of equipment he would need. He immediately replied, requesting the loan of a grating spectrograph if possible, a vacuum pump and transformer for operating a discharge tube, and a comparator for measurement of spectra. Herzberg apologized for writing in German, saying that he could read English well but he could neither write nor speak it as well as he would like and would work very hard to learn. Because only prism spectrographs were available, the grating instrument would have to be built. Within a month, Herbert W.B. Skinner, a young lecturer at Bristol, was in contact with Herzberg to plan the building of a two-metre vacuum spectrograph, with gratings to be ordered from the National Physical Laboratory in Teddington. Skinner's own research was in X-rays, but he was a consummate experimentalist and sufficiently interested in Herzberg's vacuum spectrograph to want to design and build it himself.

Towards the end of the summer semester, Professor Paul Ehrenfest of Leyden visited Göttingen with Hendrik Casimir and George Uhlenbeck, two of his students, both of whom became famous physicists. They spent three weeks in Göttingen and held daily meetings with staff and students to catch up on the most recent applications of quantum mechanics to atomic and molecular physics. Herzberg had a chance to review his own work with this group and found that Ehrenfest had an incisive way of asking questions and clarifying by them some obscure points in the discussions, a most stimulating experience for Herzberg. August turned out to be a quiet month in Göttingen with most of the staff and students on holidays, and Herzberg was able to complete the last of the papers based on his work there. He left on 1 September 1929 to spend two weeks in Nürnberg to visit Luise and her family.

Luise's parents were Paul Oettinger and Elsbeth (nee Eichenberg). Mr. Oettinger was a veteran of World War I. He first worked for the export company Eichenberg & Co. based in New Orleans but soon had his own company, the Radium–Bronze Paint and Sheet Metal Works, and travelled widely in the United States, Canada, and South America. Luise was born in Nürnberg in 1906, and her sister Lotte was born four years later. Luise attended the Realgymnasium of the Civic High School for Girls in Nürnberg from 1919 to 1925. She studied German, English, French, and Latin languages along with mathematics, physics, and chemistry, as well as history, geography, and religion. Her academic record was laudable with outstanding grades in physics, history, and geography, and she realized that her interests were focused on science. In spite of family pressures to be "feminine" she was determined to pursue a career in mathematics and science and enrolled in the Technische Hochschule in Munich. After a year in Munich, she left to visit relatives in Austin, Texas, and attended the State University of Texas during the year 1927–1928. On her return to Germany in the summer of 1928, Luise registered in the physics program at the University of Göttingen. She enjoyed her two and a half years there, attending classes and seminars given by the extraordinary group of mathematicians and physicists already mentioned. The fortuitous meeting, friendship, and love of Gerhard was a supreme bonus.

Gerhard was warmly welcomed into Luise's well-to-do family, and he perceived no hesitation on their part to accept an Aryan son-in-law. As he soon discovered, the family retained little of Jewish culture or religion, even though Luise's paternal grandfather had been a Rabbi and would not

Luise Hedwig Oettinger at the time
of her engagement to Gerhard.

have permitted close friendship with Gerhard, let alone marriage. The young couple became engaged and planned to marry in December. By that time Gerhard would be established in Bristol and would have completed his *Habilitation* in Darmstadt, so that he would be ready to take up an academic position on his return to Germany. Luise planned to complete her studies in Göttingen in the spring of 1929 and then join Gerhard in Bristol. On learning of her son's engagement, Gerhard's mother congratulated him on finding an educated and beautiful partner and never mentioned Luise's Jewish ancestry, neither did Walter. In announcing his engagement to Alfred and Hans-Werner, Gerhard reminded them of their boyhood discussions on the qualities in the women they would marry. He hinted humorously that Luise fulfilled almost all of their conditions: she was a physicist and a pacifist and had her hair cut short in the latest vogue, but she was not a vegetarian and she was Jewish.

On 15 September Herzberg attended the German Physical Society Meeting in Prague and gave a presentation titled "Bonding and anti-bonding electrons in diatomic molecules". He was pleased with the reception of this paper and the many scientists he met as a result of this work.

There are few hours in life more agreeable than the hour dedicated to the ceremony known as afternoon tea.

Henry James

4. A YEAR IN BRISTOL

Herzberg's trip to England was his first outside of the Continent. His ship landed at Dover on 22 September 1929, and he was permitted to proceed to Bristol on the conditions that on arrival he obtain a Registration Certificate from the police and that he not remain in the United Kingdom longer than twelve months. He was also to check with the Bristol constabulary every few months, noting any change of address. With these formalities completed, Herzberg took the train to Bristol where he was met by Herbert Skinner, who had helped to design the new spectrograph for Herzberg's research. Herzberg was then settled in the home of Mr. and Mrs. Painter on 42 Windsor Road in St. Andrew's Park. He joined the group at the University of Bristol the next day.

The H.H. Wills Physics Laboratory

The H.H. Wills Physics Laboratory was a spacious new building located in a fine botanical garden of the Royal Fort Estate of the University on a hilltop overlooking the city. It was named after its benefactor Henry Herbert Wills of the cigarette manufacturing firm of the same name. The Laboratory was officially opened just two years earlier on 21 October 1927 by Sir Ernest Rutherford. On this occasion, he and other physicists of great fame, including Sir William Bragg, Sir Arthur Eddington, A. Fowler, Pierre Langevin of France, and Max Born of Germany, were awarded honorary degrees. By 1929, the small staff comprised the chairman Arthur M. Tyndall, who worked on ion mobilities with his assistant Cecil F. Powell (later, of cosmic rays fame), J.E. Lennard-Jones the molecular theorist, S.H. Piper and H.W.B. Skinner working on X-rays, W. Sucksmith interested in magnetism, and L.C. Jackson a solid state physicist, among others. Herzberg found that Max Delbrück, his colleague from Göttingen, had also been invited to Bristol. He recalled that Max fitted in very well with the group of younger physicists in Bristol because of his gregarious ways and the ease with which he made friends. Herzberg and Delbrück were the first from the Continent to be given research fellowships in Bristol, followed later by K. Wieland from Switzerland, W. Heitler, M. Stobbe, and H. Bethe

The H.H. Wills Physics Laboratory, University of Bristol.

from Germany, C. Zener from the United States of America, and D.C. Rose from Canada. These were all judicious choices as three, namely Bethe, Delbrück, and Herzberg, were later awarded Nobel Prizes.

Just two days after Herzberg's arrival in Bristol, the University was host to a Faraday Society Meeting titled "Molecular Spectra and Molecular Structure" (24–26 September), organized by Professors W.E. Garner of the Chemistry Department and J.E. Lennard-Jones of Physics.[1] Many of the world authorities attended, most from foreign lands (ten from the U.S.A., six from Germany, four from France, and one or two from each of Canada, India, Italy, Poland, Sweden, Switzerland, and the U.S.S.R.), and fifteen from the United Kingdom. In all, thirty-nine papers were submitted for discussion.

This was Herzberg's first meeting in the English language, and he was somewhat dismayed on opening day to find that he did not understand a word of what the first speaker, the distinguished O.W. Richardson, who was to be awarded the Nobel Prize in Physics that year, was saying about the spectrum of hydrogen.[2] Herzberg began to wonder whether he would ever be able to understand English. He soon realized, however, that the problem was not simply his own deficiency in English, but that this great physicist mumbled. The next speaker was Sir C.V. Raman, destined to receive the 1930 Nobel Prize in Physics for his work on light scattering and for discovery of the effect named after him.[3] As he presented his paper "Investigation of molecular structure by light scattering", he spoke clearly and lucidly in beautiful English, and Herzberg could understand every word and found Raman's enthusiasm infectious. Herzberg had the opportunity to meet Raman several times during the meeting and to discuss with him the meaning for nuclear theory of the intensity alternation (strong/weak) for the even- to odd-numbered rotational lines in the Raman spectrum of nitrogen, observed by Rasetti. Raman was very interested in this result and understood and accepted the explanation of Heitler and Herzberg. At the meeting, Herzberg presented a brief report on his work with Scheibe on the continuous spectra of the methyl halides and participated in the formal discussions during the session on electronic spectra. Although he was initially concerned about his limited speaking capability in English, he felt that he had communicated his thoughts reasonably well at his first public meeting in England. Also, he was pleased to meet for the first time several senior spectroscopists with whom he had corresponded, including E.F. Barker, R.T. Birge, G.H. Dieke, and O.S. Duffendack of the U.S.A., C.F. Goodeve and W. Jevons of the U.K., V. Henri, J. Cabbanes, and J. Lecomte of France, and R. Mecke of Germany, among others.

Herzberg was quite happy with his stay in England and managed to acclimatize rather quickly to living in Bristol. At first, it was naturally difficult to get started in new surroundings with a somewhat unfamiliar language. As might be expected, he also found differences in Anglo-Saxon attitudes from those he was used to in Germany, far less formality among colleagues at the university and much more open discussion and criticism of local and federal politicians and governments. In many ways Bristol reminded him of his home town of Hamburg. Bristol was situated at the confluence of two rivers, the Avon and Frome, flowing into the Severn River and the Bristol Channel. It had extensive dock facilities and was one of England's major trading centres since the twelfth century. He enjoyed hikes in the wooded hills of the countryside, although he found cycling on the steep hills of Bristol quite a challenge, even on his lightweight bicycle outfitted with bamboo fenders.

The faculty of the H.H. Wills Laboratory in 1930.
First row: W. Sucksmith, – , G. Herzberg, G. McKenzie, J.E. Lennard-Jones, A.M. Tyndall, L. Herzberg, A.P. Chattock, S.H. Piper, H.W.B. Skinner; Middle row: L.C. Jackson, – , C.F. Powell, M.G. Bennett, – , T. Malkin, – , H.H. Potter; Back row: W.R. Harper, – , –, – .

In the laboratory, he was essentially on his own because there were no experimental spectroscopists in Bristol. However, the atmosphere at the Wills Laboratory was relaxed and friendly, and Tyndall's attitude and support stimulated creativity and hard work. The laboratories were spacious, well equipped, and much better supported than even in Göttingen, and the freedom for research was the same as in Göttingen and Darmstadt at that time. The small staff of twelve included some brilliant physicists, although Herzberg felt that the Bristol people couldn't quite match some of the very powerful minds working in Göttingen. Of course, he did not expect to find the equal of Göttingen here, since he knew that the University of Bristol was one of the newer universities in England, having been established as University College Bristol in 1876 and gaining university status only in 1909. Twenty years later its enrollment was almost one thousand students in the Faculties of Arts, Science, Medicine, and Engineering. Thanks to Tyndall's efforts, the university had already achieved great strength in science. As in Göttingen, there was also much interaction between theorists and experimentalists and, in Herzberg's case primarily in discussions with Lennard-Jones and Delbrück on molecular problems. Also there were many visitors from nearby universities and the Continent, among them Fritz London and Neville Mott, both of whom he came to know well.

A new and particularly enjoyable experience for Herzberg was the ritual of afternoon tea that brought together most of the people of the Wills Laboratory every day at 4:30 P.M. Tea was provided by Mrs. Greed, the porteress, who along with her other duties found time to prepare delicious breads, cakes, scones, jams, and biscuits.[4] These meetings gave the opportunity for much informal discussion of research and scientific activities around the world and made a deep impression on him. There was never afternoon tea in Darmstadt or Göttingen. Added to these daily gatherings were frequent Sunday walks in the Somerset hills with Prof. Tyndall and his staff.

The first few months in Bristol were spent in preparing a program of research while awaiting the completion of the two-metre grating spectrograph. This included the installation of a discharge tube for excitation of emission spectra of various diatomic and polyatomic molecules he wished to study and in preliminary experiments using the two prism spectrographs (a Hilger E_1 and E_2) at his disposal. He also immersed himself in reviewing the available literature on predissociation, the diffuseness of certain lines in a molecular spectrum, a topic which had piqued his interest at the Faraday Meeting. In the evenings, he was preoccupied with preparations for the *Habilitation*, a procedure characteristic of German universities and the outcome of which would determine his future. It was the formal entry to an academic career, a course in research he had set for himself long ago. The *Habilitation* required a thesis and a lecture, followed by discussion and a question period. He was scheduled to make his presentation in mid-January at the Technische Hochschule in Darmstadt.

On 13 December 1929, the University of Bristol celebrated the installation of a new chancellor, Winston (Leonard Spencer) Churchill. He was met at the train station by students singing "Why was he born so beautiful? Why was he born at all?" And Herzberg joined the townspeople who lined the streets to welcome Churchill to Bristol.

Marriage

Just before Christmas, Gerhard returned to Nürnberg for his marriage to Luise on 30 December 1929. Because they were of different sects, Lutheran and Jewish, and neither of them practised their faith, a religious service was out of the question. They were married by a magistrate in a civic ceremony. Only the Oettinger family was in attendance; Gerhard's mother was in America and Walter was working in Hamburg. After a week's holiday in the Alps, the couple returned to Nürnberg and travelled to nearby Erlangen. At the invitation of Professor Scheibe, Gerhard gave a colloquium on the meaning of modern spectroscopy for chemistry. He then went on to Darmstadt for the *Habilitation* which was held on 15 January. For the thesis requirements, he submitted his paper on molecular orbital theory, "The bonding of diatomic molecules".[5] He also gave the lecture "An introduction to modern spectroscopy and its meaning for chemistry" (*Einführung in die moderne Spektroskopie und ihre Bedeutung für die Chemie*) and "Selected topics in atomic physics" (*Ausgewöhlte Kapitel aus der Atomphysik*). With the successful completion of the *Habilitation*, Herzberg earned the right to lecture (*venia legendi*), and Professor Rau, now the Rector, offered him the post of *Privatdozent* at the THD, equivalent to an Assistant Professorship, to begin on completion of his Research Assistantship in Bristol.

The newlyweds proceeded to Göttingen, where they spent a few days with surprised colleagues, who were only then personally informed of the marriage. Luise and Gerhard managed to attend a Physics Colloquium and to visit and admire the new home of the Institute of Mathematics nearby, which had been formally dedicated on 2 December. Gerhard was due to return to Bristol on 23 January, the very day of David Hilbert's mandatory retirement at age sixty-eight. Luise would remain in Göttingen to continue her studies until the end of the winter semester (at Easter) and then join Gerhard in Bristol.

Return to Bristol

On his return to England, Herzberg was pleased that the immigration authorities had approved a month's extension of his stay to 1 November 1930. In Bristol, he was invited by Tyndall to give a course of lectures on molecular spectroscopy to begin in April. At the same time, the vacuum spectrograph was completed and ready to be tested and used. Also, Max Born invited him to participate at the Congress of Scientific Research to be held in Königsberg in the beginning of September, with Hund as the keynote speaker and Herzberg to follow with a shorter paper and discussion titled "The term specification of diatomic molecules". In addition, the first letters from the publisher Theodor Steinkopff concerning his book on atomic and molecular spectroscopy began to arrive, inquiring when the manuscript might be ready. There was no doubt that this would be an extremely busy year. However, with his disciplined approach to these duties and his determination and hard work, much would be accomplished before returning to Darmstadt to take up his post as Privatdozent.

A few days before he was to meet Luise on her arrival in London, Gerhard took the opportunity to visit the University of Cambridge and King's College and Imperial College in London. A letter of introduction from James Franck paved the way for Herzberg to meet some of Rutherford's brilliant associates in the Cavendish Laboratory, all young men of his own age who were to make great strides in our knowledge of nuclei. These included P.M.S. Blackett, J.D. Cockroft, E.T.S. Walton, and the Russian Pyotr L. Kapitsa, all future Nobel Prize winners, and M. Oliphant, who after some years in England returned home to Australia as a professor of physics at the National University and later served as Governor of the State of Victoria.[6] Herzberg also became acquainted with the college system at Cambridge, which was completely different from the way of life for students in German universities. In the King's College laboratory of R.C. Johnson, whom he had met at the Faraday Society Meeting, he was introduced to R.K. Asundi of Pune, India, who was working on the spectra of CO for his Ph.D. degree. He became a lifelong friend and was to introduce Herzberg to Indian culture and philosophy in addition to Indian contributions to spectroscopy. This visit to King's College turned out to be the beginning of a very important connection for Herzberg, as later events were to prove. On Luise's arrival in London they enjoyed a few days of sightseeing and took advantage of the opportunity to attend some musical events.

Back in Bristol, Herzberg gained much valuable experience with his first grating spectrograph. This was to be of enormous help in his future studies. He obtained definitive plates of P_2 showing diffuse rotational lines, which he correctly interpreted as caused by predissociation. While trying out various light sources for exciting the spectrum of P_2, he obtained and identified a spectrum of CP, arising from an organic impurity, possibly stopcock grease in the cell filled with phosphorous. He was also able to observe emission spectra of $^{14}N^{15}N$ in an overexposed plate of $^{14}N_2$. The isotope ^{15}N had been detected from band spectra of NO by S.M. Naudé in Chicago, within a year of the first discovery of the isotopes ^{17}O, ^{18}O, and ^{13}C from band spectra.[7] Since not much was known about the ^{15}N isotope, Herzberg published a brief note on his findings.[8] Luise collaborated with Gerhard on a number of these problems. This was the beginning of several joint projects over the years, with Luise receiving full credit for her contributions as a co-author in numerous publications. At Gerhard's suggestion she attempted to look for a spectrum of C_2^+, but this was an idea before its time, and the spectrum was only found about fifty years later.

Herzberg turned his attention to obtaining absorption spectra of polyatomic molecules. So as not to duplicate work being done or planned in Göttingen, he wrote to James Franck informing him of the fine qualities of the two-metre spectrograph and of his work on P_2, CP, and N_2, and inquiring whether there was continuing interest in Franck's group in the methyl halides. Otherwise he would try to obtain improved spectra of CH_3I.[9] He also wanted to look for spectra of other organic molecules such as acetylene (C_2H_2) and formaldehyde (CH_2O). Franck wrote back that Scheibe was continuing work on CH_3I, but that Herzberg should certainly study the other polyatomic molecules.[10]

Herzberg knew that no grating instruments were available in Darmstadt and that his time for experimental research would be limited while preparing for his first series of lectures, so he decided to forego evaluation of spectra while in Bristol and concentrate on obtaining good plates of spectra of C_2H_2 and CH_2O. These he could measure and analyze later in Darmstadt. This took so much of his time that he was not able to devote any time to the promised book. Moreover, progress in spectroscopy was moving at such a rapid pace that he realized he would have to change his original plan of including both atomic and molecular studies in one volume, even though this book was meant to be an introduction to the field. In fact, his own research work and responsibilities at the THD were to prevent him from completing a satisfactory manuscript for another four years. He also gave up plans to participate in Born's meeting in Königsberg because of the travel costs involved. Instead, he attended a meeting of the British Association held at the same time in Bristol. The meeting itself was not very exciting for him as most of the presentations had already appeared in publications, but he had a chance to meet many scientists and, in particular, Robert Mulliken of The University of Chicago with whom he had corresponded on many occasions. They had already developed mutual respect and admiration for each other's contributions, and this increased over the years, in spite of some friendly competition during their lifetimes.

As the time for their return to Germany approached, Luise and Gerhard were assisted by friends in their search for suitable accommodation in Darmstadt. In particular, Gretel Goldstein, the widow of Gerhard's philosophy professor Julius Goldstein was most helpful, with several suggestions of friends who rented out rooms near the THD.[11] Luise and Gerhard selected the home of the Juda family when assured by Mrs. Goldstein that they would find this household of family and roomers to be cultured and interesting people. They rented two upstairs rooms with a small kitchen and bath and were to be provided with breakfast and an evening meal, all at a cost expected to be within their means. Costs were a concern since it had not been possible to save much from the Bristol stipend. Also, Luise planned to continue her studies towards a Ph.D. degree at the THD and Gerhard's post of Privatdozent was not a salaried faculty position, with remuneration coming only from the fees paid by students for special lectures.

Much to their delight, towards the end of their stay in Bristol, James Franck presented the 1930 H.H. Wills Memorial Lecture "Spectroscopy and Chemical Binding" and was awarded an honorary degree by the University of Bristol. The thirteen month period in England proved to be a long absence from Germany for Gerhard. As much as he and Luise enjoyed their English friends and living in Bristol with the sea nearby, they were anxious to be home and counted the weeks and then the days until their return. They left Bristol and England on 31 October 1930.

The characteristic danger of great nations, ... which have a long history of continuous creation, is that they may at last fail from not comprehending the great institutions they have created.

Walter Bagehot

5. PRIVATDOZENT IN DARMSTADT

The Germany that the Herzbergs returned to was one they neither remembered nor expected. After only a year's absence they found the Weimar Republic reeling economically and threatened politically. While the heavy burden of the Versailles Treaty of 1919 had crippled German industrial capacity by stripping Germany of its colonies and merchant fleet, loans from the United States had helped bring some semblance of prosperity and stability to the country in the late 1920s. However, this was threatened by a slowdown in business activity in 1929, and the crash of the New York Stock Exchange on "Black Friday", 24 October 1929, started the worldwide Depression that hit Germany the hardest of any European country. Loans were withdrawn after the stock market collapse, and bankruptcies became commonplace, with three million unemployed by the end of 1930.[1]

The Years 1930 and 1931

In Darmstadt, the closure of printing, heating, and metal companies put 25 percent of the workforce into unemployment.[2] The unemployed held demonstrations to protest against the government, and the poverty and despair made agitation by the National Socialist German Workers' Party (NSDAP, the Nazis) much easier. In the election of 1930, the NSDAP gained 24.4 percent of the votes and became the second strongest political party in Darmstadt. At the Technische Hochschule, students had also become increasingly active politically, and the "People's Students" gained seven seats in the student elections of 1930.[3]

Under these severe economic conditions, Herzberg was fortunate to have an academic position of any kind. Many of the young scientists had to make do with postdoctoral positions, without remuneration, living on what their families could provide.[4] Privatdozents like Herzberg did not receive a stipend either. Their only income came from the opportunity to give special lectures from which they would receive a fee paid by the attendees. These lectures were in addition to the normal course requirements and were selected by students as electives, depending on their specialized interests. Herzberg gave a series of such lectures in his chosen field of spectroscopy. He had not been able to devote the necessary time to prepare these lectures during the last few months in Bristol and now worked incessantly to be ready for his inaugural lecture, which he gave in mid-January.[5] He chose the title "Cosmic Ultraviolet Radiation" for his course and was disappointed with the poor attendance and the resulting low fees which he received. He surmised this lack of attendees was owing to his choice of an unattractive and general title for the course. A regular contribution from Luise's father was most welcome at this time, as was the research stipend from the Emergency Association of German Science (*Notgemeinschaft der deutschen Wissenschaft*) awarded for his first year as privatdozent.

On returning to the THD, Herzberg's top priority for research had been to build high-resolution grating spectrographs for the far-ultraviolet and near-infrared regions.[6] He spent whatever time he could afford in the design of these instruments, with the help of Herr Sting, the head of the Physics Institute's machine shop. Herzberg hoped to obtain gratings for these spectrographs from Adam Hilger Ltd. in London, which had supplied the good two-metre grating in Bristol, but he encountered difficulties. The quality of the first grating received was a far cry from what he expected. He tried to rectify this by letter, without much success. In desperation he wrote to Professor Tyndall in Bristol and asked whether someone from the department could look into this problem for him when in London. Tyndall took up this matter himself with Frank Twyman, the Managing Director, and within a few months a satisfactory two-metre grating was received. Herzberg also considered alternative sources and inquired of others about the availability of good gratings in the United States. He was informed by Francis W. Loomis of the University of Illinois in Urbana that "gratings by Robert W. Wood of the Johns Hopkins University in Baltimore were very good, though you could never be sure of getting a grating from Wood until you had it in your hands".[7] Herzberg negotiated with Wood for a three-metre grating and was told to expect one within a year. In due course, he received a grating of remarkable quality, which Wood claimed was one of his best; it provided high intensity along with the anticipated high resolution. Although money was tight, funding for the gratings was provided through Rau by the Helmholtz Society for the Advancement of Physical–Technical Research (*Helmholtz Gesellschaft zur Förderung der physikalisch–technischen Forschung*) and the Association of Friends of the THD (*Ernst-Ludwigs-Hochschulgesellschaft*).[8]

While preparing lectures and waiting for the spectrographs to be built, Herzberg managed to resume studying some of the spectra photographed in Bristol. On completing the analysis of the P_2 spectra, he found evidence of predissociation, a topic that had perked his interest in the Faraday Discussion Meeting. To better understand this effect and to prepare a discussion for his book, Herzberg decided to write a detailed paper about this subject, including his own and other spectra as examples. He proposed this idea to the editor of *Naturwissenschaften*, who immediately approved, with the proviso that the paper be completed within a few months in order to be included in the annual volume of new results in the natural sciences. Herzberg managed to submit this long paper at the end of May.[9]

Luise had set her mind on preparing for a Ph.D. degree, with Gerhard's blessing. The degree required independent research, and she awaited the completion of the spectroscopic instruments for her experimental work. In the meantime, she enrolled in several courses in the Physics Institute of the THD and continued her collaboration with Gerhard by measuring and analyzing some of the spectra they had recorded in Bristol.

Within the first few months of his return to the THD, Herzberg was invited to participate in several conferences and to give colloquia. In February, he was invited to attend the next Faraday Society Discussion Meeting on Photochemical Processes to be held in Liverpool in April 1931. He declined because of the high travel costs and lack of time, but he submitted a brief paper on the absorption spectra of acetylene (C_2H_2) and formaldehyde (H_2CO) taken in Bristol.[10] Shortly after the winter term, he gave a one week course "The spectra and structures of atoms and molecules and their significance in chemistry" in Erlangen. This was at the standing invitation of Günter Scheibe, Professor of the Institute of Applied Chemistry, with whom he had worked in Göttingen. The course was essentially a shortened version of his winter lectures at the THD, with much better attendance, presumably because of the more specific title.

Several weeks later Herzberg participated in the prestigious "Week of Physics" held in Leipzig 3–5 July.[11] Peter Debye, famous for his work on X-ray diffraction, had organized small meetings each year since 1928 dealing with special fields of current research, with presentations given by the most active researchers in the field. On the advice of his Leipzig colleagues Werner Heisenberg and Friedrich Hund, Debye had selected the topic molecular structure for 1931. The speakers were to be Rudolf Mecke of Heidelberg on "Experimental studies of the band spectra of polyatomic molecules", Franco Rasetti of Rome on "The Raman spectra of gases", George Placzek of Leipzig on his newly developed "Polarizability theory of Raman spectra", Hertha Sponer of Göttingen on "Band spectra and dissociation", Victor Henri of Paris, who had discovered and named the effect, on "Predissociation", R. de L. Kronig of Groningen also on "Predissociation", and Herzberg on "Electronic structure of molecules and valence". With Hund expected to be present, Herzberg chose to discuss molecular orbital theory and its connection with valence, as well as his own version of bonding and anti-bonding electrons.

This conference turned out to be extremely interesting for Herzberg, particularly for the opportunity to discuss the latest developments in molecular science with the participants and the many eminent Leipzig scientists. Here, he met for the first time Werner Heisenberg, one of the founders of quantum mechanics, who was to be awarded the 1932 Nobel Prize for this work. He also met Edward Teller, a young Hungarian who had just completed his Ph.D. under Heisenberg. Teller's and Herzberg's discussions during this meeting led to their work on an important paper on the vibrational structure of electronic transitions in polyatomic molecules.[12] This was written within the next two years, while Teller was an assistant in Göttingen, with frequent visits to each other's institutes. Working with Teller was an experience that Herzberg would not forget: Teller had the ideas and shared them liberally, and Herzberg served as the midwife, trying to get these out of Teller by describing experimental results. In turn, Teller developed a great deal of affection for Herzberg. He found that "Herzberg's systematic approach and his great knowledge of the experimental material turned into concrete success what otherwise would have been no more than a number of more or less disjointed discussions. The collaboration was a great pleasure due to the discipline that was evident in everything that Herzberg undertook."[13] To Herzberg's surprise, Teller also insisted that the authors' names should be listed in alphabetical order on the paper, even though Herzberg felt that Teller's contributions were far more important and according to tradition Teller's name should be first. Herzberg was to follow the alphabetical order of names in all his later publications.

Following the conference in Leipzig, Herzberg visited the Kaiser-Wilhelm Institute for Physical Chemistry and Electro-Chemistry in Berlin-Dahlem, at the invitation of Professor Michael Polanyi, and gave a lecture at the weekly colloquium.[14] This was on the same topic as his presentation in Leipzig, with a tutorial introduction for the benefit of the younger students.

On his way back to Darmstadt, he stopped off in Göttingen to attend a conference of the German Physical Society, where he met many colleagues. These first two weeks in July, with visits to colleagues in Leipzig, Berlin-Dahlem, and Göttingen, were very important for Herzberg, although they occurred during an extremely busy summer term. On his return to the THD, he lectured on selected topics in atomic physics with emphasis on radioactivity and completed the paper for the proceedings of the Leipzig Conference.[15] At the end of September he also participated in a cramming course, preparing students for their physics examinations, a well-established system at the THD, which also helped the assistants and privatdozents to add to their low incomes. Before the start of the winter term the Herzbergs travelled to the South Tyrol for much-needed relaxation.

Luise and Gerhard were delighted with their home at 4 Heidenreichstrasse in Darmstadt. The location was ideal, in a fine residential neighbourhood, near a large park with a lake, the Grosser Woog, for boating and swimming, and bordering on a forest area that provided ample opportunities for hiking. A short walk around the lake brought them to Mathildenhöhe on the way to the THD, or skirting the lake and through the old town was another way to the THD. Either way, it was a pleasant fifteen minute walk from home to the laboratory. Their attic apartment was comfortably furnished and private for work and study in the evenings. Best of all, the

The Juda home, 4 Heidenreichstrasse, Darmstadt.

Juda family were very accommodating and friendly. Frau Juda, a widow, and her daughter Lise ran an efficient household with the help of a cook and cleaning lady. Several other paying guests included a banker's widow, a retired lawyer, a teacher, and some students. Frau Juda's brother, known to all as Uncle Victor, lived there, confined to a wheelchair by muscular dystrophy. He sketched and was very good company, always full of humour. The Herzbergs were served their breakfast and evening meal at home. Sunday breakfasts were a special treat, with a variety of baked goods, cheeses, jams and preserves, boiled eggs, and tea and coffee. Sundays were spent in long walks and often writing letters to parents and friends and working at home.

During that summer the political situation deteriorated rapidly in Darmstadt and especially in the rest of Germany, with brutal confrontations of Communists and Fascists. In mid-June more than a thousand SS (*Schutzstaffel*), Hitler's personal guards, in black uniforms and SA storm troopers in brown uniforms marched into Darmstadt, a clear threat to the Communists and to the local government. On 13 November the NSDAP held a large assembly as part of an election campaign, with Adolf Hitler present, and more than twenty thousand people in attendance.[16] Gerhard and Luise did not participate. While they had experienced hardship during earlier economic crises in their youth, the present scene was more disturbing and somewhat threatening. The mood was subdued in the Juda home that

Gerhard and unruly hair, by Uncle Victor.

Luise, the Egyptian princess, by Uncle Victor.

"German Day", 13 November 1931, celebrated by the NSDAP in front of the Landesmuseum in Darmstadt.

evening; there was no discussion of the tense situation. In the election two days later, 45 percent of the voters chose the NSDAP—an indication of the precarious situation for the Hessian Parliament and, indeed, for the Weimar Republic itself. With more than four million unemployed in Germany in 1931, people felt that only Hitler and his Nazi Party could save the country and return it to the strength and honour it enjoyed before the Great War. The Darmstadt Landtag remained as the government, but Nazi propaganda, rallies, and brawls made work in Parliament increasingly difficult. At the THD, nineteen representatives of the People's Student Party were elected to the Student Government, more than doubling the strength of the right-wing element of the university.

1932 and the New Spectroscopy Laboratory

In the new term, Herzberg was given the position of assistant to Professor Rau, with responsibilities to oversee the experimental physics laboratories and to advise and supervise students. His stipend was 300 RM (e.g., about $75) per month, barely enough to cover living expenses, so the continuing support from Luise's father was helpful.

Herzberg was now able to devote more time to establishing his laboratory in anticipation of completion of the two spectrographs. He also undertook the supervision of several students proceeding to the Diplom Ingenieur degree and a few working on their Doctorate degrees. Luise was continuing experimental work on the spectra of BeO, which she had started in Bristol, and considered that this project could serve as her Doctorate thesis. The first guest worker from North America was Dr. James Curry, a chemist who had just completed a year with Michael Polanyi in Berlin-Dahlem and, having heard Herzberg's lecture there, wanted to do some spectroscopic research.[17] He arrived in January 1932 and spent eight months at the THD studying the spectra of NO_2, PN, and O_2. In February Dr. Sho-Chow-Wu of Shanghai, then at the California Institute of Technology in Pasadena, California, working with Professor R.M. Badger, asked if he could spend a year with Herzberg.[18] Wu was highly recommended by Badger and, moreover, had a "China Foundation" fellowship, which would cover his travel and living costs in Germany. Herzberg accepted Wu and wrote to him about the laboratory and spectroscopic work, mentioning that Curry was there, along with several students. Herzberg also mentioned his interest in the challenging study of extremely weak spectra of molecules, known as "forbidden transitions", and had built a 12.5-metre-long gas cell for this purpose.[19] Wu arrived in early summer and stayed for a year, learning the new spectroscopic techniques while obtaining spectra of carbon disulfide (CS_2).

Much was accomplished during 1932, despite having to work with the available prism instruments rather than the two new grating spectrographs. In particular, with the long absorption path, Herzberg observed a forbidden

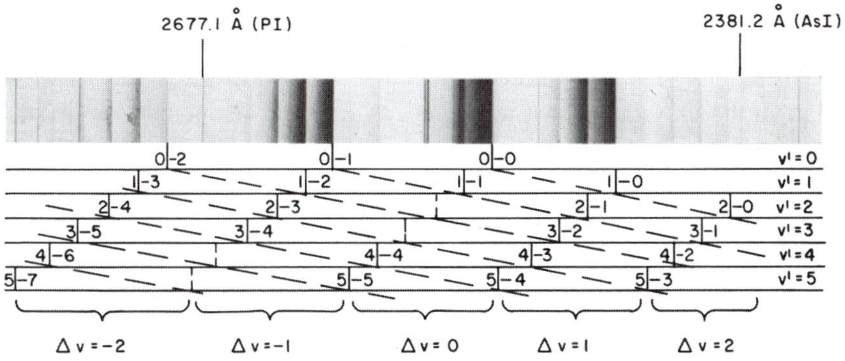

Band System of the PN molecule after Curry, Herzberg, and Herzberg, 1934.

Herzberg's two-metre far-ultraviolet grating spectrograph, Darmstadt, 1932.

spectrum of oxygen showing structure, which later became known as the "Herzberg Bands".[20] This transition in oxygen is of unique importance as it gives rise to the total absorption by the atmosphere, from 2200 to 1900 Å, and provides a shield against ultraviolet radiation. Publication of this work almost led to a quarrel with Wolfgang Finkelnburg, a colleague and a privatdozent in Karsruhe. Finkelnburg had earlier informed Herzberg of an oxygen spectrum in this wavelength region taken by himself and a colleague and felt their work had been slighted when Herzberg had not mentioned it in his paper. While Herzberg apologized for this omission, he was also able to show that in fact the two spectra were quite different: one was observed at high gas pressure and the other at very low pressure. He was to confirm the difference later, at higher resolution. This incident made such an impression on Herzberg that he vowed to remember details of discussions with colleagues and to give proper acknowledgement where due. A preliminary study of the spectrum of formaldehyde (H_2CO) with his student K. Franz was also published that year. This too was taken up at higher resolution when the grating spectrographs were completed.

Luise was nearing completion of the analysis of the BeO spectrum, which she had first observed in Bristol. She published a brief paper on this work and, on the basis of this study, felt it was now time to prepare for her

Herzberg's three-metre spectrograph for visible
and infrared regions, Darmstadt 1932.

Doctorate degree.[21] Although she had enrolled in a number of courses at the THD during 1931–1932, it was not possible to register for a Doctorate degree because she had not spent the years for a diploma degree at the THD. Another university had to be found for this purpose. Gerhard wrote to Professor Karl W. Meissner, an atomic physicist and director of the Physics Institute in Frankfurt, enquiring whether there was such a possibility in Frankfurt. Thus it happened that Luise registered with the University of Frankfurt in the fall semester, with her oral examination scheduled for May 1933.

Herzberg and his group frequently attended spectroscopy colloquia held monthly in nearby Frankfurt and Heidelberg, with Bonhoeffer, Mecke, Weizel, Ebert, and Hückel, among others, present. Moreover, he also managed

Robert Mulliken's visit at the THD, 1932.

to keep up an extensive correspondence with spectroscopists the world over, receiving and sending reprints, and discussing fine points in nomenclature and the meaning of observed features in spectra. Molecular spectroscopy was in its infancy and flourishing, with many ideas and results to be questioned and confirmed. Fortunately mail service within European countries and to Great Britain was essentially an overnight matter, and publication in scientific journals took only a few weeks, so new results were distributed rather quickly within Europe and a few weeks later in North America. As the work of Herzberg's spectroscopy laboratory became known, a steady stream of visitors from various countries came to Darmstadt, including Francis A. Jenkins of California and Robert S. Mulliken of Chicago, who were in Europe on Guggenheim Fellowships. Other events, however, were soon to intrude on this exciting period in the development of molecular spectroscopy, and of science in general, in Germany.

1933 and the Nazi Nightmare

The first indication of possible difficulties for the Herzbergs came immediately after the Nazis came into power in January 1933, with Adolf Hitler as Chancellor. Two months later, Germany became a dictatorship through the "Enabling Act", and Hitler its Führer. Events moved quickly as the Nazis put forward their progressively harsh anti-Communist and anti-Semitic programs. The Communist press was banned, and house-to-house searches and ill-treatment of leading members of the Communist Party and Socialist Party took place, with some being murdered and others placed in concentration camps. In the elections of 5 March, the Nazis obtained 44 percent of the vote in Germany, and 50 percent of the vote in Darmstadt. The following day the flag of the Reich was burned at the Darmstadt Legislature, and all official buildings were bedecked with Swastika flags.[22] The radio blared *Ein Volk, Ein Reich, Ein Führer.*

On 31 March, Jewish judges and lawyers were summarily dismissed because of their religion. On the next day a government-sponsored "National Boycott" took place; Jewish stores were placarded, Jews were kept from entering their offices and public buildings, and many were beaten in the streets. Within a week, the "Law for the Restoration of the Career Civil Service" came into effect, removing all non-Aryans from the civil service. Because the government funded the universities and held authority over them as part of the civil service, "non-Aryan" scholars and scientists and "politically unreliable" persons were dismissed from their university posts, twelve hundred in the first two years and seventeen hundred by the end of 1935. "Non-Aryan" included anyone with a Jewish parent or grandparent, or who practised the Jewish religion. Exempted were "non-Aryans" who were in office before the beginning of the Great War, those who had fought at the front, and those whose father or son was killed in the war. The term "politically unreliable" referred to people who had conducted themselves in what was considered a communist manner, whether or not they were in any way connected with the Communist Party.[23]

At the time, the 600,000 German Jews constituted barely 1 percent of the population of 65 million. Most families had lived in Germany for several generations, had fought its wars and contributed to its renowned culture, and thought of themselves as Germans first; many had converted to Protestanism. The majority lived in cities and were thus seen as a larger proportion of the civic population, amounting to about 7 percent in Berlin and 1.5 percent in Darmstadt. While anti-Semitism was prevalent in most of Europe, with growing animosity especially in Poland, Austria, Germany, and Hungary (where anti-Semitism had been legal since 1920), the concerted charge by Hitler and the Nazis that Jews were the cause of all of

Germany's past and present problems unleashed a simmering hatred that was unchecked by any form of civility or law.

No organized movements or societies existed in Germany to help the dismissed scholars, and they had to look outside their homeland for assistance in finding employment and in continuing their careers. In 1933–1934, 650 scholars and their families emigrated. As a result, physics proved to be one of the most severely damaged disciplines, with a loss of at least 25 percent of its 1932–1933 personnel, including many of the finest scientists in Germany.[24] Albert Einstein, in America on a lecture tour when the Nazis came to power, resigned his membership in the Prussian Academy of Sciences, stayed in Belgium on his return, and vowed never to return to a Germany that no longer observed civil liberty, tolerance, or equality of citizens before the law. He was invited to join the Institute for Advanced Study in Princeton University, where he remained until his death in 1955. Michael Polanyi relinquished his senior post in the Kaiser-Wilhelm Institute in Berlin-Dahlem and accepted an appointment in Manchester. Erwin Schrödinger, who was not Jewish, left Berlin disgusted by the Nazi regime and went successively to Oxford, Graz, and eventually to Dublin, to head the School of Theoretical Physics in the new Dublin Institute for Advanced Studies.

Herzberg was shocked to learn that most of the students and a considerable number of the faculty of the University of Göttingen supported the Nazi Party. A further blow was the resignation of James Franck and the exodus of Max Born, along with their assistants Walter Heitler, Edward Teller, Heinrich Kuhn, and Hertha Sponer (not Jewish), with all of whom Herzberg had collaborated. More recent arrivals in Göttingen, Eugene Rabinowitch and Arthur von Hippel were also affected. Max Born, who had never felt particularly Jewish, found his name in the *Göttinger Zeitung* on 25 April, along with those of the mathematicians Felix Bernstein, Richard Courant, and Emmy Noether, as being unsuitable to be civil servants and teachers because of their Jewish descent and were placed on leave.[25] Born left Germany the following month for the Italian South Tyrol. He accepted an invitation by Cambridge University for a year and then spent half a year at Raman's Institute in Bangalore, India, before joining the University of Edinburgh, where he remained until his retirement seventeen years later.

James Franck, whose Sephardic Jewish forebears had lived in Hamburg for over two hundred years, was a patriotic German and Nobel Laureate and was awarded the first and second Iron Crosses for bravery in the Great War. He could have remained at the university for the time being because of service to his country, but he protested publicly and his was one of the rare voices to be raised against the new laws. On 17 April Franck resigned his distinguished post.[26] He stressed to the Rector of the University, "We Germans of Jewish descent are treated as aliens and enemies of our Fatherland. It is required that our children grow up with the knowledge that they will never be allowed to prove themselves as Germans. Those who fought in the war are granted permission to continue to serve the State. I refuse to avail myself of this privilege, even though I understand the position of those who consider it their duty to remain at their posts." Next day, the text of Franck's resignation was published in the *Göttinger Zeitung*, and forty-two members of the University, mainly from the Faculty of Agriculture, condemned his public resignation as an act of treachery to inflame anti-German propaganda.[27] On learning of Franck's resignation Herzberg immediately wrote a strong note:

> Highly esteemed dear Professor Franck:
>
> In these days in which by your magnanimous decision you show the world where the insane oppression of the Jews leads to, I as one of your students would not like to be missing among those who declare their sincere thanks and unlimited veneration to you, and who especially now are filled with the highest admiration by your present step and the reason given by you, and who at the same time are filled with horror that such a thing is necessary.
>
> I am at a loss for words to express what both my wife and I always and especially now feel for you. Please remember us to your wife and children and accept our sincere greetings.[28]

Franck received hundreds of such letters from friends, colleagues, and concerned strangers in Germany and abroad. He had hoped to remain in Germany to fight the Nazis from within, but the rapidly deteriorating situation forced him to leave in the fall of 1933. He spent a year with Niels Bohr in Copenhagen before immigrating to America. He joined the Johns Hopkins University in Baltimore but left after three years as he found that life there was being made very difficult for Jewish faculty. He accepted a professorship at The University of Chicago and during the war years participated in the Manhattan Project in Chicago and Los Alamos.

In mathematics, Richard Courant, Felix Bernstein, Emmy Noether, and Hermann Weyl (who had a Jewish wife), among many others, left the University of Göttingen. The mathematician Edmund Landau was prevented from entering his classroom by about seventy of his students, some in SS uniforms, and was requested by the Nazi student commander to refrain from lecturing since "Aryan students want Aryan mathematics and not Jewish mathematics".[29] Within a few months of Hitler's ascendancy, the internationally renowned "Mecca" of Mathematics and Physics in Göttingen was destroyed. With such dismissals and departures from the principal universities of Berlin, Munich, Leipzig, Frankfurt, and Heidelberg, Germany instantly lost its preeminence in all fields of science.

In Darmstadt, these severe measures were applied more slowly, but the THD was not spared, and several senior faculty members were dismissed, along with privatdozents and assistants.[30] Among them were Edmund Stiasny, dean and professor of electrochemistry, Ernst Berl, a former dean and professor of chemistry, Erich Aron, dean, and Peter Leser, privatdozent, both of the Department of Cultural and Political Science, Michael Evenari, a biologist, Fritz Curtis, an architect, and William Prager, a privatdozent in mechanical engineering.[31] Jewish colleagues closer to Herzberg were Kurt Lion, an assistant in Rau's research group, and Hans Baerwald, a professor of theoretical physics who was a veteran, a baptized Protestant, and had a non-Jewish wife. Not being a *Beamte* (an official civil servant), Herzberg was not required to fill out the questionnaire giving dates of employment, type of war service, and the racial membership of his four grandparents. As a precaution he kept in touch with his cousin who was collecting the material needed to prove that the Herzberg family was Lutheran and of non-Jewish descent. He wrote to his friend Alfred Schulz that he never would have thought that one day he might have an advantage because of that and be able to protect Luise.[32]

On 1 May 1933, the President of Hesse announced a new "German Students' Law", decreeing that only students of German descent and mother tongue could study in the Hessian universities. Accordingly, the registered students at the THD dropped from 2,543 in 1931–1932 to 1,803 in 1933–1934 and to 1,219 a year later, and most foreign students left Germany. On that day in 1933, Heinz Hackert, the THD student leader, announced a rally and march through the city to the Marktplatz. Students, docents, and workers at the THD did not dare miss this all-day celebration, frequently punctuated with the *Horst Wessel* song, the rousing Nazi anthem. This was followed on 21 June, at the solstice festivities, with a torch parade to the music of an SA band and the burning of a truckload of books of "un-German spirit" authored by Jews, pacifists, and foreigners in a ceremony repeated all over Germany during May and June.[33] The names of squares and streets were changed, with Luisenplatz becoming Adolf-Hitler-Platz, Friedrich-Ebert-Platz becoming Dietrich-Eckart-Platz, and Rathenau Park becoming Horst-Wessel Park.

Very quickly, conditions at the THD became difficult for Herzberg. A Nazi member of the Physics Institute and some students noticed that Herzberg had not participated in the huge May Day parade of the THD community to the city centre, or in the book-burning festivities in June. Moreover, he did not begin classes with the required *Heil Hitler* salute. Rumours began circulating around the university that he had many Jewish friends and had Communist leanings. Herzberg's colleagues were too embarrassed to tell him directly and asked the workshop staff to inform him that he was no longer wanted at the THD. He felt forced to defend himself. Like many Germans, he regarded Naziism to be a passing phase, as several earlier governments had been. He had worked so hard to establish his laboratory, now known and respected internationally, that he was loathe to give it up. Moreover, in his political naiveté, he assumed that his Aryan ancestry would protect Luise in the short term. In answer to his tormentors he posted a notice in the lobby of the Physics Institute on 6 May 1933.

> In order to counter various rumours, I affirm herewith:
>
> - that I am of pure Aryan descent and that I can establish proof of this at any time through the necessary official documents,
> - that I am prepared at any time to take an oath and declare I am not a member of any political party nor ever was. In particular, I have never had any relations with the Communist Party.
> - The rumour that "I am a Communist" apparently stems from my correspondence with some Russian scientists, which was purely about scientific matters, and further that I received an invitation towards the end of last year from Dr. Bach at the Karpov Chemical Institute of Moscow State University to give lectures there on my special field, "The Spectra and Structures of Molecules". I did not accept this invitation, and I am prepared to furnish proof of this from the complete correspondence.[34]

Although originally Herzberg had seriously entertained the idea of visiting Moscow State University, he took the advice of Professor Rau that this would be unwise and in February asked Dr. Bach for a postponement.

These events severely dampened Herzberg's enthusiasm for work and he became unsure of his own and Luise's future, even though he was not immediately affected by the new laws because he was not Jewish, as the church records of Langensalza proved. So, despite the dire forewarnings of the first few months of 1933, he tried to remain calm and to trust that Germanic reason would eventually restore law and order. He was also concerned about Stephan Gradstein, whom he considered to be his best student, and his friend Kurt Lion, both Jewish. Gradstein, who was born in Germany of Polish parents, left the THD immediately after Hitler came to power and, on Herzberg's recommendation, was employed by *Der Naturforscher* (an illustrated monthly journal for the natural sciences). Although highly praised for his work, Gradstein was reluctantly discharged after only three months as a precautionary measure against possible economic sanctions under the new regime, and he fled to Holland.[35] He had worked on the fluorescence spectrum of formaldehyde at high resolution and had applied the theory of Herzberg and Teller in the analysis. However, when the paper was to be submitted for publication, Rau, fearing for Herzberg's future in this threatening political situation, recommended that Herzberg's name should not be included in the paper.[36] While it was understandable that a dictatorship would immediately take control of the public press and radio and ban all publications of conflicting parties, it came as a surprise to many that even the technical journals were being monitored by the Nazis. Karl-Friedrich Bonhoeffer had invited Herzberg to co-author a book on chemical spectroscopy, but the overly cautious editor refused to consider a book with Herzberg's name on it and received a stern rebuke from Bonhoeffer.

Kurt Lion had just completed his Doctorate in engineering with *summa cum laude* but was dismissed as an assistant from the THD and had difficulty finding employment.[37] Herzberg wrote to Arthur Tyndall in Bristol and to James Franck in Copenhagen, seeking their help in finding positions for Gradstein and Lion. In July, Herzberg wrote to John E. Lennard-Jones, now in Cambridge, congratulating him on being elected a Fellow of The Royal Society and noting:

> … the development of conditions here is quite depressing. It is a consolation to us to know of the extraordinary generosity the English nation

> shows to our dismissed scientists. We read the leading article in one of the recent numbers of Nature with a feeling of deep thankfulness.[38] I personally have as yet not been affected by the new laws, since I am purely Aryan, but it is probable that I shall lose my post in the near future. My wife is of Jewish descendence, and that is enough according to the latest proclamations to consider a man not worthy to serve his country and to do scientific research.[39]

Lennard-Jones answered immediately, offering that "if at any time you feel impelled to leave your present post, I should be glad to help you, and would put your case before the Academic Assistance Council". To which Herzberg replied:

> ... even if I can keep my post for the present, the future outlook for me is not very hopeful since according to the new laws I cannot improve my present position which as you probably know is a very low paid and dependent assistant post. On the other hand, working conditions are pretty good here until now, and the spectroscopic outfit of this laboratory is now quite exceptional.[40]

In fact, with both grating spectrographs in operation by the end of 1933 and several students and visiting scientists working in his laboratory, the next year and a half proved to be the most prolific for Herzberg's research in Darmstadt, even under these unpredictable and threatening circumstances.

Amid all this uncertainty, Luise passed the oral examination for her Doctorate thesis "Spectrum and structure of BeO" with a *cum laude* on 29 May 1933. She received the diploma for the Ph.D. degree, dated 30 August 1933, from the University of Frankfurt, thanks to the sponsorship of Karl W. Meissner.[41] She was most likely the last woman, and one of the last Jewish people, to receive the Doctorate degree in Nazi Germany.

In the spring of 1933 Herzberg received another request for permission to work in his laboratory for a year. This came in a letter from Dr. John W.T. Spinks, a young chemist from the University of Saskatchewan.[42] On coming home that evening, Herzberg showed the letter to Luise and asked, "Where on Earth is Saskatoon, Saskatchewan?"[43] They looked for it in their atlas and found that such a place actually existed, in the vast western prairies of Canada. That this tiny dot on the map of a far-off, unknown country would within two years provide them with a safe haven from a turbulent Germany and a welcome home was of course unforseen by them.

Spinks had graduated from King's College, London, having worked in photochemistry under Professor Arthur J. Allmand, and had accepted a junior faculty position in Saskatoon in 1930. The beginning of the Great Depression had a devastating impact on the prairie farms and on the university. After three years of government cutbacks, the President of the University of Saskatchewan called the younger faculty of the university to his office and gave them two alternatives: either to resign gracefully or to take a year off on five hundred dollars, with a reasonably good probability of returning to a job the following year.[44] Spinks chose the second alternative and decided to go to Germany to learn the language and to work in spectroscopy. He had read Herzberg's paper in the *Leipziger Vortrage* and that of Curry and Herzberg in *Nature* and chose Herzberg's laboratory as a possible workplace. In an introductory letter to Herzberg, Spinks noted that in order to understand the primary processes in photochemistry, he would have to study more physics and would like to work under a physicist for a time to extend his knowledge of light absorption and spectroscopy.

Herzberg inquired of Allmand, whom he had met on his visit to London in 1930, about Spinks and was assured that he should accept Spinks without hesitation.[45] In his reply to Spinks, Herzberg welcomed him to the group in Darmstadt, noting that Curry and Wu, who had been with him, were now both back in their native countries and adding that there were monthly colloquia in nearby Heidelberg and Frankfurt.[46] Spinks left Saskatoon in September, spent a few weeks with his parents in England, and arrived at Darmstadt in mid-October. Despite the ominous political atmosphere, Spinks spent a most profitable eight months with Herzberg.[47] He found that working with Herzberg was just about ideal:

> He was full of ideas, had excellent equipment, didn't mind showing me how to use it, helped me to make calculations, and was most generous with his time. Herzberg was a hard worker, very methodical and thorough, a perfectionist—every last decimal point had to be exact—and possessed of a first-class brain. He knew just what could and could not be deduced from the information at hand. Yet he was most modest and unassuming, and had a pleasant and friendly approach to everyone, and a constant stream of interesting visitors came to see him in Darmstadt. For my part, I often pinched myself to reassure myself that I had been so lucky. If you will gather from this that I had a fabulous year in Germany, you will have guessed right, I did.[48]

Spinks rented a room in the same house as the Herzbergs, so they spent much time together. Herzberg and Spinks often took a calculating machine home and spent the weekend calculating results. Every few weeks they finished a research project and carried out the analysis, and eventually they wrote eight papers based on their work in 1934. Spinks and the Herzbergs often went to concerts and operas in the Landestheater. They also attended seminars together at neighbouring universities and enjoyed hiking in the nearby woods.

Spinks experienced such favourable conditions at home and in the laboratory that Darmstadt seemed a most pleasant place to live. But he also saw the coming debacle as SA men trooped through the streets, as Germany withdrew from the League of Nations, and as new decrees by the Nazis continued throughout the year. Looking back on his year in Darmstadt, Spinks later wrote:

> It had within it all the elements of a Greek tragedy—people going about their daily work in a somewhat stoical fashion, yet knowing that political activities were leading Germany along a collision course which would inevitably and inexorably lead to wholesale destruction and tragedy for millions. On the one hand there was a highly civilized and cultivated existence, books, music, theatre, and on the other—Storm Troopers marching with a heavy tread through the cobbled streets, and the regular items in the weekend papers *Im flucht er so hossen*—telling of a political prisoner being conveyed to an interrogation centre who tried to escape and was, sad to relate, shot in flight.

On 21 October 1933 the *Darmstädter Zeitung* reported that the Rector would be the *Führer* of the THD, and the leader of the Student Council would be a *Führer* too, with a seat in the University Senate. The THD was being politicized by the Reich Education Ministry, established that year to govern academia and to align it with the Hitler movement. One of the THD Professors of Philosophy, Hugo Dingler, became a prominent spokesman for German science versus Jewish science, led by the extreme nationalists Philipp Lenard, formerly professor in Heidelberg and now retired, and Johannes Stark, president of the Imperial Institute of Physics in Berlin, both Nobel Laureates in physics in the early 1900s. An even bigger shock for Herzberg was seeing his colleague Günter Scheibe of Erlangen wearing the Nazi emblem at a meeting in 1933.

1934–1935 and Thoughts of Leaving Germany

On the dismissal of his teacher and colleague Hans Baerwald in July 1933, Herzberg was asked to take over the course in theoretical physics for the rest of the year.[49] This was an unexpected opportunity to delve into classical theoretical physics and include contemporary advances, an experience he enjoyed immensely. It proved to be an important lesson for him, and he was reminded of the Roman author Petronius Arbiter who wrote "docendo discimus"—"by teaching, we learn". Moreover, Herzberg was paid for giving this course.

However, the situation in Darmstadt worsened considerably for the Herzbergs with the receipt by the Rector on 27 April 1934 of an order from the Hesse State Ministry that all assistants must immediately (by 16 May) submit copies of the following documents:

> The birth certificate of your wife.
>
> The marriage certificate of your wife's parents.
>
> Your own marriage certificate.[50]

Herzberg complied and wondered what the next new Nazi law would bring. He did not have long to wait. He was informed by the local Ministry of Education that he could not teach in the following semester, as he was deemed unfit to teach German youth, a *Jüdisch versippt* (of the Jewish clan), because of his wife's Jewish ancestry, but he could carry on with research work for the time being.[51] Unknown to Herzberg, students petitioned the Culture Ministry of Hesse for the continuation of Herzberg's course in theoretical physics—his lectures were so popular—and for permission for him to give examinations at the end of the semester. Teaching was denied, but he was allowed to examine students who had taken his course. Another ominous sign was Hitler's announcement in March 1935 of the establishment of an air force and of conscription to expand the army, which was in direct violation of the Versailles Treaty.[52]

Herzberg had already launched an ambitious program of research. A major incentive was the arrival of Spinks from Canada, Gösta W. Funke from Sweden, and Heinz Verleger, a German, who along with Luise and the many good students formed one of the strongest groups in the THD Institute of Physics.[53] Another plus was the discovery in 1932 of heavy hydrogen, or deuterium, by Harold C. Urey and co-workers at Columbia University. Herzberg immediately recognized the importance of deuterium for the study of molecular structure. Moreover, special Agfa photographic plates, rated as sensitive in the infrared out to 10.5 microns (μ), became available to Herzberg (who had been a consultant to Agfa), and he found

Institute of Physics faculty, students, and visitors.
From left: John Spinks, Georg Müller, Helmut Bumann, Koelsch,
– , – , Prof. Dr. Hans Rau, – , Adam Walz, Heinz Verleger,
Fraülein Pfersdorf (Secretary), Werner Maurer, Herzberg, and Simon, 1934.

that the wavelength range could be extended even further, to 13 μ, with long exposure times.

On his way to Darmstadt, Spinks had visited Urey's group at Columbia University and came to Herzberg's laboratory prepared to produce some heavy water (D_2O) for use in making various isotopes of hydrogenic molecules. After several months of considerable effort, he succeeded in producing about a teaspoonful of this precious material. Soon after, commercial heavy water became available from Norway, but at a high price. During a visit to the University of Vienna, Spinks met the chemist Franz Patat, who was experienced in preparing deuterated compounds, and Patat joined Herzberg and Spinks in the preparation and study of heavy acetylene (C_2HD).

With both grating spectrographs in operation, one for the extreme ultraviolet wavelength region and the other for the visible and near infrared regions, the spectra of many molecules were obtained. Among the diatomic

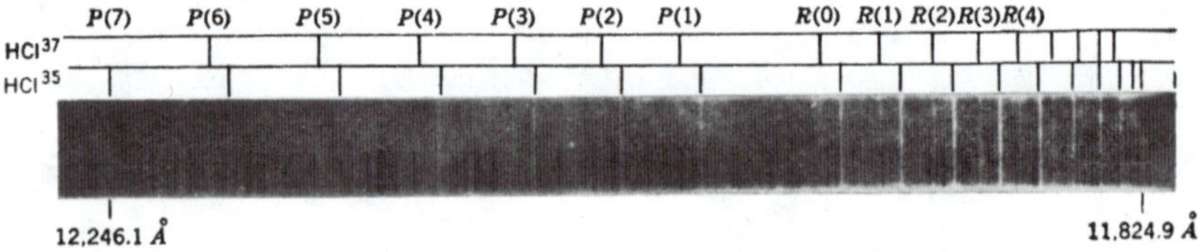

The 3-0 infrared band of HCl, after Herzberg and Spinks, 1934.

molecules were N_2, O_2, CN, CO, HCl, P_2, CP, and PN. For the spectum of O_2, Herzberg set up a mirror system on the roof of the Institute to bring sunlight into the three-metre spectrograph and, with a very long exposure time, was able to photograph the solar spectrum out to 12.9 μ (the longest wavelength ever recorded photographically). A variety of polyatomic molecules were studied, including CO_2, CS_2, HCN, H_2CO, B_2H_6, C_2H_2 and its isotope C_2HD, and CH_3CCH with its isotope CH_3CCD. Many of these spectra were obtained with a twenty-five metre absorption path, others in emission, and some by fluorescence. Herzberg even had plans to excite Raman spectra at high resolution, but time was running out for him, and measurement and analysis of many of the spectra had to be put off for a few years.[54]

With Herzberg's very successful research program in full swing, Rau had been able to secure a contract from the government for him to serve as his assistant until October 1935. In all probability this would not be renewed, and the possibility existed that he would be dismissed even earlier. The decision to deny Herzberg the opportunity to teach was made by bureaucrats at the local level, who were aware of the forthcoming "Nürnberg Laws" to be announced in September 1935. These laws would affect all Jews and Germans married to Jews, making them second-class citizens in Germany. With this rejection of teaching at the THD and only a tentative contract as assistant, Herzberg finally realized he had no choice but to look outside his fatherland—and better still, outside of Europe—for a research position, or for work of any kind.

Come my friends. 'Tis not too late to seek a newer world.

Alfred Lord Tennyson

6. SEARCHING THE WORLD FOR AN ACADEMIC POSITION

Gerhard and Luise could hardly believe that within three years of their happy homecoming, their dreams would be shattered. They reached an inescapable conclusion: the Nazis and the Third Reich would stay—they were not just a fleeting episode in Germany's history, as many had thought based on the repeated changes of government in the previous decade. Resigned to their fate but determined to succeed, Gerhard and Luise began a worldwide search for other opportunities.

The Emergency Society of German Scholars Abroad in Zurich

In November 1933, Herzberg began regular correspondence with the Zurich office of the *Notgemeinschaft Deutscher Wissenschaftler im Ausland* (Emergency Society of German Scholars Abroad), which contacted him after learning from Max Born of his plight.[1] This society for mutual assistance was founded in Zurich in March of 1933 by German intellectual exiles under the leadership of Professor Philipp Schwartz, a Hungarian who was dismissed from his post in Frankfurt. The Notgemeinschaft was financed by contributions from displaced scholars whom it had helped to re-establish. An early success was its negotiation for the placement of fifty-six German scholars on the faculty of the recently established University of Istanbul in November 1933, with a final total of over one hundred in academic positions in Turkey. It also helped to place dismissed scholars in Asiatic and South American countries where no national committees had been established. With the charge to university teachers placed abroad to look for openings for other exiles in professional life or academia, it eventually placed about two thousand persons all over the world. The activities of the Notgemeinschaft were known to the Gestapo and deemed to be anti-German. Thus a notice was sent to rectors of all universities in November 1934 requiring that all correspondence received from the Society not be answered but be sent directly to the Reich Minister of Science, Education and National Education in Berlin.[2] Herzberg avoided this dictum by carrying on all correspondence with the Notgemeinschaft from his home. In these early years of the Nazi regime, censorship seemed rather lax, and he survived the risk of detection.

When his colleague Professor Ernst Miescher of the University of Basle learned that Herzberg was to attend a conference in nearby Freiburg, in February 1934, he invited Herzberg to give a seminar at his institute, knowing full well that this would give him the opportunity to visit the Notgemeinschaft in Zurich.[3] Herzberg accepted the invitation, gave a seminar on recent research, and then made his way to Zurich. From then on, the Notgemeinschaft continually notified him of opportunities for lecturing and for research in theoretical and experimental physics in a number of countries, including China, India, New Zealand, Ecuador, and Burma. Although Herzberg was concerned about the adequacy of research facilities at these distant institutes, in desperation he applied to all but China. He asked that his name not be sent to Nanking, because he had already been invited to go to Shanghai by his postdoctoral fellow Dr. Wu. Wu had just returned home after a fruitful year in Darmstadt and on learning of Herzberg's predicament had wanted to help in some way. He asked Herzberg whether he would come to help set up a laboratory when conditions in China improved.[4] However, within a year, Wu was embroiled in his own country's invasion by Japan and later in the civil strife in China. In applying to the Indian Institute of Science in Bangalore, Herzberg was torn by the rumour that his dismissed colleague Baerwald had also applied for this post, and he beseeched Raman: "As he was a teacher of mine and as I am well acquainted with him, I would of course not like his chances to be decreased by my application and would not apply under these circumstances."[5] Professor Tyndall of Bristol wrote to many institutes giving his support for Herzberg, but he was not optimistic about Herzberg's chances because British subjects would be given preference in the Dominions and Colonies in this difficult period of worldwide depression.[6] As it turned out, not one of Herzberg's applications was successful.[7]

Herzberg followed advertisements for academic positions in the English journal *Nature*, and on learning of a reader position at Cambridge University, he applied for it. Professor Lennard-Jones, who had just left Bristol for the Chair of Theoretical Chemistry at Cambridge, supported him, but understandably Cambridge graduates and British subjects were preferred. Regarding an advertised Assistant Professorship at the University of Manchester, Herzberg chose first to ask Michael Polanyi about his chances. Polanyi had voluntarily resigned from the Kaiser-Wilhelm Institute in Berlin-Dahlem and had been appointed to the chair of Physical Chemistry in Manchester.[8] However, the University of Manchester had been violently attacked by the press for this appointment of a foreigner, no matter how distinguished, and it was obvious that any new positions had to be filled by British subjects. Polanyi replied within two days and suggested that he would write to Werner Heisenberg to ask him to look into possibilities for Herzberg.[9] Herzberg replied:

> Of course I have nothing against you discussing my affairs with Heisenberg, but I do not believe that in my case the professors are to blame. Professor Rau, the Director of the Institute, and Professor Busch, the Rector, do indeed champion my cause. Furthermore, I had the intention of applying for a Rockefeller Award with the possibility of going to The University of Chicago to work with Professor Mulliken. For this the Rockefeller Foundation requires a statement that I will again be employed here on my return. Upon inquiry by the Rector, he was told by the government agent in charge that such a confirmation was completely out of the question. Upon further inquiry as to the customary renewal of my employment contract as assistant, which expires in the fall of next year, it was stated that this was extremely unlikely, and that I might even be laid off earlier. According to the Hesse Government, the renewal would mean a new contract, which by the civil service law says that new appointments of civil servants married to non-Aryans are disallowed. However, as assistant I am not a Beamte or civil servant, so this does not apply to me. It would be very gratifying if Heisenberg would succeed to bring about a clarification on this point. Maybe the State government is more holy than the Pope![10]

A request by Polanyi[11] to help Herzberg was answered by Heisenberg within a month, after contacting Rau in Darmstadt:

> According to what Rau has written to me, there are hardly any hopes for Herzberg in Germany. It is certain that in the foreseeable future he cannot get an academic position because of his wife's descent. Furthermore, according to unofficial but unfortunately quite clear statements by relevant government authorities, he will lose his position as assistant, probably by October of this year. While his dismissal as assistant cannot be explained by the law governing professional civil service, nothing can be done legally speaking since the government has the right of giving notice vis-à-vis non-tenured employees. Rau writes further, that so far all efforts to find something for H.—especially with the help of the Zurich Notge-

> meinschaft and the Academic Assistance Council—have not led to success. Also the hope for a Rockefeller Fellowship has not been fulfilled since H. would not have a definite position after such time.
>
> We would therefore be very grateful to you if you could approach the relevant authorities in England regarding help for H. In Germany, help is already becoming much more difficult because the Notgemeinschaft der deutschen Wissenschaft has now passed into the hands of Stark. I shall look for new possibilities for Herzberg in Germany as hard as I can, but I ask you not to count on success when making any decisions.[12]

Heisenberg was clearly aware of the general situation in Germany for young scientists seeking employment and spent much time doing his best to help. Research jobs in institutes and industry were possible by decrees for those experiencing Herzberg's problem, but with the rabid Nazi Johannes Stark at the head of this science agency, any hope of such a job was out of the question.[13] It was clear that Herzberg had to seek opportunities outside Germany.

The Academic Assistance Council in London

At the suggestion of James Franck, Herzberg also applied to the Emergency Committee in Aid of Displaced Foreign Scholars in New York and to the Academic Assistance Council in London in June 1934.[14] Although a quick response from the Emergency Committee regretted that no action was possible at present, the Academic Assistance Council immediately offered help.[15] This agency was formed in May 1933 by the heads of English universities and learned societies and was one of the first to come to the aid of academics and other intellectuals who "by reason of race, religion or political views were unable to carry on their investigations in their own country". The aims were "the relief of suffering and the defence of learning and science". It had offices in The Royal Society at Burlington House in London, with Lord Rutherford as its first President. The Council acted in a double capacity: it served as a centre of information and as an organization to put the teachers concerned in touch with the institutions where they could work, and it raised funds (with many faculty members contributing by deduction from their salaries) to be used primarily in providing maintenance for displaced teachers and in finding them work in universities and scientific institutions. As the exodus from Germany continued and refugees from other European countries (including some from Russia) asked for help, the Council was placed on a more permanent basis and in 1937 was renamed the Society for the Protection of Science and Learning.[16]

When the Council asked Herzberg what country would be agreeable to him, he promptly replied, "I am ready to go to any place where reasonable research facilities are available. I could take over a teaching position as well as an experimental or theoretical physics or chemistry research post."[17] As references, he included the names and addresses of Hans Rau, Karl-F. Bonhoeffer, Friedrich Hund, Max Born, James Franck, Arthur M. Tyndall, and Robert S. Mulliken. With the acknowledgment of his letter within a week, Herzberg was informed of a position at the University of Leningrad. Professor J. Frenkel of the Physical Technical Institute wrote to Herzberg (via the Academic Assistance Council) that Professor Semenoff, the Director of the Institute for Chemical Physics, would offer Herzberg a position and that "he would find a most hearty welcome and very good conditions both for scientific work and general living".[18] Herzberg was duly informed of other positions at colleges and universities (Louisville, Kentucky; Cape Town, South Africa; Ghent, Belgium; and Giza, Egypt). He applied for all these positions, though not the one in Leningrad.[19] Franck recommended him highly stating "I really believe we have not many physicists of his age who can compare with him." Although the Louisville position was solely a teaching post, Herzberg thought of it as a possible later entry to the larger universities in the United States. Of these several openings, only the University of Ghent offered him an appointment, a two year research fellowship in January 1935, based on the strong recommendation of Born, who nominated Herzberg for the position.[20] Herzberg visited the University and Professor Verschaffelt's Institute and seemed disposed to accept this post, even though the stipend was minimal.

Herzberg was touched by a helpful letter he received from his former student Stephan Gradstein in Holland.[21] He had written to William Prager, a former THD privatdozent ousted from Karlsruhe University in 1933 and now a professor in the University of Constantinople, telling him that Herzberg was looking for a position. Prager replied immediately that Istanbul was not suitable, although the Chair of Theoretical Physics in Istanbul was not yet filled, and that the new University of Teheran in Iran had many openings. The chance of gaining one of these positions was still rather good, though many enquiries were being received daily from Germany. When Herzberg learned that James Franck and Richard Courant had paid a brief visit to Turkey to check on positions they had been offered, but did not accept, he chose not to apply to Turkey or Iran. A letter from the Dutch spectroscopist Dirk Coster of Groningen, co-discoverer of hafnium in 1923, sadly reported his lack of success at finding Herzberg a position in Holland, even after alerting senior scientists in his country of Herzberg's achievements and present plight.[22]

A Search in North America

Leaving no stone unturned, Herzberg contacted science colleagues in North America for possible opportunities. One of the first to offer assistance was Robert Mulliken of Chicago.[23] However, this was based on obtaining a Rockefeller Fellowship, for either one or two years, and it required a post to return to. Hertha Sponer, the former senior assistant to James Franck, remarked during this period, when she and Herzberg were working on a joint publication and both were looking for academic positions: "Berkeley is a thousand times more beautiful than Chicago, you should try there."[24] She, too, had left Göttingen, although she was not Jewish, because it was clear that women had no future in the new German scientific establishment: according to the Nazis, women belonged in the home raising children. With Heisenberg's help Sponer found a temporary post in Madrid and then in Oslo, before settling in the United States in 1936. Herzberg's search at the University of California, Berkeley, was not successful: there was no possibility because of the Depression, as Raymond T. Birge commented. Joseph Kaplan could not give encouragement at Los Angeles, nor could Wolfgang Finkelnburg (a Rockefeller Fellow soon to return to Germany and the THD) in Pasadena. Herzberg's name was suggested by H.L. Johnson to the Chairman at Ohio State University, but he had someone else in mind for the available position. James Franck also wrote about Herzberg to Rudolf Ladenburg at Princeton and to Karl Herzfeld at Johns Hopkins in Baltimore, both of whom had left Germany before the Nazis came to power—all to no avail. On his return home to Saskatoon from Darmstadt, John Spinks stopped off at the University of Toronto to check on possibilities there but found no available opening for Herzberg. With the Depression wreaking havoc in North America, any openings would naturally favour Americans and Canadians.

As every one of these possibilities from all six continents resulted in negative responses, Herzberg realized that he was too late. Those who had been part of the early exodus from Germany had filled the few positions available to foreigners. He was left with only the offer of a fellowship from Ghent. He took this opportunity to clarify his future at the THD one last time by writing to the Dean of the Faculty of Mathematics and Natural Sciences. He apprised the Dean of the Ghent offer, stating that his decline of this offer was dependent on whether the Reich Education Ministry would extend his job as assistant for the continuation of his research and would promise that he could lecture at least on his special field of research.[25] The Ministry's answer to the Dean's request and to Herzberg was immediate and, while not unexpected, crushing: no teaching.

In the meantime, with the ever-increasing displays of brown shirts, swastikas, and anti-Semitism at the THD and in Darmstadt, his future with the fellowship in Ghent, or with any position in western Europe, took on the appearance of a repetition of his present predicament.

Recognized internationally as one of the pioneers of molecular spectroscopy and molecular structure at the age of thirty, Herzberg had nowhere to turn.

PART TWO

A SAFE HAVEN IN CANADA (1935–1947)

A sparrow in the hand is naturally better than a pigeon on the roof.

Anonymous

7. GUEST PROFESSORSHIP AT THE UNIVERSITY OF SASKATCHEWAN

Carnegie Corporation Fellowship

A glimmer of hope was raised with Herzberg's receipt of a strictly confidential message from the Notgemeinschaft Deutscher Wissenschaftler im Ausland in January 1935.[1] This stated that the Carnegie Corporation of New York would assist displaced German scholars by providing fellowships tenable for two years in universities of the British Dominions and Colonies, the application to be made by the university for the services of the refugee. Herzberg immediately wrote to John Spinks in Saskatoon, mentioning that this might be a wonderful opportunity to go to Toronto, with its prominent spectroscopy laboratory.[2] He suggested that this also might be a way of continuing their collaboration, even though he was aware that there was no work in spectroscopy being carried out at the University of Saskatchewan. Herzberg fixed on the University of Toronto and its Physics Department because he knew of the spectroscopic work on light-scattering spectra (the Raman effect) of liquid hydrogen, oxygen, and nitrogen by Professor John C. McLennan, whom he had met briefly at the Faraday Society Meeting in Bristol in 1928. He did not know that McLennan had retired in 1932 and was living in England. Herzberg was also familiar with the work on the Stark effect by Professor J. Stuart Foster at McGill University in Montreal, and he considered the best approach to seeking a position there would be through his friends James Franck and Hertha Sponer, who knew some of the faculty.

On receiving Herzberg's letter, Spinks discussed the matter with Thorbergur Thorvaldson, the Head of Chemistry in Saskatoon, and within a day, the two notified the President of the University, Walter Murray, of Herzberg's difficulties in Germany. Murray had already been made aware of the wonderfully productive year that Spinks had enjoyed in Germany, thanks to Herzberg's expertise and drive, and he immediately grasped the gravity of the situation for Herzberg, as well as the opportunity for Canada to obtain a very distinguished scientist. The next day he sent letters to

President H.J. Cody of the University of Toronto and to Eli F. Burton, the Head of its Physics Department.

> Dear President Cody:
>
> A member of our University staff spent last year in Germany working under Dr. Herzberg at Darmstadt. Dr. Herzberg is a very brilliant physicist, who is recognized as an international authority on spectroscopy. He has, according to Hitler's standards, the misfortune of having married a Jewish woman and is now rated as a second-class citizen of Germany and barred from promotion in German institutions. His appointment terminates this June of this year. He has the prospect of receiving a fellowship at a university in the British Dominions, ... conditional upon a university making application for his services.
>
> Your equipment for spectroscopic work is the best in Canada and you could give him a much better opportunity than any other university. Should you not wish to invite him to come, kindly let me know and I will take the matter up with Dr. H.M. Tory and Dr. R.W. Boyle of the National Research Council. Should neither be willing to invite him, we would do so with joy, although we have not the equipment that is worthy of his ability and his work.
>
> I believe this is one of the opportunities of securing a very brilliant scientist, and he will make a very acceptable member of the university forces in Canada.
>
> Would you kindly let me know as soon as possible what you think of this suggestion? Dr. Herzberg's letter arrived the day before yesterday and action should be taken somewhat promptly.[3]

While Murray had no idea if Herzberg would consider an appointment at Saskatchewan, he did not wish to lose this rare occasion to add to Canada's scientific stature. On the other hand, although he knew that his own university was without funds, being a most resourceful person, he felt that something could be worked out to build up science and research in Saskatoon.[4]

Spinks immediately informed Herzberg of Murray's interest in securing Herzberg for Canada and of his letters to Toronto and Ottawa.[5] Spinks also added:

> Dr. Thorvaldson wrote a short appreciation of your scientific reputation, and I wrote something from what I had seen of you and what I heard of you from other physicists and chemists in Germany and other countries.

> Just now, having no thought for your blushes, I can say that what I wrote was sufficiently glowing to serve as your passport should you be thinking of going to Heaven at any time!—and I think that I never wrote anything with greater pleasure, apart from the slight embarrassment caused by the fact that I was writing about someone so much brighter than myself!

The University of Toronto was already aware of the Carnegie Fellowships and was involved in obtaining support for Bernard Haurwitz, a mathematical meteorologist from the Geophysical Institute of Leipzig, to join the Physics Department. In fact the Physics Department had been urged by the French physicist Leon Brillouin to accept two refugee students, Michel Magat and Walter M. Elsasser. Toronto applied to the Carnegie Corporation for Haurwitz and the young Elsasser.[6] President Cody replied to Murray that if the Carnegie Corporation acceded to the present request, he could not ask for further support, and as for McLennan's replacement, Burton had in mind a brilliant young Canadian spectroscopist, now in Europe.[7] At that time, only the appointment for Haurwitz was granted by the Carnegie Corporation; a position with the Dominion of Canada Meteorological Service was to be made available to him after his two year appointment as a guest professor.[8] Later that year, the University of Toronto succeeded in obtaining a second Carnegie Fellowship for Peter Brieger of the University of Breslau, a historian of fine art and architecture, who helped to establish the Department of Fine Art at Toronto.[9]

Murray's letter to President H.M. Tory of the NRC also brought a negative reply: "I am sorry but there is no possibility at present of our using Dr. Herzberg's services. We have no work going on in spectroscopy, nor have we any equipment at the moment for such work."[10] In February, Herzberg himself wrote to the University of Toronto and to McGill University, and he learned that James Franck in Copenhagen and Karl Herzfeld of Johns Hopkins University in Baltimore had also written to give their support and that Niels Bohr had discussed Herzberg's plight with McLennan—all to no avail.[11] Enquiries on Herzberg's behalf at McGill by Hertha Sponer and James Franck, through the Danish physicist Dr. Svien Rosseland who was visiting McGill, elicited a similar negative reply from Professor J. Stuart Foster.[12] Meanwhile, weekly letters between Spinks and Herzberg kept each side informed. The letters were also full of science, of their joint research papers submitted for publication, and of proofs or reprints received, along with local news.

Offer from the University of Saskatchewan

On learning that there were no possibilities for Herzberg's employment at Canada's major research centres, Murray called in Spinks and asked if he was absolutely certain of his high recommendation of Herzberg.[13] On hearing Spinks's assurance, Murray instructed him to send Herzberg a telegram offering him a position as Guest Professor in the Department of Physics at the University of Saskatchewan. Murray realized that his university did not have sufficient means to provide him with proper equipment for his work, but he was certain that a man of Herzberg's power and resource could make much of little. He was not to be disappointed.

Spinks had already laid the groundwork for acceptance of Herzberg in Saskatoon by talking incessantly about his wonderful year in Darmstadt, mainly because of Herzberg. He had also addressed the Faculty Club in November of 1934 on his year in Darmstadt, attesting to Herzberg's brilliance and pioneering research. He wrote about the occasion to Herzberg, "I culled for them passages from my diary bearing on German universities, the civil service, theatre, cinema, experiences, and jokes. It seemed to keep them interested for a couple of hours and a lively discussion followed. Fifty profs including the President and Dean turned out to hear the baby of the faculty, so I felt duly flattered."[14]

Spinks later wrote Herzberg a long and forthright letter, noting that a look at a map would show him that Saskatoon was a long way from anywhere and that visits to and from research centres in Canada and the United States were apt to be few and far between.[15] Moreover, there was no apparatus for his particular work, although the Department of Chemistry had a Hilger prism spectrograph and a calculating machine. A good workshop and an instrument maker were also available. The University Library had the usual technical journals and even some from Germany. Spinks sent him photographs of the campus and the Physics Building and commented that Dr. Ertle L. Harrington, the Head of the Department of Physics, was a pleasant, rather shy, individual. Spinks also described the northern lights and drew "sun dogs" and other optical phenomena prevalent in the extremely cold winter in Saskatoon. "For our sake, I hope you will come, and if you have nothing better in view, at least this will give you a two year breathing space in which to look around North America."

In the meantime, Murray clarified the conditions and stipend of the Carnegie Fellowship with J.M. Russell, Assistant to the President of the

Carnegie Corporation.[16] He learned that the Corporation had not set up a formal system of fellowships but would consider, on their merits, proposals from individual universities in the British Dominions and Colonies.[17] The conditions were that "if the German scholar will fill a gap on the staff of the university as a guest professor, and if the university believes there is a reasonable possibility of providing a permanent position for him, then the Corporation will be glad to give consideration to a grant to cover the salary of a guest professor for a period not to exceed two years". Murray immediately applied for a grant to cover the salary of a guest professor, with priority given to Herzberg, also mentioning Dr. T. Plaut, formerly of Hamburg, who would fill a position in the Department of Economics.[18] On 8 March, Murray was informed of the resolution adopted by the Carnegie Corporation that the sum of $4,500, payable in two annual instalments of $2,250, be appropriated to the University of Saskatchewan for a professorship in Physics.[19] The money was to come from the British Dominions and Colonies Fund, established by Andrew Carnegie in 1912 (with the first grant awarded a year later to Queen's University in Ontario).[20] Spinks sent Herzberg a telegram with this news, and Murray formally offered Herzberg the Guest Professorship, to take effect from 1 July 1935. Herzberg was to report for duty on 15 September "to do some teaching and be given such opportunities for research as are available in our laboratories".[21] He ended the letter by noting that Spinks could give him a better idea of the facilities for research, and almost as an afterthought, he mentioned that he had spoken about this matter to Dr. Harrington, the Head of Physics, who had concurred with the invitation.

Herzberg welcomed the firm commitment of President Murray and cabled Spinks on 15 May that acceptance was probable.[22] Yet he was worried about the conditions for research at the University of Saskatchewan, so far removed from any of the large research centres in Canada or the United States. Also he was somewhat taken aback that all of these hurried negotiations for a senior appointment in the Department of Physics had been carried out by the president himself with a junior staff member of Chemistry, not with the Head of Physics. Before accepting this offer, Herzberg wrote to Hertha Sponer about his concerns and as a last resort asked her if she would telegraph Rosseland at McGill and implore him one more time to check on Toronto. Feeling somewhat at a loss that the only offer had come from the University of Saskatchewan, Herzberg added that as much as he would have preferred Toronto or Montreal, *Anderseits ist naturlich der*

Sperling in der Hand besser als die Taube auf dem Dach ("on the other hand it is naturally better to have a sparrow in the hand than a pigeon on the roof").[23] As luck would have it, the very next day a letter arrived from Karl Herzfeld of Johns Hopkins University, noting that he had had a reply from Eli Burton in Toronto "that in view of its present state of finances, the University of Toronto could not assure the Carnegie Corporation that it could take a visiting professor on its permanent staff after the two year term."[24] As this dashed any further hope of an appointment at Toronto, Herzberg promptly informed Hertha Sponer of this message and reviewed the offer from Saskatchewan.[25]

During this period of indecision, Herzberg was in constant communication with James Franck, who was at the Bohr Institute in Copenhagen and himself at the point of deciding whether to leave Europe for America. In mid-March, as he groped for a solution to his problem, Herzberg was in very low spirits and summarized his future in a cheerless letter to Franck. In Darmstadt, he had built an outstanding spectroscopy laboratory, but when his probable departure loomed, the only offers he had were for two temporary positions in laboratories far less well equipped than his own. In a long letter to Franck, he concluded with a note of resignation:

> The outlook for me in Darmstadt is extremely uncertain. Even as I write to you, my Privatdozent may be taken away. If I am permitted to stay longer, sooner or later I will be dismissed and forced to leave Germany, and by then it will be far more difficult to be accepted in a foreign country. So which is it to be, Ghent or Saskatoon? The facts for Ghent are: essentially better spectroscopic means are available; the nearness to Germany; further, the physicists and physical chemists there, and those nearby, are interested in the modern questions. For Saskatoon: mainly better possibilities from there to find employment in the United States; the considerably better financial situation (at the present exchange rates, a factor of two); on this basis, most probably without further arrangements, I could go for a week to a research centre in the United States (for example, Chicago) at least once a year, whereas from Ghent, a trip to even a neighbouring institution would be difficult without financial help. The fact that in Saskatoon there is no spectroscopic equipment at present doesn't mean that this will always be the case. Once there, I can evaluate plates that I would bring with me. Besides I can obtain new spectra as a visitor to some American institution, and I can devote some time to theoretical problems. Finally, it is not necessary that I spend all my life

> working on molecular spectra; with modest means, I can try to begin something else.[26]

This last thought must have been excruciatingly difficult to consider and to write about, but it indicated the seriously depressed state Herzberg was in. Franck answered the next day, urging him to take up the Saskatoon post with both hands; he tried to comfort him with the remark that being young, Gerhard and Luise had little furniture to transport but could pack much good humour.[27] In the meantime, on the basis of this new offer from Canada, Rau approached the Hesse Ministry to get a more secure position for Herzberg, but his effort was in vain.[28]

Acceptance of Guest Professorship

Herzberg accepted the University of Saskatchewan offer on 2 April. He cabled Spinks and sent Murray a letter stating "It was extremely kind of you to make enquiries about the possibility for me to come to Toronto. I am certain however that I shall spend a very profitable time at your University, and I hope that I may be of some use to you."[29] When he learned that the Board of Governors of the University had confirmed the appointment, Herzberg wrote to Murray, "I am extremely glad to accept your kind invitation. I shall be in Saskatoon on 15 September, the date mentioned in your letter. I am looking forward to my work at your University. Thanking you again for your very kind endeavours."[30]

During all of this period of looking worldwide for a research position, Herzberg kept his friend Alfred Schulz informed of his many failures and finally of the offer from the University of Saskatchewan, along with his concerns. Alfred tried to console him with the thought that a smaller university might give him a better chance to do his own work, but also noted that he couldn't find Saskatoon on his map. Gerhard wasn't too surprised but chided Alfred that if he couldn't find the province of Saskatchewan either, then he must have a rather bad map. He added that the university seemed all right, even if not important, and the possibility of going to the United States from there was much better than from Darmstadt. What would be very different was the winter climate with temperatures of −40°C not a rarity, and there were no beautiful forests, as in Germany, for hiking.[31]

Herzberg realized that he now had at most four months in which to wind down his research and responsibilities at the THD; to complete his book on atomic and molecular spectra and conclude arrangements for its publication; to plan whatever he could for any research activities in Saskatchewan; and to proceed with details of immigration to Canada and the organization of his passage to the New World.

Herzberg immediately informed Professor Verschaffelt of his decision to go to Saskatchewan and thanked him for the offer of a research fellowship in Ghent.[32] He wrote to Max Born, James Franck, Karl-F. Bonhoeffer, and many other colleagues of his acceptance of a guest professorship in Canada, thanking them for their concern and assistance during this difficult period. From the many letters he received from Hertha Sponer in Norway, Herzberg learned that in September of 1935, Edward Teller would be on his way to join George Gamow at George Washington University, and she to Duke University in January 1936, so that they could all meet in the U.S.A. some day. She noted that "my Duke is in North Carolina and seems to be as significant as your Saskatoon".[33] Duke University had been founded in 1924 as an expansion of Trinity College in Durham, North Carolina, and President William P. Few used the support provided by the New York based Emergency Committee in Aid of Displaced German Scholars to bring six major figures to the university. Sponer was the first in Physics, with the theoretical physicist Lothar Wolfgang Nordheim, her colleague from Göttingen, arriving in 1937. A year later the pioneer in quantum chemistry and superconductivity, Fritz London, joined them. These three helped to establish the Physics Department at Duke as an important centre for graduate studies and research.

Herzberg also notified the Academic Assistance Council in London and the Notgemeinschaft in Zurich that he had accepted a Carnegie Guest Professorship at the University of Saskatchewan.[34] He thanked them for their kind and effective help while looking for a suitable post and asked them not to drop his name from their lists, since for the time being, the post in Saskatchewan was not a permanent one. Being uncertain of his future in Canada after the guest professorship of two years, he did not resign from the THD but formally requested of the Rector a leave of absence for the period 1 September 1935 to 31 August 1937.[35]

His next step was to write to Dr. E.L. Harrington, the Head of the Department of Physics in Saskatoon, who had also written Herzberg—their letters crossed within a day of each other.[36] Herzberg suggested that he could give courses in atomic spectra and structure, molecular spectra and structure, nuclear physics, radioactivity, and atomic physics in general, as well as wave mechanics or advanced optics or electrodynamics, with the selection left completely up to Professor Harrington. In his letter Harrington wrote: "Perhaps you would like a word of greeting directly from the Department of Physics. While I had no part in making the arrangements which culminated in your decision to join us next autumn, I do want to assure you that your welcome here will be no less cordial on that account."[37] He then went on to suggest that Herzberg could give two courses (rather than the usual three) of three one-hour lectures each week, one in general physics and half courses in theoretical spectroscopy and wave mechanics. He also recommended that Herzberg should consider supervising one or two students working towards the Master's degree (the university was not yet prepared to offer Doctorate degrees). He ended with "If I can be of any assistance in a personal way, in facilitating your adjustments to the life and work in this new atmosphere, feel free to mention anything you would like for me to do."

On receiving this surprisingly friendly and cordial letter, Herzberg was relieved and sensed that he would get along well with Harrington. This feeling of helpful co-operation was strongly confirmed as letters continued to flow back and forth, dealing primarily with the availability or possible purchase of laboratory equipment. Herzberg was bringing special optics to build a fluorite prism spectrograph for the far-ultraviolet region but needed a comparator for the measurement of spectra. He also inquired about the possibility of obtaining a grating, of building mountings for a grating spectrograph, and of procuring space for a three-metre instrument.[38] Harrington sought gratings at the universities of Toronto, Chicago, Michigan, Iowa, and Minnesota without success, but a room was available for the grating instrument. He also visited the Gaertner Company in Chicago concerning the comparator and received authorization from President Murray for Herzberg to choose one and order it. Harrington also suggested that Herzberg visit The University of Chicago on his way to Saskatoon to discuss grating availability and price with Dean H.G. Gale; the two of them could then present the matter to President Murray.[39] Herzberg was surprised to experience such instant rapport with someone he had not met.

Preparations for Emigration

Unexpectedly, emigration matters proceeded smoothly in Germany. Officials saw only that a German Guest Professor was off to Canada for two years. He would be a *Tarnkappe*, a good ambassador for the Fatherland who would spread the gospel of pan-Germanism and help to counter the anti-Nazi propaganda that was being spread by the Canadian media. Nevertheless, Herzberg was informed that while he could purchase return passage in Marks, including the ocean crossing and train to Saskatoon, each traveller was permitted to take only 10 M cash (i.e., $2.50) out of the country. Indeed, the purchase of return fare seemed a good idea at the time; after all, this whole Nazi situation might be over in a year or two, and if not, the tickets could be sold later. As a Guest Professor, he found that the customs inspection was perfunctory and he was allowed to ship books, optical equipment, photographic plates, and other small apparatus that he felt would help him in his research. From Saskatoon he was informed that such shipments sent directly to the university would be duty-free.

Herzberg was completely unaware of the strict immigration rules in force in Canada at that time.[40] When his application for entry into Canada was received, A.L. Jolliffe, the Commissioner of the Department of Immigration and Colonization, wrote to Murray informing him that Herzberg would not come within the classes ordinarily admissible to Canada under existing immigration regulations. To determine whether special facilities would be warranted on behalf of the Herzbergs, he asked for assurance that the appointment as Guest Professor of Physics was correct and, if so, whether his term with the University would be limited to a period of two years.[41] Murray assured Jolliffe that Herzberg's appointment was for two years, with salary to be paid by the Carnegie Corporation, and arrangements were made for temporary admission on a non-immigrant basis for two years.[42] After making numerous enquiries of the Canadian Immigration Office concerning the delay in receiving visas, the Herzbergs finally learned on 29 July that they were granted temporary entry into Canada under non-immigrant status for a period of two years.[43] With passage booked on the SS *Hamburg* leaving Hamburg for New York on 22 August and the return fare as well as train fare to Saskatoon paid for in Marks, Herzberg turned his attention to scientific matters at the THD.

His first concern was the status of the book on atomic and molecular spectra. Originally this was to be a brief elementary introduction to the subject for the beginner in the field, based on the courses he had given in Göttingen, Bristol, and Erlangen. However, even the part on atomic spectra was now over two hundred pages, and the preliminary draft of molecular spectra was at least twice as long. Herzberg decided to split off the atomic part to stand alone as *Atomspektren und Atomstruktur*, even though several books on atomic spectra had already appeared in German as well as in English in the early 1930s. Having obtained the approval of Th. Steinkopff, the publisher, Herzberg proceeded to complete the smaller volume on atomic spectra to his satisfaction, with the intent of submitting it for publication before leaving Germany. This he succeeded in doing on 30 June, with the hope that he would not be asked to shorten it.[44]

In spite of the meagre equipment he expected to find in Saskatoon, Herzberg was determined to build a spectroscopy laboratory to rival the best available. Since it would take several years to duplicate some of his Darmstadt instruments in Saskatoon, he now concentrated on obtaining photographic plates of high-resolution infrared spectra of oxygen, the deuterated acetylenes, and methylacetylene for a number of studies he had in mind. These plates would be measured and analyzed in Saskatoon and would keep him active in research while the fluorite prism and a grating spectrograph were being built. Also as time permitted, after classes and lecture preparations, he planned to continue writing his book on molecular spectroscopy and molecular structure, on which a very good start had already been made in Darmstadt.

Farewell to Family and Friends

The time for embarkation arrived all too soon. The Herzbergs had brief visits with friends in Darmstadt and with the Oettinger family in Nürnberg. Luise was particularly concerned about the future welfare of her parents, living in this national shrine of the Nazi. However, her father felt they were exempt from the anti-Semitic turbulence because he was a war veteran, and he was determined to continue managing the growth of his company. The Herzbergs then spent three days in Hamburg, their port of departure. Visits with brother Walter and longtime friends Alfred and Hans-Werner were a disheartening reminder of their carefree years at the Johanneum and of hiking in the mountains and forests in the summers. Now they discussed the unthinkable—the low level to which their once great country, the bastion of Western culture, had sunk in a few short years. Education was no longer the high ideal of German youth; the attendance at universities and gymnasia was dramatically reduced, and the outstanding Johanneum of Hamburg, their Alma Mater, was reduced to a training centre, with many of its famous professors driven out, in conformity with the Nazi hygienic policy, to be replaced by those embracing the National Socialist Party. It was unbelievable that all of this could be happening in the country of Heine, Goethe, Schiller, Mozart, and Beethoven.

Walter and Alfred wondered how was it possible that a Herzberg whose family had lived in Germany almost four hundred years was now considered a traitor and forced to leave his homeland. Walter was also experiencing difficulties: he had lost most of his piano students and a recent concert was poorly attended simply because of his name. The *Hamburger Tageblatt*, organ of the National Socialist Party, reviewed Walter's concert as "No idea about art", although the *Hamburger Fremdenblatt* gave a very favourable review. Alfred, too, was having difficulty continuing with his research for the Historical Reichscommission and was given a teaching job at the so-called Jewish school, the famous Heinrich-Hertz Gymnasium. Later, because of his hearing impairment, he was moved to the Library of the Hochschule for Teachers' Education. Gerhard saw his friend Hans-Werner Döring only briefly. Although Hans-Werner had no socialist leanings, his father was an ardent Nazi and kept pushing him to join the Party so he could get a teaching job. Hans-Werner was obviously sensitive about the discussions of present-day Germany and sadly left this gathering at Alfred's home early with the excuse of a previous appointment, staying only long enough to catch up on the latest news and to bid his friend a safe journey and *auf wiedersehen*.

For Gerhard and Luise, not knowing what the future would bring, and to be so far from friends and family, meant that leaving Germany with only a few personal belongings was an acutely painful experience. There was little to look forward to: they were headed for a small university in an isolated prairie town in far-off Canada where they knew only one person, their friend of one year, John Spinks. As they boarded the SS *Hamburg* on 22 August, Gerhard clutched his luggage containing letters from friends and colleagues which he had saved and cherished as his only mementos of the lonely, yet happy years in his homeland, now a godforsaken country. A telegram with "Best Wishes" from their friend Walter Heitler, meant to cheer them on their way, only reminded them of the many friends they were leaving behind as they sailed out along the Elbe River to the North Sea and into the boundless Atlantic Ocean. Little did they realize how extremely lucky they were.

Arrival in the New World

The Atlantic crossing proved uneventful, except for rough seas on the first day followed by dense fog for several days, with better weather only after passing the Gulf Stream.[45] Arrival in New York seven days later was on schedule on a beautiful clear morning with the imposing skyline familiar from the many postcards sent by visiting friends. The Herzbergs were met at the dock and brought to their hotel by James Curry, his first postdoctoral fellow in Darmstadt, now working at Columbia University. A thoughtful advance from the University of Saskatchewan and a gift from Luise's sister Lotte and husband Hans Thurnauer, who had settled in the United States a year earlier, awaited Gerhard and Luise on arrival. This money made it possible for them to spend a few days in New York and to make some additional trips in the eastern part of North America. For the next two days they toured downtown New York, marvelling at the large number of skyscrapers, the blazing lights of Times Square, and the onrushing cars and pedestrians. They viewed the sea of slim towers and houses from atop the newly built Empire State Building, which they had been told had 102 stories and was higher than the Eiffel Tower.

On Sunday, 1 September, Luise left by train from the Pennsylvania Station to visit Lotte in Chattanooga, Tennessee, while Gerhard started on a series of rapid trips with brief visits to various universities and research laboratories in the northeastern United States and in Montreal, Canada. Early September proved to be an unfavourable time for such visits, as most people were still on vacation just before the start of the new academic year. Nevertheless, he encountered a number of scientists, some of whom he had met in Germany and England, and was able to see many spectroscopy laboratories. On this whirlwind tour Herzberg managed to squeeze in visits to ten research institutes of spectroscopy, fearing that it would be a long time before he might have the opportunity to come east again. He was also pleased that he had managed to make these visits at minimal expense, with hotel costs ranging from $1.00 to $1.75 per night.[46]

His first visit was to Columbia University, which impressed him with its vast extent and its Physics Department housed in the Pupin Tower. There he met for the first time Isidor Rabi of atomic-beam fame and Harold Urey, Nobel Laureate in 1934 for the discovery of heavy hydrogen. Urey had just been named editor of the *Journal of Chemical Physics*, a new journal devoted to publications of interest to chemists and physicists, and he asked Herzberg to referee a submitted paper. This was a new experience for Herzberg since papers in the German *Zeitschrift für Physik* were not refereed. Next, he was in Boston and the Massachusetts Institute of Technology, where he was shown the activity in the new field of electronic computers. He took an overnight train to Montreal and visited J. Stuart Foster at McGill University and discussed his work on the Stark effect. He also met the chemist Edgar W.R. Steacie, who was to play an important role in Herzberg's career many years later. Another overnight train took him to Princeton University where he visited Edward U. Condon (of the Franck–Condon principle). This was a fortuitous meeting, as Condon had just taken on the job of general editor of a series of physics texts to be published by the Prentice-Hall Company. When he learned of Herzberg's book *Atomspektren und Atomstruktur*, he immediately invited Herzberg to produce an English translation for publication in the series.[47] At Johns Hopkins University in Baltimore, Herzberg saw the grating ruling engine of Robert W. Wood but missed him as well as James Franck, who had recently accepted a professorship there. In Washington, Herzberg toured the extensive laboratories of the National Bureau of Standards and walked to the Capitol and to the Lincoln and Jefferson monuments. In Pittsburgh he visited his former colleague Ernest Berl, who had been dismissed from the THD in 1933 and was now a Professor at the Carnegie Institute of Technology. He and his wife had adapted quickly to the American way of life and felt entirely at home in the United States. A day's visit to the Ohio State University in Columbus was followed by one to the University of Michigan in Ann Arbor. Herzberg enjoyed the latter visit best of all because the work in Michigan was almost exclusively spectroscopic and he sensed the pleasant co-operation within the group headed by Harvey M. Randall and David M. Dennison. At the University of Illinois in Urbana, he visited Francis M. Loomis, with whom he had corresponded for several years about gratings and spectrographs. Herzberg was disappointed on finding no one at The University of Chicago, not even Robert Mulliken. Next morning, he awaited Luise's arrival from her visit in Tennessee.

On to Saskatoon

The Herzbergs left Chicago at noon on Saturday, 14 September, on the "Hiawatha", the fastest train in North America, which covered the eight hundred kilometres to Minneapolis in five hours. Unfortunately, the trains to Winnipeg, Regina, and Saskatoon did not move with even half this speed, so that they did not reach their destination until Monday morning, 16 September. The trip was not as dull as they had expected because the vast wheat fields of the Prairies and the farm houses and barns with tall silos were all new to them. Nevertheless they became increasingly concerned as the train often stopped at places with only a few houses, and they began to wonder what Saskatoon would be like. But when they arrived in Saskatoon in splendid sunshine, they were pleasantly surprised to find an attractive small city, decked out in beautiful autumn colours. This welcome impression of their new homeland was enhanced beyond measure when they saw their friend John Spinks waiting for them at the railway station.

The University of Saskatchewan is apparently half a century ahead of Cambridge in science and of Oxford in common sense.

George Bernard Shaw

8. BEGINNINGS IN CANADA

Gerhard and Luise instantly felt comfortable in Saskatoon and never forgot the kind hospitality and friendliness with which they were received by faculty members and neighbours. Within three weeks of their arrival, they sent off letters to friends in Germany describing their new homeland:

9 October 1935

Saskatoon was a pleasant surprise for us. The city lies on the South Saskatchewan River, which is as broad as the Elbe at Dresden, which of course does not mean that I want to compare Saskatoon to Dresden. There are five bridges across the river, two of which are very beautiful. The riverbed lies rather deep, and consequently the coastline looks very nice. The university is on the opposite side of the river from the main part of the city, and its institutes are built far apart, so there is still a lot of room for additional buildings. The physics building is relatively large, about as large as the Institute in Darmstadt, but the biologists are also housed in the building, and many more rooms than in Darmstadt are used for classroom purposes. Moreover, teaching takes over a much larger share of time, indeed I have to lecture for six hours, and other colleagues even teach nine hours. I have a very nice office, and already two students want to take their Master's degree for research work in spectroscopy. The means for research are, however, rather limited, but everyone here shows the utmost accommodation for my wishes. All of the people here are especially nice. With the English lectures I manage quite well, but of course it is more work.

The first fourteen days, we stayed in a small hotel since the apartment we found was not available until October 1st. We now have a furnished apartment with a kitchen–dinette, a bedroom, and sitting room.

On our second day here, we saw a wonderful display of Northern Lights, in several colours, very bright and constantly changing. Northern Lights are frequent here since we are rather close to the north magnetic pole, which lies in northern Canada. Nevertheless, Saskatoon is not much more northerly situated than Berlin. A few days later, we had a temperature of –8°C at night, but during the day it is most pleasant since the sun is shining most of the time. About the winter with its –40°C, we have already been told all kinds of things, although some say it is not so bad—well, we shall see.[1]

Saskatoon and its University

Within a short time, Gerhard and Luise learned the early history of this remote community and the founding of its university. Settlement in the district of what was to become Saskatoon began in earnest in 1882 when the Temperance Colonization Society received a land grant from the Dominion Government, with the colony to be settled within five years. The townsite was named Saskatoon, a shortened version of the Indian name Mis-sask-quah-too-min, meaning "carpet of flowers". Within a few years the colony became a supply base for government troops, and men were employed as farmers, freighters, couriers, and scouts for the rapidly expanding northwest. By 1890 the railroad had reached Saskatoon, and the first railway bridge was completed across the South Saskatchewan River to serve this village of 113 souls in 1901. The Province of Saskatchewan was formed in September 1905, and the City of Saskatoon was inaugurated a year later, after losing a hard-fought campaign to the City of Regina as the provincial capital. Nevertheless, railway activity continued with the building of tracks in all directions from the village, then another bridge, and a railway station and yards, making Saskatoon by 1907 the "Hub City" and the "Hub of the Hard Wheat Belt". After another lengthy political battle, Saskatoon was awarded the University of Saskatchewan in April 1909. This decision was greeted with the ringing of church bells, the blowing of steam whistles, and the shouts and screams of half the population in a torchlight parade of burning brooms.

Saskatoon, 21st Street, facing east to the railway station.

The campus of the University of Saskatchewan, 1935. At lower left is the chemistry building, then the physics, administration, and arts buildings.

With the granting of the charter for the University of Saskatchewan and the selection of the beautiful site overlooking the city, the prestige of a university added a new pride to this pioneer community of 12,000 inhabitants and advanced its cultural life. An extensive building program at the university and city brought trade, increased capital, and skilled labour to the city, and Saskatoon enjoyed a period of booming growth up to the time of the Great War.[2]

Walter Charles Murray (1866–1945) of Dalhousie University was selected as the founding president of the University of Saskatchewan in August 1908. He was born in Studholm, New Brunswick, and was educated at the University of New Brunswick. He distinguished himself in philosophy at the University of Edinburgh and, after a brief period of study in Berlin, returned to his alma mater at the age of twenty-five to take up the Chair of Mental and Moral Philosophy and Political Economy. Within a year he was offered and accepted the George Munro Professorship of Philosophy at Dalhousie University, the leading university of the Maritimes. During the next sixteen years he carried out his university teaching and administrative duties with distinction and served the Church, the School Commission, and the City Council; he wrote about educational and municipal affairs and was active in many clubs and committees. In a farewell tribute, his friend of Edinburgh days, James Falconer, wrote in *The Dalhousie Gazette*:

> But as attractive as he is as a lecturer he is yet more noteworthy because of his broad humanity. Few in college had a larger circle of friends than he; and these were drawn from every quarter. He was *persona grata* in every society. He would breakfast with philosophers, dine with doctors, and sup with theologians, and whenever he came his happy laugh and ingenious discussions were the life of the company.... He is essentially a peacemaker; and whether in college or city council or church courts, it is ever the same that he refuses no labour, counts nothing too much trouble, if only he can bring people to see eye to eye. Energetic to the last degree, ready for hard work, sane in judgement, he is a man who is always sure to come to the front in the counsels of men.

Such was the man chosen to build the University of Saskatchewan.[3] Murray came with firm ideas on the nature of the university he would build:

> What is the sphere of the university? Its watchword is service—service of the State in the things that make for happiness and virtue as well as in the things that make for wealth. No form of that service is too mean or too exalted for the university.... Teaching, Research, and Extension are the three forms of its service. As it cares for the different phases of public well-being it increases in usefulness and merits the support which the people generously give.

Although Murray originally strongly supported Regina as the site of the University of Saskatchewan and expressed his disappointment with the decision to locate it in Saskatoon, he was quickly reconciled. Murray envisioned a large university with faculties of arts, science, engineering, agriculture, education, law, medicine, and probably dentistry and commerce. He understood the importance of agriculture to the people of Saskatchewan and stressed this in his plans:

> The College of Agriculture, while distinct from the other Faculties and probably more isolated and independent, should yet be within the University, receiving from the liberal studies a humanizing influence and giving to the whole life of the University a close relationship between the daily life of the people and the pursuit of the scholar and the scientist.

The early 1900s was an exciting period in the Canadian West. "A mood of exhilarating optimism was abroad in the Prairies. Nearly everyone was young, and had come from some other part of the world to seek new fortune in a land of promise. Immigrants were fanning out from Winnipeg to take up homesteads, and abundant harvests were yielding quick returns. Life was one long, expanding boom with advances and recessions it is true, but nobody dared to place any limits on the possibilities of the future."[4] While Murray hailed from the more cultured Maritimes with close ties to Great Britain, he easily fell in step with this adventurous mood of the West and fuelled its spirit at the University. The establishment of a first-class university in the service of the people of Saskatchewan became his life's mission and a challenge as the population of Saskatoon increased to 25,700 in 1921 and to 43,300 a decade later. By the time the Herzbergs arrived in Saskatoon, the major work of planning and building the first phase of the campus had been accomplished, and about two thousand students had already been awarded degrees.

The Department of Physics

Within two weeks of arriving in Saskatoon, Herzberg was teaching two courses, one in elementary mechanics to undergraduates and the other in atomic and molecular spectroscopy to students in the Master's degree program, the highest degree given at the university. Having spent a year in Bristol, he was comfortable lecturing in English. But he found it rather hard work to prepare the undergraduate course and especially to set problems for the students and provide solutions to them—something he had never done in Darmstadt, where much less time was devoted to problem-solving by the students. To his pleasant surprise, he found the standards at this little university to be remarkably high; the pioneer immigrants in the farming community believed that their children should have a good university education and sent them to university in spite of economic hardships. These were eager students who competed strongly to see who would be at the top of their class, and they performed exceptionally well for the Bachelor's and Master's degrees and in postgraduate studies in the United States or the United Kingdom. Herzberg learned that of the almost two thousand students who had graduated in the past twenty-five years, over eighty had gone to other universities to obtain Doctorate degrees and were employed in universities, colleges, and national laboratories. Of the sixteen Rhodes Scholars from Saskatchewan, nine had received Firsts and Higher degrees at Oxford and none less than a Second, a better performance than Rhodes Scholars from any other province.[5]

Among the students in his first graduate class were William G. Schneider and Henry Taube from neighbouring farms in Wolseley, Saskatchewan, both enrolled in chemistry. After his Master's degree, Schneider obtained a Ph.D. in physical chemistry at McGill University; he carried out research at Woods Hole Oceanographic Institute in Massachusetts from 1943 to 1946 and then joined the NRC in Ottawa and served as its President from 1967 to 1980. Taube obtained his Ph.D. at the University of California at Berkeley, and being unable to find a position at a Canadian University, he joined Stanford University. He received the 1983 Nobel Prize in Chemistry for his work on the mechanisms of electron transfer reactions, especially metal complexes.

Herzberg's colleagues in the Department of Physics were Ertle L. Harrington, the Head of the Department, Balfour W. Currie, Newman Haslam, and Charles MacKay. They taught physics to a total of about eight hundred students, a large proportion of the less than three thousand enrolled in the university. In addition to lectures, the students specializing in physics spent much time in laboratories that were well equipped, so they had very good background training in experimental as well as theoretical physics. Student interest in physics was encouraged by the activities of the Physics Club, with biweekly supper meetings of staff and graduate students. Papers were read by student members, and special experiments were performed by staff, with the annual highlight being the Physics Show, essentially an open house full of striking demonstrations for the audience.

From its beginnings in 1910, the department focused on teaching as its first duty and pioneered new undergraduate courses in electron theory and atomic structure in 1924, in medical physics in 1928, and in meteorology and climatology in 1936–1937, long before some of the larger universities took up these themes. On completion of the Physics Building in 1921, the first research activities were studies of soil temperatures at various depths, with results of interest to soil scientists, and of the motion of curling stones and the effects of sweeping, which stirred up considerable publicity for the university. Notable recognition for research came to the department with George R. Henderson's research in radioactivity and Thomas Alty's work in surface physics. Alty was the Research Professor of the department for ten years and left Saskatoon on being appointed Kelvin Professor of Applied Physics at the University of Glasgow, at the time of Herzberg's arrival.

Harrington headed the department from 1925, and through his inspired leadership and planning, the University of Saskatchewan became widely

The Physics Club, University of Saskatchewan, 1936.
Front row: Prof. Haslam, Prof. Harrington, Dr. L. Herzberg, Prof. MacKay, Prof. Herzberg, Prof. Currie. Second row: G.G. Milne, L.G. Mundie, G.J. Thiessen, R.B. Sutton, J.G. Fox, R. Anderson, R. Fournier, K.N. Barnard, J.L. Stewart. Third row: S. Standen, A.E. Douglas, K.T. McLeod, A. Morrison, W.C. Fisher, B. Stannard, C.M. Penner, R.F. Pattison.

respected in physics. He was raised on a farm in Missouri and was educated at the universities of Missouri, Harvard, and Chicago. He was a confirmed gadgeteer and believed that students from the farms made the best physicists because they were practical and resourceful and could construct almost anything with a piece of barbed wire, angle iron, and a stick of wood. Along with his administrative duties and teaching, Harrington was noted for his development of new apparatus and for building the first radon plant in Western Canada. Atmospheric physics and studies of the auroras and earth currents were Currie's main interests. Haslam had returned to the university in 1935 after obtaining his Ph.D. at McGill under John Foster and spending two years in Leipzig with Werner Heisenberg of quantum mechanics fame.

As Currie noted, among the various universities to which Herzberg might have gone, one of the most unlikely was the University of Saskatchewan.[6] The university lacked suitable equipment for spectroscopic research, and funds to purchase equipment and make additional appointments to the staff were almost non-existent as the university was operating under drastically restricted budgets because of the Great Depression and the years of drought leading to a succession of poor crops for the province.

These problems were well known to Herzberg, but after some initial hesitation he accepted this temporary position since it was the only safe haven he had been offered. Moreover, with the full support of Harrington, Herzberg was allotted $1,800 to equip his laboratory and to purchase a comparator for the measurement of the spectra he had brought from Darmstadt; secretarial services were provided for the writing of papers and books, and he was given space to build a large spectrograph when adequate funding became available. He could not ask for more!

Research Professor of Physics

Harrington immediately recognized the good fortune of the department in the new recruit, and within a month of Herzberg's arrival he was strongly recommending to President Murray an increase in Herzberg's salary. Herzberg had already set up an active laboratory with the equipment Harrington had ordered for him and the optics he had brought from Germany. His lectures were well received by the students in spite of his accent, and he worked long hours, regularly and efficiently. As one of his students recalls:

> Oh, Herzberg was a marvellous fellow. I always appreciate people who have super-brilliant minds, which Herzberg obviously had, and yet who are down-to-earth and human. And he was also, I think, a very kindly man.… There were several of us in this first year class, who quite plainly belonged to the Awkward Squad, and while Herzberg didn't have to, he organized extra classes for us at 4:30 in the afternoon. And I think that was a very generous thing for him to do, to help out people who were having all sorts of trouble.[7]

Luise, too, was warmly welcomed to the Physics Club and was able to pursue her interests in spectroscopy and work with Gerhard in the laboratory.

President Murray himself was much impressed and wrote to Professor Alty in Glasgow that Herzberg "is proving to be a genuine treasure". Just three months after Herzberg arrived, and much to his surprise, he was called to Murray's office and given a permanent faculty appointment with the title of Research Professor, together with a very substantial raise in salary.[8] The Herzbergs could hardly believe their good fortune: all of their worries about the future were eliminated. This was a most welcome relief from the thought of having to return to a troubled Germany after the two years as Guest Professor. Life in Saskatoon turned out to be rather special

The first winter in Saskatoon, 1935.

for them. They quickly came to know the hundred or so faculty members and became close friends with many of them. They were invited to Sunday afternoon teas and to musical evenings at friends' homes. Even the challenge of the severe winter did not daunt them. They walked across the 25th Avenue bridge many mornings and evenings when bus service was disrupted because of heavy snows. There was now no doubt in their minds that Canada was to be their home. It was time to start a family.

Having decided to remain in Canada, Herzberg applied for permanent landing in January 1937, long before the expiry of the temporary visa as Guest Professor. This provoked serious enquiries from A.L. Jolliffe, the Canadian Commissioner of Immigration, who instantly wrote to President Murray asking for an explanation.[9] He wanted to know whether Herzberg's position had been made permanent and, if so, the nature of the appointment and whether he would be displacing any Canadian resident. Murray responded immediately.[10] He explained that on the departure of Dr. Alty for the University of Glasgow, his position was taken up by Drs. Herzberg and Haslam and that the arrangement was working out well, with the department now having five staff members in place of the previous four. In a second letter Murray came straight to the point in his usual effective manner:

> In your letter of January 26th you raise an interesting question. You ask if Dr. Herzberg would be displacing any Canadian resident. Does that imply that a Canadian University cannot appoint to its staff any person, no matter how distinguished, who would in any way displace a Canadian resident? Does it mean that we are restricted to Canadian residents for the filling of academic positions unless no Canadian resident has the peculiar qualifications required? If so, I fear it may prove fatal to higher education.
>
> While we are all most anxious to give our Canadian students a good chance and in making appointments actually give them a preference, we must from time to time bring in from outside of Canada distinguished scholars to strengthen our staff. Does this suggestion mean that from Great Britain we should not bring scholars if it displaces a Canadian resident, or from the United States, or from any country in Europe? If this is a matter of settled policy its seriousness for higher education and research in Canada is very great.

Jolliffe replied that in view of Herzberg's special qualifications, the department had decided to extend favourable consideration in the matter of a permanent landing. However, because the Herzbergs did not come within the ordinarily admissible classes, it would be necessary to make a special recommendation to Council on their behalf, an action he had already taken up.[11] Landed-immigrant status was authorized by Order-in-Council on 17 March 1937 to Gerhard and Luise, thanks to Murray's strong intervention. No sooner was Herzberg's two year leave of absence over (on 1 September 1937), and with him not having returned to Darmstadt, the Rector of the Technische Hochschule notified him that his position as Privatdozent no longer existed.[12] In 1936 Herzberg began to repay his student bursary in Germany by sending 16 M at a time to the Reichstudentenwerk until 1939, and he contributed $30 quarterly to the Emergency Society of German Scholars Abroad in Zurich for help to other refugees.

Elsbeth Oettinger, Luise's mother, was granted permission to visit the family in Saskatoon for several months in the summer of 1936, and she was delighted to be there for the birth of her grandson Paul Albin, born on 23 September 1936. She had sailed from Hamburg to Halifax on the luxury liner *St. Louis*. One of the passengers happened to be Henry R. Calvert, one of the many visitors at the University of Göttingen in its heyday, who remembered Herzberg making the daily rounds with Professor Franck. He wrote to Herzberg that he enjoyed the company of Mrs. Oettinger as they dined at the same table on the *St. Louis*. Calvert also mentioned that on this trip he had revisited the Institute of Physics in Göttingen, but sadly all of

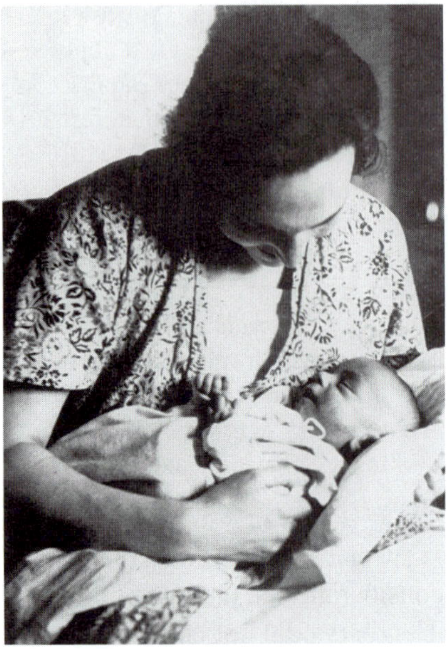

October 1936

May 1937

Proud parents with Paul.

the familiar faces were gone. Mrs. Oettinger's visit in Saskatoon was extended to the end of 1936 when Gerhard accompanied her on the long train trip to her daughter, Lotte Thurnauer, in Chattanooga, Tennessee. After a brief visit with Lotte's family, she sailed home to an increasingly troubled Germany. Two years later, Luise's parents would plead for help to arrange for their immigration to Canada.

A daughter, Agnes Margaret, was born on 12 December 1938. The growing Herzberg family then moved to a small house at 813 Colony Street, within easy walking distance of the university. Both Paul and Agnes were baptized in the United Church as protection against future "Nazis", even though Gerhard and Luise were not keen on the religious aspect, nor did they expect to return to Germany or Europe. In fact, the Herzbergs were for all intents and purposes atheists, but they could not acknowledge this since it would raise problems even with the educated people in Saskatoon. There were strict observances of religious decorum in this city of many churches, one precept being that tennis could not be played before noon on Sundays. During the next few years, Luise gave up her work in the laboratory to take care of the children, yet she managed to keep abreast of devel-

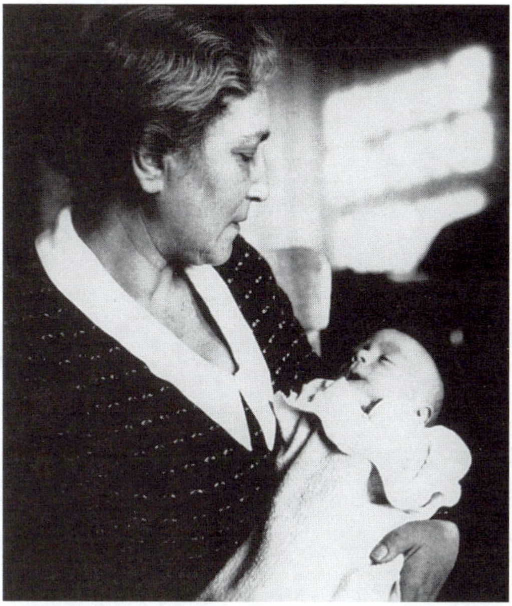

Grandma Elsbeth Oettinger with Paul, October 1936.

opments in spectroscopy and to contribute to some of Gerhard's research by preparing figures and tables for his books. She was often sighted on campus during good weather, wheeling the baby carriage, then the stroller, as the family visited Gerhard and brought him lunch.

Invitations to Scientific Meetings

The constant stream of letters to and from friends and scientific colleagues in Europe and North America was quickly resumed in Saskatoon. From colleagues who had to leave Germany, he received inquiries about the Carnegie Guest Professorships and of the chances of academic or research posts in Canada. He informed Hans Beutler of his own experiences, and Beutler, who had applied to universities around the world, eventually joined Mulliken's group in Chicago. When Herzberg learned from letters of Hertha Sponer that Eugene I. Rabinowitch was at loose ends because his fellowship from Imperial Chemical Industries had expired in London, England, Herzberg asked Rabinowitch for a vitae and publications list to help in an inquiry at the University of British Columbia. However, no positions

Luise and Agnes, March 1939.

Uncle Victor's greetings on the birth of Agnes.

materialized in Canada, and Herzberg wrote that he would discuss Rabinowitch's problem with colleagues at Princeton University.[13] Finally an opening at the Massachusetts Institute of Technology became available and Rabinowitch thanked Herzberg for his help. Herzberg was also informed by Sponer that Edward Teller had visited Duke University, that Lothar Nordheim, her former colleague from Göttingen, was to join Duke as theoretical physicist in 1937, and that Fritz London, who along with Walter Heitler pioneered the field of quantum chemistry, was to come a year later as a guest professor.[14] In fact, London remained at Duke until his untimely death in 1954, and his contributions to the physics of extremely low temperatures, superconductivity, and superfluidity won him much acclaim and helped raise the stature of physics at Duke University.

Soon after his arrival, Herzberg was invited to participate in scientific meetings in Canada and the United States. In spite of the long distances involved and having to pay his own costs, he took every opportunity to attend, as long as his absence from home was brief and the time away did not interfere with his classes. The latter restriction didn't hinder him unduly, since most science conferences were held during school breaks at Christmas, Easter, or summer holidays. His first chance to travel came in June 1936, when he attended the Seattle–Victoria Meeting of the Astronomical Society of the Pacific and combined this with a visit to his mother in Seattle, Washington. At this conference he met many American and Canadian astronomers for the first time, among the latter were Carlyle S. Beals and Andrew McKellar of the Dominion Observatory in Victoria, British Columbia, who were soon destined to make important contributions in astronomy and would become Herzberg's close friends.

He visited his mother whom he had not seen since her brief visit in Germany, at least ten years before. In the meantime, she had met and married Oscar Svendsoy, a longshoreman in Seattle, and had raised a daughter. Herzberg met his half-sister Charlotte but, having little in common with her or Oscar, did not relate well to them on this visit, as noted and commented on by his mother. On the journey home, he visited the Observatory in Victoria and came to know a few more Canadian astronomers and their work.

Herzberg was invited to participate in a conference on molecular structure, organized by the American Chemical Society and being held in Princeton, New Jersey, in January 1937. He presented the results of recent work on the spectra of methyl acetylene and diborane. There he met the leading American astronomer Henry N. Russell of Princeton University and discussed with him a project of possible importance in astronomy concerning the absorption of radiation in the infrared region by water vapour in the atmosphere. Herzberg's point was that in the Saskatoon winter with temperatures as low as –40°C, the water vapour in the air would be frozen out, so that the radiation from the Sun would not be absorbed, and there would be a good chance of extending our knowledge of the Sun's spectrum. Russell was very interested, thought this a good idea, and suggested that Herzberg apply for a grant from the Penrose Fund of the American Philosophical Society, which he would support.[15]

On the basis of his paper at the Princeton meeting, Herzberg was invited by H.D. Smyth, Chairman of the Physics Department, to join Princeton for the second term (10 February to 18 June 1937) to give a graduate course on molecular spectroscopy, but he declined because of his duties and graduate students at the University of Saskatchewan.

Herzberg's next conference proved to be an important introduction into the circle of American astronomers. It was held at Yerkes Observatory in Williams Bay, Wisconsin, from 22 to 25 June 1938. The conference was organized by Robert Mulliken of The University of Chicago and Otto Struve, the Director of the Observatory, with discussion on "Recent Progress in the Interpretation of Molecular Spectra and in the Study of Molecular Spectra in Celestial Objects". This was the first of several such conferences at Yerkes Observatory with astronomers, astrophysicists, and physicists in attendance.[16] Herzberg met many American spectroscopists and astronomers and was re-acquainted with Edward Teller, Robert Mulliken, Hans Beutler, and John Winans, all of whom he had last seen in Germany. He presented the paper "Forbidden Transitions in Diatomic Molecules". In particular, he predicted the possibility of detecting molecular hydrogen in planetary atmospheres by investigating an extremely weak spectrum, known as the quadrupole spectrum, a major discovery he was to make a decade later by simulating the extremely long depths of planetary atmospheres in the laboratory.

That year, Herzberg had to forego meetings in Pittsburgh and Berkeley because of travel costs and visa problems. The following year, he was invited by the American Chemical Society to visit the universities in Minneapolis, Madison, Urbana, Lafayette, Columbus, and Ann Arbor where he lectured on a variety of molecular topics. This was a whirlwind trip lasting from 8 to 17 May 1939 and was a good introduction to many American chemists and physicists. Within three years of his coming to North America,

Herzberg had visited most of the very active centres of spectroscopy and had met many of the distinguished astronomers, chemists, and physicists.

Early Accomplishments

Along with his teaching duties and the analysis of spectra he had brought from Darmstadt, Herzberg kept busy writing and revising the volume on diatomic molecules. In the meantime he reviewed the galley proofs of the German edition of atomic spectra, and the book was published in 1936. With the help of John Spinks this was translated into English, and *Atomic Spectra and Atomic Structure* was published by Prentice-Hall Company in New York a year later, with due credit being given on the title page to Spinks for the translation. The first volume in the series *Molecular Spectra and Molecular Structure*, titled *Diatomic Molecules*, was published in 1939 in both the English and German editions. Herzberg then turned his attention to the second volume in the series, on polyatomic molecules, writing in longhand at every possible opportunity.

In addition to the time-consuming work of reading and correcting proofs and writing, Herzberg was most anxious to begin experimental research. Two students began research work on his arrival in September, and he wanted to get them started right away and to spend as much time as possible with them. J.G. Fox set up a high-voltage discharge cell for studying the emission spectrum of CO, and L.G. Mundie built an absorption cell 2.5 metres in length and examined spectra of NO. Fox completed his Master's degree in the spring of 1937, and Mundie in the fall of that year. W.S. Herbert and G.A. Mills (graduate students in chemistry) worked on active nitrogen during the summer months of 1936. In the meantime another two students joined the group, C.M. Penner studying the emission spectra of B_2 and Si_2 and R.B. Sutton who helped in setting up the new grating instrument. A steady stream of students asked to join in Herzberg's research, and he elected to have two working in the laboratory at any one time, along with Luise and himself.

With strong recommendations from Henry Russell and James Franck, Herzberg was awarded $1,500 by the American Philosophical Society to build a spectrograph for his molecular research.[17] It was the first research grant he received in North America and opened the way for his early studies in high-resolution spectroscopy. He chose to design and build a six-metre grating spectrograph to provide sufficient resolution for the problem he had discussed with Russell and to study the spectra of other molecules. He used $500 for a grating, which he ordered from R.W. Wood of Johns Hopkins University who had supplied him with the efficient grating for the instrument in Darmstadt. The rest was needed for the shopwork in building the instrument. This was efficiently pursued by the technician Bert Cox, who had joined the department in 1924. Herzberg was in constant contact with Wood about details of the grating and was assured in early June 1938 that it was finished and that it was a "beauty". Finally, after four years in Saskatoon, Herzberg had the necessary equipment, and the best instrument in Canada, to continue his spectroscopic studies. He first carried out the experiment he had proposed to Russell, only to find that there was no difference in the summer and winter spectra of the Sun. The explanation was that even though the winter temperature on the ground was −40°C, there was an inversion layer in the upper atmosphere at about +10°C so that the water vapour contained there still blocked out part of the Sun's spectrum in winter as it had in summer.

Although this project seemed to be a complete flop at the time, it later proved to have some importance for astronomy. Astronomers were constantly on the lookout for the best locations for observatories, places far away from city lights and atmospheric disturbances. When the American astronomer Gerard Kuiper was making a survey of various possible locations for observatories with better viewing, he used Herzberg's results to decide that there was no use in going to colder places to observe, rather one must go to higher places. In this way he found Mauna Kea at an altitude of four thousand metres in Hawaii to be an ideal place for astronomical observations, and over the years, a large number of observatories were built there.

A major result for the understanding of chemical bonding was the discovery by Herzberg in 1937 that the length of the C–C single bond was dependent on its environment. When the spectra of methyl acetylene (CH_3CCH and CH_3CCD) taken in Darmstadt were finally analyzed, the length of the C–C single bond was not found to be constant at the value 1.543 Å accepted for ethane (where the C–C bond is surrounded by six single bonds). In methyl acetylene, the C–C bond is adjacent to three single bonds on one side and to a triple bond on the other, and its length is shortened to 1.460 Å.[18] This was the first recognition that the C–C bond length depended on the number of adjacent atoms, a topic that was pursued by Herzberg and his colleagues and by several other groups. The difference in bond length was so striking that Linus Pauling, who was developing his theory of the chemical bond, did not believe this result until it was confirmed by R.M. Badger of the California Institute of Technology.[19]

During the period 1935–1939, Herzberg published twenty papers, half were based on spectra he had taken in Darmstadt, many of which had been analyzed in Saskatoon, and the rest were based on experimental research carried out in Saskatoon. Luise completed the analysis of an infrared spectrum of HDO that she had produced in Darmstadt and published the results as her last paper in German.

With these many accomplishments in the few years that Herzberg had been in Canada, his colleagues and friends decided it was time to nominate him for Fellowship in The Royal Society of Canada. Harrington submitted the nomination papers, supported by Gordon M. Shrum and Frank B. Kenrick, along with the following letter:

> Professor Herzberg is now in his fourth year with us as Research Professor in the Department of Physics, having come to us in 1935 as a successor to Professor Alty. His work in spectroscopy has been of such outstanding importance that little comment is necessary, particularly in view of the fact a complete list of his publications is being submitted. While of German training, he had already spent a year in England before coming to Canada. He is a most excellent lecturer, speaking clearly with well chosen words and having the gift of knowing whether or not his audience is able to understand what is being said. He is very popular with the research students and with other members of the staff, as well as with faculty members outside our department. He is most cooperative and tactful in his dealings with everyone.
>
> His book on atomic structure has been well received and is published in both English and German. A second volume is in proof stage. This too will appear in both English and German editions. I believe there are comparatively few who can be considered such an authority on atomic and molecular structure. His several invitations to participate in symposia is ample recognition of his standing. I consider him to be not only well qualified, but thoroughly Canadian in his outlook and interests.[20]

Although there were twelve nominations that year, the Selection Committee put forward three, with Herzberg as the leading candidate. There was some comment regarding the fact that he had been in Canada only since 1935 and was not a Canadian citizen, but the Committee felt he was so outstanding, and according to Harrington would remain permanently in Canada, that a mere counting of years was not of importance. When this slate of candidates was announced to the Fellows, a very strong objection was raised by Eli F. Burton of the University of Toronto, who sent a letter to all members of Section III (the scientists in the Society). He raised the point that Herzberg had been in Canada only a few years, and although there was nothing in the by-laws of the Society confining membership to Canadian or British citizens, he thought it very unfortunate that this choice should be made in view of the fact that there were a great number of Canadian scientists who deserved election and whose nominations had been renewed year after year and who now were being passed over for a comparative newcomer. After stating that this matter should be given very careful consideration by the Society, Burton added that if the election of this candidate was carried through at the present time and confirmed by the Society, in justification of his interest in Canadian scientists, he would resign as a Fellow of the Royal Society of Canada.[21]

To some members, Burton's objection smacked of anti-Semitism, an attitude deplored by many who found it to be gaining ground in Canada. This was perhaps an unjustified criticism of Burton's concern, who was told pointedly that Herzberg was not Jewish, and one colleague even went so far as to state that Herzberg was a good Christian. The strong support for Herzberg's many contributions assured his election to Fellowship in The Royal Society of Canada that year at the age of thirty-four, one of the Society's youngest members. Burton attended the Annual Meeting of the Society, was polite to Herzberg, and did not resign.

Volume I of *Molecular Spectra and Molecular Structure*, *Spectra of Diatomic Molecules*, was finally completed to Herzberg's satisfaction and immediately translated into English by Spinks. Luise prepared all of the drawings and tables, with the final figures being drafted by Lorne Gray, an engineering student (who many years later became the President of Atomic Energy of Canada Limited). Gray was recommended to Herzberg by Chalmers Jack Mackenzie, the Dean of Engineering (who left the University of Saskatchewan in 1939 to become Acting President and in 1944 President of the NRC in Ottawa). Again, Haslam read the proofs and contributed many stylistic improvements to the text. The German and English versions were published in early 1939 by the same publishers that produced the books on atomic spectra. This volume was dedicated to Walter Charles

Murray, First President of the University of Saskatchewan. On receiving a copy of the book, Murray was overwhelmed:

> Dear Dr. Herzberg:
>
> I cannot tell you how much I appreciate the great honour which you and Dr. Spinks have done me in dedicating your book to me. The beauty of its external appearance is far surpassed by the beauty of your gracious act.
>
> You and Dr. Spinks have brought great honour to this University by your researches and your teaching.
>
> Dr. Spinks has the added honour of having brought you to this University. Everything which he said about you has been more than justified by what you have done since coming to Saskatchewan. Like him, you have contributed much to the life of the University as well as to Advancement of Knowledge.
>
> May this University long enjoy the benefit of your great services is the sincere wish of your grateful friend.[22]

Family Reunion

As conditions in Nazi Germany steadily degenerated and became unbearable for the Oettingers by September 1938, they sought the help of the Herzbergs to emigrate to Canada. One might wonder why they made this decision so late, yet one could understand their inner turmoil. They were both Germans, born and bred in Germany, he was a front-line veteran of the Great War, his company was flourishing, and they retained little of Jewish culture and religion. Yet living in Nürnberg, the national shrine of the Nazi, with the pomp and glory of torchlight parades and Hitler often addressing zealous crowds of one hundred thousand or more, they should have realized much sooner that their presence would not be tolerated for long. The disastrous Kristallnacht all over Germany on 10 November 1938, the atrocities that followed, and the mandatory use of the names "Israel" and "Sara" after their first names on all official documents shattered any dreams they may have had for their continuing survival. The final blow was Paul "Israel" Oettinger's ouster from his own company by his Aryan partners.

Herzberg's first enquiry on seeking entry of Luise's parents as permanent residents brought an immediate reply from A.L. Jolliffe, the

Commissioner for Immigration, that the Oettingers were not in a position to comply with the Immigration Regulations and that Canada was being inundated with such requests.[23] Walter Murray, now retired from the presidency but ever active, stepped in again with his strong support. The Investigative Officer in Saskatoon reported that circumstances were favourable for admission of the Oettingers but that special authority would have to be secured by Order-in-Council, and Jolliffe informed Herzberg that appropriate action was being taken. In view of the terrible news of Kristallnacht, Herzberg sent a night letter asking for acceleration of the final papers, only to be told that because of the large number of such requests, the Department could not give precedence to the Oettingers. On 8 December, Murray sent Herzberg a telegram stating that he had been to the Immigration Department in Ottawa and that a cable would be sent to Germany regarding permission for the Oettingers to come to Canada. After further delays, Murray was informed that the Order-in-Council had been passed and that the Canadian agent in Hamburg had been informed to proceed with the permits for entry into Canada. Passports stamped with a large red "J" were issued in March, and the Oettingers finally sailed from Hamburg on 22 March, arriving safely in Halifax on 3 April 1939.

Thanks to the persistent and persuasive efforts of Murray, the Oettingers found a safe haven in Canada. One might well have asked why would Murray have gone to so much trouble? As his successor, President James S. Thomson wrote of Murray: "There was a phrase that often slipped from him as he spoke about the practical solution to some problem—It's the human thing to do."[24]

The Oettingers moved in with the Herzbergs, but living conditions with two young children and grandparents in their small home proved difficult for all, and the increased expenses became a concern. A move to a larger house at 814 Temperance Street a year later eased the strain somewhat. Also, Lotte and her husband, now American citizens, were able to contribute a monthly allowance towards the living expenses of her parents. To Gerhard's surprise, he found that Mr. Oettinger expected much more than just a home: he insisted on total devotion and service from Luise. Thus, she essentially had to give up any thought of serious scientific work for a few years, until her parents moved to Ottawa in 1943. Although only English was spoken at home after Paul and Agnes were born, Gerhard and Luise now felt they had to switch to German since Elsbeth was not comfortable in English. Luise's father on the other hand spoke English fluently and in

1943 was offered a job as a Censorship Examiner in the Department of National War Services in Ottawa. The Oettingers became naturalized British subjects in 1945.

As the daily newspapers reported increasingly ominous news from Germany, Herzberg worried about Walter, whose infrequent letters told little about his employment and even less of living conditions in Hamburg, presumably because of fear of censorship. The main personal news was that he had not joined the National Socialist Party, nor was he drafted into military service because of an arm injury in a motorbike accident in 1939. Gerhard wondered how long it would be before Walter would be mobilized.

Life in Saskatoon

The small university community was a friendly, close-knit group that organized picnics in the northern lake district, visits to each others' homes, and a children's Christmas party in the President's home. After Murray's resignation in 1937, these parties were hosted by the Physics Department, with Mr. Oettinger being Santa Claus in 1939 and 1940. The Herzberg family enjoyed outings to Lake Waskesiu and Emma Lake, still in their natural state, and the good hiking in the forests around them, where the silences were broken only by the sound of a loon or the splash of fish. They attended the winter series of concerts of the young Saskatoon Symphony Orchestra and the art exhibits and other cultural events that toured Western Canada, giving them the opportunity to meet colleagues and distinguished guests. Through Spinks, Gerhard struck up a friendship with the artist Ernest Lindner and was invited to the "Saturday Night" salons at the Lindner's home on 9th Street. These were attended by professors from a variety of departments, Spinks from Chemistry, David from French, Steinhauer from German, Bentley from English, and Saunders from Biology, as well as by people from the press, the cooperative movement, school teachers, visiting dignitaries, and artists. Discussions during these long evenings were intense and animated and covered a broad spectrum of topics, philosophic, religious, scientific, and artistic.

Gerhard was especially moved by a radio broadcast by Lindner on the theme "No Civilization without Creation". His concluding remarks resounded strongly with Herzberg's ideas, which years later he would espouse at university convocations:

> Let us not just be contributors to the world's stomach with our wheat, and to the world's industry and armament with our minerals. Let us contribute to the world's cultural life with our thoughts, with literature, music, folk songs, handicraft, and art—grown on our own native soil. Only if we do that, will we live a full life, will we truly appreciate the accomplishments of other nations and other times and become a full member of the family of the great nations of the world.[25]

Others who became best of friends of the Herzbergs in a short time were Rudolph and Anni Altschul, Austrian refugees who arrived in Saskatoon in 1939, having survived the torpedoing of the liner *Athenia*. He was a neuropsychiatrist in private practice in Vienna but switched to anatomy in Saskatoon since it was the only position available at the time. He became internationally recognized for his research in arteriosclerosis, the hardening of the arteries in humans, as well as experimentally induced arteriosclerosis in animals. Frederick Mendel was another Jewish refugee who settled in Saskatoon just before the start of the war. He had operated a meat processing plant in Czechoslovakia and soon started the very successful Intercontinental Pork Packers plant in Saskatoon. He donated the Mendel Art Gallery to the city, a noteworthy cultural centre for exhibiting the work of Canadian and international artists.

The prospects of better crops towards the end of the thirties encouraged a mood of optimism at the university and in the city and province, and this mood was strengthened in Saskatoon with the major celebrations for the Royal Visit of King George VI and Queen Elizabeth in June of 1939. Within three months this jaunty atmosphere was shattered as Germany pounced on Poland to precipitate the Second World War and the Saskatoon Light Infantry embarked for Great Britain with the First Canadian Division in December 1939.

I'm a great believer in luck—and I find the harder I work the more I have of it.

Stephen Leacock

9. THE WAR YEARS IN CANADA

Friendly "Enemy Aliens"

As soon as Canada declared war on Germany on 10 September 1939, the Herzbergs became "enemy aliens". They reported to the Royal Canadian Mounted Police each month and remembered it as a friendly affair. They were not maltreated in any way by the university community or neighbours because they were known to be refugees from the Nazi regime that had now started the Second World War. Before long, they became accustomed to the rationing of food; however, restrictions on gasoline and liquor and the "meatless Tuesdays and Fridays" did not affect them, as they did not own a car, were teetotallers, and most of their meals were vegetarian, with Luise adding the occasional meat supplement to her diet. Like their neighbours, they tended a small garden plot in the area used as a skating rink in winter and canned much of the produce.

By September 1940, the Herzbergs had lived in Canada for five years, the necessary period to claim citizenship. In fact, they could have applied a year earlier because they had spent a year in England. Herzberg submitted an application, supported by a strong letter of recommendation from President James S. Thomson, who noted that Herzberg was a scientist of great international distinction, a Fellow of the Royal Society of Canada, and one who was much impressed with the democratic character of Canadian life.[1] Herzberg was informed that the Court would hold a sitting in Saskatoon to consider his application for naturalization in January 1941. The Court gave its approval but the certificate was not granted at that time. A possible reason for the delay was stated in a letter received by Thomson in October 1940 from the Under Secretary of State:

> When the present Secretary of State assumed office on May 1940, he laid down the policy that he would not sanction the issue of certificates of naturalization to persons of enemy nationality and has extended this to nationals of countries contiguous to countries in the war zone. This ruling may be regarded as being to some extent provisional and temporary, but the Minister has not felt it expedient up to the present to make any exceptions. It is quite possible that in the course of the next few months the policy may be reviewed and certain exceptions permitted.[2]

Another request was made by Herzberg two years later, and once again in May 1945, stating that his father-in-law, who had come to Canada four years after himself, had already received his certificate of naturalization.[3] This long delay in the Herzbergs' naturalization was explained away as a loss of his application, which had never been received from the Court in Saskatoon.

Conferences and Molecular Astronomy

During the war years, travel to conferences in the United States became much more difficult, but still possible. In May 1940 Herzberg spent a week at Purdue University as visiting lecturer and was especially pleased to find Edward Teller there. Their host K. Lark Horowitz, an Austrian refugee, invited both to his home for dinners to catch up on news and to enjoy evenings of discussions as well as Teller's virtuoso piano performances. Teller had not lost his musical touch from the last such sessions that Herzberg remembered attending in Göttingen in the early thirties. That summer, Herzberg returned to the University of Michigan at Ann Arbor for the months of July and August to give a summer course on molecular spectroscopy. His hosts at this centre for infrared spectroscopy were Harvey Randall and Edward F. Barker, both pioneers of this field. While there, Herzberg had the help of a technician to search for emission infrared spectra of HD^+ and H_3^+ in an electrical discharge, but without success. This visit gave him the opportunity to attend the famous Summer School in Michigan, with lectures by prominent physicists, Enrico Fermi and John Wheeler among them. Much of the discussion pertained to nuclear physics, highlighted by the newly discovered fission of uranium, and to the possibility of a sustainable chain reaction. Leo Szilard, a refugee Hungarian and one of the first to suggest a chain reaction, was there too, and he proposed that all work on chain reactions should be kept secret and not be published because it might help the Germans develop an atomic bomb.[4] This was the first indication to Herzberg that there might be research on production of an atomic bomb. Only after the war's end did he learn that John G. Fox and Roger B. Sutton, two of his students, had worked on the bomb project in Los Alamos, New Mexico. Fox later wrote to Herzberg about having experienced the first test on 16 July 1945 in New Mexico, when he felt the heat and blast of the explosion even though he was nine miles away, lying flat and face down.

On his next visit to The University of Chicago in late 1940, with the United States not yet involved in the war, Herzberg noticed that much of Mulliken's laboratory was closed off. He was unaware that Fermi and others had moved to Chicago for work on fission and atomic energy in the so-called Metallurgical Laboratory. On the way home, Herzberg was taken off the train at Emerson, on the border between Minneapolis and Winnipeg, and informed that the American government had decided to close the border to all aliens and that he, travelling with a German passport, was not eligible to leave the country. The immigration officer was a kindly old man who didn't want to lock Herzberg in a jail cell but told him he would lose his job if Herzberg walked across the border and escaped. Herzberg didn't attempt to escape but became rather nervous as it took three days to straighten out his predicament, with negotiations between Saskatoon, Chicago, and Washington.[5]

One of Herzberg's most important meetings turned out to be a small informal conference at Yerkes Observatory on interstellar molecules, held in June 1941. This was organized by Otto Struve and was attended by a group from Chicago including Mulliken, Teller, and Beutler, Pol Swings (a distinguished astronomer from Liège, Belgium), Herzberg, and the small staff of the observatory. The purpose was to discuss a series of spectral lines at wavelengths near 4000 Å that had been observed in the absorption spectra of distant stars by the astronomers Theodore Dunham and Walter S. Adams at Mount Wilson Observatory in 1937.[6] In the same year Swings and Rosenfeld had identified one of the lines to be due to the diatomic molecule CH, and its presence in the interstellar medium was confirmed in 1940 by the Canadian astronomer Andrew McKellar.[7] That year McKellar also established the presence of the diatomic molecule CN in interstellar space through his identification of three lines found by Adams.[8] CH and CN were the first molecules to be identified in the interstellar medium, and their discovery proved to be a major breakthrough for astronomy. However, four lines found by Dunham and Adams remained unidentified and their origin posed an important puzzle for astronomers and spectroscopists. At the meeting, Swings suggested they might belong to an ionized diatomic molecule such as C_2^+, CH^+, CN^+, NH^+, or NO^+, whereas Mulliken, who was then working on his theory of spectra of polyatomic molecules, thought they could be due to the free radical CH_2. Herzberg and Teller had good reason to favour the ion CH^+ instead. Although its spectrum was unknown, they surmised that it would have an electronic band of the required type near 4000 Å because of the similarity of CH^+ to the iso-electronic molecule BH, whose spectrum was known to be in this wavelength region. The solution to this spectroscopic puzzle was certainly worth pursuing.

On his return to Saskatoon, Herzberg decided to try to reproduce these unidentified lines in the laboratory. The six-metre grating instrument was ready, he had a good student, Alex Douglas, and apparatus for the study of spectra of various gases and mixtures of gases was available. Within a short time, a discharge in helium with a trace of benzene produced a spectrum in the region of the unidentified lines. The spectrum was clearly of a molecular type, and closer examination showed that three of the lines (the only three expected to occur at the extremely cold temperatures of space) were exactly at the positions of the unidentified interstellar lines.[9] There was no doubt that the laboratory spectra duplicated the interstellar line spectra. However, the question remaining was what molecular species produced

Graduate student Alex Douglas preparing for the spectrum of CH^+, University of Saskatchewan, 1941.

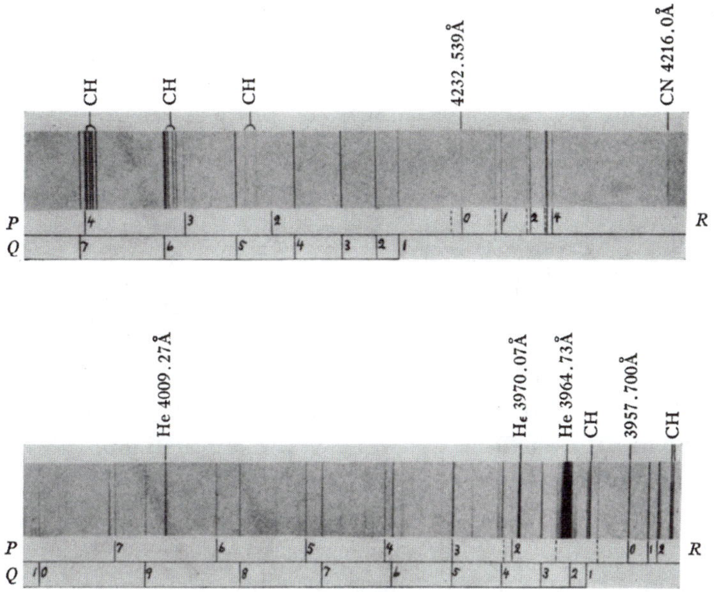

Spectrum of CH^+ obtained by Douglas and Herzberg, 1941. The R(0) lines labelled 4232 and 3957 Å are two of the lines found in interstellar absorption.

these lines? Further experiments and analysis convinced Herzberg and Douglas that the spectrum was due to the ion CH^+. This result was published and was of great interest to astronomers because it was the first molecular ion to be identified in the interstellar medium.[10] This discovery was even reported in *The New York Times*. Such publicity was a rare event for Saskatchewan, and Herzberg only learned of this news when he met a delighted Chairman of the Board of Governors of the University, who noted: "I've seen an article in *The New York Times* where you were mentioned about CH^+."

The next meeting at The University of Chicago was a conference on spectroscopy organized by Mulliken, Struve, Franck, and Weldon G. Brown, held from 22 to 25 June 1942. There, Herzberg met Brown for the first time and learned that he was a graduate of the University of Saskatchewan. This meeting dealt with a variety of problems in atomic and molecular spectroscopy, including the spectra of comets, of planetary atmospheres, and of dyes and large organic molecules. Herzberg presented two papers: one was on a new effect he had discovered in the spectra of polyatomic molecules, which he called *l*-type doubling, and the second was on evidence for the presence of CH_2 in comets.

Alone in the Laboratory

Herzberg's work on CH_2 first started when he received a letter (and a photograph of spectra) from Pol Swings in Belgium stating, "We observed in a comet a group of features around 4050 Å, and we can't understand what they are.[11] Can you tell us what these spectra are?" Herzberg was just then writing his book about polyatomic molecules and thought that the spectrum looked like that of a triatomic molecule. One of the simplest triatomic molecules is CH_2, and he had the idea that this 4050 Å group of lines in comets might be due to CH_2, a free radical with a very short lifetime.

He decided to try to reproduce the spectrum of the 4050 Å group and started experimenting with a discharge of methane (CH_4), thinking that as the methane was destroyed in the discharge, at some stage there might be some CH_2 formed. He carried out these experiments by himself since he had no students after 1941. The young people no longer stayed on for Master's degrees but enlisted in the military services or became involved in the war effort. W.R. Ham and G.G. Milne completed their degrees in the spring of 1940, A.E. Douglas and N. Olson in the fall of that year, and W.J. Hushley and A.S. McKay were his last students receiving their degrees in 1941. With some of the professors giving courses in radio and radar to the armed services, Herzberg was asked to give an extra undergraduate course. His contributions to teaching and research continued to be appreciated and he received a salary increase to $4,500 per year, with an additional $500 for research purposes.

Herzberg's initial experiments on the comet bands were a total failure, with production of only H_2 and CH spectra. However, he noticed that the colour of the discharge looked very different at the moment the discharge was turned on than when it ran continuously. So he obtained spectra as he turned the discharge on and off about two hundred times by hand. To his surprise a new feature in the spectrum (apart from known H, H_2, and CH lines) appeared at 4050 Å, identical to that observed in comets. Having observed the spectrum from a discharge in CH_4, it seemed natural to assume that it was due to CH_2, although he did not rule out CH_3 or CH_4 at that time.[12] This result on the comet bands and the earlier identification of CH^+ in interstellar space quickly established Herzberg's reputation among

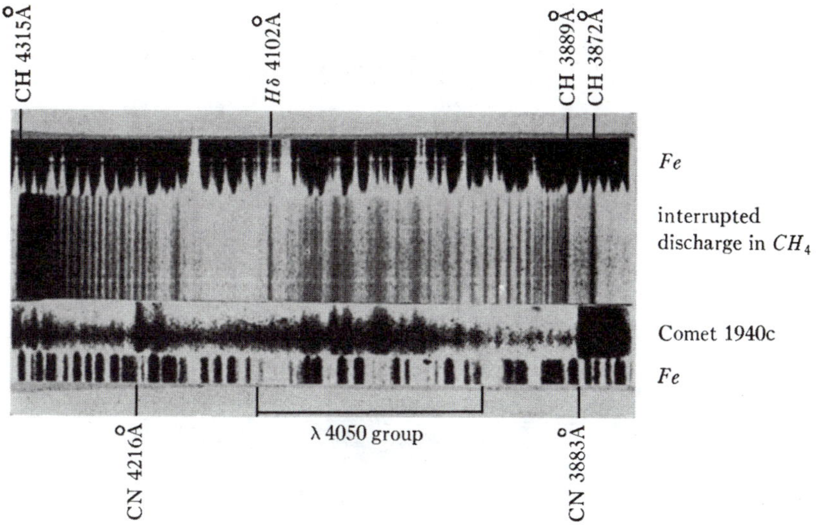

The 4050 Å group found in a comet and the spectrum obtained by Herzberg, 1942.

the astronomers. Even so, his identification of the 4050 Å group with CH_2 was shown to be wrong about seven years later, but it forced Herzberg to continually think about the free radical CH_2 and to search for its spectrum until he discovered it two decades later.

With no graduate students to supervise, Herzberg had more time to devote to writing his book on polyatomic molecules, and he pressed ahead, completing a first draft in English by early 1942. Having achieved this major goal, Herzberg decided to give himself a treat. He had always loved music and had played the violin before attending university, his brother was a pianist, and his gymnasium friends were good musicians. In Darmstadt he had taken every opportunity to attend concerts and opera. Now he decided it was time to take up a hobby, something he would do for pleasure, away from his work. He chose to take singing lessons. He found a good teacher, Mrs. F.B. Morrison, and began taking lessons to control and make the most of his resonant bass–baritone voice. The more he sang, the more he enjoyed it. He became especially fond of Schubert lieder, songs based on the poetry of Heinrich Heine, whose work he enjoyed as a youngster in Hamburg. Later he took up lieder by Brahms and arias by Mozart and Verdi. This hobby was a closely kept family secret. Being naturally very shy, Herzberg insisted on closing all of the windows at home during

Grandparents Elsbeth and Paul Oettinger and Ella Svendsoy
with Paul and Agnes, summer 1942.

practice so that neighbours would not hear him singing. In time, his regular absences from the university for one or two hours while at singing lessons were noticed and commented on, raising some eyebrows. However, all was clarified when he gave his first concert, much to the surprise and delight of his friends.

In the summer of 1942, Gerhard's mother Ella came for a brief visit. She was delighted to see her son, meet Luise for the first time, and to coddle her grandchildren. This was also her first meeting with the Oettingers, Luise's parents. While catching up on news of life in Seattle and in Saskatoon during wartime, their thoughts naturally centred on Walter and his family in Hamburg. Neither Ella nor the Herzbergs had heard from Walter since the start of the war, and so far, there was no inkling of the coming devastation of German cities by Allied bombing. For the time being, they could only hope that Walter was not actively involved in the war.

Explosives Research

In 1943, Herzberg was invited to take up work on the spectroscopy of explosives by George Wright, Professor of Chemistry at the University of Toronto, who had invented some new explosives. Wright convinced

E.W.R. Steacie, Chairman of the National Research Council Committee on Explosives, that such secret war work could be carried out in Saskatoon even though Herzberg was technically an "enemy alien". Herzberg signed an Oath of Secrecy, and Wright arranged for Herzberg to attend classified meetings on explosives in the United States by using a Certificate of Identity issued by the Department of External Affairs instead of his German passport.[13] These meetings were organized by the U.S. Navy Bureau of Ordnance, and Herzberg met several of the key explosives scientists, including George B. Kistiakowski of Harvard University, Henry Eyring of Princeton, George Gamow of Carnegie Technical University, and Bryce Crawford of the University of Minnesota. Herzberg was astonished to see that his former student John G. Fox was also a member of this group. At the end of the war Herzberg learned that many in this group were participants in the Los Alamos Laboratory.

By July of 1943, Herzberg had a bunker built at the back of the Physics Building, with walls made of sand bags and a roof of loose planks. In an adjoining hut were housed a fast rotating mirror camera for photographing spectra at one microsecond intervals, and delicate detecting instruments. As his colleague Currie noted, "While this research was classified as 'secret' it did not go unseen and certainly not unheard." The explosions were remembered as a feature of day-to-day life by the citizens of Saskatoon, who could hear a "whoomp" from the university campus from time to time. On campus, these explosions would go off without warning, and the planks were propelled upward and off the bunker by an acoustic wave that rattled and sometimes cracked windows in nearby buildings. Finally, in order to

Bunker and lab for explosives research,
University of Saskatchewan, 1940s.

alert those on campus of the coming boom, Herzberg's assistant, George Walker, who happened to be a bugler, would sound the "Last Post" before each detonation. One of Herzberg's first year students, Bill Cameron, described one such occasion:

> Dr. Herzberg was lecturing away in his usual fashion and suddenly his assistant came charging across the space between the little shack and the back door of the Physics Building and came running into the classroom. And there was an urgent and unintelligible conference between Dr. Herzberg and the assistant, at which Herzberg excused himself in great haste, and the two of them went charging out the door and into the little shack. They came out running four times faster, charged into the classroom, hair dishevelled, a smudge of dirt on Dr. Herzberg's face. And just as they got in the door, there was a *tremendous* explosion. The planks of the bunker went right up in the air and quietly settled back again. Herzberg breathed a profound sigh, turned to the classroom and said: "My! Dat vas a good one, vasn't it?"[14]

The results of this research were published in classified reports and finally in a brief paper in *Nature*.[15] As Herzberg was to say on later occasions, although this explosives work was challenging and interesting scientifical-

Agnes and Paul on a visit to Daddy in physics.

Herzberg in front of the physics building.

ly, it did not help to end the war. Yet this research must have been useful since it was carried on for two years after the war had ended and Herzberg had left Saskatoon.

Herzberg continued to work at his office on Sunday mornings, and Paul and Agnes would go to the university to take him home for lunch. They threw pebbles at his window to alert him of their arrival and he would hand them a chocolate bar while he packed his briefcase with work for home. Sometimes the family would visit the bunker or the university farms to see the animals before heading for home. They spent the afternoons tending their vegetable garden or walking along the river banks.

Offer from Yerkes Observatory, The University of Chicago

There is no doubt that Herzberg's contributions in the several meetings at The University of Chicago, and especially his work on CH^+ and CH_2, had impressed astronomers, particularly Otto Struve, Director of the Yerkes Observatory. Thus as Struve thought of the possibility of increasing research activity in astrophysics after the war, if not in the interim, Herzberg was much on his mind. After discussing his thoughts with Mulliken in the Department of Physics, he wrote to Herzberg enquiring informally, yet rather specifically, whether he would be interested in joining The University of Chicago:

> In connection with our spectroscopic work at the McDonald and Yerkes Observatories the question has often been discussed whether it would not be possible and advisable to secure for our group someone who, like yourself, is a recognized authority in band spectroscopy and line spectra.... I have nothing very definite in mind, but it occurred to me that in view of your phenomenal success in solving certain astrophysical problems you might not be averse to establishing a closer connection with the astronomical kind of spectroscopy. I know that Robert Mulliken and other members of the physics department would be tremendously interested in some such arrangement, though under the present wartime conditions all of their own time is, of necessity, devoted to war work.... What I am saying is based purely upon two or three casual conversations which I have had with Mulliken. In so far as the astronomy department is concerned, however, I can assure you that President Hutchins would be exceedingly enthusiastic about the plan and would welcome an arrangement whereby you could work in our organization....

> Please feel entirely free to tell me how the matter strikes you. Perhaps you are perfectly happy in what you are now doing, in which case I shall certainly not try to induce you to give up your connection with the University of Saskatchewan. On the other hand, if a change should be indicated it might be profitable for me to know that fact and then go a little more into the matter with the university administration on one side and members of the physics department on the other.... It is more than likely that President Hutchins would also like to meet you and talk to you, if and when a definite proposition can be made to him.
>
> It is probably premature to discuss further details, but I might say that the rank of Professor Swings (who left the observatory some months ago to undertake research on war problems) was that of a visiting full professor, with the understanding that the designation "visiting" referred to his express wish to return to Belgium. It is entirely possible that this could be dropped in your case, though, of course, I am without authority to speak for the administration. I can only say that, in the past ten years they have been extremely favourable to our department and have usually acted in accordance with our recommendations....[16]

This letter came as a complete surprise to Herzberg. For him this would be the ideal situation, an opportunity to be a member of a major research institution, to interact daily with world-class scientists of similar interests, and to become an astronomer, a career he had dreamt of long ago. Moreover, it would be a welcome change from the present loneliness he was experiencing in his laboratory without students. Yerkes Observatory seemed to be very active scientifically even during wartime. On receipt of Struve's unexpected letter, and in his excitement considering it to be a proposal, he replied immediately:

> I am delighted to have your very kind offer to join the staff of the Yerkes Observatory. It is a great honour for me that you have considered me for such an appointment. While I have here a position that is in many ways very satisfactory, I have always envied those working in the larger research institutions with large research funds and their possibilities of ready exchange of ideas with other workers in the same field. The history of the identification of the interstellar CH^+ lines has demonstrated to me particularly strongly how necessary for one's work personal contacts with others interested in the same subject area are.
>
> Even before my recent astrophysical work, I had always hoped that one day I might have a much closer connection with astrophysics and these hopes have been greatly enhanced by this recent work. Thus I am greatly attracted by your plan and I shall be very glad to accept it

provided that the questions explained below can be satisfactorily settled as I trust they will be....

You will realize that my position here is quite permanent in character and that I would be somewhat reluctant to accept one that is not permanent no matter how attractive it would otherwise be. However, I take it from your letter that the appointment offered to me is a full professorship and as such permanent....

May I again express my sincere appreciation for your very kind offer. I am looking forward with keen anticipation to your further letters in this matter.[17]

Herzberg went on to raise several conditions, such as desiring to set up a spectroscopy laboratory for the study of molecular spectra as well as astrophysical problems, and enquired about salary.

In further letters, Struve suggested that he would be only too glad to have Herzberg do some laboratory work at Yerkes but that the original spectroscopy laboratory had been completely dismantled twenty-five years ago, and he wondered whether a new facility could be organized without undue expense. Struve also indicated that Mulliken hoped Herzberg would spend two-thirds of his time in the Physics Department in Chicago after the war, but that this division of time could be left open for the time being. Of more immediate concern was that President Hutchins wished to meet Herzberg in view of the requested permanent position at the full professor rank. A visit was planned for early December.

In the meantime in order to obtain a visa, various forms had to be completed and notarized, and letters from sponsors (Struve and Mulliken) were requested by the State Department. Also, Herzberg wanted assurance from the Canadian Government that he would be re-admitted to Canada. Finally, all was in order for Herzberg's brief visit to Chicago. Together with Struve he met Hutchins and was charmed by the man and his directness. He visited James Franck, Weldon Brown, and Mulliken and the staff of Physics and Astronomy, and in both departments he gave colloquia that were exceedingly well attended. Herzberg was thoroughly satisfied with all aspects of his visit and was particularly impressed with the Astronomy Department and its faculty. On returning home, he wrote to Struve thanking him for making the arrangements and for his kind hospitality, noting that he appreciated the definiteness and straightforwardness of Struve's proposals and was looking forward to an intimate association with him and his colleagues at the Observatory.[18]

But this enthusiasm was cut short just at Christmas by the return letter from Struve, accompanied by copy of a letter from Arthur H. Compton, Dean of the Division of Physical Sciences. In this letter, Compton asked Struve to invite Herzberg to come to The University of Chicago as Associate Professor of Astronomy at a salary of $5,500. Struve was clearly embarrassed and regretted that the administration did not accept his recommendation for a full professorship. He noted that the complication with the rank arose solely in the Physics Department and bore no relation to the appreciation Herzberg would receive in the Astronomy Department.[19] Herzberg was sorely disappointed and obviously offended by Compton's letter. In his confidential reply to Struve the following week, and contrary to his usual good nature, Herzberg expressed his chagrin in no uncertain terms:

> Naturally Dean Compton's letter was a great disappointment to me, the more so since I was entirely unprepared for such a turn of events....
>
> If I were to accept Dr. Compton's offer as it stands I could not help feeling, particularly in view of our conversation with President Hutchins, that in a way my association with The University of Chicago would start with a demotion. Certainly Hutchins, at the time, did not say anything that in the least could be construed as his not agreeing with your recommendation of a full professorship for me.... I remember clearly that Hutchins made it a point (quite unexpectedly to me) that steps should be taken that I would not be just one of Mulliken's men. Obviously Dr. Compton's offer represents a step in exactly the opposite direction. I think I would enjoy greatly collaborating with Mulliken and I believe it would be to the good of spectroscopy, but I do feel that it should be on an equal footing.
>
> Accepting an associate professorship would certainly put me in an awkward position toward the administration of this University who have treated me in the most generous fashion and given me a senior professorship with a salary near the top for that rank. Naturally everybody here will agree with me that the standing of The University of Chicago is far superior to that of the University of Saskatchewan. But will they agree that it is so far superior that an associate professorship there is much more desirable than a full professorship here, or will I not by my acceptance imply that I consider the standing of this University to be very low and thus seriously offend people who have been real friends to me? I might add here that C.D. Ellis (the well-known collaborator of Rutherford), who a few years ago visited all Canadian Universities staying at each for a week or more expressed the opinion to the sponsors of his trip that the science

> departments of the University of Saskatchewan are at or certainly near the top of all in Canada (including Toronto and McGill). Other competent observers have expressed similar opinions....
>
> With regard to a future promotion Dr. Compton says "that we consider the way open to him for advancement in rank as he takes his place in the activities of the department". It is very difficult for me to understand the exact meaning of this clause.... Does it simply mean that I would become one of four (or more) physicists waiting for promotion to full professorship, but the one with the least seniority, looking the youngest, with the least desirable citizenship, and with the least aggressiveness in these matters, working in a field least interesting to the head of the physics department, and so forth? ...
>
> Does Compton's offer leave me the option to be full-time with the Astronomy Department even after the war (without of course losing contact with the Physics and Chemistry Departments)? ... Should I see my way through the difficulties against accepting an associate professorship, I would want to be full-time with the Astronomy Department—since I would rather be where I am really wanted and appreciated, quite apart from the fact that it has always been my desire to become an astronomer. I do feel that I would be happy in your department and that a harmonious and fruitful collaboration would ensue.[20]

On receipt of Herzberg's letter Struve replied immediately, noting that because of the Christmas holidays he had not been able to discuss the matter with the university authorities. Also he did not feel justified in urging Herzberg to accept an associate professorship but had to send him Compton's letter. Nevertheless, he hoped that it would be possible for Herzberg to come in spite of this disappointing restriction. Struve informed both Mulliken and Compton of Herzberg's hesitancy in accepting the offer and urged them to write to Herzberg, particularly to clarify the wishes of the Physics Department.

Weldon Brown wrote to Herzberg immediately: "I think they played a hell of a trick on you but it doesn't surprise me. It is rather typical of Compton's style of administration."[21] James Franck wrote a long letter trying to explain Compton's decision and suggesting that the title was not important. He thought that Herzberg would not like everything in Chicago; the town was dirty and the climate was disagreeable, but living in that nice place at Lake Geneva with his family would be something that could be enjoyed, and he would have nice colleagues and a real scientific atmosphere. Later he wrote again:

> One thing I may mention since there may be a misunderstanding on your side. You regarded Dr. Struve's letter as an offer, while it was none; he only made preliminary contacts with you to find out if you would be interested. He mentioned his opinion that the position would probably be a full professorship and apparently he was too optimistic. You are therefore not quite right in stating that the "offer" was changed.[22]

It must be remembered that while these negotiations to bring Herzberg to The University of Chicago were proceeding, but unknown to Herzberg, Compton, Franck, and others from the university were intensively involved in the Manhattan Project at Los Alamos, New Mexico, working on the atomic bomb. With Compton away from Chicago, Mulliken answered Herzberg that according to his understanding,

> The department would leave the path open for your free collaboration in the work of the department both in research and in teaching, … and the time spent in Chicago will depend primarily on you. Many of us here (witness the audience at your colloquium talk) are hoping that it will prove to be a considerable fraction. I want to express again my sincere hope that you will decide to join the faculty of this University. I personally am sure that you will have a real opportunity whether at Williams Bay or at Chicago to continue and extend your fine work of past years.[23]

Within a few days, Mulliken wrote again that he had shown this letter to Compton and that it agreed very closely with Compton's point of view. Struve also forwarded a copy of a letter from Compton stating explicitly that Herzberg should be informed at once that an appointment to the rank of associate professor had the same implication of permanence as an appointment to a professorship and that Herzberg could be assured of a cordial welcome by the physicists and could divide his time between the Astronomy and Physics Departments by mutual agreement of all concerned. Struve sent a long letter to Herzberg reviewing the complete situation and question of rank from his first discussions with Mulliken. He emphasized that he would accept with good grace if Herzberg should decide that under the conditions suggested in Compton's letter he could not accept, but if on the other hand he could accept, Struve would do everything in his power to bring about a promotion.[24]

On receipt of these quick and friendly replies to his several concerns, and after considering what Franck had written and Struve's detailed review of the circumstances, Herzberg accepted the position of associate professor but chose to work in the Astronomy Department, noting that he would prefer a title of Associate Professor of Spectroscopy.[25] Now remained the task of applying for and gaining entry into the United States for the purpose of employment. This turned out to be a formidable task during wartime.

Herzberg applied to the Canadian National Selective Service for a Labour Exit Permit. He was duly informed that the Wartime Bureau of Technical Personnel recommended that a permit not be granted "in as much as there is no evidence that Dr. Herzberg's proposed transfer will be in the National interest, and there are no grounds other than personal desires". Herzberg appealed to the Unemployment Insurance Commission, giving his reasons that the President of the University of Saskatchewan did not offer any objection to his leaving the university, the appointment at The University of Chicago was in response to an unsolicited invitation, his wartime research could be carried out at The University of Chicago, and indeed, scientific teachers in Canada had been granted permits, e.g., Dr. J.L. Synge of Toronto had gone to Ohio State University and Dr. Ralph Hull of the University of British Columbia had moved to the University of Nebraska.

The appeal was denied since Herzberg was in the category of Science and Technical Personnel so his movement was controlled exclusively by the Wartime Bureau of Technical Personnel and a ruling had already been made in his case.[26] The University of Chicago also made a strong presentation to the Canadian representative in Washington, noting that Herzberg would be given space and facilities to pursue his war research on explosives at the university. Finally, Herzberg appealed to the Director of the Wartime Bureau—but all of these efforts were in vain—he would have to wait until the war's end.

On 23 March 1945, Walter Charles Murray, President Emeritus and Founding President of the University of Saskatchewan, died at the age of seventy-nine. The Herzbergs recalled the crucial role he had played in their lives in a letter to Mrs. Murray:

> Dear Mrs. Murray,
>
> The sad news of Dr. Murray's passing came as a great shock to me and my wife. We realize the magnitude of the loss that you have suffered. To us his passing means a very personal grief since it was Dr. Murray who gave us a secure haven and a new home here when we could not stay in our own country. This and the recognition that Dr. Murray gave me from

> the very beginning have meant more to me than I can express in words. His kindness and humanity have been an inspiration that neither my wife nor I will ever forget. It has been a very real privilege to have known him and to have worked under him.[27]
>
> Gerhard Herzberg

With Walter Murray's passing a momentous era had come to a close in Saskatoon. In his honour the university was closed on the day of his funeral.

Walter C. Murray (1866–1945),
President of the University of Saskatchewan (1908–1937).

Good scientists study the most important problems they think they can solve.

Sir Martin Rees

10. INTERLUDE AT YERKES OBSERVATORY, THE UNIVERSITY OF CHICAGO

With the approaching end of hostilities in Europe, the Herzbergs had several concerns on their minds, not only the possibility of an eventual move to Williams Bay and the Yerkes Observatory, but especially of the welfare of family and friends in Germany from whom they had not heard for over five years. Had Walter and his family survived the saturation bombing of Hamburg in 1943, and if so, had he been mobilized in the final futile effort to defend Germany from the Allied onslaught? Answers to these constant worries would have to wait.

Once again, Herzberg inquired of the Wartime Bureau of Technical Personnel what his chances were for release by the National Selective Service in order to take up the position he was offered at Yerkes Observatory. He was informed that chances were excellent for lifting of the manpower restrictions as soon as the European war was over. When the end came in May 1945, formal proceedings for entry to the United States moved rather quickly. First, Herzberg was notified by the National Selective Service that he was exempted from obtaining a labour exit permit before departing from Canada, and he was authorized to leave Canada not later than 1 November 1945 with permission to remain outside Canada indefinitely.[1]

He informed Otto Struve of this news and made plans for a quick visit to Williams Bay in early July to look into the housing situation. This visit was conveniently arranged to coincide with a conference of the Explosives Group of the U.S. Navy Bureau of Ordnance at Cornell University, which Herzberg was to attend. In Struve's absence Herzberg was met at the railway station in Williams Bay by Subrahmanyan Chandrasekhar, whom he had met on earlier visits and who was to become his closest friend at Yerkes. Herzberg looked over the housing on the Observatory grounds and in the nearby area but found that the only available accommodation consisted of three houses, all rather large and all for sale. He felt that the cost of buying any of the houses was beyond his present means and decided that it would be best to rent a cottage while waiting for the university to provide something better. He also spent several hours touring the entire Observatory building with W. Albert Hiltner to check on the available space and consider the possible location of the new spectroscopy laboratory.[2]

In the meantime, Gerhard and Luise were granted naturalization certificates and became Canadian citizens on 28 June 1945, having waited five years since their first application in October 1940.[3]

Astronomer Herzberg

Herzberg received an official notice of appointment as "Associate Professor in the Department of Astronomy at The University of Chicago, on indefinite tenure from 1 September, 1945, on a full-time four-quarter basis, with a salary of $5,500 per annum" and accepted the position, although he would have preferred the title Associate Professor of Spectroscopy.[4] He had finally achieved his boyhood ambition of becoming an astronomer. With the necessary papers for crossing the U.S. border in hand, he then wrote to President Thomson:

> As you know, it is only on account of the special opportunities for research in my field offered in Chicago that I am leaving this University. The ten years of my stay here have been very pleasant and fruitful indeed. I have greatly enjoyed my work here and the associations with the members of the staff have been very stimulating.
>
> Many special considerations have been given me by the University authorities in providing opportunities for my research work and for these I am most grateful. I shall never forget the fact that this University gave me a safe haven when I came here as a refugee. Please be assured of my continued interest in, and affection for, the University of Saskatchewan.[5]

Harrington was disconsolate at losing a friend and stimulating colleague and wrote to President Thomson: "No matter how long one has expected the death of a friend—the event always comes as a shock, so too, with respect to the news of the loss of Herzberg from the department."[6] As their many friends came to wish them well and with a large group to send them off at the railway station, the hurried leave-taking in Saskatoon was almost heartbreaking for the Herzbergs. They arrived in Williams Bay on 20 September 1945 and were met by Struve and his driver, who took them to the Rest Cottage Resort, where Herzberg had rented a cottage for the first few months while awaiting renovations in one of the faculty houses.

Yerkes Observatory[7]

Yerkes Observatory was located next to the village of Williams Bay on Lake Geneva in Wisconsin, about one hundred miles northwest of Chicago. The Observatory was built on a vast expanse of flat land, separated from the lake by a wooded hill. It had good viewing, with little smoke or bright lights because of the relatively low population density and the absence of factories. George Ellery Hale (1868–1938) had designed and built Yerkes Observatory and was its first director. Hale and William Rainey Harper, the founding president of The University of Chicago, were successful in convincing Charles Tyson Yerkes, the patron, to fund the building of the 40-inch telescope on fifty acres of land donated by John Johnson, Jr., a wealthy Chicago real-estate speculator. At the time, Yerkes had the largest telescope in the world and indeed the largest refractor ever used (since a larger lens would begin to distort because of the pull of gravity). The Observatory was in operation and dedicated on October 1897. Its main purpose was research in astrophysics, the study of the nature and composition of planets, stars, and nebulae. It was the first observatory devoted to such studies, in contrast to the more usual work at observatories of that time of determining positions and motions of heavenly bodies. Only six years later, Hale left Yerkes to follow his lifelong ambition to build a succession of the world's largest telescopes: the 60-inch reflector (1908) followed by the 100-inch reflector (1919), both on Mount Wilson, and the 200-inch reflector completed in 1948 on nearby Mount Palomar in California. To honour this pioneer of astrophysics, the 200-inch was named the Hale Telescope, and the observatories on Mount Wilson and Mount Palomar were named the Hale Observatories.

Yerkes Observatory, winter 1945.

Geneva Lake from the Observatory, 1945.

Otto Struve (1897–1963) was the director of both the Yerkes Observatory and the McDonald Observatory in Texas at the time of Herzberg's stay at Williams Bay. Struve, who was born in Kharkov, Ukraine, was the fourth generation of an eminent astronomical family and was a refugee, having survived the civil war of 1919–1920 in Russia. He was given an assistant position at Yerkes in 1921 on the basis of the high regard for his family held by Edwin B. Frost (1866–1935), who took charge of the observatory when Hale left. Struve was appointed director in 1932 at the age of thirty-five and is credited with assembling one of the world's finest groups of theoretical and observational astrophysicists at Yerkes. Struve also assumed editorship of the *Astrophysical Journal*. He was instrumental in the negotiations and the building in southwest Texas of the McDonald Observatory with its 82-inch reflector. The University of Texas paid for the land and observatory, and The University of Chicago provided the staff and salaries. On its completion in 1939, the McDonald Observatory was operated jointly by the two universities, with Struve as director of both observatories. He accomplished these tasks with his phenomenal drive and brilliance and the full support he had gained from the young president of The University of Chicago, Richard Hutchins, who was himself a powerful personality.

Immediately after World War II, Yerkes was a thriving research centre with a large and dedicated staff and many visitors from abroad. It was strongly oriented towards research, with very little teaching. This was the golden age at Yerkes with exceptional scientific output on stars, interstellar matter, and planets. During those years, the staff consisted of the Director Otto Struve, who worked at every opportunity on spectroscopic binaries and massive stars, William W. Morgan with interest in the hottest, bluest stars, and Gerard Kuiper concentrating on planetary astrophysics. Subrahmanyan Chandrasekhar worked on the theory of radiative transfer in stellar atmospheres and quantum mechanical calculations of the opacity of H^-. Other members of the staff were Jesse L. Greenstein, W. Albert Hiltner, George Van Biesbroeck, Thornton L. Page, Louis G. Henyey, Guido Münch, William P. Bidelman, and Herzberg. Visiting professors for various periods of time included Bengt Strömgren and Kaj A. Strand of Denmark, Pol Swings of Belgium, and Marcel Minnaert, Jan H. Oort, Hendrik C. van de Hulst, and Adriaan Blaauw from Holland. Postdoctoral fellows such as George H. Herbig, who came from Lick Observatory, and many graduate students complemented this illustrious group of astronomers and astrophysicists.

The staff at Yerkes Observatoroy, May 1946.
Front row, left to right: Mrs. S. Deutsch, Mrs. M. Carlson, Ann Underhill, Guido Munch, Doris Blakely, Mrs. W. Krogdahl, Nancy Roman, Carleton Pearson; Middle row: P. Swings, G. Herzberg, L. Herzberg, W.W. Morgan, O. Struve, J. Greenstein, G.P. Kuiper, S. Chandrasekhar, G. Van Biesbroeck, L. Henyey; Back row: Paul Ledoux, Arne Slettebak, Mrs. J. Phillips, F. Pearson, John Phillips, Armin Deutsch, Roy Wickham, Merle Tuberg, Wm. Bidelman, Marshall Wrubel, Irene Hansen, Mrs. W. Breen, Arthur Code, Alice Johnson, Gertrude Peterson, Mrs. G. Van Biesbroeck, Carlos Cesco, Edith Janssen, Victor Blanco, John Vosatka, Harold Bernstein.

Struve also dreamt of building another large telescope and made plans with Robert Mulliken for an Institute of Spectroscopy on the Chicago campus after the war. Instead, based on its wartime success in atomic energy, The University of Chicago chose to establish an Institute for Nuclear Physics headed by Enrico Fermi and an Institute for the Study of Metals led by Harold C. Urey on their return from Los Alamos.

Life in Williams Bay

Williams Bay was a very small village situated on the north shore of lovely Lake Geneva. It was the location of the summer residences of many wealthy Chicago families and was exclusively a summer resort. The small permanent population of about seven hundred was mainly of Scandinavian stock, with their primary occupation being tourism. Understandably, there was very little in the way of intellectual life outside the Observatory in this village, so the faculty and their families formed a small, close-knit group.

Most of the faculty lived in homes on a handsomely treed avenue bordering on the extensive lawns of the Observatory, in an area known as Frost's Woods, between the lake and main building. Students were housed in dormitories on the third floor of the Observatory and took their evening meals at the Van Biesbroeck home. The location was an ideal neighbourhood and playground for the faculty children, with nearby swimming and picnic areas, along with hiking trails along the lakeshore and nearby woods. Just before winter, the Herzbergs moved into the old home of the former director Edwin B. Frost, which had been renovated to form two apartments. The Hiltners occupied the second apartment. Paul and Agnes soon found congenial and constant friends in their neighbours Emily and Billie Morgan; they walked together to school in the village and enjoyed many ball games in the playground, so much so that Paul's early ambition was to become a baseball player—a shock for his parents. There, Paul and Agnes learned how to ride bikes and to make and fly kites with their dad. On Sunday evenings the family would gather around the radio to listen to Edgar Bergen and Charlie McCarthy, with Mortimer Snerd being Gerhard's favourite.

The Herzberg home on the campus of Yerkes Observatory, shared with the Hiltner family.

Otto Struve, Carl Beals, and Lalitha and Subrahmanyan Chandrasekhar.

A warm friendship developed between Gerhard and Chandrasekhar (called Chandra by students, colleagues, and friends), which they both valued highly and continued for the rest of their lives. Luise and Lalitha Chandrasekhar also became good friends, and Dr. Chandra and Mrs. Chandrasekhar became Paul's and Agnes's favourite seniors. Agnes recalled that "the children of Dr. Chandra's colleagues liked him, and said he was 'magic', because once on a picnic, everyone had rolled up their shirt-sleeves in the hot afternoon. In the cool evening hours, when they rolled down their sleeves, everybody's sleeves had a crease but not Dr. Chandra's."[8] An annual treat for the faculty children was an Easter egg hunt organized by Dr. Chandra in the Morgan's large garden. Another yearly event enjoyed by families, visitors, and students was Thanksgiving Dinner at the Hiltners, with tables featuring roasts and vegetables, and cakes and pies prepared by all the participants.

Some of the Yerkes faculty took part in the local politics of Williams Bay to ensure a voice in village affairs and especially to make sure that adequate schooling for their young children would be provided. The Herzbergs limited their visits in the village to the barber, baker, and grocery store. They found that the townspeople viewed the strange mix of Russian,

German, Dutch, Indian, Mexican, and South American population of the Observatory with some amusement and continued to charge them all year long what the traffic would bear for groceries and supplies in the busy tourist season.[9] What troubled the Herzbergs most about the villagers was that on arrival, shortly after the war's end with some rationing still in effect, they found a flourishing black market all over town.[10] This was in complete contrast to Saskatoon where they had not detected any such underhanded dealings throughout the war years. Astronomers with cars purchased their groceries and furnishings in the nearby towns of Elkhorn and Delavan, where they obtained far better value for their limited funds.

The Spectroscopy Laboratory

Herzberg's new laboratory was set up in the basement of Yerkes Observatory between the two small domes.[11] The funding provided by Struve, $5,000 for establishing the spectroscopy laboratory and $3,000 for ancillary instruments, was sufficient for the essential equipment. A replica of the 21-foot grating spectrograph he had built in Saskatchewan was installed in such a way that with the aid of a heliostat and one mirror, the solar spectrum could be studied. The grating was supplied by R.W. Wood and had excellent concentration of intensity in the first-order of 11 000 Å or second-order of 5500 Å. An infrared spectrometer with photoelectric detection, built by G.P. Kuiper, was sometimes brought from the McDonald Observatory for specific studies. A medium Hilger quartz spectrograph was also purchased for work at lower dispersion. Other much needed instruments were borrowed for limited periods.

In order to emulate planetary atmospheres, Herzberg designed and built two cells to provide extremely long absorbing paths. One was a glass cell of 150 centimetres length and 5 centimetres radius, and the second was an iron pipe 22 metres long and 25 centimetres radius, the latter running under the ceiling, through almost the whole length of the observatory basement between the two small domes. Each cell was fitted with concave mirrors that were carefully aligned and adjusted to produce multiple traversals of the cell and thus provide extremely long absorbing paths.[12] The mirrors were fabricated at the observatory's optical shop by Fred Pearson, who years before had been Albert Michelson's optician in the Physics Department on the Chicago campus. Up to 40 traversals were obtained with the short tube, giving a path length of 60 metres, and up to 250 traversals, or a

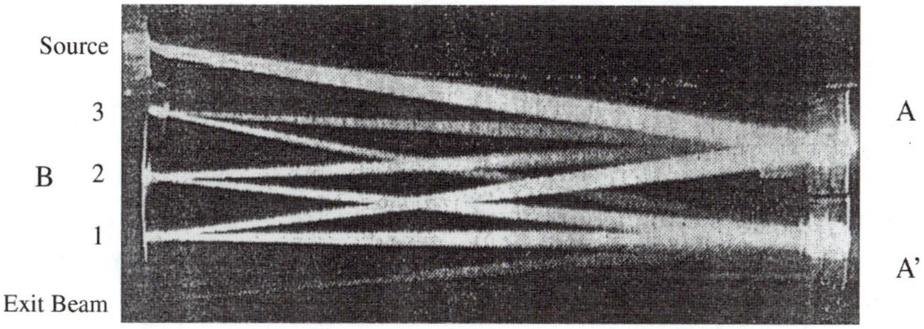

Schematic diagram of a multiple-transversal gas cell.

path length of 6000 metres, was obtained with the 22-metre tube. These long optical paths made possible the study of absorption spectra of astrophysical interest and quickly became the standard method for laboratories involved in reproducing planetary spectra, as well as for the study of very weak or forbidden spectra.

Herzberg supervised the research of two graduate students and two postdoctoral fellows. His first student was K. Narahari Rao, who had received a three-year fellowship from the Government of India to develop skills for the future benefit of India, which was about to gain independence.[13] He chose to work in spectroscopy with Herzberg and completed his Ph.D. in 1949 with a thesis on spectra of CO and CO^+. When he returned to India to take up a position at the National Physical Laboratory, he found that there was no plan to make use of his training, and after two years he returned to the United States. He spent a year as Research Associate with Dr. Sponer at Duke University and another year at the University of Tennessee before joining the Department of Physics at The Ohio State University in Columbus, Ohio. There, Rao built an internationally renowned laboratory for infrared spectroscopy, developing reliable wavelength standards for the infrared region and supervising the research of more than fifty Ph.D. students. Together with Harald H. Nielsen of The Ohio State University, he started and established *The Journal of Molecular Spectroscopy*, which quickly became the most important international journal in spectroscopy. For about forty years Rao continued to organize the annual International Symposium on Molecular Spectroscopy. This was always held in Columbus, Ohio, and continues today, contributing immensely to the field of molecular spectroscopy.

John G. Phillips, Herzberg's second student, was initially given the problem of checking whether a broad interstellar absorption line at 4430 Å was due to the iron hydride molecule FeH. However, this problem proved to be intractable. This feature was one of several broad bands, known as the diffuse interstellar bands, first observed in 1910 and shown to be interstellar two decades later. Its identification was to haunt Herzberg and many others up to the present day. Phillips earned his Ph.D. in 1948 working on the spectrum of the carbon molecule C_2. On the basis of the analysis, Herzberg pointed out that this spectrum arose from a fundamental transition in C_2 and labelled it the Phillips system.[14] As noted by Phillips, "this designation became ingrained in the subsequent literature according my name an immortality enjoyed by few others. Any lesser thesis adviser would have found a way to take credit for himself. It was a lesson I have taken to heart." Phillips remained at Yerkes until June 1950, when he joined the Astronomy Department of the University of California at Berkeley. There, he had a distinguished career in spectroscopy and astrophysics.

Harold J. Bernstein, a Canadian and new staff member of the NRC in Ottawa, was a Research Associate. He had been interned during the war while on a scholarship in Copenhagen, where he worked with George Placzek, and survived five years of malnutrition in prison camps in Denmark and Germany. E.W.R. Steacie, the Director of the Division of Chemistry at the NRC, suggested that while Bernstein waited for space and equipment to establish his own laboratory in Ottawa, he should join Herzberg at Yerkes to catch up on progress in molecular spectroscopy. He arrived in January 1946 and remained for almost a year, helping to set up the long absorption cell and carrying out the first experiments with it. On his return to Ottawa, he led a group in infrared and Raman spectroscopy and later in nuclear magnetic resonance spectroscopy. S.P. Sinha, another postdoctoral fellow, who was from Patna University in India, joined the group for a year in 1947 to gain experience in molecular spectroscopy.

Luise was also a member of the group; she served as a Volunteer Research Associate and took up the study of the atmospheric bands of oxygen. In the exciting scientific atmosphere of Yerkes, Herzberg's group flourished and carried out many important studies in astrophysics and molecular spectroscopy.

Within six months of his arrival at Yerkes, Herzberg's laboratory was in full operation, photographing a variety of molecular spectra of interest in planetary astronomy. His group began by examining spectra of carbon dioxide, CO_2, observed on Venus and of methane, CH_4, observed on Jupiter. These spectra were reproduced in the laboratory with remarkable fidelity using the long absorption cells, permitting estimates of gas pressures and depths of the planetary atmospheres. Studies were also made of the ultraviolet spectrum of oxygen, O_2, important for upper atmosphere physics.

In 1946, the Office of Naval Research (ONR) was founded as the first U.S. government agency to support basic research in universities. This new source of funding provided a much needed boost in morale to the universities, which were desperate for funds to replenish laboratory equipment and finance the many students enrolling in graduate studies in science and engineering in the postwar period. The ONR immediately began to solicit proposals for research grants and contracts. Struve submitted applications for three grants on behalf of his staff: one for a photoelectric project to be developed by Greenstein, another for an infrared study suggested by Kuiper, and a grant for Herzberg to help equip his new spectroscopy laboratory.[15] This would be a good opportunity to purchase much needed ancillary instruments for the laboratory and to assist graduate students and postdoctoral fellows. Discussions with ONR personnel indicated that only the grant for Herzberg had any chance for approval. Herzberg applied for salaries of a research assistant, a laboratory technician, and an occasional stenographer, capital equipment and supplies, and travel to conferences, the total amounting to almost $25,400. Eventually, even Herzberg's proposal was turned down, much to the surprise of the university administration and to the utter disappointment of Herzberg, who wondered whether the importance of spectroscopic work for astrophysics was appreciated in the U.S.A. This negative result left an indelible impression in Herzberg's first year at Yerkes, especially when he learned of the success of other spectroscopists, Mulliken among them, in obtaining generous ONR grants. He began to wonder if he had made the right decision in coming to Yerkes.

Early Misgivings

No sooner were the Herzbergs settled in Williams Bay when letters began to arrive from many friends in Saskatoon emphasizing how much they were missed. Mention was also made that Professor Harrington, Head of the Physics Department, would retire in a year or two, and colleagues wanted Herzberg to take up the position. In fact, Herzberg received an offer from Harrington himself in March of 1946.[16] However, in all fairness to the efforts and expenditures that Struve had made in bringing him to Yerkes, Herzberg could not possibly consider such an immediate departure from Yerkes.[17] The move to Yerkes was a good one scientifically, and moreover, in June of 1946, he was informed that the promised promotion to Professor of Spectroscopy would become effective 1 September, with indefinite tenure, at a salary of $6,500 per annum. Even so, he was beginning to have qualms about remaining at Yerkes after the rejection by ONR, and on several occasions, he called himself a fool for leaving Saskatoon, a place with so many friends and opportunities and a nice home. His yearning to return to Canada manifested itself when after decades of good health, he was suddenly stricken with a bad flu. The severe pain caused him to think the end was near, and with Luise at his bedside he implored her to take the children back to Saskatoon. This illness passed as quickly as it came, and he was back at work the next day. Nevertheless, following this episode and after barely a year at Yerkes, he wrote to the Canadian Naturalization Department of his desire to remain a Canadian citizen and asked about the regulations for this purpose.[18] He mentioned that after having a few years' experience at a large institution like the Yerkes Observatory, he would like to return to Canada if a suitable position at a Canadian university should be offered. He was assured there would be no problem in retaining Canadian citizenship.

At the same time, in September of 1946, his staunch friend John Spinks wrote that he had attended a physics conference in Montreal, where many friends had asked about Herzberg:

> We wondered how we could get you back to this country, by fair means or foul. Don't be shy about letting us know of any change of heart on your part.[19]

The receipt of such letters reinforced the recurring thoughts of Gerhard and Luise of returning to Canada, much to the astonishment of their American friends, who joked about the Herzberg's desire to return to living in an igloo. While they enjoyed their new home and the wooded countryside around Lake Geneva, which formed an ideal place for raising their children, the tiny village lacked the amenities of music and theatre that the Herzbergs valued so highly. Apart from visits from a few close friends, Williams Bay turned out to be a lonely and impersonal community. Moreover, they were becoming concerned about the lack of adequate educational opportunities beyond public school in the vicinity of Yerkes for Paul and Agnes.

Activities at Yerkes and The University of Chicago

During Herzberg's stay at Yerkes, he taught a course on atomic and molecular spectra. His students liked him, considered him to be a good teacher, a person who knew his subject well, worked hard, gave good lectures, and was fair and friendly.[20] His office was on the first floor of the Observatory next to the main telescope, affording the students easy access, and Chandra's office was across the hall. Being of like mind and both being prodigious workers, they soon developed a very close and lasting friendship. To Herzberg the close association with Chandra was the most rewarding result scientifically and personally of the years he spent at Yerkes Observatory:

> Sometimes when Chandra felt he needed a break he came to my office and we had a long chat either there or on a walk along the shore of Lake Geneva. We usually discussed some of his work or mine, or indulged in some reflection of the history of our subjects. Chandra, with his incredible memory, was able to recite almost verbatim some of the conversations he had with Eddington, Milne, Rutherford, Chadwick, Blackett, etc., during his Cambridge years, which coincided with one of the most exciting periods in physics.[21]

Chandra was one of the greatest theoretical physicists and astrophysicists of modern times. Born in 1910 in Lahore, India (now Pakistan), he was educated in Madras, receiving a Bachelor's degree with honours in physics in 1930 and a Government of India scholarship for graduate studies in Cambridge, England. He obtained his Ph.D. degree there in 1933 and was elected a Fellow of Trinity College for the period 1933–1937. In 1936, Chandra returned to India to marry his college friend Lalitha, and they came to the United States where Chandra had been offered a position by Struve as a Research Associate at Yerkes Observatory. He was soon invited to join many other universities and accepted an offer from Princeton but finally chose to remain with The University of Chicago, moving from Yerkes Observatory to the main campus and the Department of Physics in 1952.

Chandra had a unique style of work best described in his own words:

> After the early preparatory years, my scientific work has followed a certain pattern motivated, principally, by a quest after perspectives. In practice, this quest has consisted of my choosing (after some trials and tribulations) a certain area which appears amenable to cultivation and compatible with my taste, abilities, and temperament. And when after some years of study, I feel that I have accumulated a sufficient body of

> knowledge and achieved a view of my own, I have the urge to present my point of view, *ab initio*, in a coherent account with order, form, and structure.[22]

In this manner, Chandra contributed notably to theoretical physics and astrophysics, publishing seven seminal volumes on a variety of topics in the period from 1939 to 1983. Herzberg thought of Chandra as a mathematical genius; his brilliance had been amply demonstrated when Chandra worked out the limit of star mass while on his long voyage from Bombay to Cambridge, when only nineteen years old. His theory opened the way to the present theories of neutron stars and black holes; this was the first time in the history of physics that the theories of gravitation, quantum mechanics, and relativity were used simultaneously in deriving a formula.[23] Chandra received the 1983 Nobel Prize in Physics (shared with the astrophysicist William A. Fowler) for his theoretical studies of physical processes of importance to the structure and evolution of stars. The main body of this work was accomplished in the early 1930s when Chandra was nineteen to twenty-six years of age, with additional contributions to this topic in 1964 and 1970.

Herzberg also developed a close friendship with Gerard Kuiper, who spent much of his time at the McDonald Observatory in Texas applying his infrared spectrometer to the study of planetary atmospheres. When Herzberg joined Yerkes Observatory, Kuiper had just returned from service with Alsos, an American intelligence mission that entered Germany in late 1944 to ferret out and destroy any German fission project. Kuiper told much about the conditions he found in Germany and its universities at the end of the war. Among other events, he mentioned how he had encountered Max Planck among some refugees and saw to it that he was installed in Göttingen, where Kuiper also helped in re-establishing the university, once the world centre of mathematics and physics. Kuiper was a pioneer of solar system astronomy and was the first to detect a Martian atmosphere of carbon dioxide and an atmosphere of methane on Jupiter and the outer planets. He also examined many mountain sites as possible locations of observatories and selected six superior sites where major observatories stand today. He and Herzberg shared their interests in planetary spectra, and later Kuiper used the long-path absorption tube built by Herzberg to compare laboratory spectra with those of Venus and Jupiter.

Subrahmanyan Chandrasekhar, 1947.

Gerard Kuiper, 1948.

Herzberg attended seminars on the main campus, occasionally giving talks on his own research, and spent time with Mulliken and his group, keeping in touch with the newest advances in spectroscopy. He was pleased to resume discussions on molecular problems and astrophysics with Edward Teller, who left Los Alamos in February 1946 to return to teaching and basic research at The University of Chicago. It amused Herzberg to find that Teller also participated in the World Federalist movement and worked hard giving lectures across the country on world government and world peace, so much so that his colleagues in the Physics Department were upset that he was neglecting his duties.[24] However, after about six months Teller gave it up, and in 1952 he helped to develop the Lawrence Livermore National Laboratory, a second nuclear weapons laboratory. Teller was soon to become known as "the father of the hydrogen bomb", a label he disliked, and he maintained that his greatest contribution was in molecular spectroscopy, especially on "the vibrations of polyatomic molecules" and wished he could have spent more time on it.[25] Among his many contributions in molecular physics, all in the 1930s, are the Jahn–Teller and Renner–Teller effects, the Teller–Redlich product rule, and the paper he wrote with Herzberg on the vibrational structure of electronic transitions in polyatomic molecules. Herzberg claimed he only served as the midwife for

Teller's brainchild. He recalled Teller's early brilliance, his complete unselfishness and sincerity, and the freedom with which he gave ideas to others, without worrying about credit and priorities. The theorist Eugene Wigner, another of that eminent group of Hungarian physicists who came to the United States of America and served in the Manhattan Project, said of Teller, "He is the most imaginative person I ever met—and this means a great deal when you consider that I knew Einstein."[26] In the late 1980s, Teller convinced President Ronald Reagan to launch the Strategic Defense Initiative (SDI), known as the "Star Wars" program, designed to destroy incoming missiles before reaching their targets. This plan was severely criticized by scientific colleagues, and Teller responded with *Better a Shield Than a Sword.*[27] Herzberg always thought it most unfortunate that one as truly gifted as Teller, and from whom he had learned so much in the early years of his own scientific development, would spend his life supporting the military establishment and that his other great contributions to our knowledge should not be recognized and rarely be mentioned.

Herzberg often visited his mentor and friend James Franck, supervisor of his year in Göttingen, who had also returned to The University of Chicago to resume research in photosynthesis after having led the chemistry division at Los Alamos during the war years. Franck's wife had died soon after their arrival in the United States, and in 1946 he married his former pupil, co-worker, and family friend, Hertha Sponer, then Professor of Physics at Duke University in Durham, North Carolina. Franck divided his time between Durham and Chicago and moved to Durham on his retirement in 1949. Just before the test of the first atomic bomb on 16 July 1945 at Alamogordo in New Mexico, Franck had submitted to the Secretary of War what became known as the "Franck Report", urging the U.S Government to consider the use of the bomb as a political decision and not merely as a matter of military tactics, and "to reveal the bomb to the world by a demonstration in an appropriately selected, uninhabited place." However, this was not to be, and the dire predictions of the Franck Report came to pass, "If the United States were to be the first to release this new means of indiscriminate destruction of mankind, she would sacrifice public support throughout the world, precipitate the race for armaments, and prejudice the possibility of reaching an international agreement on the future control of such weapons."[28]

In 1947, Yerkes Observatory celebrated its fiftieth anniversary, and *Science*, the weekly magazine of the American Association for the Advancement of Science, devoted most of its 5 September issue to articles written by the faculty on the history of Yerkes and on astrophysical research.[29] Herzberg contributed a brief paper on the early history and present revival of spectroscopy at Yerkes, noting that Hale had realized the importance of laboratory investigations for the elucidation of astrophysical problems and had designed the building with space for laboratories in experimental physics, chemistry, and spectroscopy. Two conferences added to the anniversary celebrations.[30] "Stellar Atmospheres" was organized by Struve at the annual meeting of the American Astronomical Society and was held in nearby Northwestern University. This was followed by an expedition to Yerkes and a second meeting, "Planetary Atmospheres", organized by Kuiper. The papers of both conferences were published in the books *Astrophysics: A Topical Symposium*[31] and *The Atmospheres of the Earth and Planets*.[32] Herzberg's paper "Laboratory absorption spectra obtained with long paths" appeared in the latter.

Thoughts of Leaving Yerkes

In spite of the many scientific activities and a light teaching load, Herzberg soon came to realize there was little possibility of enlarging his group in spectroscopy, since Yerkes was primarily an observatory. Also, the budget was limited, and it took time to obtain equipment and supplies. Most perplexing was the constant problem of waiting for supplies, since Williams Bay was inconveniently far from the large cities of Madison, Milwaukee, and Chicago. Herzberg complained strongly when he ordered liquid air from Milwaukee and found that half had evaporated by the time it arrived at the laboratory. The rejection of his grant application by the Office of Naval Research continued to trouble him.

Herzberg was anxious to have more personal contact with colleagues interested in fields other than his own. As a student, he had originally set his sights on being an astronomer, but now he found that to live only with astronomers at an isolated observatory was not what he had expected: he longed for the daily discussions with chemists, physicists, and humanists he had enjoyed in Saskatoon, and this was not possible at Williams Bay. His contacts with colleagues Struve and Kuiper even for scientific discussion were all too few, and only his friend Chandra had broad general interests in literature, philosophy, and music. Visits with Mulliken, Franck, and Teller on the distant Chicago campus turned out to be a rare experience, since Herzberg did not drive, but travelled by bus or train. He was continually being invited to join the Physics Department of The University of Chicago, but living in the centre of this huge city did not appeal to him or Luise. Moreover, his colleague Mulliken had already established a large theoretical and experimental spectroscopy group on the Chicago campus, and it would neither be wise nor possible to duplicate this effort.

To these concerns were soon added the noticeably increasing anti-Communist feelings being propagated in the United States with the escalating cold war.[33] In 1946 Herzberg learned that Eugene Rabinowitch, who had joined the Manhattan Project during the war, was denied the security clearance needed to become Head of the Chemistry Department of Clinton Laboratories at Oak Ridge. That same year, Harlow Shapley, a prominent astronomer at Harvard University, was subpoenaed to appear before the House Committee on Un-American Activities. Both had been outspoken in their criticism of the cold war and of postwar anti-Communism. In March of 1947, President Harry Truman barred Communists (or those aiding or sympathetic to Communism) from the Executive Branch, and the Taft–Hartley Act, passed in June 1947, over Truman's veto, denied the facilities of the National Labour Relations Board to unions that failed to file affidavits affirming that their officers were not Communists. A year later Edward U. Condon was attacked by the House Committee on Un-American Activities but was successfully protected by the Emergency Committee of Atomic Scientists. These events raised many unpleasant memories of the activities of the Nazi regime in Germany and set Gerhard and Luise to wondering whether they were in the right place.

The culminating reason for Herzberg's decision to leave Yerkes so soon after his arrival came with the rising tension among his colleagues amid plans for a re-organization of the Department of Astronomy proposed by Struve. If accepted by the University, these plans would have far reaching consequences for the department. As Struve wrote in a confidential letter to Herzberg in January 1947, he wanted to recognize the brilliance of Kuiper and Chandrasekhar and the fact that the department had grown and needed a new structure.[34] Thus, he proposed that Kuiper be made the Director of both the Yerkes and McDonald Observatories and Chandrasekhar be made the Director of an Institute for Theoretical Astrophysics. Hiltner would remain as Assistant Director of the observatories, and Morgan would become the Managing Editor of the *Astrophysical Journal.* Struve mentioned that he deliberately refrained from suggesting that Herzberg's laboratory become a separate group because it would look like an independent department of physics was being set up at Yerkes. This would arouse jealousies on the Chicago campus, and the administration would almost certainly refuse. For himself, Struve wanted to be relieved of the many day-to-day administrative duties, so that he could spend more time on his own research. These suggested changes were all laudable: Struve had served as Director of Yerkes for fifteen years, during difficult times, and had advanced it to world recognition. It was time for him to hand over responsibilities to others so that he could pursue his research.

However, Struve also maintained that he should be the "Chairman" of the new structure and have control of general policy, overall planning, and final responsibility for budget, personnel, and promotions in the department. As might be expected, the strong personalities of the senior group at Yerkes, with their egos and ambitions, could not accept the suggestion that Struve should retain supreme power. Nevertheless, the re-organization at Yerkes came into effect in July of 1947. It brought dissension and acrimony to the small staff of the Observatory, an atmosphere which Herzberg deplored but could do little to alleviate.

With the receipt of Struve's letter and foreseeing the divisive consequences of the restructuring plans, Herzberg finally accepted the thought that his stay at Yerkes would be short-lived, dependent on when he felt he had adequately discharged his obligations to Struve and the Observatory. On receiving an enquiry that January from E.W.R. Steacie, Director of the Division of Chemistry at the NRC, as to his possible interest in a research position in Ottawa, Herzberg pursued this unexpected opportunity with alacrity, and within a few months his return to Canada in the following year was assured.[35] Several of the younger members of the Yerkes Observatory were also lured away within the next two years, and in 1950 Struve himself resigned to become Chairman of the Astronomy Department at the University of California at Berkeley.

Having made the decision to return to Canada, Herzberg immediately turned his attention to the formalities for crossing the border and to the attainment of his research objective at Yerkes, namely the search for the so-called quadrupole spectrum of hydrogen, a very weak and normally forbidden spectrum. He was also determined to complete the revision of the second edition of *Diatomic Molecules*. These concerns were reminiscent of those he had faced on leaving Darmstadt for Canada over a decade earlier.

The Final Year at Yerkes Observatory

In the laboratory, Herzberg was successful in observing the quadrupole spectrum of hydrogen, and this turned out to be his major achievement during his brief stay at the Yerkes Observatory. While hydrogen is the most abundant element in the universe, molecular hydrogen (H_2) is difficult to detect because it is transparent in the infrared region, where its vibrational spectrum is expected to occur; its absorption spectrum is exceedingly weak because a molecule consisting of two identical atoms interacts negligibly with infrared radiation. He had predicted ten years earlier that the large amounts of H_2 present in planetary atmospheres would make up for the weak quadrupole spectrum and had set his heart on finding this spectrum of hydrogen in laboratory experiments.[36] He had built the long absorption tube expressly for this purpose.

No one had yet reported the observation of a quadrupole spectrum, and he considered its detection to be a major challenge. In his mind, this would be the only way to confirm the presence of molecular hydrogen in planetary atmospheres and in interstellar space. His two students Phillips and Rao were busy with their own research problems, so Herzberg worked on the experiment by himself. For the 3-0 band, which he calculated would occur in the 8000 to 8600 Å region, he adjusted the mirrors in the 22-metre cell for 244 traversals to give an effective path length of 5370 metres and raised the hydrogen gas pressure to 9 atmospheres. He observed four of the lines in their predicted positions. Another four of the expected lines were found for the 2-0 band (11 300 to 12 400 Å). All eight lines were extremely sharp, as anticipated for a quadrupole spectrum, even at the high pressures used in the experiments.[37] This observation proved that it would require high-resolution instruments to detect these sharp lines in the spectra of the outer planets, whose atmospheres were expected to contain large quantities of hydrogen.

It was to be another twelve years before the H_2 quadrupole spectrum was observed in the atmospheres of the giant planets, first in Jupiter and somewhat later in Uranus.[38] Later still, this spectrum was observed in emission in the Orion nebula and in the hot gases of other nebulae, planetary ionospheres, and superluminous galaxies.[39]

Herzberg also photographed the spectra of several polyatomic molecules, namely CH_3CF_3, CH_3I, and N_2O, for study and analysis at the NRC while waiting for completion of the instruments being built for the new

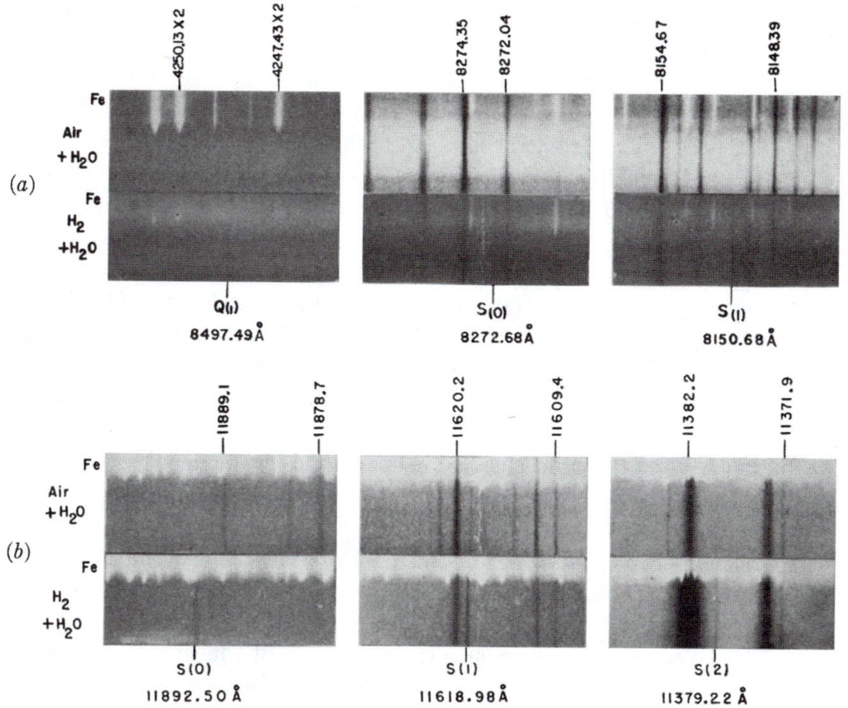

The quadrupole spectrum of H_2: (*a*) the 3-0 band, (*b*) the 2-0 band, after Herzberg, 1948. (In each case, the bottom strip shows the spectrum obtained with H_2 and the upper strip with air.)

laboratory. The spectra of the two latter molecules were measured and analyzed with the help of Luise, and they published the results as joint authors. A thorough analysis of high-resolution spectra of the atmospheric oxygen bands photographed at the Mount Wilson Observatory was carried out by Harold D. Babcock and Luise and remains today as one of the most important papers on the oxygen molecule.[40] Over the years many spectroscopists have mistakenly credited this paper to Gerhard Herzberg.

Long after Herzberg's departure from the Yerkes Observatory, his friend Chandra was to summarize Herzberg's accomplishments there:

> The years after World War II were years of exceptional growth in the physical sciences at The University of Chicago; and Herzberg's appointment as a professor of spectroscopy in the Astronomy Department at the

Yerkes Observatory contributed in no small measure to that growth. Even though Herzberg's association with The University of Chicago was short and lasted only three years, it is startling to realize the many lasting initiatives of those years besides what was accomplished.

In two years, Herzberg built up a laboratory that was capable of unique and important experiments involving long absorption paths. An absorption tube 75 feet long was built with an optical arrangement that could achieve many traversals (as many as 250 in some of the later experiments); and with this tube Herzberg was able to study the absorption spectra of many molecules of astrophysical interest including CO, CO_2, NO, C_2H_2, and CH_4 with path lengths comparable to those in planetary atmospheres. For example, the CO_2 bands in the spectrum of Venus were reproduced with remarkable fidelity.

The methods which he initiated and developed at the Yerkes Observatory have since become standard in laboratories devoted to the study of planetary spectra.... While many results of significance on individual molecules were obtained at the Yerkes Observatory, perhaps the most spectacular accomplishment was Herzberg's observations of the 2-0 and 3-0 bands of the quadrupole spectrum of the hydrogen molecule: a prize that had been sought in vain before.

The Yerkes Observatory and The University of Chicago can hardly lay claim to any substantial fraction of Herzberg's total accomplishments ... but they can, with some justice, lay claim to the deepening of his interests in spectroscopic problems with astrophysical overtones.[41]

A curse on this false fatherland, teeming
With nothing but shame and dirty scheming,
Where every flower is crushed in a day.

Heinrich Heine

11. NEWS OF FAMILY AND FRIENDS IN WAR-TORN EUROPE

With the end of the war in Europe in May of 1945, the Herzbergs immediately tried to contact Walter and their many friends in Germany, particularly those who had lived in Hamburg, Darmstadt, Frankfurt, and Berlin when these cities were devastated by aerial bombardment. However, communication by mail or telephone to any of the four occupied zones of Germany was not possible until almost a year later.

First News

The first news from Europe came from Herzberg's former student Stephan Gradstein, who had fled to Holland in 1933 and whose last letter in 1940 ended, "War is on—have suitcases ready!" Now a postcard dated 13 August 1945 arrived, just as the Herzbergs were preparing to leave Saskatoon for the Yerkes Observatory.[1] They learned that Stephan had a Dutch wife and that she and their two children had lived through the war and the German occupation with her parents in a small village, and Stephan, who was Jewish, had survived by lying in hiding with them for the four years. After the war, he was quickly reinstated in his editorial job with the Philips Company, and the family was now waiting for the repair of their bomb-damaged home in Eindhoven. Herzberg immediately answered, thankful that Stephan and his family were alive, and then added some news of their youngsters Paul and Agnes and the move to Yerkes. He asked Stephan to note in his next letter what items of food or clothing would be helpful. On receipt of a list of small supplies the following month, the Herzbergs sent a package to the Gradsteins and were gratified to learn that it arrived safely:

> Dear Dr. Herzberg:
>
> Perhaps you do not know that the 6th of December is the day of Santa Claus, which is always greatly celebrated in this country by surprising one another on that day with little gifts of all kinds. Well, this parcel of yours was one of the most capital Santa Claus surprises I have ever seen.

> I suppose it must be somewhat difficult to make you understand with what joy a box of shoe-polish, say, or a little sewing cotton, safety pins and shoe laces, or some knitting wool may be welcomed! All these things are very, very helpful, and my wife and I thank you very sincerely for the trouble in assembling these different articles.[2]

Later, the Herzbergs sent clothing and shoes to the family and a parcel of children's clothes to the astrophysicist Jan H. Oort, also in Holland, for distribution to the needy. Herzberg also tried to reach his brother and friends in Germany through these Dutch colleagues and through friends in Switzerland, but learned that this was still not possible even from these neighbouring countries.

The Destruction of Darmstadt and the Technische Hochschule

When mail service to and from Germany re-opened on 1 April 1946, the first letters came from former colleagues at the Technische Hochschule in Darmstadt. General Patton and the Third Army had liberated Darmstadt, which was now in the American zone of Germany. Letters from Hans Rau, his supervisor, Heinz Verleger, a co-worker in 1934–1935, and Oswald Walther, Professor of Mathematics, with a long letter from Walther's wife to Luise on life in Darmstadt, told of unbelievable conditions in the bomb-ravaged city.[3–5] In one night of saturation bombing on 11 September 1944, using a new system called *Der Todesfacher*, "The Death Fan", 80 percent of the city was destroyed by fire, with over 8,000 dead and most of the Technische Hochschule in ruins. Further bombings demolished the chemical works and increased the death toll to about 12,000.[6] Half of the population had abandoned Darmstadt, and because the city was not expected to be reconstructed, the capital of Hesse was quickly moved to Wiesbaden.

Miraculously, the Juda house on Heidenreichstrasse, where the Herzbergs had lived for five years, was the only one to survive in the immediate area. However, the Juda family had left their home after the horrors of Kristallnacht (10 November 1938) and lived in Paris with Frau Juda's brother Otto for several months. This had been described by Hedwig Juda in a modest and understated letter to the Herzbergs in November 1939, as usual without any mention of the hardships they had suffered but inquiring of Paul and Agnes and life in Canada. A year later, when France was

The remains of the Technische Hochschule Darmstadt
after bombardment, September 1944.

attacked by the Germans, the Judas moved to the village of St. Sulpice in the middle of France as a measure of safety from aerial bombing. This was the last message to be received from the Judas.[7] During the occupation of France, Uncle Victor died in his own bed, but Frau Hedwig Juda and her daughter Lise perished in Auschwitz just a month before hostilities ended. Of the 1,427 Jews living in Darmstadt in 1933, about half had left for North and South America or Palestine by 1938, and only 360 remained in 1940. And with Himmler's proclamation of the "Final Solution", they were transported to Theresien Concentration Camp in 1942 and 1943.[8]

Although no specific reason for the destruction of Darmstadt was given by Bomber Command, it was known that the Technische Hochschule was involved in V-1 and V-2 rocket development and that the chemical works were of strategic importance, and on the night of 11 September, a munitions train was left at the railway station. Immediately after Germany's surrender, some of the university's senior professors, Hans Rau, Oswald Walther, Carl Wagner, a professor of physical chemistry, and Richard Vieweg, the Rector, were taken to London, England, and interrogated about the rocket program. They were invited to go to the United States with the first group of rocket scientists, but only Wagner accepted. The others returned to Darmstadt with the hope of restoring the university. In spite of the ruined buildings, classes were soon in progress in the old workshop and in whatever rooms were usable in the main building, with students sitting on the floor or on chairs found in gardens and bombed restaurants. The letters of Rau and Verleger informed Herzberg that the spectroscopy laboratory was completely destroyed, including all of the instruments, and that the metal coatings on the gratings had evaporated in the heat of the fire bombing.

Herzberg could never forget Rau's kindness and unfailing encouragement in the difficult days, so Rau's letter was especially heartwarming; yet its beginning was momentarily puzzling:

> Dear Dr. Herzberg:
>
> Your letter took a long time for its journey; it not only had to cross the vast space but also an almost endless time-span. It was indeed a greeting from a different world, and an especially great joy. I am very happy that you not only succeeded to save your family from a great danger, whose whole atrocity only became clear after the war, but that you obviously have found working possibilities over there, that you could hardly ever have found in Germany, even under different circumstances.[3]

As Herzberg thought deeply about this last statement, he finally came to understand its meaning. All of his professors and colleagues at the Technische Hochschule in Darmstadt, as well as in Göttingen, and all of the scientists he met in Germany were offspring of professors, bankers, or doctors, the "Mandarin" families of Germany. He was clearly not one of this elitist group; without a father, with a mother working in America, and with no family background in learning to speak of, he obviously did not belong in this upper class. No matter how hard he would have worked in Germany, only a miraculous discovery in science could have led to an opportunity for him to rise to the rank of a research professor in a major university, even though he was recognized internationally as one of the pioneers in molecular science.

Heinz Verleger was having difficulties in de-Nazification and in resuming his former position in the University of Tübingen, which was in the French Occupied Zone. He asked Herzberg for help by writing to the administration in the American Zone to support his transfer to a university post there. If possible, of course, he would prefer to be permitted to enter Canada or the U.S.A.[4] Unfortunately, Herzberg's letters were of no help in getting him transferred or in finding him a job, even though Herzberg vouched for his character and made it clear that to the best of his knowledge, Verleger had not the slightest sympathy for the Nazi cause. The problem was that after his year with Herzberg in Darmstadt in 1934–1935, Verleger had the misfortune to be employed until 1941 at the Physikalisch-Technischen Reichsanstalt in Berlin-Charlottenburg, under the supervision of the fanatical Nazi Johannes Stark, and this was not readily forgotten or forgiven by the Allied military governments. After receiving letters from French and American authorities, who had investigated the wartime activities of Verleger, even Herzberg began to have some doubts of his former friend's sincerity. Eventually, Verleger found an academic position in South Africa.

Hans Baerwald, Herzberg's teacher and friend, had survived a difficult period in England during the war years, shuttling from one year teaching posts at the universities of Aberdeen, St. Andrews, and Cardiff and living alone as his Aryan wife remained in Germany. At the end of the war, he returned to Darmstadt and sought reinstatement to his former position as theoretical physicist, but because he was past the retirement age of sixty-five, this was denied. He died in England in 1946. Another colleague Hans Jüngst, a Privatdozent in geology and minerology at the THD, who was horrified at the atrocities of the Nazis, was conscripted and killed in action towards the end of the war.

Herzberg was sympathetic to the difficulties experienced by G. Valt. Schmitt, one of his former undergraduate students, who wrote asking for a letter to help in obtaining a certificate of exoneration towards his de-Nazification. Much to his surprise, Herzberg learned that in 1934 Schmitt had petitioned the Culture Minister of Hesse to permit Herzberg to continue teaching the theoretical physics course and moreover had asked the examination commisioner to let Herzberg undertake the examination of the candidates in the course. In time, this petition became an obstacle for Schmitt, and he was not able to find a job in spite of his excellent academic record. Finally, against his inner conviction, he became an SS candidate in order to gain "political correctness" but left voluntarily in 1938. He served in the war for six years and was wounded. After rehabiltation he returned to the THD to improve his standing in mathematics for entry into teaching.

Herzberg was also informed of some colleagues who had joined the Nazi Party. One was Wolfgang Finkelnburg whom Herzberg had introduced to Rau and to the Technische Hochschule Darmstadt. On being appointed Chief Assistant at the Physical Institute in Darmstadt in 1936, Finkelnburg had been pressured by the Rector, Karl Lieser, to join the Nazi party in order to moderate the activities of the "Aryan physics" group within the THD and in the University Teachers League. In 1947 he wrote a friendly letter to Herzberg mentioning that he and his wife loved Rau and his fatherly kindness and that Rau was now in better health. He then described his own scientific activities following the war, writing a large textbook on atomic, nuclear, and molecular physics. He said that he was unemployed, because former National Socialist Party members had undermined his efforts in academia. Herzberg did not reply. Quite by chance they met at the Watergate Opera in Washington, D.C., in 1951, when Finkelnburg was a consultant to the Engineering Research and Development Laboratories in Fort Belvoir, Virginia, but Herzberg was not inclined to renew their former friendly relationship.[9] Only many years later did Herzberg learn of the courageous role Finkelnburg had played in an offensive against the proponents of "Aryan physics", who had enjoyed immense political influence in academic affairs on Hitler's rise to power. In 1940 Finkelnburg had accepted the leadership of the University Teachers League under the condition that he could use his position to combat the threat posed to professional physics by the "Aryan physics" proponents. By this time, he was director of the Institute of Physics in Strassburg and had the power to organize a debate in Munich with the best young physicists left in Germany to confront the politically minded Aryan physicists led by Lenard and Stark. The outcome began a splintering of the ranks of the Aryan physics adherents and eventually led to the demise of politicized physics in academia in 1943–1944.[10]

Although this defeat of the Aryan physicists came long after the decimation of the scientific establishment in Germany, it nevertheless helped to maintain some semblance of professional recognition among the remaining scientists and may have led to an earlier acceptance of German scientists into international conferences and organizations after the war.

News from Hamburg

Finally, Herzberg received news of his brother Walter and friends in Hamburg. Walter and his family, living in the outskirts of Hamburg, had survived the saturation bombing of their city in 1943. Alfred Schulz had also survived and lived with his sister Hertha, whose husband was declared missing. Neither Walter nor Alfred had served in the war, both being declared unsuitable for military service: Alfred was almost totally deaf, and Walter had damaged an arm in a motorbike accident but was conscripted towards the end of the war for the defense of Schleswig-Holstein. After the war, Alfred was more withdrawn than ever, isolated by his deafness and his heavy responsibilities in taking care of an ill mother, an unemployed father, and a widowed sister. Without children of his own, Alfred became very attached to Monika, aged six, the daughter of his sister. The needs of his family required all of his attention.

Hans-Werner Doering, Gerhard's and Alfred's former close friend, had served with the army on the Russian front and was wounded three times; he had lost one eye in 1944 and was left with only partial vision in the other eye. In his first letter, Hans-Werner emphasized the wonderful and enduring friendship they once had and noted how difficult it was to renew their relationship after these many years, and after what had happened, "Perhaps he was crossed off the list of Herzberg's friends." His letters were full of guilty feelings as he tried to recount his life in those terrible years. He was married with two children, a son and daughter. He did not understand or share his father's rigorous belief in the Nazis, and as a teacher and civil servant, Hans-Werner was himself put under moral pressure; a summons from the authorities forced him to become a party member and he finally joined the National Socialist Party in 1937. He understood Herzberg's compassion with the terrible fate of the Juda family and wondered if this caused Herzberg to be disinterested in finding out about other friendships in this unholy land, this country of ruins, misery, hunger, and desperation. Although he and his family were profuse in their thanks when food parcels arrived along with two hundred cigarettes, Hans-Werner wondered whether the parcels were really a sign of redemption or just a generous gesture of charity towards the needy and miserable without wanting to have anything more to do with them. He thanked Herzberg for his sympathy in the loss of his mother and brother-in-law and recalled the purity and happiness of their innocent youth in the hope of renewing their old friendship.[11] Herzberg found it difficult to answer such sad letters of despair and regret and hoped that time would help to heal Hans-Werner's conscience of the terrible years of the Nazis and the war.

Parcels of Food and Clothing

In early 1946, an appeal was launched by James Franck and a group of colleagues and was sent to President Truman, the State Department, and members of Congress of the United States. The appeal asked that relief should be provided and charitable organizations be admitted into the occupied countries to reduce suffering in Europe. This was signed by 180 distinguished scholars, scientists, and artists of German and Austrian origin, all enemies and victims of Naziism who had found refuge and opportunity in free America.[12] Herzberg was one of the signers. Soon a limited program of relief to Germany by private welfare agencies was announced, and Gerhard and Luise spent whatever time and money they could afford in preparing and sending a series of parcels of clothing and food packages to their relatives and friends in Hamburg, Langensalza, Darmstadt, Frankfurt, and Berlin.

Herzberg's cousin Emmy Langemak, a dentist in Frankfurt, had lost her home twice during the war, once in bombardment and again to America troops for use as an operations office. She had survived the bombing of Frankfurt along with her daughter Christa, but her son Fritz had been conscripted after graduating from the gymnasium. He was sent to the eastern front and was missing since February 1945. The Herzberg's sent her a series of parcels with food to tide them over, as well as several packages of dental instruments and supplies so that Emmy could resume her professional practice.[13]

Herzberg also wrote to Karl-Friedrich Bonhoeffer to offer his sympathy on the execution of his brother Dietrich, the theologian and Confession Church leader, and of his brother-in-law Hans von Dohnanyi, a former Reich Supreme Court Counsellor.[14] Dietrich had returned to Germany after lecturing for a month in New York in July 1939. He gave up his own safety to take care of his theologian students and to organize a church-based resistance group, calling on clergymen to oppose Adolf Hitler as the "Antichrist". He also took part in one of the most active resistance centres in Germany, founded by Dohnanyi, who had served in military intelligence (the *Abwehr*) and who along with Colonel Hans Osler, his superior, had organized an underground railroad for Jews to escape Germany. All three were imprisoned in 1943 for their role in the plot to assassinate Hitler and were sentenced to death by an SS tribunal. They were hanged in April 1945, just a month before the war ended.[15] Later, Herzberg was to learn that other members of the Bonhoeffer family, namely the jurist Klaus Bonhoeffer and brother-in-law Dr. Rüdiger Schleicher, had been executed by the Gestapo that April.[16] Karl-Friedrich managed to avoid incarceration, although he knew about the plot against Hitler, and he succeeded in protecting the remaining Bonhoeffer families, all ardent anti-Nazis, from the Nazi regime. He was in poor health after a heart attack in 1946 and had to care for the large number of children of his dead relatives as well as his own four children.[17] Food parcels were quickly sent to the Bonhoeffer family.

Food parcels were invariably dispatched to former colleagues who had many young children, even though Gerhard and Luise did not know of their political beliefs or activities during the war. As they added their thumbs in the tying procedure, young Paul and Agnes were impressed with the heaps of boxes being packed and neatly wrapped on evenings and weekends. And they wondered about the many people their parents knew in Europe.

Uncle Victor's last greeting, Christmas 1941.

PART THREE

THE GOLDEN YEARS
(1948–1971)

A great day in the history of the NRC and of Canadian science in general.

C. Jack Mackenzie

12. RETURN TO CANADA

In the two decades following World War II, Canada was a country of great optimism economically and culturally. Its abundance of natural resources was a boon to international trade, and the vast growth of its industrial plant symbolized the promise of a country on the move to major achievement. Science also enjoyed this spirited progress, and because of its accomplishments during World War II, the National Research Council of Canada (NRC) became the engine to drive science to greater heights in academia, government, and industry. This period was justifiably called the "Golden Age" in Canadian science.

In early 1947, only a little more than a year after his start at Yerkes Observatory, Herzberg received an offer from the NRC in Ottawa that was an opportunity not to be missed: he was invited to establish a major spectroscopy laboratory for basic research. Matters quickly came to a head with visits to Ottawa and much correspondence, culminating in his appointment as Principal Research Officer in the Division of Physics. The position was to be taken up in mid-1948. At the NRC, Herzberg would realize his full potential.

How Did This Happen?

Again, Herzberg's good friend John Spinks played a key persuasive role. In the words of Chalmers Jack Mackenzie, President of the NRC at that time:

> To some not familiar with scientific research in Canada, it may seem rather unusual that Dr. Herzberg should have given up an established professorship at The University of Chicago and returned to a Canadian government research institution, where at that time, facilities in his special field were limited. This occurred not by any elaborate planning but by a series of fortuitous events and timely interlocking personal associations very similar to those which first brought Dr. Herzberg to Canada.
>
> John Spinks, after a wartime stint with the Royal Canadian Air Force, had been attached to the NRC's atomic energy project for some time before returning to the University of Saskatchewan. Dr. E.W.R. (Ned) Steacie had become Director of NRC's Division of Chemistry in 1939. In

> the fall of the same year, I had left the University of Saskatchewan, where I had been associated with John Spinks and Gerhard Herzberg, to become Acting President of NRC. Consequently, the three of us were familiar with the operational flexibility and working environment of NRC. Also, we were all friends and admirers of Herzberg and collectively possessed intimate knowledge of his research activities and, in addition, had the power to get quick action.
>
> Finally, it should be noted that the wartime performance of the NRC's scientific staff had won general public approval, and generous financial support for post-war research became available. During the post-war reconstruction period, the most immediate and urgent task facing the NRC was reconversion to its original civilian status. During the war, the Physics Division had been deeply and almost exclusively involved in important applied research projects. At war's end, several senior scientists left for other posts, and others were approaching retirement. The need was obvious: reorganization of the research units and strengthening of work on fundamental research. The immediate decision was to find a distinguished and active reseach physicist to stimulate original work and possibly succeed the Director when the latter retired. The search was on.[1]

While in Ottawa in January 1947, John Spinks mentioned to Mackenzie and Steacie the long-term hopes of the Herzbergs to return to Canada. This confirmed the recent message Steacie had received from Professor Donald LeRoy of Toronto, who had learned from his close friend Harold Bernstein that Herzberg felt badly about having left Canada and would like to come back.[2] Steacie immediately wrote to Herzberg:

> Dr. Spinks told me that he had recently had a letter from you from which he got the impression that you wished you were back in Canada. Is there any possibility that you would be willing to work here if a suitable offer could be made? You would, of course, have complete freedom to do what you wished, and I am sure that anything you wanted in the way of equipment could be obtained.
>
> We would very much like to have you with us.... As Bernstein has probably told you, we have succeeded in building up a very good group in the Division of Chemistry. It is absolutely essential that we do likewise in Physics, and it would be of inestimable value to us if we could get you here.
>
> I hope you will excuse my writing to you on the basis of a mere rumour, but I felt that we shouldn't pass up the opportunity if there was the slightest chance of your being interested.[3]

Herzberg replied instantly:

> I was very glad to have your inquiry with regard to the possibility of my joining the Research Council. I should say at the outset that I am indeed interested in such a possibility and would seriously consider a suitable offer if one were made....
>
> There are of course many questions that arise in my mind in connection with your suggestion. For now, I will only mention two of them: Would the appointment be of a permanent nature? And precisely how great will the freedom of choice of my research problems be? Or, in other words, for what routine matters would I be responsible, and how much administrative work would be involved? I should perhaps say that I have very little experience in administrative work.
>
> In concluding, may I express to you my sincere appreciation of your thoughtfulness in considering me for a position at the National Research Council. I am sure that I would profit greatly in my scientific work by an association with you and your group.[4]

Mackenzie then took up the correspondence:

> Dr. Steacie has shown me the correspondence which he has had with you, and I am very interested in the possibility of your returning to Canada and joining the staff of the National Research Council....
>
> The two questions you raise can be very definitely answered; first, the appointment would be definitely permanent, and secondly, you would not be responsible for any administrative work and you would have, within very broad terms, complete freedom of research problems. Dr. Steacie in his Division of Chemistry is operating under a similar scheme....
>
> In brief, our philosophy is that in every Division there should be a modest group of scientists who are essentially engaged in fundamental work which is in no way directly focused on practical problems. We feel that not only will such a group make valuable contributions to science, but in addition, the presence of such activity will maintain higher standards in other sections of a more applied nature and generally stimulate scientific work in the Division.
>
> I will be very glad to hear from you as to whether or not you would be interested in such a position, and if you are, I think it would be a wise plan for you to come to Ottawa for a day or so in order that you could look over the situation in detail.[5]

In the meantime Herzberg had received several other unofficial offers. In March of 1947, Carl S. Beals, the Acting Dominion Astronomer, who had recently moved to Ottawa, wrote to Herzberg that the position of Head of the Solar Division of the Observatory in Ottawa would be vacant. He asked Herzberg to write to him confidentially if he would be interested.[6] The following month, Herzberg was approached by Dean A.H.S. Gillison of McGill University about his possible return to Canada and the University, and somewhat later, Professor W. Bentley asked whether or not he would let his name stand as Professor of Physics and Director of the Electronics Research Laboratory at McGill.[7,8] Herzberg was also approached by Dr. N.S. Gingrich of the University of Missouri regarding an appointment there.[9] Later he even received an enquiry from the Ministry of Education of North Rhine – Westphalia concerning a full professorship at the University of Bonn, which had an established tradition in spectroscopy.[10] This he declined.

Herzberg focused his efforts on the NRC and visited Ottawa in April. He had a long discussion with President Mackenzie that continued through lunch, and he spent the afternoon with Steacie.[11] He was won over by the activity and excitement in the Division of Chemistry and with the potential in the Division of Physics, although he only met briefly with R.W. Boyle, its Director. Mackenzie noted Herzberg's visit in his diary: "I was very much impressed with him and there is no doubt of his quality, and if he comes to us, it will be a great triumph." While in Ottawa, Herzberg took the opportunity to speak with Beals about the various offers he had received. He thanked Beals for inquiring whether he had any interest in a position at the Observatory but considered that he would be out of place as a solar astronomer. Also, the McGill position did not quite fit in with his immediate plans. Herzberg felt that after the interruption because of war work and the time spent writing his books, he was just beginning to hit his stride in research and was concerned that even a small teaching load would divert him from his main interests. Moreover, the offer from McGill included the policy that first contracts were only for a limited time, in spite of the fact that Herzberg had had tenure at the Universities of Saskatchewan and Chicago and was an internationally renowned scientist.

There was no doubt in Herzberg's mind that the NRC offered the best opportunities for spectroscopic research and for freedom in research. Moreover, he and Luise had found Ottawa to be very much to their liking; the city was a comfortable size, in a lovely setting of rivers and canals, and there were good schools for their children. Proceedings moved quickly by correspondence and another meeting in Ottawa, and issues of budget, staff, freedom from administrative responsibilities, salary, and moving costs were discussed and resolved.

Acceptance of Appointment as Principal Research Officer

In June 1947, Herzberg informed Mackenzie that he was ready to accept the position in the newly created category of Principal Research Officer in the Division of Physics, and he summarized the various conditions of his appointment as agreed to in their personal discussions.[12] Briefly, these included appointment on a permanent basis with a starting salary of $6,500 per year. He was to carry out research in fundamental physics and allied subjects, with the choice of problems left entirely to him, and would have no routine duties of the type being carried out in the sections dealing with applied physics or applied chemistry. Space and funds would be available to set up a new Section of Spectroscopy in the Division of Physics. An annual budget of $25,000 exclusive of salaries was estimated to be adequate, with an additional $50,000 over the first two years for installation of the laboratory. Funds would also be available to hire research staff, perhaps two at the outset increasing later to four or five, and service personnel such as laboratory technicians and helpers for computational and secretarial work. Such magnanimous support would have been impossible to obtain as a university professor through the usual granting channels. Finally, and perhaps most surprising of all for someone in his prime of activity, Herzberg asked for and was to be provided with an opportunity for continuing his scientific work after retirement at the age of sixty-five. The appointment was to be taken up about July 1948.

Within a week, Mackenzie replied that he was delighted with Herzberg's acceptance and agreed that all of the conditions regarding freedom in research, facilities, staff, and work after retirement represented his own understanding of NRC's offer.[13] Also, Luise would be welcomed in every way to pursue research interests with the spectroscopy group. Next day, Mackenzie informed Boyle that Herzberg would join the NRC. In summarizing this happy turn of events, Mackenzie later commented:

> I have always thought that Dr. Steacie's advice and persuasions were the clinching factors in Herzberg's decision, as he probably became convinced that if the conditions of work were agreeable to Steacie he could

> accept our offer with confidence. As President of NRC, I had the responsibility alone of recommending the appointment to the Right Honourable C.D. Howe who promptly (22 July 1947) obtained formal Government approval.... This was a great day in the history of the National Research Council and of Canadian science in general.[14]

On receiving Mackenzie's letter, Herzberg confirmed his acceptance of the appointment and added: "I feel certain that I have made the right decision and I do hope that I will be able to justify the confidence you have put in me."[15]

Notice of Impending Departure

Herzberg immediately notified Otto Struve (who was carrying out observational work at the McDonald Observatory in Texas at the time) about his decision to take up the position at the NRC in about a year's time:

> I have had some further correspondence with Ottawa.... Naturally, I have thought the matter over very carefully and many times. I fear that the reasons for accepting the Ottawa offer outweigh by a considerable margin the many reasons that would induce me to stay at Yerkes.... I would certainly not want to resign from my appointment at Yerkes earlier than July of next year and possibly as late as September.
>
> I am confident that in the next twelve months the laboratory will yield some worthwhile results, which in themselves will justify the expenditures that the University undertook in establishing the laboratory.... Therefore, I do hope you will not feel that the time and thought you have spent on establishing this laboratory and getting me here (with all the troubles involved in that) were wasted, even if I should leave after only three years' stay. I for my part have found this time exceedingly stimulating. It has increased my knowledge of, and interest in, astrophysical problems and I am sure that I shall continue to be interested in them.[16]

When Mulliken learned of Herzberg's decision to leave Yerkes Observatory, he personally did his best to persuade Herzberg to come to the Chicago campus, and he strongly recommended to the President that Herzberg should be given a Professorship in the Department of Physics:

> I feel it would be a tragedy if we did not make every reasonable effort to keep at this University a man who, I am convinced, is one of the best in the Physical Sciences Division.... I have no hesitation in expressing the opinion that Herzberg is the most competent and productive worker in his field today.[17]

Herzberg thanked Mulliken for his endeavours to arrange favourable conditions for him to join the Physics Department since it would have offered the possibility of close collaboration with Mulliken and the other molecular physicists there, but he regretted that considerations of a personal nature made him decide in favour of the position in Ottawa. However, he hoped that there would continue to be many opportunities of contacts, stimulating discussions, and collaboration.[18]

It was arranged that Herzberg would resign his position as Professor of Spectroscopy at the Yerkes Observatory as of 1 September 1948; he would take his year's vacation during August and therefore leave Williams Bay sometime between August 5 and 10. This would also mean the resignation of Luise Herzberg as Voluntary Research Associate on the same date.

Herzberg next checked with the Immigration Branch in Canada as to the necessary steps he should take in order to ensure his and the family's re-admission into Canada in 1948 to take up the NRC position. He was informed not to anticipate any difficulty in re-entering Canada.[19] This news was a most welcome relief, and Herzberg turned his complete attention to his obligations to Struve and Yerkes in the remaining year at Williams Bay. To this commitment was added the need to plan the new Spectroscopy Laboratory and to decide on the staff and begin to order equipment. The search for a suitable home in Ottawa was also on his agenda.

While actively pursuing his ultimate research on the spectrum of hydrogen, Herzberg was considering who he might like to have as his principal assistant in Ottawa. He immediately thought of Alex Douglas, whom he regarded as his best graduate student at Saskatoon. Douglas was employed by the NRC in the Acoustics Section of the Division of Physics but had taken a leave of absence after the war to complete his Ph.D., working with David Rank at Pennsylvania State University. Rank was a noted optical physicist with an interest in infrared spectroscopy and light scattering. Herzberg wrote to Douglas in late 1947, informing him of his plans to set up a spectroscopy laboratory at the NRC and inviting Douglas to join him. Douglas expected to complete his thesis on light scattering by the end of May 1948, but he had resolved not to return to his position at the NRC because of unsatisfactory Council policy and low salaries, which caused many of the best scientists to leave the Division of Physics after the war. Following an exchange of several letters in January and a visit with Herzberg, Douglas realized that promising changes were taking place to improve the situation at the NRC. He was willing to return to the NRC to work with Herzberg in a pure research position provided that he was allowed to transfer to this new Spectroscopy Section and that the salary was adequate. Within a month, Herzberg had discussed Douglas's situation with President Mackenzie and was able to inform Douglas of his promotion to Associate Research Officer in the Spectroscopy Section with an annual salary of $4,050. This was gratefully accepted by Douglas, and Herzberg was delighted and relieved to know that he had a brilliant co-worker to get the Spectroscopy Laboratory started.[20] They met on several occasions in Ottawa and at Yerkes to plan the new laboratory and to discuss staff and equipment.

Just a few months before the Herzbergs' return to Canada, Luise's sudden deteriorating health was the cause of much anxiety. Gerhard and the children were stunned to learn of her serious illness. A biopsy proved Luise had breast cancer, and an operation was performed at Billings Hospital, affiliated with The University of Chicago. Life at home was quiet and lonely for Paul and Agnes without their mother and with their father's frequent visits to the hospital. While Luise was recuperating at the hospital and at home, Herzberg took on the household chores of shopping and laundry, and he even became adept at braiding Agnes's hair. Cooking was not such a problem since the vegetarian meals were simple, and he and the children often dined at the Van Biesbroeck home, along with the graduate students. Lalitha Chandrasekhar was a constant companion to Luise during this stressful period.

Farewell the Astronomer

A most memorable event was a farewell garden party at the home of Chandra and Lalitha, and many members and children of the Yerkes community were present. On the morning of 8 August 1948, the Herzbergs were accompanied to the railway station at Williams Bay by Chandra and Lalitha and Gerhard's students Rao and Phillips. After fond farewells, they boarded the train for Chicago and spent the afternoon and evening visiting with friends at the university. The next day, they attended the Chicago Railway Fair, where they admired the different locomotives and coaches of the past. Then they were off on the return trip to Canada. As Paul remembers: "After we had crossed the border and had completed all the immigration matters, Mom and Dad sat together on the Pullman car seat and were smiling and very pleased to be back in Canada. I don't think I understood or appreciated at the time how much this meant to them, but I was struck with their obvious satisfaction."

On Arrival in Ottawa

Anxious to get to their new home as quickly as possible after a brief stop in Toronto, the Herzbergs took an overnight train to Ottawa. This skirted the north shore of Lake Ontario, passing through many small towns to Kingston, and then headed north through flat farmlands, with glimpses of the Rideau Lakes and Canal system all the way to the west end of Ottawa. The train then crossed the Ottawa River at the Chaudière Falls Bridge into the city of Hull, with its lumber mills, huge pyramids of logs, and piles of yellow sulphur, and then circled back to Ottawa via the Royal Alexandra Bridge. As the train chugged slowly into the Ottawa Union Station, there was a stunning view of the limestone cliffs of Parliament Hill crowned with the majestic Peace Tower of the Parliament Buildings.

Aerial view of the Parliament Buildings, War Memorial, Chateau Laurier Hotel, and the railway station in foreground.

The Herzbergs were met by Alex Douglas and Adair Morrison, former students of physics at the University of Saskatchewan, both working at the NRC. On emerging from Union Station on the south side of Rideau Street, Paul and Agnes had a quick first look at the hub of their new city. Across the street was the grand Chateau Laurier Hotel, to the west was the imposing War Memorial on Confederation Square, and beyond they had an oblique view of the Parliament Buildings dominated by the high Peace Tower of the Centre Block. Once settled at home, a visit to this highest point in Ottawa would give them a bird's-eye view of the city and surrounding countryside.

With luggage bags packed in two cars, Douglas and Morrison drove the Herzbergs to their new home on Sunnyside Avenue in Ottawa South. This house was purchased sight unseen after months of careful real-estate searching by Adair Morrison and numerous letters back and forth describing the family needs and details of the property. It proved to be satisfactory in most respects, with nearby schools for Paul and Agnes, although it was somewhat distant from the NRC Laboratories situated in the north end of the city.

Within a week of their arrival in Ottawa, letters went between Luise and Gerhard and their cherished friends Lalitha and Chandra.

Dear Lalitha:

I do not want to let this first week pass without writing to you.... First of all, I would like to thank you and Chandra for the friendship and great kindness extended to us during our time in Williams Bay, and especially during my illness last month and then before we left. We enjoyed very much the party you gave for us.

I am very pleased with the house. It is in very good condition, everything smooth and modern. It should be easy to run once we are organized.... The only serious drawback is that it seems to take Gerhard about forty minutes to get to and from the laboratory....

I hope you will pardon me for saying at this occasion, that having come to know you and Chandra is the most enjoyable and valuable experience we had during our time in the Bay. On your account we regretted very much to leave. We now hope that you will soon make good your promise to visit us here.

Life here seems to flow rather quietly and peacefully. It is an advantage for a nation not to be burdened with the responsibilities that come to the mighty.[21]

Luise

Dear Chandra:

Strange to say, we arrived here on schedule, and without the slightest difficulty with customs or immigration.

At home we are fairly well settled, but at the Council I have thus far only a provisional office. My plates and other office equipment which were sent by express have not yet arrived, but the plates which came with my luggage are unharmed. I have measured the H_2 plates and expect to write up the note for *Nature* in the next few days....

Luise has already expressed our appreciation for all you and Lalitha have done for us during our stay at Yerkes Observatory and particularly during the last months. It was a great experience for me to have so many opportunities of discussions with you, and I shall certainly miss them here. Your gift will always remind us, if that were necessary, of your friendship.[22]

Gerhard

Dear Gerhard:

I have kept your and Luise's letters for the past three weeks, feeling utterly inadequate to say how much your letters have meant to me and Lalitha. We have been long enough in this country to appreciate kindness and kindliness and to value friendship when it rarely comes. Luise has kindly said that knowing us was one of the things you cared for, during your time in the Bay; on our side, it is <u>most</u> certainly true that Lalitha and I have valued the friendship you generously gave us, more than any other personal experience during our twelve years of "exile" here. You know this country and you know Yerkes well enough not to require any elaboration on the dryness of the air which can choke one here. And now that we are again left alone, I am beginning to wonder, what I had not for three years, whether it is worth giving up all things personal for the abstraction of science. I am afraid this sounds dangerously close to self pity: but there is always an ingredient of self pity in any feeling of personal loss: and your leaving <u>has</u> been one, deeply....

I forgot to acknowledge your letter enclosing a copy of your letter to *Nature* on the "Quadrupole Rotation—Vibration Spectrum of the Hydrogen Molecule". It is certainly something Yerkes can be proud of; it crowns, fittingly, your record of achievement here.[23]

Chandra

Dear Chandra:

It was a very great pleasure indeed to have your letter and to find in it your fine expression of friendship. Both of us certainly hope that our mutual visits will not be too rare events and that perhaps, as we suggested once before, we could even spend our vacations together at some nice place in the mountains.

We had Boenhoffer here three weeks ago. He is a very fine person. Steacie offered him a position similar to my own. Boenhoffer would like to hold out in Germany unless the Russians make that impossible. He stayed with us at the house, and one night told us some of the gruesome story that led to the execution of his brothers. It is a miracle that he himself survived since he knew all along about the plot against Hitler and helped the conspirators....

Kindest regards to you both, also from Luise.[24]

Gerhard

Canada's Capital and Home of the NRC

No sooner were the Herzbergs comfortably settled in their home towards the end of August, when they were visited by the Thurnauers from Chatanooga, Tennessee, Lotte (Luise's sister) and Hans with their children Peter and Dorothy. Lotte especially wanted to catch up on the latest news of Luise's health and to see her parents, Paul and Elsbeth Oettinger, who had moved to Ottawa in 1943. This proved to be a timely visit, since Elsbeth died a year later.

The visit was a lively one for the children, since Paul and Agnes were about the same age as Peter and Dorothy. One sunny Sunday, the two families decided to explore the downtown area of government buildings and then visit the NRC Laboratories. The first order of business was to view the city from the balconies atop the Peace Tower of the Parliament Buildings. Once there, just under the clock face and sixty metres from the ground and about a hundred metres above the Ottawa River, all of the Capital City lay before them outlined by its several waterways, many parks, and abundant greenery. With a map of the city in hand, they immediately located the NRC building on the south banks of the Ottawa River and noted its location relative to various landmarks and major buildings. The Ottawa River flows from the northwest, pours down the Chaudière Falls at Hull, and carries on to the horizon in the east on its way to meet the grand St. Lawrence

Grandpa Paul, Agnes, Grandma Elsbeth, Peter, Dorothy, Hans, Lotte, Paul, and Luise, during a visit of the Thurnauers in Ottawa, 1948.

River. The Ottawa River is joined by the Rideau Canal with its eight locks between the East Block of the Parliament Buildings and the Chateau Laurier Hotel, and further east the Rideau River drops fifteen metres into the Ottawa River. On the north side of the Peace Tower, the Gatineau Hills, foothills of the Precambrian Shield, dominate the view, with Brewery Creek pouring into the Ottawa River at Hull and the Gatineau River with its many logs joining it east of the NRC Laboratories. On the south side could be seen Wellington Street with the United States Embassy opposite the Tower. Past the city, at the rapids at Hog's Back, the Rideau River and Canal separate on their different paths through the city.

Apart from the striking Supreme Court Building and classic Confederation Building, both on Wellington Street just west of the Tower, most of the interesting parts of the city appeared to lie on the east side of the city. Clearly, the centre of the Capital was Confederation Square with its War Memorial, around which all traffic circled whether going south, east, or west in the city. Past the locks and the Chateau Laurier Hotel with Major's Hill Park behind it lay the long and curved Sussex Drive with the Bytown Market and some of the oldest buildings in Ottawa. Following north on Sussex Drive the Herzbergs noted the grey wooden "temporary" buildings, built during World War II to house the expanding government and still in use. Just where Sussex Drive makes a sweeping turn eastward stood Notre Dame Basilica, a prominent landmark of Gothic design with high twin towers. Further east, the large NRC building was situated in a park-like setting near the Rideau Falls, with Earnscliffe, the home of the British High Commissioner, on its west side and the Embassy of France to the east. Next along Sussex Drive was the residence of the Prime Minister, and east of it on the south side of Sussex was Government House (Rideau Hall) with guarded gate and vast parkland, the home of the Governor General of Canada, resident representative of the Crown. The NRC Laboratories building was on the ceremonial route from Rideau Hall and the Prime Minister's home to Parliament Hill.[25]

One might well wonder as the Herzbergs did, why the city of Ottawa, far from the main population of this vast country, would be chosen as the capital of Canada rather than the larger cities of Montreal, Quebec, or Toronto. As early as 1610, French explorers had navigated the Ottawa River, and the first white settlement was established only two hundred years later, on the north shore at Chaudière Falls, by Philemon Wright, an American from Massachusetts. Loyalists and others from the Thirteen Colonies settled in the area and developed a thriving timber industry. However, after the British–American War of 1812, a large garrison was established in the area as a defensive measure against further attacks by American forces, and in order to deploy the army quickly to the border regions, the Rideau Canal system was built to connect Ottawa to Kingston and Fort Henry. Work started on the canal in 1826 and was completed in 1832 under the direction of Lt.-Col. John By. At that time, the city was known as Bytown, formerly Richmond Landing, and finally in 1857 was named Ottawa after the original native tribe of the area, the Algonkin or Outaouais in French.

Ottawa became the capital city of the United Province of Canada in 1857. Earlier, the capital had been moved from Quebec City to Toronto and back again. Finally, Ottawa with a population of about ten thousand English, French, Irish, and Scots was selected by Queen Victoria as the permanent seat of the future government since it combined more advantages than any other place in Canada. Ten years later, with its population doubled and growing, Ottawa was confirmed as the Capital of the Dominion by the British North America Act. With expansion of the Dominion and the necessary growth of the federal government, especially during and after two world wars, the city flourished, and by 1948 its population numbered almost two hundred thousand. Ottawa was to be the Herzbergs' home for the next half century.

Much to their surprise the Herzbergs found that Canada's Capital did not possess a theatre or concert hall. But with their love of music, they attended many of the concerts held in the auditorium of Glebe Collegiate on Monday evenings under the auspices of the "Morning Music Club" (founded in 1892). Concerts by Glenn Gould, the Virtuosi di Roma, the Melas Ensemble, and American and Continental trios and quartets would pack the auditorium. From time to time, concerts were also held in the Capitol Theatre (one of the great movie palaces of North America, seating twenty-three hundred), with some of the world's major artists, the small Ottawa Philharmonic Orchestra, and the beautiful singing of Paul Robeson, Marion Anderson, Lois Marshall, and Maureen Forrester being memorable occasions for the Herzbergs. They saw some plays at the Ottawa Little Theatre (a former church) and especially enjoyed the performances of the Canadian Repertory Group directed by Amelia Hall at the De Lasalle Academy, next to Notre Dame Basilica.

At Home in Ottawa

After two years of travelling back and forth between home and the NRC by bus, Herzberg decided it was time to buy a car and learn to drive. With much practice under the watchful eyes of friends, he finally became reasonably comfortable driving in traffic to the NRC. While he felt that this saved some time and was convenient, since he could readily return to the office in the evenings when necessary, he missed all of the reading he used to do on the bus.

In a short time, the Herzbergs found their home to be too small. Visits from Gerhard's mother from Seattle in the summer of 1949 and from Chandra and Lalitha in 1950 convinced them that they could use more space to properly host visitors. They built a new house near their first home, but this part of Ottawa South soon became heavily populated and noisy as many houses were built, all very close together. The Herzbergs then bought a spacious lot in Rockcliffe Park, a quiet and wooded, rural neighbourhood, and had a split-level home built by Heinrich Kroeger, one of Ottawa's best-known developers.[26] After several delays the Herzbergs moved into their new home at Christmas in 1955. They came to enjoy long walks through the woodland around MacKay Lake and along the Ottawa River, and swimming in the lake in summer was an added pleasure. While the Rockcliffe

Gerhard holding a skein of wool for his mother in Ottawa, 1949.

Gerhard, Agnes, and Grandma Ella on a boat tour in Montreal, summer 1949.

The new Herzberg home, 190 Lakeway Drive, in Rockcliffe Village, 1955.

home was too far from the NRC to walk on a daily basis, the meandering drive along the Ottawa River and wooded area to Sussex Drive, past Rideau Hall, the Prime Minister's home, and the French Embassy was a welcome change from the earlier heavily travelled routes through the downtown and market areas of Ottawa.

Decorating the Christmas tree, 1955.

A game of deep thought.

At home in the evenings, Herzberg would review technical papers and reports he had brought from the office and then relax by playing chess with Paul and practising his singing for half an hour, accompanied by Luise on the piano. He especially enjoyed reading biographies and listening to his favourite recordings of vocal and orchestral music. He would seldom spend much time with newspapers or the radio, except for listening to broadcasts of the Metropolitan Opera performances on some Saturday afternoons. There was no television in the home; he felt that one could become addicted and waste much time with this medium. There were much better ways to use any spare time, especially outdoors, walking, jogging, mowing the lawn, working in the garden, and shovelling snow from the walkway and driveway in winter, usually helped by Paul and Agnes.

He took singing lessons once a week, usually on Sundays, with his vocal teacher Dave Galbraith. One year he also attended the master class of the choral impressario Nicholas Goldschmidt. At a meeting of the Canadian Association of Physicists in Vancouver in 1965, on an evening featuring a recital by physicists and members of their families, Herzberg sang Schubert lieder and arias of operas by Mozart and Verdi. This being his first public performance, he was surprised that he was not as nervous as he expected. He sang at Kingsway United Church in Ottawa several times and sang Handel's "Judos Maccabaes" with a choir at Ottawa's Jewish Community

Centre. His singing became familiar to members of the NRC since he was often invited to perform at staff parties and at Christmas, but carols were not in his repertoire. Often when interviewed for radio and television he did not hesitate to add an aria or two.

Vast improvements were soon to take place in cultural and sports facilities across Canada as the country prepared for Expo'67 in Montreal and the celebration of Canada's Centennial in 1967 with a new flag. In Ottawa, a new city hall was built in 1957 on Green Island, just east of the NRC; a broad east–west expressway, the Queensway, was dedicated by the Queen and opened in 1965; and in 1969 the National Arts Centre with its magnificent Opera House seating twenty-three hundred was opened. Ottawa also became the home of Carleton University in 1964 at the city's southern extremity on the Rideau River, a welcome addition to the University of Ottawa, which was established in 1910 in the city centre. Later, Herzberg was to play an important role as Chancellor of Carleton University where the Physics Building would be named in his honour.

The NRC was one of the striking examples of the growth of national spirit in Canada after 1914.... This successful experiment of the NRC seems to me one of the miracles of our modern Canadian democracy.

Frank H. Underhill

13. NATIONAL RESEARCH COUNCIL OF CANADA: THE TEMPLE OF SCIENCE

The National Research Council (NRC) had been in existence for only three decades when Herzberg joined it in 1948. Prior to its establishment, Canada's scientific resources and manpower were meagre in most sectors of the country and non-existent in some. Industrial research was essentially unknown, and the supply of scientists and engineers was woefully inadequate. Even university research was rare, so that talented students carried out their postgraduate studies in foreign universities, usually never to return to Canada. Thanks to dedicated and determined leaders who foresaw the needs of the country for research in science during war as well as in peacetime, the young NRC survived the debilitating years of the Depression and thrived during World War II to become a major scientific resource for Canada and an institute admired around the world for its research in basic and applied science.

A New Era For Research In Canada[1]

As early as the mid-1800s, the Canadian Government had established several scientific organizations to deal mainly with the country's natural resources. Some of these agencies are still in operation today, although under different names or departments. The earliest were the Geological Survey of Canada for mineral exploration, the Meteorological Service for gathering climate data, the Central Experimental Farm for agriculture, the Dominion Observatory as a time service, and the Marine Biological Station for fisheries.

The genesis of the NRC was a recommendation from the British Advisory Board in 1916 that each Dominion should set up an organization to develop scientific and industrial research. This charge was based on the experience that Germany's superior organization in scientific research had given it a distinct military advantage over the Allies. In Canada, an Honourary Advisory Council was appointed by the Government in the autumn of 1916 and given the mandate "to promote and undertake scientific and industrial research" for national development. It was to report to the Minister of Trade and Commerce. Eleven members made up the Council, mostly university scientists and a few representatives of business and industrial interests. The Council's general functions were threefold: to advise the government on matters of science in general; to encourage and promote fundamental science, especially in the universities; and to operate laboratories of its own, especially in fields that were not the responsibility of government departments and with reference to the problems of secondary industry.

In a 1917 survey of existing research facilities across the country, the Council found that there were fewer than fifty full-time researchers in the physical sciences in Canada; that scientific research was practically confined to the laboratories of two or three universities and one or two government departments; and moreover, that there was little research activity to co-ordinate in Canada. As a result, the Council stressed the need to establish a program of grants and scholarships to encourage students to remain in Canada for postgraduate research. Also foreseen was the need to develop a central research institute for fundamental problems and standards.

From its inception, the Council also conceived of the novel idea of Associate Committees—advisory panels of leading authorities in Canada set up to examine specific problems facing industry and the country. Committee members would review the state of knowledge about a topic by organizing a conference of the foremost experts, then propose a research program for its solution, and recommend by whom and where the research should be carried out. The services of the advisory members were voluntary and unpaid, except for travel expenses to meetings. In the early years, committees on long-standing concerns in chemistry, mines and metallurgy, grain research, and forestry were established. Special committees for timely problems such as tuberculosis, animal and plant diseases, biology, flax cultivation, cold storage research, and underground water in the prairies were some of the first to be activated. By 1952, there were thirty-two Associate Committees in operation, and thirty-six ten years later. This mechanism proved to be an efficient and economical way of using the best expert advice in the country, and much of the progress in scientific and industrial research in the early years of the NRC was thus a free gift of busy men and women.[2]

Henry Marshall Tory (1864–1947), a mathematical physicist and founding president of the University of Alberta, was appointed the Council's first President in 1924. He assumed the role at a difficult time, when many on the Council were discouraged with the lack of support for science by some powerful members of Government. The Senate had rejected a central laboratory as being too costly, older senators saw no need for research, and the Civil Service was fearful that the Council would undertake work that government departments could be doing. At age sixty, Tory accepted the post with the statement: "I believe with all my heart and mind that Canada needs today more than any other thing, the multiplication of scientific work in connection with our natural resources and our industrial development."

The name National Research Council (NRC) was authorized in 1925. The NRC was set up not as a Department of Government but as a Crown Corporation outside the Civil Service, with a governing body of the most distinguished scientists in Canada. This was an unprecedented move by the Government of the day. Tory set the tone for the operation and control of the NRC by scientists, namely, people who understood what it was for; they set the regulations for appointments, promotions, and salaries. In the early decades, the NRC enjoyed "arm's-length" treatment from the government, which left it free from many of the normal aspects of government control and interference. This independence was deemed to be absolutely essential for the operation of a first-rate scientific organization and was the vital element that helped the NRC to promote and nurture science in Canada.

In-house research was started in 1925 in rented quarters, and research activities gradually increased, so that four years later the National Research Laboratories were created with Divisions of Chemistry, Physics and Engineering, Applied Biology, and Research Information. In 1929, Tory inaugurated the *Canadian Journal of Research* for dissemination of the results of research from universities and the NRC. After years of pressing for a major national laboratory, but experiencing considerable opposition in Parliament, Tory finally succeeded in persuading Prime Minister W.L. Mackenzie King of the necessity of central laboratories, and a new building was approved by the Government in 1928.

The National Research Laboratories

The magnificent building of the National Research Laboratories at 100 Sussex Drive sits on a ten acre plot on the high banks of the Ottawa River, immediately west of the Rideau River and Rideau Falls, overlooking the Gatineau Hills to the north. Construction of the building began in 1930, but by the time the building was completed, the Depression and a change of Government produced severe cuts in budget, and the laboratories were not adequately staffed or equipped. The dire circumstances were compellingly described by the historian Wilfrid Eggleston:

> Perhaps nothing illustrates more vividly the desperate state of the times and the hopeless nature of the unemployment problem—especially for the younger men and women just entering the labour market—than the provision which was made in the spring of 1933 for "employing" persons in the new laboratories without pay.[3]

Under these conditions the new laboratories made little impact on the national science scene in the early 1930s.

Nevertheless, for the official opening of the NRC Laboratories on 10 August 1932, at the time of an Imperial Economic Conference in Ottawa,

The National Research Laboratories on Sussex Drive, 1935.

addresses were given by the Governor General, His Excellency the Earl of Bessborough, by the Prime Minister, the Right Honourable R.B. Bennett, and by NRC President H.M. Tory, with the proceedings broadcast to the Empire. Obviously, great importance was attached to the new building, and the Canadian press named it "The Temple of Science". A bronze plaque was unveiled in the front hall to proclaim the Laboratories' mission:

> This building was constructed for the purposes of fostering the scientific development of Canadian industry for Canadian needs and for the extension and expansion of Canadian trade at home and abroad.

On Mackenzie King's return as Prime Minister in late 1935, the words he had originally chosen for the new building were carved into the stone high above the main entrance of the Laboratories: they gracefully convey the essence and wonder of research.

NATIONAL RESEARCH LABORATORIES
GREAT IS TRUTH, AND MIGHTY ABOVE ALL THINGS:
IT ENDURETH, AND IS ALWAYS STRONG:
IT LIVETH AND CONQUERETH FOR EVERMORE
THE MORE THOU SEARCHEST, THE MORE THOU SHALT MARVEL.[4]

This building was to be NRC's home for research activities until World War II, when the rapid increase of staff and new programs, mainly in applied research, necessitated expansion to a new four hundred acre site, the NRC complex on Montreal Road, about ten kilometres east of the Sussex Laboratories. The cornerstone for its first laboratory, the Aerodynamics

Front lobby and entrance.

Corridor, showing laboratory doors of steel and glass panels.

Building, was laid in July 1940. By the end of the war, the new campus was thriving as a home to nine new laboratories.

The War Years

General Andrew G.L. McNaughton (1887–1966) served as the second president of the NRC from 1935 to 1944. He obtained Bachelor's and Master's degrees in electrical engineering from McGill University in 1910 and 1912, respectively, enlisted in the Great War, and advanced as an artillery officer to the rank of Brigadier-General. He joined the permanent forces and became Chief of the General Staff. In this role he became familiar with the NRC by frequently drawing on its resources and by being the driving force in establishing Associate Committees in surveying, radio, and aerial navigation. As President of the NRC, his inspired foresight that war was imminent, and that scientific research and technology would play a major role, helped to prepare the NRC for research that would prove to be indispensable in war. Two years before World War II erupted, he encouraged work in radar, ballistics, gas masks, optics, chemical warfare, and aeronautical and medical research, among other projects. During the war, the NRC staff swelled from three hundred to three thousand, and all of the facilities of the NRC were directed to research on defence problems. The main task for the NRC was to serve as science adviser and research wing for the Army, Navy, and Air Force, and Canadian scientists and engineers rose to the challenge.

When war broke out, the NRC had its one laboratory operating on an annual budget of $900,000. Immediately after Canada declared war on Germany, McNaughton left the NRC to assume the position of Officer Commanding the First Canadian Division. It was Chalmers Jack Mackenzie (1888–1984), Herzberg's colleague and former Dean of Engineering in Saskatoon, who as Acting President (1939–1944) steered the NRC through this dramatic epoch, which in essence was its formative period. At first, there seemed to be scant progress in executing wartime programs because of government inertia in providing the needed funds. However, with the fall of the Low Countries, Norway, and France, a gift of $1,300,000 from a few patriotic and wealthy Canadians was made available for war research, without strings of any kind. Work was immediately started on many projects, without the need to justify expenditures. Radar was given highest priority, and work accelerated with a quarter of the "free fund" and a staff of two hundred. Mackenzie kept McNaughton well informed of the activities of the staff and progress in wartime projects, and he noted:

> One thing which pleases me very much is the realistic view which all members of the staff here take. We all feel keenly that unless our endeavors produce equipment and findings of use to the man in the field we will not be achieving our fundamental purpose, for we all realize that in modern warfare based on science, technology and mass production, there are three stages—research and development, production, and use in the field.[5]

Towards this end, the NRC helped in setting up twenty-one additional research laboratories, manufacturing companies, and test sites from the Atlantic to the Pacific. One of the foremost successes was Research Enterprises Limited, established in Toronto as a major radar and optical factory. Many sophisticated devices were developed there, including radar, gun sights, and magnetometers for anti-mine and anti-submarine defence. Many important contributions in aeronautical engineering and aviation medicine, explosives, chemical warfare, protective clothing, nutrition, and packaging and transportation of foods were credited to the NRC. As the war proceeded, there was a crucial need for the transfer of research in atomic energy from Britain and France, and teams of nuclear scientists came to Canada to develop a nuclear reactor and eventually to set up the Chalk River Laboratories.

The Climate for Postwar Research

During World War II and immediately after, Canada was fortunate to have two great men at the helm of the NRC, C.J. Mackenzie and the chemist E.W.R. Steacie (1900–1962), on whom Mackenzie relied heavily for advice. Mackenzie became President in 1944, serving as such to 1952, and Steacie served as Vice-President from 1950 to 1952 and then as President until his untimely death in 1962. The two were outstanding individuals, exceptionally talented administrators, and acknowledged leaders in their respective fields of expertise. They envisioned a bright future for Canadian science and saw eye-to-eye on the methods to bring this about. With their leadership and vision, Canadian science came of age during World War II.

The wartime accomplishments of the NRC staff were praised by the military and politicians and won strong support for increased research activity in peacetime. Suggestions were even put forward that all of the scientific laboratories of the federal government should be placed under the aegis of the NRC. Mackenzie wrote about this to McNaughton:

C. Jack Mackenzie (1988–1984), NRC President (1944–1952).

E.W.R. "Ned" Steacie (1900–1962), NRC President (1952–1962).

> The work of the Research Council during the war years has created a favourable impression and the Government as a whole is kindly disposed to us and rather favours all scientific work being done under our auspices.[6]

However, Mackenzie believed that the NRC's most productive role would be to return to its prewar objectives of fundamental research in the natural sciences and expansion of applied research to assist industry. In keeping with this belief, Mackenzie later also declined an invitation for the NRC to be responsible for social science research. The Minister accountable for the NRC was Clarence Decator Howe (1886–1960), also an engineer, who had the highest regard for Mackenzie. After much discussion, he was convinced that Mackenzie was right about what should be done by the NRC in the period of reconstruction after the war. According to Mackenzie:

> As victory became certain, the most important immediate task was to prepare specific estimates for the first postwar budget. After discussions with Mr. Howe, I appeared before Treasury Board, outlined our long-term plans, and submitted the following recommendations for immediate action:
>
> 1. Continue the budget for the NRC on the same scale of expenditures as in the last year of the war, on the understanding that it would be doubled within five years as the necessary staff of competent scientists became available.

2. Give highest priority to the setting up of a military research organization to take over responsibilities for defence research policies.
3. Continue and expand our existing nuclear-energy programs for the peaceful use of atomic energy.
4. Expand medical research.
5. Establish new research divisions of building research, radio and electrical engineering, applied chemistry, and applied physics, and laboratories in the Prairie and Maritime regions, to serve the special needs of those areas of Canada.[7]

The government accepted in principle this postwar science policy and provided the budget to cover the immediate expenditures to bring an expanded NRC back to peacetime activities. In a radio broadcast to the nation on 13 October 1944, among other news, Prime Minister Mackenzie King announced that research would be extended and more liberally supported in the postwar period, a commitment never before made by any Canadian politician. Given such unstinting encouragement by Government, science and engineering experienced unprecedented growth of research in universities and government institutions and a modest beginning in industry.

Mackenzie was impressed by the ease with which the NRC staff changed to war work and back again to peacetime research with a minimum of serious disruption.[8] Not long afterwards, the off-shoot programs envisaged in items 2, 3, and 4 began to be separated from the NRC according to plan; they became the Defence Research Board in 1947, the Atomic Energy of Canada Limited situated in Chalk River, Ontario, in 1952, and the Medical Research Council in 1960. In 1947, the Electrical Engineering Section in the Division of Physics became the Division of Radio and Electrical Engineering, the Division of Building Research was formed, and the Technical Information Service was assigned to the NRC. In 1952, the applied research branch of the Division of Chemistry became the Division of Applied Chemistry. These new divisions were all housed on the NRC Montreal Road campus at the eastern end of Ottawa. The Prairie Regional Laboratory was established in Saskatoon in 1947, and the Maritime Regional Laboratory in Halifax in 1952 (with a name change to the Atlantic Regional Laboratory in 1955). Eventually, the aeronautical research of the Division of Mechanical Engineering was re-organized as the National Aeronautical Establishment in 1959 and was located near the Ottawa airport.

One of the spectacular achievements of the NRC was to catapult Canada into the forefront of nuclear science and peaceful uses of atomic energy.[9] This began serendipitously in wartime, when Winston Churchill and Franklin Roosevelt at the Quebec Conference in 1943 agreed that the development of a heavy-water reactor system should be carried out in Canada in cooperation with Britain and the United States. The NRC was already involved in nuclear research, with provisional laboratories at the University of Montreal where scientists from Britain and France were working on designs of reactors. Even earlier, George C. Laurence had attempted to build the first man-made chain reaction at the NRC Laboratories using uranium and graphite. Once Canada's responsibility for the heavy-water project was authorized, NRC's priority was to find a major new site as quickly as possible, away from populated areas and near a large water supply. In 1945, the Chalk River Nuclear Laboratory was established on the Ottawa River, about two hundred kilometres north of Ottawa, and was operated by the NRC under the newly created Atomic Energy Control Board. Under the leadership of the English scientists John D. Cockroft (who received the Nobel Prize in 1951 for transmutation of atomic nuclei) and W. Bennett Lewis, the Chalk River Laboratory became a centre for leading-edge research in nuclear physics, chemistry, and biology. Among its many successes was the development of NRX, an experimental atomic pile with the highest neutron flux density of any pile in the world. This led to Canada's pre-eminence in the field of neutron scattering in the 1950s, resulting in the award of the Nobel Prize in Physics to Bertram Brockhouse in 1994. Also the CANDU atomic-power system was designed and built at Chalk River, and CANDU reactors now supply most of the electric power in Ontario, about 15 percent in Canada, and are in use in several other countries. Mackenzie served as president of the Atomic Energy Control Board (1948–1961), and following his retirement as president of the NRC in 1952, he was president of Atomic Energy of Canada Ltd. in 1953–1954.

The NRC Postdoctoral Fellowships

Another laudatory initiative of the NRC was the Postdoctoral Fellowship Program, which was to have far-reaching consequences for research both at the NRC Laboratories and in Canadian universities.[10] It began in 1946 through the efforts of Steacie, who never forgot his exhilarating experience of spending a year in Europe and England in 1934–1935. Steacie had earned his Ph.D. in physical chemistry in 1926 from McGill University and continued his research as a postdoctorate fellow. He accepted a position as Lecturer and was promoted to Assistant Professor in 1930. In the summer of 1934 he took a leave of absence and spent half a year in Frankfurt, Germany, working with Karl-F. Bonhoeffer at the time that Herzberg and his Darmstadt group attended seminars there. Steacie then joined the laboratory of A.J. Allmand at King's College, London, for several months in 1935. On returning to McGill, he was promoted to Associate Professor, and four years later he accepted the appointment as Director of the Division of Chemistry at the NRC.

With the rapid expansion of the NRC after the war and the increasing need for scientific manpower, Mackenzie discussed with Steacie the problems of finding inspiring leaders for the new divisions and sections, maintaining an active youthful staff, and providing a stimulating atmosphere as experienced by the NRC during the war years. He was concerned about the possibility that, in time, an aging permanent staff would become less efficient and less creative.

Steacie's year in Europe and England had impressed him with the opportunity of meeting many scientists, young and old, some very famous, others upcoming, all having different interests and expertise and willing to talk about their work and share their experiences. Based on this experience, Steacie was confident that what was needed to keep the NRC dynamic was a continual flow of young talent with top-notch education in modern science and engineering from universities and research institutes in Canada and abroad. Thus was born Steacie's scheme of postdoctoral fellowships, tenable in the NRC Laboratories for up to two years. Mackenzie quickly endorsed the Program, and with final approval of Council and Government, the Fellowship Program was launched in 1948, just before Herzberg's arrival in Ottawa. This Program proved to be so successful at the NRC that it was expanded in 1949 to include the funding of postdoctoral fellowships tenable in Canadian universities.

Growth of University Research

In order to meet the needs of a developing nation, the vital prerequisites were the education and training of first-class scientists and engineers, which required the build-up of robust research infrastructures in universities across the country. This became Mackenzie's and Steacie's objective, and they continually emphasized throughout their years in office the need for increased scholarships and grants-in-aid for university research.

Before the existence of the NRC, only McGill University and the University of Toronto had research programs leading to the Ph.D. degree, while eleven universities granted Master's degrees in Arts or Science. It was understandable that most graduates seeking further advancement would continue their studies in the United Kingdom, the United States, or Europe. One of the first tasks of the Honourary Advisory Council was to promote graduate research in Canadian universities, to assist students showing superior ability and interest in order to keep them in Canada, and to expand the use of science in Canadian industry. Thus began the NRC program of grants and scholarships. By 1931, scholarships had been awarded to 324 students, and of these 303 had obtained Master's degrees and 152 Doctorate degrees, having published about twelve hundred scientific papers. By 1939, the total budget for grants and scholarships had increased to about $250,000 and remained almost constant until the end of World War II. With increasing enrollment and the return of many veterans to universities, the grants and scholarship allocation rose to about $2 million by 1952. At that time there were fifteen institutions offering Master's degrees in the sciences and seven of these had Ph.D. programs in research.[11]

There is no doubt that NRC's support of grants for the provision of equipment, facilities, and assistants for research, as well as scholarships for postgraduate studies and research, played a crucial role in building up Canadian graduate schools in science and engineering. From 1954 to 1963, the number of institutions carrying on graduate work in the sciences increased to twenty-four, and the expenditures for scholarships and grants increased dramatically by an average of almost 30 percent each year, reaching $34 million by 1966. This raised the standard of scientific and engineering faculties and accelerated the quantity and quality of university research. Moreover, as the schools turned out graduates with experience in research, a supply of trained scientific workers became available for government, university, and industrial laboratories.

A World Centre for Basic and Applied Research

Mackenzie and Steacie cherished the freedom of scientists and engineers to pursue their own ideas. They stressed the work of the individual over that of team research and opposed organization by projects. Moreover, they insisted that administration was there to serve the scientist and engineer:

> The fundamental feature of the administration of the NRC … is to make sure that the administration can never issue any instructions to scientists in connection with any technical subject whatever. It is the exact opposite of the administration of most government departments, where the administrative head is in charge.… It is up to the administration to make sure that things can be worked out with the scientific divisions, so that the administration acts as a service to the divisions, rather than as a control. The result is a highly decentralized organization.[12]

Steacie in particular was outspoken about this credo and reiterated his belief in it at every opportunity. He went on to say:

> In the operation of a scientific laboratory, nothing matters much except the competence of the staff: the fundamental policy is to write the organization chart after you have employed the staff and to ignore it beforehand.… I think that the NRC is almost unique from the point of view of scientific organizations, and I might say that almost every government research laboratory in the world is trying to copy it—in some cases successfully, and in other cases, unsuccessfully.

Both Mackenzie and Steacie were held in such high regard by the scientific community and by politicians and bureaucrats that the NRC was allowed the freedom to operate without undue interference by the Government. This independence in planning and operation of research was to last almost two decades after the end of World War II. During this unparalleled era, Mackenzie and Steacie were able to establish the NRC as the principal scientific resource of Canada and as an international centre of basic and applied research. The recruitment of Herzberg proved to be one of the major ingredients in their plans for he epitomized the dynamic leadership and basic research focus that was needed to bring world recognition to the NRC Laboratories.

A noted English chemist has said that the only institutions which have previously played such a role were the Cavendish Laboratory in Cambridge and Bohr's institute in Copenhagen.

Stig Claesson

14. THE SPECTROSCOPY LABORATORY

The NRC Spectroscopy Laboratory was to be Herzberg's fifth and final laboratory following his earlier initiatives at Bristol University, the Technische Hochschule Darmstadt, the University of Saskatchewan, and Yerkes Observatory. His constant dream had been to establish a major spectroscopy laboratory and he now was given this opportunity. The NRC Spectroscopy Laboratory would become recognized as one of his supreme accomplishments and the one of which he was justifiably most proud.

New Developments in Spectroscopy

The years immediately following the end of World War II, referred to by many as the physicists' war, were propitious for the establishment of a spectroscopy laboratory. Many new devices and techniques developed during the war were now available for peacetime use. The most important for

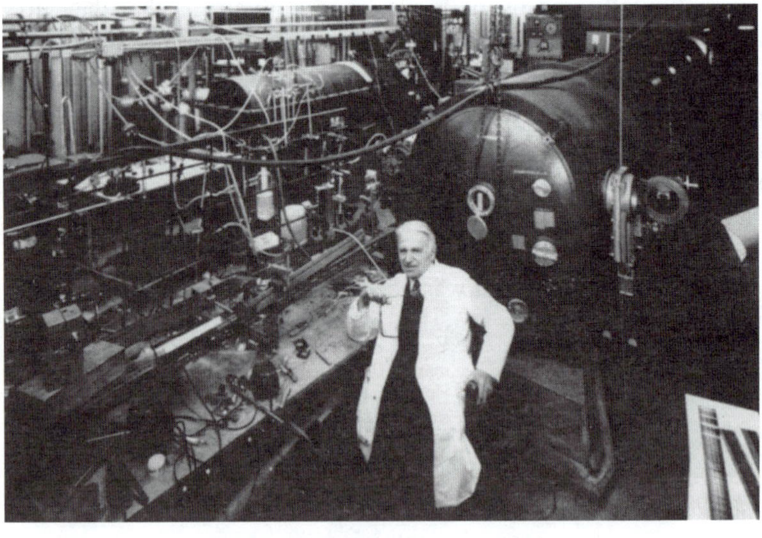

Herzberg in his laboratory.

spectroscopy was radar, developed primarily in the United Kingdom and the Radiation Laboratory of the Massachusetts Institute of Technology and manufactured in Canada by Research Enterprises. Radar's offspring was microwave spectroscopy, which opened a whole new field for precision measurements of rotational spectra of molecules, leading to knowledge of the dimensions of molecules. Several laboratories in the U.S.A., including those of Duke University, Columbia University, and the Massachusetts Institute of Technology, and Cambridge University in the U.K. were pioneers of these techniques. Extremely sensitive detectors for the infrared region and photomultipliers for the visible and ultraviolet regions had also been developed and were now available for general use. Such detectors would be essential for high-resolution instruments, which normally have very low light-gathering power. There was also substantial improvement in the sensitivity of photographic plates for the visible and ultraviolet regions. For light-scattering experiments, a powerful mercury arc lamp was produced at the University of Toronto. All of these developments helped to once again bring research in atomic and molecular spectroscopy to the forefront of science. The invention of masers and lasers a decade later would provide sources of unimagined high intensity and monochromaticity, rekindling this advance.

Planning the New Laboratory

Given the encouragement by President Mackenzie, with substantial financial support and space, Herzberg seized this opportunity to establish a major spectroscopy laboratory, second to none in quality. It would concentrate on studies of fundamental problems, mainly in spectroscopy and the structure of simple gaseous molecules, but also would include some atomic spectroscopy and make use of the most modern techniques available. Thus, the new spectroscopy laboratory was being planned to achieve the highest resolution possible, with access from the longest to the shortest wavelengths of the optical spectrum.

Herzberg had recruited Alex Douglas, who was working on his Ph.D. at Pennsylvania State University, to be his principal assistant. They met several times at the Yerkes Observatory and in Ottawa to plan the new laboratory and to discuss the main equipment to be designed and built. Plans were made for three major spectrographs to cover the infrared, visible, and far-ultraviolet regions of the spectrum. All were to be high-resolution instruments and so would make use of diffraction gratings. While smaller spectrographs were available commercially, and some were ordered for survey work at lower dispersion, any laboratory expecting to do forefront research in high-resolution spectroscopy of gases had of necessity to build its own instruments. This would take time, be expensive, and be dependent on obtaining good gratings.

For the spectral region 2000 to 12 000 Å, a 7-metre concave grating spectrograph was designed, similar to those Herzberg had built in Saskatoon and Yerkes. A 3-metre concave grating was chosen for the vacuum ultraviolet below 2 000 Å, and a plane grating for the infrared region with wavelengths longer than 12 000 Å. The infrared spectrometer was designed to incorporate the most recent developments in sensitive detectors and to operate under vacuum in order to eliminate absorption by water vapor in the air.

While adequate space had been allotted for the Spectroscopy Laboratory in the NRC Laboratories on Sussex Drive, this turned out to be on the third floor of the building, absolutely unsuitable for the large instruments being planned. Thus, time-consuming building alterations became necessary to house the spectrographs in the basement, where heavy concrete foundations could be built on solid bedrock to ensure stability for the gratings and the other optical elements of these sensitive instruments. On completing his Ph.D., Douglas returned to the NRC in May 1948, three months before Herzberg's arrival in Ottawa, and began to supervise these alterations. He also ordered much of the necessary ancillary equipment with the help of two senior scientists, Donald Rose, Head of the Cosmic Ray Section, and Leslie Howlett, Head of the Optics Section.

At the time of Herzberg's arrival in Ottawa, two spectroscopy laboratories were already operating in the Division of Chemistry. One group under the direction of R. Norman Jones was engaged in the study of infrared and ultraviolet spectra of large molecules, with particular interest in molecules of biological significance. The second group, led by Harold J. Bernstein, who had worked with Herzberg at Yerkes, concentrated on infrared and Raman spectra of simple molecules with emphasis on measurements of intensities of Raman spectra. Both groups were well equipped with commercial spectroscopic instruments of low to medium resolution, suitable for their research programs. While the interests of the three spectroscopy laboratories were focused on different problems, all three were located in the same building, and the scientists began to co-operate as partners by lending equipment, helping with techniques, and often collaborating on research problems of common interest.

The Founding Staff

With the building of the major instruments being overseen by Douglas, the major task facing Herzberg on arrival was finding the key scientific and technical staff for the extensive laboratory he had in mind. He was determined to establish a group of active young scientists who had shown promise of working independently and who had expertise in fields and techniques of modern spectroscopy that would complement his and Douglas' competence in the visible and ultraviolet regions. Based on his own experience and bolstered by the advice of Steacie, Herzberg's plan was to find the best scientists and allow them the freedom to work on atomic and molecular problems of their own choosing. Thus, for the founding staff, Herzberg sought an experimentalist to set up a laboratory in the new field of microwave spectroscopy, another with expertise in the infrared, and one to work in atomic beam spectroscopy. Each was to be assisted by a technician and up to two postdoctoral fellows. Finally, in order to operate efficiently, the laboratory would require a small machine shop with two or more staff members, as well as a secretary and later, possibly, an assistant for computational work.

Herzberg was intent on getting the Spectroscopy Laboratory into operation expeditiously, in spite of the required renovations and building of the large spectrographs, but other urgent matters intervened. He had barely settled in a temporary office in the chemistry end of the building when he was reminded of the upcoming retirement of the Director of the Division of Physics and was strongly urged by Steacie to accept the directorship when it was offered to him. Such an administrative commitment was never in Herzberg's plans, but finally he was persuaded to accept this position when given considerable administrative assistance to look after the day-to-day business affairs of the Division. But in spite of this support in management, the added responsibilities inevitably delayed his bringing the laboratory into an active mode as quickly as he would have liked.

Alexander Edgar Douglas, FRS, FRSC (1916–1981) was one of an eminent band of scientists raised on homestead prairie farms and educated at the University of Saskatchewan who played a major role in the development and enrichment of science in Canada. He was born near Melfort,

Alex Douglas analyzing a spectrum.

Saskatchewan, and lived with three siblings in a log farmhouse with no running water or electric power and with a wood-burning stove for heat. He attended a one room country school and then high school in town, taking one year by correspondence to save expenses during the Depression. First year university courses were also completed by correspondence and summer school, before he attended the University of Saskatchewan, taking physics courses with Herzberg. Douglas graduated with honours in 1939 and received a National Research Council bursary to continue studies for a Master's degree in physics. He was accepted by Herzberg for research in molecular spectroscopy and published papers on spectra of B_2, as well as on BN and BH.

After spending only half a year on Ph.D. courses at the University of Minnesota, Douglas returned to Saskatoon to work with Herzberg during the summer. It was at this time that he obtained the spectrum of CH^+, four lines of which coincided with an unidentifed interstellar spectrum. This was proof that the ion existed in interstellar space. He then decided to enlist in the Armed Forces but was persuaded by Harrington, the Head of Physics, and by Herzberg to join the National Research Council, which was recruiting new staff for wartime research. Douglas worked in the Acoustics Section, spending four years on anti-submarine research during the war, followed by one year in echo sounding for geophysical exploration. He then carried out research on light scattering with David Rank at Pennsylvania State University and obtained his Ph.D. within two years. Herzberg contacted Douglas at about this time to tell him of his plans for the Spectroscopy Laboratory at the NRC, and Douglas agreed to assist him in this new venture. Douglas served as Head of the Spectroscopy Section from 1949 to 1969, while Herzberg was Director of the Division of Physics and then the Division of Pure Physics.

Thus began the fruitful collaboration in the development of the Spectroscopy Laboratory of the NRC, which propelled Canada into the forefront of research in molecular spectroscopy and structure. This close intellectual friendship was to last Douglas' thirty-three years with the NRC (having also served as Director of the Division of Physics in 1969–1973), a period of which Herzberg wrote, "Douglas made a towering contribution to the Spectroscopy Laboratory as well as to the NRC and to Canadian science generally".[1] Other examples of two outstanding scientists working in such harmony in the same field and in almost daily contact over so many years are extremely rare.

The next member to join the group was Donald Allan Ramsay, CM, FRS, FRSC. He was born in 1922 in London, England, and educated at Latymer Upper School before going on to St Catharine's College in the University of Cambridge. There, he came under the influence of Fred S. Dainton and Gordon B.B.M. Sutherland, two of England's notable chemists, and obtained his B.A. in 1943 and Ph.D. in 1947. At the time, there were two major laboratories for infrared spectroscopy in England, one in Cambridge under the supervision of Sutherland and the other in Oxford under H.W. Thompson, both involved in wartime research and in friendly competition. Ramsay studied the infrared spectra of a series of sugars for his Ph.D. On being offered several research opportunities in the U.S.A., Australia, Sweden, and Canada, Ramsay chose to work with R. Norman Jones at the NRC and arrived in July of 1947. His research concerned the intensities of infrared spectra of steroids, on which he presented a paper at the Molecular Spectroscopy Symposium in Columbus, Ohio, in June 1948. There, he heard a paper by Herzberg and was so impressed that when he learned of Herzberg's appointment to the NRC, Ramsay discussed with Steacie the possibility of transferring from the Division of Chemistry

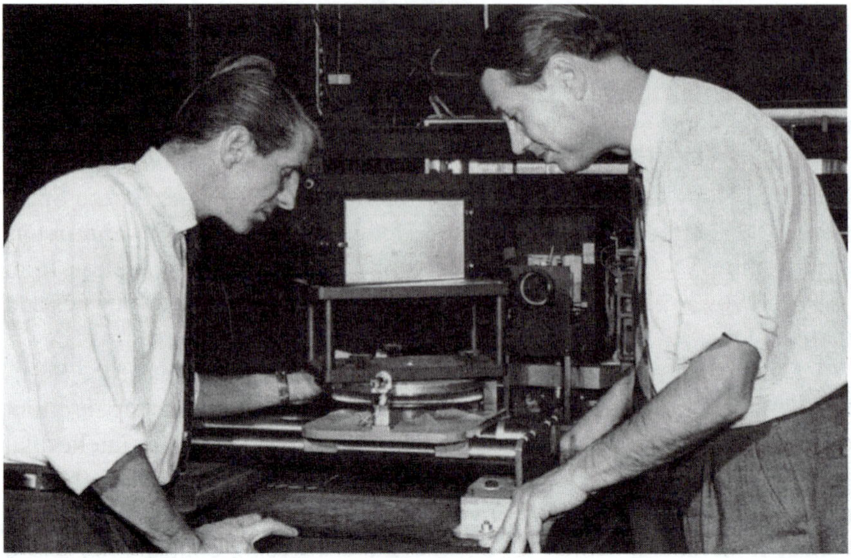

Don Ramsay (right) and his assistant Werner Goetz lining up a spectrograph.

to Physics. Ramsay joined Herzberg's laboratory in July 1949 and worked with him in developing a flash-photolysis apparatus (first used by Reginald G.W. Norrish and George Porter at Cambridge University) for the production and detection of free radicals.[2] The first free radicals to be identified in Ottawa were NH_2 and HCO, and while Ramsay went on to analyze their complex spectra and to produce others, Herzberg pursued his intensive search for spectra of CH_2 and CH_3. In the early 1960s, Ramsay became head of a separate group devoted to the study of spectra of large molecules and later (1984–1988) served as Head of the Spectroscopy Section.[3]

Hin Lew, whose parents had immigrated from China, was born in 1921 and educated in Vancouver, obtaining his B.A. at the University of British Columbia. For graduate studies, he joined the University of Toronto in 1941 but found little research in progress because of the war and so obtained a Master's degree by taking courses. He was employed by the National Research Council in Ottawa a year later to work on ultrasonics with Arnold Pitt, and it was there that he met and became friends with Alex Douglas. Lew left the NRC in September 1945 for the Massachusetts Institute of Technology (MIT), where he received his Ph.D. (1948) on research with atomic beams under the supervision of Professor Jerrold R. Zacharias. During the following year, which Lew spent as a Research

Hin Lew and his atomic beam apparatus.

Associate at MIT, he was contacted by Douglas with news of Herzberg's Spectroscopy Laboratory and the suggestion that he apply for a position there. At the interview with Herzberg, the main question asked was "Are you sure that you can build an atomic- and a molecular-beam apparatus?" Since Lew had built and operated a beam machine at MIT, he was confident that he could and was hired to begin in September 1949.

On arrival in Ottawa, Lew was given a huge empty room (10 metres by 10 metres), a completely free hand in the design and building of the necessary apparatus, a full-time technician, and no fixed budget but full support by Herzberg and Douglas to build a molecular-beam machine as quickly as possible. Who could ask for anything more!

Cecil Clifford Costain, FRSC (1922–1991), given the name C^3 (i.e., C cubed) by his colleagues at the NRC, was another of the graduates from Saskatoon to seek his fortune in Ottawa. He was born in Alberta, and when the family moved to neighbouring Saskatchewan, he studied physics at the University of Saskatchewan and obtained a three year B.A. degree. Having attended Herzberg's classes during those years, Costain later remarked "Herzberg made scientists of us farm boys." In 1941, Costain instructed recruits of the Royal Canadian Air Force at the university and a year later joined the Canadian Navy as a Radar Officer. He rose to the rank of

Lieutenant Commander in the British Admiralty at age twenty-two and was awarded the Distinguished Service Cross. He returned to the University of Saskatchewan for his Master's degree and then joined Cambridge University to work with Professor G.B.B.M. Sutherland in microwave spectroscopy. In 1950, Sutherland transferred to the University of Michigan in Ann Arbor, taking a group of students with him. Costain received an NRC scholarship and completed his Ph.D. in Michigan in 1951. He eagerly accepted the opportunity to establish a microwave laboratory in the Spectroscopy Laboratory and arrived in Ottawa in the autumn of 1951. His wartime radar experience served him well, and his laboratory soon became recognized as a major centre for the accurate determination of molecular structures and was a home to many postdoctoral fellows. Costain left the Spectroscopy Laboratory in 1972 to head the Time and Frequency Section of the NRC, where his group developed Canada's primary standards of time, cesium clocks, with accuracies equivalent to those of the U.S.A., France, and West Germany with which they were compared.[4]

An excellent technical staff was also acquired, beginning with James Potter who joined Douglas in the summer of 1948 and assisted him in planning the building renovations and setting up the first spectrograph. Potter was an acknowledged master in solving mechanical problems of the most intricate laboratory apparatus and was instrumental in designing and supervising the construction of most of the large spectrographs. Frank Doren and Paul Frechete managed a small machine shop and took care of the

Cec Costain, Boris Stoicheff, Gerhard Herzberg, and Don Ramsay.

immediate needs for apparatus, whether machined by them or by the main NRC workshop. Franz Alberti, Werner Goetz, Peter Flainek, and Cecil Burgess assisted Douglas, Ramsay, Lew, and Costain, respectively, and were of enormous help in devising apparatus and specialized techniques for these research groups.

Herzberg was most fortunate in obtaining a superb technical assistant, Jack Shoosmith, a senior technician at King's College, London, who was keen on coming to Canada. Shoosmith was highly acclaimed by Professor A.J. Allmand, who had recommended John Spinks to Herzberg years earlier. Herzberg found Shoosmith to be efficient and intelligent and a self-starter. He helped Herzberg achieve many experimental successes, as indicated by the acknowledgements in countless papers as well as by being designated a co-author on some of Herzberg's most important papers. Shoosmith worked with Herzberg for twenty years, until his retirement in 1969.

In the early years of the Spectroscopy Laboratory, Luise Herzberg was a guest worker, measuring and analyzing spectra that had been brought from the Yerkes Observatory. Her insights and pleasant manner appealed to the young women who were helping Herzberg and others in the lab by analyzing spectra and carrying out complex calculations on desk calculators. While they were university graduates in physics or chemistry, these women were not familiar with spectra but quickly learned the methods of analysis and were of immense help. The first to join was Ruth Craig, who arrived in 1950 and left three years later as the wife of Keith Innes, a post-doctorate fellow. She was followed by Lila Howe, who could operate two desk calculators simultaneously and was so quick in their use that she often had to stop to let them cool down. Howe also served as receptionist for the lab office, tending the telephone and ensuring that the office ran smoothly. Her usual salutation in answering the telephone was "Hello, Molecular Spectroscopy". One day, with sudden silence at the other end of the call, she repeated her greeting, only to be asked to her surprise "Does anyone speak English there?" She was appointed to the scientific staff and during her eight years was a co-author on several papers with Herzberg and Douglas. Beulah Wadsworth and Izabel Dabrowski joined the laboratory later and became proficient in the use of computers in analysis of spectra. Dabrowski worked with Herzberg for almost thirty years. She became a member of the scientific staff in 1984, and through her skill in analysis of spectra of hydrogen and rare-gas hydrides, she co-authored several series of papers with Herzberg.

Lila Howe

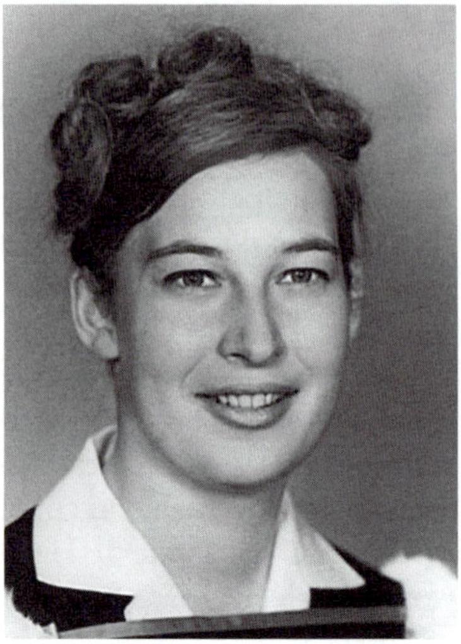

Izabel Dabrowski

The First Research and Publication

Herzberg was anxious to put the new laboratory on the scientific map as quickly as possible. Once the first spectrograph had been completed (the 7-metre grating instrument), he immediately put it into service, making use of a grating borrowed from the University of Saskatchewan. This loan made possible the functioning of the laboratory one year earlier than would otherwise have been the case. Herzberg decided to attempt an experiment he had had in mind for some time, namely the determination of the nuclear spin of the helium isotope ^{3}He; a value of 1/2 was expected from theory but an experimental measurement had not yet been made.

With the help of W.B. Lewis of the Chalk River Laboratories, Herzberg obtained a small sample of this rare isotope from the U.S. Atomic Energy Commission, and Douglas photographed the spectrum of the molecule $^3He_2$ in record time. From the measured intensity alternation of 3:1 of successive rotational lines, it was established conclusively that the spin of the ^{3}He nucleus is 1/2. The first paper from the new spectroscopy laboratory, authored by Douglas and Herzberg, was submitted for publication as a Letter to the Editor in the *Physical Review* on 5 October 1949 and appeared a month later with the title "The Nuclear Spin of ^{3}He".[5]

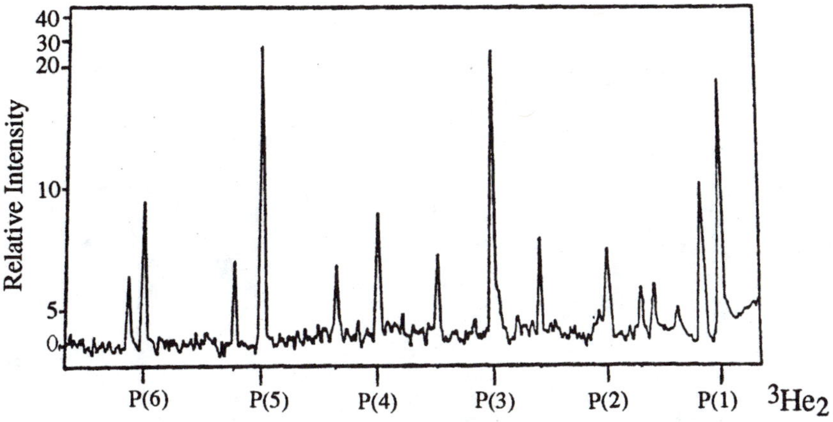

The first research of the Spectroscopy Laboratory, 1949, spectrum of He_2 showing intensity alternation.

The other spectrographs for the extreme ultraviolet and infrared regions were completed and in use within three years. Other spectrographs were soon designed: one a larger vacuum ultraviolet spectrograph using a 10-metre concave grating, and a smaller instrument for the visible region making use of a large-aperture plane grating to increase its light-gathering power and thus permit the photography of normally very weak spectra.

Postdoctorate Fellows

Herzberg approved wholeheartedly of Steacie's plan of postdoctoral fellowships, and by early 1949, young postdoctorate fellows, or PDFs, began to arrive in the Spectroscopy Laboratory. They played important roles in many phases of the development and research of the laboratory, bringing special skills and knowledge from the best laboratories around the world. They were productive scientists during their stay at the NRC, and while some chose to remain in Canada, the majority returned to their homelands (some with Canadian wives) singing the praises of the lab and Canada. In 1949, six PDFs joined the laboratory from Canada, England, India, New Zealand, and South Africa. Another four were added in each of the next two years, and on average there were five newcomers each year until the Postdoctoral Program was phased out at the NRC in 1975 to be replaced by appointments of Research Associates (RAs).[6] By that time, over 130 PDFs had participated in the work of the Spectroscopy Laboratory, and later

Staff and first group of postdoctorate fellows at tea, 1950.
From left, top row: D. Sharma, J. Shoosmith, A.V. Jones, D.A. Ramsay, C. Reid, M. Feast, J. Potter. Middle row: P. Frechette, Freddy Willans, C. Pallett. Front row: A.E. Douglas, Ghislaine Le Cours, J. Casey, Barbara Davidson, Joan Galligan, Liola Mason.

about two RAs per year joined the group. Most of the PDFs came from the United Kingdom, Canada, India, and Japan. Over the years, a small number of them were offered permanent positions in the Spectroscopy Laboratory: I was one of these lucky ones.[7] Other PDFs appointed by Herzberg before he retired from administrative duties in 1969 included George T. Ritter, John W.C. Johns, Jon T. Hougen, Takeshi Oka, Klaus P. Huber, Philip R. Bunker, and George D. Chapman after a fellowship in Oxford. In later years, several more PDFs were appointed to the scientific staff, including A. Robert W. McKellar and James K.G. Watson, along with senior scientists Michel Vervloet, Takayoshi Amano, Paul Marmet, and Benoit Simard.[8]

I first met Herzberg in 1950 when he visited the University of Toronto. At the time, I was completing my Ph.D. thesis in molecular spectroscopy under the supervision of Harry L. Welsh, a good friend of Herzberg. My intention was to do postdoctoral research in the high-pressure laboratory of the University of Amsterdam. However, on hearing Herzberg's outstanding lecture on the quadrupole spectrum of hydrogen and how it might be used to detect hydrogen in the planets and interstellar medium, I began to wonder, "Why should I go to Europe when we have such an exciting person here in Canada?" So, I applied for an NRC Fellowship, visited the Spectroscopy Lab, and joined the group in late 1951. I quickly realized how extremely lucky I was to be a member of the group of Alex Douglas, Don Ramsay, Hin Lew, and Cec Costain with a "boss" possessed of boundless energy and a resounding laugh, whom we affectionately came to know as "GH", a revered colleague.

On my arrival at the NRC, Herzberg's secretary knocked on his door and then ushered me into his large office through two padded doors, which no doubt insulated him from the noise of a clanking typewriter and mechanical desk calculator. Herzberg immediately stood up from his desk, neatly piled high with journals, and came forward to greet me. He was resplendent in his clean, white lab coat, unbuttoned over his dark vest, as he took my overcoat to hang in a closet. We sat on chairs in front of his desk while we clarified some administrative details and then discussed my planned research project. I was completely taken by surprise by this treatment as an equal in his greetings and in the long discussion that followed. As I learned over the years, this was his regular form of greeting with anyone entering his office, whether a visiting scientist, a staff member, or a PDF.

His office was on the second floor in a spacious room with a magnificent view of the Ottawa River and the Gatineau Hills in Quebec. This room reminded me of a comfortable library: it was packed full of filing cabinets, with lofty bookshelves lining the walls from cabinets to the high ceiling, filled with journals, books, and bound volumes of scientific papers, and on one wall there was a large blackboard covered in equations and molecular symbols. Behind his desk stood a tall bookcase that divided the room to provide him with a quiet area where he could study and analyze spectra. A corner of this section was covered with portraits of famous scientists, many of them his friends and colleagues. The outer office used by his secretary was similarly lined with bookshelves filled with journals, and her portion of the room was separated by a glass partition from that of Herzberg's computing assistant. In every respect, this part of the NRC building was a most impressive section of the Spectroscopy Laboratory and a fitting tribute to the leader of the lab and Director of the Division of Physics.

Herzberg gave guidance to the group in the lab by his own inimitable example. He worked long hours, six days a week, and we tried to keep up

A view of the Ottawa River from Herzberg's office.

A corner of Herzberg's office with photographs of friends and colleagues. Top left: C.V. Raman, Max Planck, Paul Dirac. Third row: Max Von Laue, James Franck, Max Born, Francis Simon. Second row: S. Chandrasekhar, a group of eminent scientists, Albert Einstein. Bottom row: Alfred Kastler, Ned Steacie, Robert Mulliken.

with him by working day and night and weekends. He was deeply immersed in his own inspiring research, and yet he found time each day to talk to us about our ideas and work. To our surprise, he somehow managed to keep abreast of the voluminous scientific literature, and he arranged for a constant stream of scientists to visit the lab and to give seminars and so keep us up to date on spectroscopic activities worldwide. And above all else, the freedom Herzberg sought for himself when first approached by the NRC, he gave to all members of the Spectroscopy Laboratory whether on staff or a fellowship. Neither he nor Douglas directed our research, but both were always available to keep us out of experimental pitfalls, or once lost in them, to gently ease us out and to put us on the right track. There were occasions, however, when we would catch only the blur of Herzberg's white lab coat as he raced up the stairs to his office, and we would be reminded that other important matters, either a meeting, a budget, or a pressing administrative problem, also had to be attended to. But seldom would such obligations be allowed to intrude on the daily progress of the lab.

The attitude of mind and the readiness of Herzberg and Douglas to raise the standards of all around them were a constant revelation to the younger members. Each PDF was free to collaborate with a staff member or to work independently, and there were a variety of problems to choose from, with excellent equipment and facilities at our disposal. There was much exciting research being done and much to be done. There were weekly group meetings, where we discussed our problems and progress, and weekly seminars by visitors or members of the lab. If by chance a layperson had entered one of these group meetings, at times it would have seemed like a court of law with learned discussion of Hund's case (a), (b), or (c) and, at other times, like a planning board for a local concert as we contemplated the Vegard–Kaplan Bands, Cameron Bands, or Herzberg Bands, all being the usual jargon of molecular spectroscopists.

Scientific life in the Spectroscopy Laboratory was intense, more so than many PDFs had ever experienced. There were daily exchanges of ideas and arguments, which were continued by the bachelor PDFs at dinner and on into the night. These led to constructive criticism of each other's work and especially of our manuscripts. Results were published independently, with only the names of direct participants as authors, in alphabetical order, and acknowledgements of those who had assisted either technically or in discussion. Herzberg read all manuscripts prepared by the group to be certain that the papers were up to his high standard. But his name did not appear on any paper unless he had contributed scientifically in a major way. And he saw to it that his own manuscripts were read by others of the group and inevitably by Douglas, whose opinion and comments he valued so highly. Herzberg published many of his papers in the *Canadian Journal of Physics* and encouraged members of the lab to do likewise, except when the topic was clearly of little interest to physicists. The recognized importance of papers from the Spectroscopy Laboratory helped immeasurably in promoting this journal internationally.

Soon after I arrived in Ottawa, I was given a completed manuscript by Herzberg at 3 P.M. one Friday, simply to check that there were no obvious errors in it before he mailed it to the publisher that afternoon. Herzberg chose to ask me because the paper was on the topic of pressure-induced absorption, an effect that had been discovered at the University of Toronto by my supervisor Welsh and his colleagues at the time of my graduate studies there. An hour later, Herzberg returned and was somewhat taken aback to find that I had noted three pages of comments. This no doubt was a brash thing for me to do at that time, but I had been schooled by Welsh to read and re-read when writing my thesis and papers in order to correct typos, grammar, English usage, and so on, and I had assumed that I should do the same with this manuscript. Herzberg realized that the paper would not make the 5 o'clock mailing and asked in his usual polite manner whether we could go over the manuscript next morning. At 8 A.M. on Saturday, he showed up at my desk, armed with the Oxford dictionary and *Fowler's Modern English Usage*. After several hours of give and take, the manuscript was revised to our mutual satisfaction. He was most appreciative and generous in his thanks and, as I learned later, acknowledged my assistance in the published paper, a magnanimous gesture to a young novice.[9] As he was leaving my room Herzberg turned to me, smiled, and said "Wait till I get hold of your first manuscript." And this is the way it was, friendly arguments, penetrating criticism, and learning together with GH. The understanding and the quality of the work were always uppermost in our minds.

My planned project at the NRC was to improve the apparatus and technique of light scattering (the Raman effect) in order to make use of the high-resolution spectrographs available in the lab, and Herzberg approved. Since this was a new experimental method for the lab, I worked by myself with the assistance of George Ensell, a skilled glassblower, to modify the "Toronto" mercury lamps to produce higher intensity and with machinists to develop a more efficient apparatus. In a year, the equipment was ready, and the initial experiments with the 7-metre spectrograph proved to be successful beyond my wildest dreams. It was time to try a crucial experiment, the rotational spectrum of benzene (C_6H_6), to attempt to determine precise values for the C–C and C–H bond lengths. After nursing the apparatus during a 48 hour exposure, I developed the photographic plate, and there it was, an extensive series of lines—the first rotational spectrum of benzene.[10] I came out of the dark room, and there by chance was Herzberg. He saw that I was beaming, and when I showed him the spectrum, he held the plate up to the light exclaiming in his excitement "By Jove, by Jove!", while I kept my hands below his, hoping he would not drop the plate. He was most generous with his compliments, and to my surprise, within a few weeks, I was given permanent appointment as a member of the staff of Herzberg's Spectroscopy Laboratory. In a short time, Eugene Pfitzer, a skilled technician, joined in my research, and like the other staff members, I was then privileged to annually choose up to two postdoctoral fellows to work with me and to invite visiting scientists to collaborate in research. While this type of research did not require expensive equipment or materials, there was never any suggestion of budgetary restraint.

Afternoon tea at three o'clock was always a special occasion in the Spectroscopy Laboratory. All members took part, scientific and technical staff as well as secretaries, in a relaxed atmosphere, with discussions on science and a variety of topics, sometimes including hockey and even cricket. Herzberg was usually there, attentive as ever, listening and engaging members in the discussions, making sure that newcomers and visitors were introduced and felt comfortable in this setting. The informality was

Jim Watson and Bob McKellar in foreground with Takayoshi Amano, Maynard Cloutier, and Wojtek Majewski.

Phil Bunker and GH in deep discussion.

Afternoon tea, June 1985.

genuine, and this pause in a long day's work was warmly welcomed. A spirit of friendship and co-operation made the lab a pleasant place to be a part of, and this atmosphere extended well beyond the lab. Newcomers and visitors to the lab were met by a member at the local airport or train station. They were taken to their hotel and helped to find living quarters and informed of local customs and activities. There were invitations to each other's homes for receptions or dinners, often from the Herzbergs or Douglases to meet distinguished visitors. Together we organized picnics with swimming in summer and skiing in winter in the beautiful Gatineau Hills. Christmas parties were a special treat, as were mock weddings and christenings on appropriate occasions. For many, the friendships developed in the Spectroscopy Lab were to last a lifetime.

Visiting Scientists

A close working relationship developed between members of the Spectroscopy Laboratory and several groups from around the world, mainly brought about by common interests in molecular puzzles, both experimental and theoretical, and through personal friendships. Some interactions were to last for several decades. In particular, three university groups in North America were involved in exchange visits, with several of the

A party at the Herzbergs, 1951. From left to right: Ruth Craig, Mrs. J. Shoosmith, Agnes Herzberg, Mrs. Herzberg, Paul Herzberg, GH, J. Shoosmith, F.E. Geiger.

Tea party, 1953. From left: Doris Shoosmith, Luise Herzberg, Cynthia Costain, Ilse Brix, and Phyllis Douglas.

Christmas party with entertainment by the "Spectroscopy Beatles". From left: Jon Hougen, Harry Kroto, Neil Travis with drummer Takeshi Oka in rear, 1964.

younger members joining the NRC as postdoctoral fellows. Robert Mulliken and his group in Chicago were prominent visitors, P. Wilkinson was a regular collaborator and guest worker at the NRC, and W. Kolos often communicated with Herzberg on theoretical calculations for hydrogen. At Harvard, E. Bright Wilson, Jr., who was interested in theory and internal rotation of molecules, sent several of his graduate students to use Costain's microwave spectrometer, among them Jerome D. Swalen, who joined the group as a postdoctoral fellow, and Dudley R. Herschbach, who shared the

Jon Hougen demonstrating molecular motion.

John W.C. Johns.

1986 Nobel Prize in Chemistry with John C. Polanyi and Yuan T. Lee for contributions concerning the dynamics of chemical elementary processes. Later, William Klemperer of Harvard provided the laboratory with its first theorist, Jon Hougen, who joined the scientific staff after a stint as postdoctoral fellow. Alexander Dalgarno of the Harvard–Smithsonian Center for Astrophysics shared many interests in hydrogen and interstellar molecules with Herzberg. The Department of Physics at Toronto contributed a number of postdoctoral fellows, with two of Harry Welsh's group becoming members of the staff, Bob McKellar and the author.

H.W. Thompson (later Sir Harold) of Oxford University, with his renowned laboratory for infrared spectroscopy, recommended many of his students for postdoctoral fellowships to the Spectroscopy Laboratory, as did G.B.B. Sutherland and Norman Sheppard of Cambridge. Herzberg's favorite theorist, with whom he frequently interacted when on visits to Cambridge, was Christopher Longuet-Higgins, who often came to Ottawa. A strong bond developed with their love of music and with his expert piano accompaniment for Herzberg's singing. H.W. Kroto (later Sir Harold), a postdoctoral fellow in the mid-1960s and later a visiting scientist, shared in the 1996 Nobel Prize in Chemistry along with Robert F. Curl, Jr., also a visiting scientist, and Richard E. Smalley for the discovery of fullerenes. Several postdoctoral fellows came from Krishna Asundi's laboratory in Bombay, India. Herzberg's friendship with Asundi began when they met at King's College, London, in 1929 and flourished over the years with visits to each other's laboratories. Ernst Miescher from Basel, Switzerland, whom Herzberg met in 1934 and had corresponded with about spectra of

A typical group of the Spectroscopy Laboratory, 1968, including scientific, technical, and office staff, visiting scientists, postdoctoral fellows, and summer students. Fourth row: C.C. Costain, M. Barnett, C. Jungen, D.A. Ramsay, L.E. Geoffrey, R.L. Fersch, P.R. Bunker, C.W. Mathews, C.M. Woodman, K.P. Huber, E. Miescher. Third row: S. Coulson, R.B. Caton, P. Daley, C.A. Harris, R.K. Lees, A.S. Pearl, E. Thiessen, J.M. Brown, F. Alberti. Second row: T. Oka, H. Lew, A. Lagerqvist, J. Shoosmith, W. Goetz, J.W.C. Johns, S. Krishnamachari, P. Flainek, G.D. Chapman, J.G. Potter, E.J. Blair. First row: M.N. Bedard, M.P. Thompson, J. Poll, B.A. Mackenzie, A.E. Douglas, GH, M. Bebbs, M.B. Wadsworth, S.K. Duke.

various diatomic molecules, was a frequent visitor, and several of his students came to Ottawa, with Klaus P. Huber becoming a staff member and Christian Jungen a co-author with Herzberg on a series of studies on hydrogen spectra. Among others with whom Herzberg collaborated were the astrophysicist Boris Rosen of Liège and spectroscopist Albin Lagerqvist of Stockholm, with whom he co-authored several papers.

Numerous other spectroscopists from major institutes around the world were attracted to give seminars on their research and to visit and spend some time in the Laboratory. Some came from as far away as Australia, India, and Japan, many from Europe and Britain, and many more from the United States.[11] They enriched our activities and helped to introduce the work and scientists of the lab to the international science community. In this way, we younger scientists became aware of the world of atomic and molecular science; we met most of the international players at work, at conferences and socially, and before long began to feel that we were part of the international set. This aura was enhanced by Herzberg's encouragement that we present papers at national and international conferences (after good preparation and rehearsal at the lab) and visit research institutes in the host country as well as in neighbouring countries.

Summing-Up the Philosophy of the Spectroscopy Laboratory

The Spectroscopy Laboratory was very successful in the study of atomic and molecular spectra and structures. In considering what led to its being hailed as "the undisputed centre for such research", it is worth recalling the words of Alex Douglas who assisted Herzberg throughout the laboratory's development and its rise to eminence:

> Certainly it was not careful organization, in the traditional meaning of the word. By the usual standards of government managers, the laboratory was chaotic. From the first, it was established that there would be no committee meetings and no rigid chain of command. Some who came to the laboratory from more formal and structured environments found it difficult to accept the lack of organized structures; others found it a great relief.... But organization also stifles initiative and it is doubtful if on balance there would have been a gain.

Also, it is clear that it was not the priorities, carefully selected by some guiding committee, which led to success. Certainly, individuals in the laboratory carried on well planned programs for years to achieve particular objectives, … but there was no detailed plan guiding the individual staff members.

The achievements of the laboratory depended on a variety of factors:

(a) The laboratory came into being and flourished in the golden years of the NRC. These were the years when adequate financing was combined with a devotion to quality to give an atmosphere most conducive to excellent science. The presidents stated and followed the principle that the administration existed to assist the scientist with his task, … a violent reversal of policy of the public service in the past.

(b) The laboratory certainly depended upon the leadership given by Herzberg in his energetic pursuit of important scientific goals and his unfailing demand for quality.… The respect he commanded from all members of the group was such that his own actions set the whole tone of the laboratory.

(c) Many other factors followed from Herzberg's influence and from the NRC policies that gave full rein to that influence. Distinguished scientists from other laboratories were encouraged to spend some time in Ottawa and they inspired much new work. The flow of postdoctorate fellows enlivened the group and gave it excellent contacts with most of the best spectroscopy laboratories of the world. Also of great importance was the fact that a technical staff gave the scientific staff time to concentrate on their programs.

(d) Finally, and perhaps most importantly, a spirit of friendly cooperation between all members of the staff, both technical and scientific, allowed a multitude of problems to be settled quickly and informally.[12]

While I wholeheartedly endorse these statements by Douglas, nevertheless I am sure that all who passed through the Spectroscopy Laboratory, either as visitors or as temporary or long-term staff, would agree with me that Douglas himself had a tremendous influence on us all. It was a privilege to work with Herzberg and Douglas for they personified the spirit of freedom and creativity that made this laboratory the wonderful place so many came to cherish. It changed the lives of many of us and placed Canada in the forefront of molecular science.

I am the Director but I don't direct.

Gerhard Herzberg

15. INSPIRING THE GROWTH OF BASIC RESEARCH

Within a month of his arrival at the NRC, Herzberg was made aware that R.W. Boyle, the Director of the Division of Physics, would retire in October 1948 at the age of sixty-five. Herzberg had barely settled into a provisional office, awaiting completion of his own, when he received several visits from Steacie encouraging him to accept the directorship. Steacie's argument was that the various Section Heads would approve of Herzberg, but that there would be difficulties if one of them were to be made director.[1] Herzberg had thought that he would decline the directorship if he were to receive such an offer. After all, he had just arrived at the NRC while several of the Section Heads had played crucial roles in the development of the Division and in the war effort. Moreover, his own interest and experience was in research, and his main objective and reason for coming to the NRC was to build a major research laboratory.

Dr. Robert William Boyle (1883–1955) was the Founding Director of the Division of Physics, having arrived at the NRC in 1929, three years before the laboratories at 100 Sussex Drive were opened. He came from the University of Alberta, where he had been a Professor of Physics since 1912 and Dean of the Faculty of Applied Science. He had been invited to head the Division of Physics by President Tory, who knew Boyle as a colleague at the University of Alberta, and was impressed with his high-quality research in ultrasonics at the university and at the British Admiralty during the Great War. Boyle's role at the NRC was to develop the Division of Physics, and he succeeded admirably by selecting young scientists who had excellent academic records and had demonstrated talent for research. All his appointees became "prime movers" at the NRC.[2]

President Tory considered Boyle to be his senior director and had him serve as second-in-command: Boyle took charge of the NRC when Tory was away. Thus, it was expected by the staff and, surprisingly, by Tory and Boyle that Boyle would be named president on Tory's retirement in 1935. However, the appointment of president was the prerogative of the

Government. Prime Minister R.B. Bennett, who had a past personal disagreement with Tory, summarily dismissed Tory at the end of his second five-year term, just a month before the newly appointed president could take office.[3] Bennett selected General McNaughton, an engineer and Chief of the General Staff, as President of the NRC in June 1935. This was a severe setback for Boyle. He was extremely disappointed and seemed to lose all further interest in his responsibilities at the NRC. During World War II, C.J. Mackenzie, the Acting President, lacked confidence in Boyle. He wrote to McNaughton about his concern: "The situation in physics is the most troublesome; the general administrative and professional direction is not in keeping with the high-grade personnel.... I feel the need for some first-class senior research directors and have canvassed the situation many times."[4] Thus, it was not surprising that after the war, Mackenzie sought the advice of the dynamic Steacie, Director of the Division of Chemistry, regarding the rejuvenation of Physics rather than discussing the situation with Boyle. There is little doubt that Mackenzie had Herzberg in mind as a possible new Director of the Division of Physics when he appointed him Principal Research Officer in 1947.

Appointment as Director

On being offered the directorship, Herzberg had misgivings about accepting and sought the advice of his good friend Chandra. Finally, Herzberg began to wonder whether it might not be better to be the boss than to be at odds with a possibly unsympathetic one. After considerable thought and discussions with Steacie and President Mackenzie, he wrote to the President:

> I feel greatly honoured by the fact that you are considering me for the position of Director of the Division of Physics. The decision is certainly not an easy one for me to make, particularly since up to now my life's work has consisted mainly in carrying out my own scientific research and, to some extent, in conducting and supervising the research of others, but not in any appreciable administrative work.
>
> I understand that it will be my primary duty to carry out and supervise research in pure physics and to raise, if possible, by example and encouragement the quality and quantity of the scientific work of the Division. Therefore, it is imperative (and a condition of my acceptance) that my administrative duties be kept to a minimum.... I am very glad that Dr. Howlett is willing to take over the direction of all the work in applied

Director of the Division of Physics, NRC, 1949.

> physics as well as all the ordinary administrative work of the whole Division so that my duty would only be a general supervision of these activities.... I realize the high responsibilities of the office of Director and I am keenly aware of my shortcomings which prevent me from fulfilling all of the requirements. But I shall do my utmost to justify the confidence you have placed in me.[5]

Although still uneasy about becoming a director so soon after his arrival at the NRC, Herzberg eventually accepted the position. On learning of this decision, Chandra immediately wrote "You sound somewhat skeptical about the wisdom of accepting such a position; but it is a measure of the confidence and trust your new associates have in you, and that certainly gives your friends the utmost satisfaction".[6] Among the letters of congratulations was one from Dirk Coster of the University of Groningen, whom Herzberg had not met but had corresponded with regularly about spectroscopic matters. He had tried to find a position for Herzberg in Holland in 1935. Coster wrote a lengthy, friendly letter ending with: "I hope you enjoy your position at the National Research Council of Canada. After all you may perhaps be thankful to the Nazis, that they did not let you stay in Germany."[7]

Herzberg was officially appointed Director of the Division of Physics on 22 December, effective 1 January 1949, to be in charge of fundamental research, with Dr. Leslie E. Howlett as Assistant Director in charge of applied research. Howlett, with a Ph.D. from McGill University, had been at the NRC since September 1931 and had concentrated on problems in photographic optics. He was instrumental in developing the Optics Laboratory at the NRC and in setting up standards of measurements for light and by the use of light. This laboratory played a leading part in improvement of aerial and night photography both during and after World War II. Moreover, Howlett and his colleagues carried out all preliminary work in organizing Research Enterprises Limited in Toronto, with the establishment of an optical factory for the manufacture of optical glass and instruments, as well as radar equipment during the war. For his contributions to the scientific war effort, Howlett was awarded the MBE.

While many wondered why Howlett would agree to carry the day-to-day administrative load in the Division, he was an able administrator and enjoyed it. Moreover, having carried out some spectroscopic research himself, he was deeply respectful of Herzberg's accomplishments in this rapidly growing field. Thus, Howlett was a most helpful co-director with

Leslie E. Howlett.

Herzberg, so that Herzberg spent very little time on general administrative matters and delegated responsibilities to Howlett, to E.R. Birchard, the Vice-President of Administration, and to F.T. Rosser, the Director of Administration and Personnel. Herzberg noted that in his first few years at NRC, he spent only one day on the annual budget for the Division.

The appointment of Howlett as co-director was a wise and practical move from another point of view. In 1950 the world situation was growing apprehensive with the intensifying Cold War, so it was not surprising that the first few meetings of the Directors of Divisions attended by Herzberg would concentrate on planning procedures for effective war research in the event of war. On such matters, Herzberg was a novice. During World War II, he was technically an enemy alien in Saskatoon, and thus his experience was limited to basic research on explosives. Howlett, on the other hand, played a major role in wartime projects of the NRC. President Mackenzie and the Chairman of the Defence Research Board (DRB) discussed the responsibilities of the DRB and the NRC and came to an agreement on how priorities between research projects should be determined. The directors reviewed the responsibilities of the NRC and recommended procedures on how decisions were to be made on wartime projects and on how the NRC could render service most effectively.

Defence projects were becoming a major part of the work in some of the NRC Divisions, as an excerpt from the 1950–1951 Annual Report of the NRC notes:

> With the growing uneasiness in the world situation that has been so marked during the past year, pressure on research for defence purposes has been rising, and once again the facilities of the NRC are being turned more and more to projects arising from the requirements of the Armed Forces. At the present time, in addition to the atomic energy project, which always has had a dual character, the divisions of electrical engineering, mechanical engineering, and to some extent building research, applied physics, and applied chemistry have turned almost exclusively to war work.

Another topic requiring considerable discussion among the directors was the maintenance of high standards in the scientific staff and especially the screening of staff in the first few years following appointment. Various recommendations were approved. The directors insisted that only the best scientists and engineers should be kept on staff and recommended that three committees, one each for scientific, engineering, and Chalk River staff, be set up and authorized to review staff at regular intervals to ensure that high standards are maintained.

Creating a Lively Atmosphere for Research

Herzberg felt that his first task was to become acquainted with the personnel and research of the various Sections of the Division, to inquire about their objectives, and to determine their needs in staff and equipment in order to achieve these aims. There were fourteen Sections in all, involved in basic and applied research covering most areas of current interest in physics. Primarily, he wanted to assist each of the Section Heads in establishing and maintaining an environment for the best research possible in their group, within the means available to the Division. Thus, he encouraged appointments of PDFs, as well as invitations to special visitors for short periods. He enticed the scientists to attend conferences and to make their work known to the scientific communities in Canada, the United States, and abroad. Also, recalling his own excitement when prominent scientists visited and gave talks at Yerkes, Bristol, and Göttingen, he initiated monthly colloquia for the Division to be given by major scientists from all over the world. He also provided funds to the various Sections of the Division of Physics to encourage established scientists to visit and give seminars and, if possible, participate in research with colleagues at the NRC. Theorists as well as experimentalists came from all parts of the world to spend anywhere from a few days to some months at the NRC. Such interactions often led to long-term collaboration on problems of mutual interest, including exchange visits by NRC personnel to other countries. As research funding for the Division increased, these various programs were implemented and, along with similar activities in the Division of Chemistry, were to develop an exciting and stimulating research atmosphere for those fortunate to work at the NRC at that time.

Colloquia were held in the grand auditorium of the NRC, which had seating for 290. On occasion, distinguished speakers gave public lectures in the evening, under the auspices of the Science Association, usually to capacity audiences. One of the first colloquium speakers was Max von Laue from Göttingen, who originated x-ray diffraction in 1912 and managed to withstand and survive the Nazi regime. Among the early visitors were Patrick M.S. Blackett from Imperial College, England, and Edward Teller from the Lawrence Livermore Laboratory speaking on the new field of plasma physics, George Gamow from Washington University on the "big-bang theory", which he advocated, Subrahmanyan Chandrasekhar on relativistic hydrodynamics, and Alfred Kastler from Paris on optical pumping, all exciting speakers and all but Gamow and Teller recipients of the Nobel Prize. Usually such visitors would spend a day or two at the NRC in discussions with colleagues.

Herzberg always found the time to greet newly arrived PDFs and to meet with the steady stream of visitors and scientific delegations to the Division. While the various outreach programs and research activities blossomed under his guidance and with improved government funding, Herzberg became concerned that there were no groups in the fast developing fields of plasma, solid-state, or theoretical physics. He set his mind to remedying this situation and immediately began inquiries in Canada and other countries for the best possible candidates to establish and lead such groups at the NRC.

He was quickly apprised of another important task being carried out by directors, namely the annual evaluation of research grant applications from university professors. Applications in physics became Herzberg's responsibility, and he and Douglas spent several days reviewing the 100–200 applications for operating and equipment grants. Their method was to assess the past performance of applicants and not to rely solely on the promises of detailed proposals. New applicants were given $5,000 a year for two years and then evaluated on their contribution, while those from non-research universities were allotted small grants to at least attend physics conferences. The directors' recommendations were then submitted to the Council for its decision.

As for his own research, Herzberg managed to find time in the evenings and weekends to complete several papers based on spectra taken at Yerkes and to plan his long-term research.

Theoretical Physics Section

Initially, Herzberg had the idea of adding a senior theorist to the Spectroscopy Group and, after clearing the idea with the President, invited Walter Heitler, his friend of the Göttingen days, to join him in Ottawa. Heitler had left Germany abruptly in 1933 for Bristol and was appointed to the Chair of Theoretical Physics. In 1941, he accepted a position as Assistant Professor at the Dublin Institute of Advanced Studies, where he

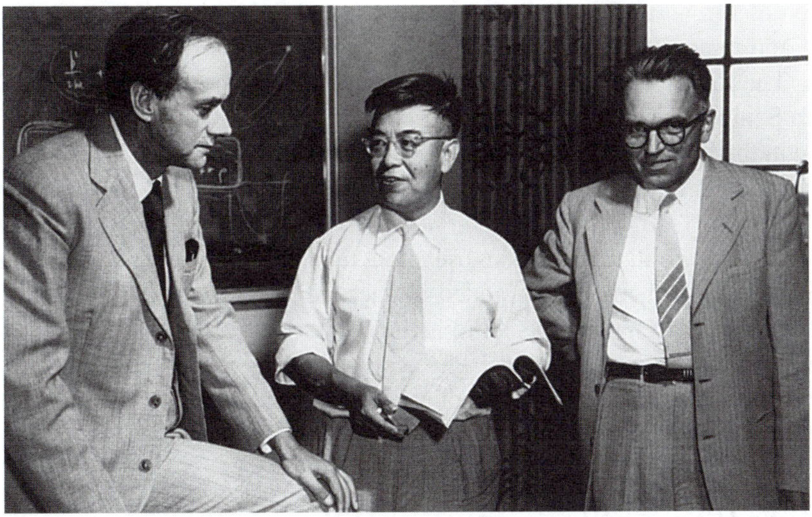

Ta-You-Wu and Herzberg with Prof. Paul Dirac
during his visit to the NRC in 1955.

succeeded Erwin Schrödinger as Director in 1946. It was in Dublin that Herzberg's invitation reached him. After considerable thought over the several offers he had received, Heitler declined the NRC position noting: "I have no doubt that the atmosphere in Canada would be very nice indeed, and it would be delightful to be with you. In fact, there is hardly anyone I would desire more as a colleague."[8] However, Heitler wanted to return to a German-speaking country and one with extensive forests for he missed his regular hikes in the Black Forest. He accepted an appointment as Professor and Director of the Institute for Theoretical Physics in the University of Zurich, a chair which had been held by such luminaries as Einstein, Debye, von Laue, and Schrödinger.[9]

Finding no suitable Canadian theorists in spectroscopy and astrophysics, Herzberg inquired of American colleagues. Isidor Rabi of Columbia University recommended Dr. Ta-You-Wu, a citizen of China and Assistant Professor at Columbia.[10] Wu had received his Ph.D. from the University of Michigan and had taught there and at Columbia. He had published many papers on atomic and molecular spectra and structures, as well as some on astrophysical problems. Wu eagerly accepted an appointment as Associate Research Officer in the Spectroscopy Section with the understanding that he would be able to develop a group in theoretical physics as soon as formal approval was granted by Council. He reported for work in the autumn of 1949.

The following year a Theoretical Physics Section was formed with Wu as a Senior Research Officer and its Head. Three PDFs joined the Section, and in the following year a junior staff member was appointed. The Section attracted many PDFs during the 1950s. Their interests were varied: most of the early investigations concentrated on spectroscopy and astrophysics, with work in solid-state physics, quantum theory of chemical reactions, and quantum field theory being added in succeeding years. As several of the Sections in the Division began to include theorists on their own staffs, the permanent staff of Theoretical Physics was not increased, much to Wu's disappointment. He took a leave of absence in 1962 and resigned two years later to join the University of Buffalo in New York State.[11]

Low-Temperature and Solid-State Physics Section

Herzberg and Howlett agreed that a solid-state physics laboratory was needed at the NRC and quickly sought an outstanding scientist to lead it. Francis Simon at Oxford recommended D.K.C. MacDonald, a brilliant young scientist of thirty with Doctoral degrees from Oxford and Edinburgh and thirty-eight publications to his credit. On a visit to the Clarendon Laboratory in Oxford in 1950, Herzberg recognized the genius and energy of

Keith MacDonald.

MacDonald and offered him the position to set up the new laboratory at NRC. MacDonald was inclined to refuse this offer, but on learning of the Postdoctoral Program that would give him the opportunity to develop a "school" of young colleagues to work with, he readily accepted and arrived in Ottawa in September 1951. As one of his friends at Oxford wrote later:

> In Ottawa he had to start from scratch as far as low-temperature work was concerned, but he was backed by an immense store of good will. The authorities at the National Research Council ... did everything in their power to help him get on with his work. The appointment turned out to be an unqualified success. MacDonald's tremendous drive was now turned to one object, to make Ottawa one of the centres of international low-temperature physics, and the result was truly remarkable.[12]

There is no question that the contributions of MacDonald's laboratory and those of the neutron scattering group at Chalk River, led by Donald Hurst and Bertram Brockhouse, quickly put Canada in the forefront of low-temperature solid-state physics in the early 1950s. MacDonald's co-workers were devoted to him for his enthusiasm, his stimulating presence, and his tremendous appetite for work, even though they found him to be quite difficult at times. Even the mild-mannered Herzberg found MacDonald to be a rather demanding subordinate, always wanting exemptions from administrative rules. He alone accounted for half of Herzberg's administrative time, but he was forgiven; his brilliance and contributions made up for his demands. MacDonald enjoyed discussion and was an excellent teacher. He lectured at the University of Ottawa and began a tradition of Christmas science lectures for children and became known to the general public for his radio, film, and television appearances. MacDonald was an inspiration to all who knew him during his short life. The progressive atrophy of muscles during the last six years of his life eventually led to his coming to the NRC in a wheelchair and then on a stretcher to dictate his final and lasting contributions of five books before his death in 1964 at the age of forty-three.[12]

Plasma Physics

Discussions with Patrick Blackett and Edward Teller during their visits to the NRC convinced Herzberg that plasma physics was a promising new area for basic and applied research, and he began to search for a leading scientist to develop a group at the NRC. At first, realizing that the NRC could not compete in building the large installations of current plasma laboratories, he sought a theorist to head the group, but was not successful. He began negotiations with Stuart A. Ramsden at Harwell, England, in 1960. After visiting the NRC, Ramsden accepted the position for a trial period of two to three years, arriving in Ottawa in June 1962 to set up the Plasma Physics Section, later renamed the Laser and Plasma Physics Section. Initial experiments aimed at the investigation of light scattering from plasmas established the importance of laser radiation in determining the densities and temperatures of dense plasmas. The group became involved in building powerful, pulsed laser systems for the production of extremely dense plasmas, as well as for their use as diagnostic tools. Large laser systems of carbon dioxide and of neodimium glass were developed and used in collaboration with research groups in universities, industry, and U.S. National Laboratories. A. John Alcock succeeded Ramsden, who returned to England to head the Applied Physics Department at Hull University. In time, the Laser Group disbanded and separated into smaller units involved in the use of lasers in investigations of surfaces, solids, and extremely short pulses to control the dynamics of atoms and molecules.

Divisions of Pure Physics and Applied Physics

As early as 1944, there were plans for the creation of separate Divisions of Applied Chemistry and Applied Physics. In 1946 a Chemical Engineering Branch was formed, re-named Applied Chemistry in 1947, and finally the Division of Applied Chemistry. This was housed on the Montreal Road campus of the NRC by 1952 in a separate new buiding designed for pilot production plant functions. Perhaps it was inevitable that the splitting of the Division of Physics would soon follow, in parallel with the separation of the Division of Chemistry.

Herzberg understood and accepted the splitting of the Division of Physics into two autonomous branches in June 1952. Howlett became Director of the Applied Physics Branch, which included the Sections of Acoustics, Electricity, Metrology, Optics, Photogrammetry, Photometry and Colorimetry, Radiology, Special Problems, and Temperature and Radiation. Herzberg was Director of the Pure Physics Branch, which included the Sections of Cosmic Rays, Low-Temperature and Solid State Physics, Spectroscopy, Theoretical Physics, and X-Ray Diffraction and Electron

Microscopy. While this break-up of the Division meant that he would lose the valuable daily assistance of Howlett, Herzberg found that he was beginning to have some doubts and to quietly disapprove of some of Howlett's administrative decisions. More importantly, he realized that it was time for Howlett to head a major laboratory at the NRC; Howlett was recognized internationally for his work on photography, and there was concern that he might leave the NRC for a much more lucrative position in industry.

In 1955, Herzberg finally accepted the definitive separation of the Division of Physics into the Divisions of Pure Physics and of Applied Physics. But two years later, he was shocked to learn by chance that architect's plans existed for a new building for the Division of Applied Physics. Steacie and Howlett had decided on a new building and had planned it for the Montreal Road complex without including Herzberg in any of the discussions. He complained to Steacie, pointing out that if the Sussex building could not hold the two Divisions with their planned expansions, then he would have preferred that both Divisions be moved to one large building on the new campus.

Herzberg recognized the strong interplay between basic research and technology and how each in turn aids the other to further advances. In fact, the two are so closely intertwined and dependent on each other that it is difficult to see how one can progress without the other. Thus, Herzberg strongly believed in having all of the physicists in one building, whether working on fundamental or applied problems; they interacted very well at the NRC and helped each other through discussions and joint seminars, as well as technical know-how. This would no longer be possible since the two Divisions would now be separated by about ten kilometres. Herzberg felt that this decision was one of Steacie's serious mistakes as President.[13] It also led to a cooling of Herzberg's relationship with Howlett. The Division of Applied Physics eventually moved into the new building on the Montreal Road campus in 1962.

On the retirement of Howlett in September 1968, Herzberg was asked to substitute as Acting Director of Applied Physics until a new director was appointed. Alex Douglas was considered to be the choice candidate, but he was reticent about assuming this title. Only when Herzberg's mandatory retirement as Director came a year later did Douglas agree to succeed him, with the proviso that the two Divisions be united to again become the Division of Physics. In spite of this heavy responsibility, Douglas managed to maintain some research activity in the Spectroscopy Laboratory.

Inspiring Leadership

As the NRC became internationally recognized as a leading centre for research in science, technology, and engineering, world centres such as the National Physical Laboratory in England, the Max-Planck Institute of Germany, the Centre Nationale de la Recherche Scientifique of France, and research institutes of many other countries sent groups of scientists and administrators to Ottawa to learn about the operation of the NRC. In addition to discussions with President Mackenzie and later President Steacie, these groups visited some of the Divisions and laboratories and invariably the Division of Physics and Herzberg. Taking his cue from the practice of both Mackenzie and Steacie, Herzberg would emphasize that administration at the NRC was there to serve the working scientists and engineers. And he liked to add his own surprise by informing visiting groups that although he was the Director of the Division, he did not direct. He saw his role as hiring the best scientists available when positions were to be filled and giving encouragement to all by providing the best facilities possible for scientists to work on problems of their own choosing. One could not ask for a more enlightened view to bring out the best efforts in people.

In scientific discovery chance favours only the prepared mind.

Louis Pasteur

16. RESEARCH AND WORLDWIDE ACCLAIM

Within a few years, the Spectroscopy Laboratory was in full swing and producing new results on atomic and molecular spectra and the properties and structures of many diatomic and polyatomic molecules. The most up-to-date techniques in atomic beam, microwave, Raman, infrared, and electronic spectroscopy were developed and used by the staff and postdoctorate fellows to obtain these data. Starting from nothing, in twenty years the apparatus grew to become the world's largest collection of high-resolution spectrographs and spectrometers, and Canada's first lasers were built there. The spin and magnetic moments of nuclei were measured and the interaction between nuclear and electronic motions were studied. Spectra of diatomic and polyatomic molecules and free radicals were obtained, many for the first time; carbon–carbon distances were shown to be dependent on the number of neighbouring bonds; a variety of very weak forbidden transitions were investigated; and spectra of molecular ions were observed and analyzed. These studies were important for the development and confirmation of atomic and molecular theory, as well as for determining molecular structures in ground and excited states. They often proved to be significant for astrophysics. In the first twenty years, over one hundred visiting scientists worked in the laboratory for periods of four months or more, and their results were presented at numerous national and international conferences and published in over 400 papers in established scientific journals.

Favourite Research

Herzberg's own interests and experiments in atomic and molecular spectra continued on a broad front, but he concentrated his efforts on obtaining the spectra of the free radicals CH_2 and CH_3, the cornerstones of organic chemistry. He was also determined to find a spectrum of H_3^+, an important ion in interstellar clouds since it appears to be the starting point for molecule formation in space. Another tantalizing problem that intrigued him was an explanation of the diffuse interstellar bands: over a hundred broad absorption lines had been observed since the 1930s, but not one had been identified or reproduced in the laboratory. While these were the main challenges Herzberg set for himself, he made major contributions on a variety of other problems. Some could be termed "bread and butter" research, carried out while waiting for improvements in apparatus for the major studies. But each investigation had good reasons to be undertaken: to either provide more precise molecular constants or to test and confirm theory and so provide examples for his Volume III. These many studies were carried out with the help of his technician Jack Shoosmith, an assistant, and two postdoctoral fellows and sometimes in collaboration with visiting colleagues. In addition, Herzberg continually worked on his remaining treatise *Electronic Spectra of Polyatomic Molecules* of the molecular trilogy and focused his attention on it from 1960 until its publication in 1966.

Herzberg's day at the NRC began with his arrival at 8 A.M. or earlier, and after donning his white lab coat, he would scan with a magnifying glass in hand the photographic plate of a spectrum he was studying at that time. This habit of perusing the riddles of spectra, where every line means something, gave him inspiration and set his mind on the main research course for the day. He then visited Jack Shoosmith in the laboratory to discuss in detail the results of their past few days and work out together the best course for the next series of experiments. Next, he would check with his computing assistant on what progress or problems had occurred in analysis or calculation of spectra and then return to his office to tackle administrative problems with his secretary, usually dictating scores of letters and reviewing the day's schedule of meetings, appointments, and visitors. Any time left over was used to visit his collaborators, analyze spectra, write papers, prepare presentations for scientific meetings, and try to catch up on reading the steady stream of technical journals and papers that crossed his desk. Yet he made a point of joining the group at afternoon tea and of always being on call to members of the spectroscopy staff and of the Division of Physics. The office day would end with him piling notes and journals into a bulging briefcase and leaving for home at about 7 P.M. Saturdays, too, were long days; Herzberg would be closeted in his office with numerous periodicals, papers, and tables of data while writing and revising the manuscript for *Electronic Spectra of Polyatomic Molecules*.

Atomic Spectra, Experiments, and Theory

Herzberg began a lengthy program of accurate measurements of absolute wavelengths for spectra of deuterium (D), helium and its ion (He, He^+), and ionized lithium (Li^+) in the vacuum ultraviolet in order to obtain experimental values to test theoretical predictions for Lamb shifts, an effect first observed in hydrogen by Lamb and Retherford in 1947.[1] For these evaluations, he also needed theoretical values of specific energy levels and ionization potentials, but the available values turned out to be far less reliable than had been assumed, and so he became involved in computations using variational methods, something quite new in his research. As told by his friend Chandra, this all started when the two of them met to discuss the problem during a conference of the American Astronomical Society in December 1952, and it soon became a cause célèbre:

> Herzberg explained to me the sorry state of the wavelength standards in the far ultraviolet and inquired whether the theoretical value for the energy of the ground state of helium obtained by the Norwegian theorist E.A. Hylleraas could be used as a guide.
>
> Some years earlier (1946–7) while engaged on the related problem of the ground state of the ion H^-, I had, in the course of some checking, found an error in one of Hylleraas's matrix elements and had concluded that his value for the ground state of helium must be in error. And when I told Herzberg of this fact he was visibly shocked. He told me that the matter should be brought out in the open; at his insistence, we collaborated on a re-evaluation of the energy of the ground state of helium with a wavefunction having eleven parameters; and this calculation showed that Hylleraas's value was indeed in error, and hence that the theoretical value was substantially higher than the experimental value.
>
> Herzberg and I later improved the calculation with a wavefunction of eighteen parameters, and that started an avalanche of wavefunctions with a continued crescendo of parameters. It is impossible to believe now, that for some 25 years it was considered as firmly established that eight parameters would suffice when in fact 1000 are needed.[2]

These results provoked many theorists to calculate the energy levels and ionization limit of He, as well as to re-calculate corrections for the fine structure of hydrogen, helium, and two-electron systems. Chandrasekhar and Herzberg also evaluated the ground-state energies of Li^+ and O^{6+}, after which Herzberg continued variational calculations of He and He-like ions for another decade with J.F. Hart of the University of Toronto.[3]

In 1954, Herzberg was invited to give a lecture at the Rydberg Centennial Conference in Lund, Sweden, and during the talk he mentioned his preliminary value of the ground-state Lamb shift for deuterium obtained from the difference of observed and calculated wavelengths for the Lyman-α line at 1215.3378 Å. The result was 25 percent lower than the theoretical prediction. Neither Paul Dirac nor Wolfgang Pauli, two of the giants of theoretical physics and Nobel Laureates, nor Herzberg's friend Walter Heitler, could believe that the shift could be lower than the calculated shift. In fact, Pauli in his usual critical yet friendly manner told Herzberg that his result was "a manifestation of experimental error". On telling of this incident after he had made more precise measurements, Herzberg roared with laughter saying "and Pauli was right". When the work on the Lamb shift of the ground state of deuterium was completed, giving a value of 0.264 cm^{-1} in agreement with theory (0.2726 cm^{-1}), Herzberg sent a copy of his manuscript to Willis Lamb for comments and congratulated him on being awarded the 1955 Nobel Prize for his discovery of the fine structure of the hydrogen spectrum.[4] In his reply, Lamb added the following anecdote, which understandably pleased Herzberg:

> I don't know if I have ever written to tell you that the first suggestion that microwaves and hydrogen atoms should be combined came from your book on atomic structure. I was teaching a summer session class in atomic theory at Columbia in 1945 with your book as text. The footnote referring to Betz and Haase put the idea in my mind.... Of course, if I had studied Grotrian's book in my college days I might have had the idea sooner, but it took the war to teach me about microwaves.[5]

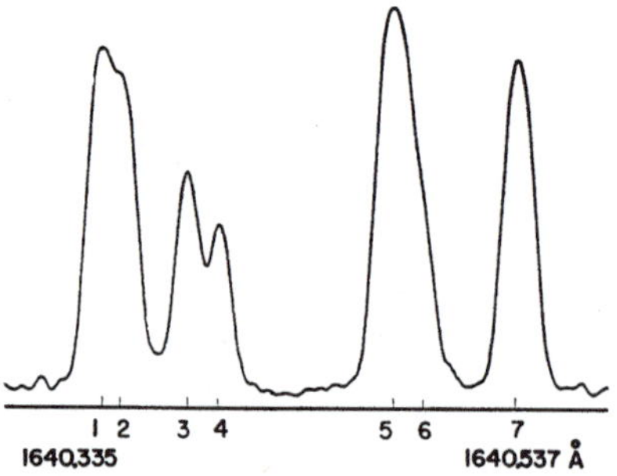

Components	Observed Splitting	Theoretical values: Dirac	Theoretical values: Quantum electrodynamics
(1)-(2)	0.47_7	0	0.4658
(2)-(4)	1.73_7	1.7312	1.7352
(3)-(4)	0.59_0	0	0.6082
(3)-(7)	5.85_8	5.8428	5.8563
(5)-(7)	2.19_6	2.3082	2.1711
	$cm.^{-1}$	$cm.^{-1}$	$cm.^{-1}$

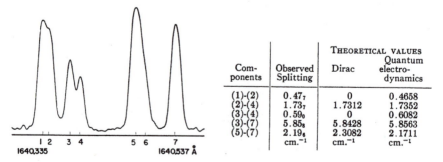

Spectrum of the 1640 Å line of He^+ and observed and predicted splittings, after Herzberg, 1956.

Herzberg was able to obtain experimental values of Lamb shifts for excited states of He and Li^+ in general agreement with theory. His measurements of the separation of components of the 1640 and 4686 Å lines of He^+, which included sums of Lamb shifts of the ground and excited states, agreed with quantum electrodynamic values of these splittings. He continued with experiments and calculations of ionization potentials until the ground states of two-electron systems were determined with sufficient precision to confirm the theoretical Lamb shifts for ^3He and ^4He. He ceased working on fine structure problems a few years later, when the new laser techniques superseded the accuracy obtainable with photographic measurements.[6]

Spectra of Hydrogen in the Laboratory, in Planetary Atmospheres, and in Space

At the time of his earliest studies of the spectrum of atomic hydrogen in 1927, Herzberg became intrigued with the spectrum of molecular hydrogen, which overlapped that of atomic hydrogen. While H_2 is one of the simplest molecules, its spectrum is far from simple. Herzberg realized that experimental data of H_2 and its isotopes would be of fundamental importance for testing quantum theory and of significance for astrophysics since hydrogen is the most abundant constituent of the universe. So began his concerted study of the infrared and far-ultraviolet spectra of molecular hydrogen.

With the publication of the quadrupole spectrum of hydrogen, which Herzberg investigated at Yerkes Observatory, he turned his attention to the mixed isotope HD. This has a small dipole moment because the centre of mass does not coincide with the centre of charge and is expected to exhibit a weak spectrum. Herzberg had suggested in 1938 that such a spectrum could be used to detect deuterium in planetary and stellar atmospheres.[7] In 1950, he succeeded in observing several rotation–vibration lines of the 3–0 and 4–0 bands of HD by using a 500-metre path of gas at atmospheric pressure and later obtained the 1–0 band in the infrared.[8] Two decades later, HD was observed in a spectrum of Jupiter.[9]

While Herzberg had expected that the presence of hydrogen in planetary atmospheres would be revealed by observation of the quadrupole spectrum that he had produced at Yerkes, the first proof came from a quite unexpected source, and he was able to capitalize on it. In 1949, Gerard

Kuiper, his friend from Yerkes, found a number of weak and broad features in spectra of the planets Uranus and Neptune.[10] These bands were not due to methane, which was known from earlier work to be present in Uranus, and Kuiper asked Herzberg whether he had any idea of what could give rise to these broad bands. A feature at 8270 Å agreed closely with a line of the 3–0 quadrupole spectrum of H_2 but was clearly not a quadrupole line since these are extremely sharp. That same year, Harry Welsh and his colleagues in Toronto had discovered in the laboratory a new, very broad spectrum of hydrogen (the 1–0 and 2–0 bands) at high gas pressure, which came to be known as the pressure-induced spectrum of hydrogen.[11] Herzberg surmised that the Uranus feature could be caused by the pressure-induced 3–0 band of hydrogen. He wrote to Kuiper about his idea, telling him that he was beginning experiments with H_2 at high pressure and a long absorbing path, cooled to liquid nitrogen temperature. Under these conditions, Herzberg observed a broad 3–0 band, in agreement with the spectra of Uranus and Neptune, and so established for the first time the presence of hydrogen in extraterrestrial atmospheres, and specifically in these planets. From a comparison of the laboratory spectrum with that of Uranus, he was able to estimate a temperature of about 80 K and a pressure of 6–8 atmospheres on the planet.[12]

A decade later, the sharp lines of the quadrupole spectrum of H_2 were observed in emission in Jupiter and, later, in spectra of Uranus and Saturn taken with high-resolution instruments.[13] Such emission spectra provide a powerful means to study the hot gases in planetary ionospheres, circumstellar atmospheres, planetary nebulae, and superluminous galaxies. Finally, H_2 was identified in the interstellar medium by its electronic spectrum in the far-ultraviolet region, first taken by rockets in 1970[14] and a few years later by means of the Copernicus satellite.[15] Even the spectrum of the isotopic molecule HD was detected in the interstellar medium.[16] These matched perfectly with spectra taken by Herzberg in the laboratory and left no doubt that molecular hydrogen is present in the interstellar medium.

Tests of the Quantum Theory of Molecular Hydrogen

The first experimental determinations of the energy required to break up the hydrogen molecule into two hydrogen atoms, that is the dissociation

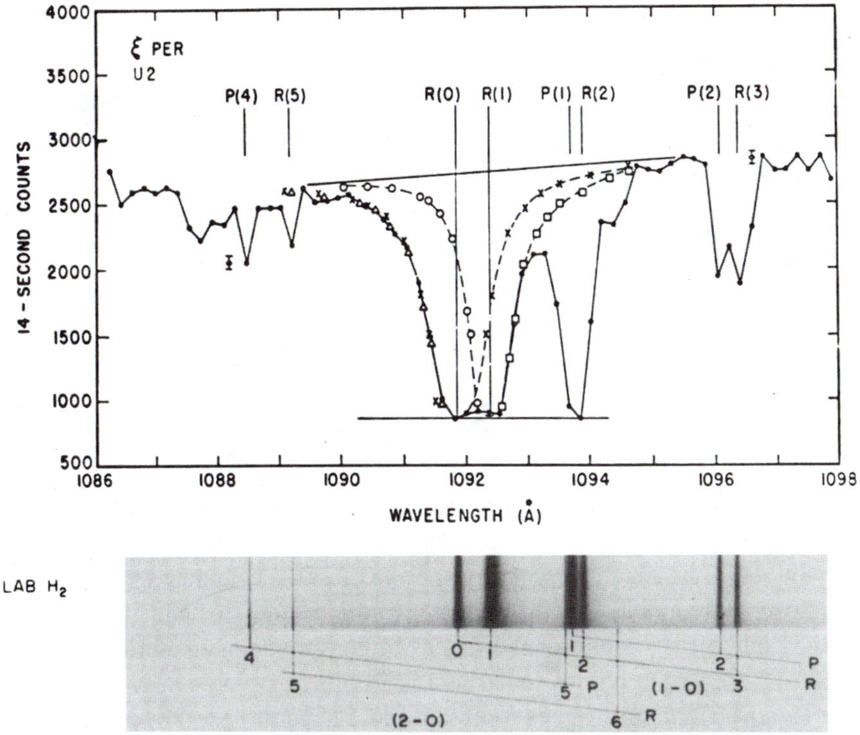

H_2 interstellar absorption lines near 1090 Å after Spitzer *et al.*[15] compared with a laboratory spectrum, 1973.

energy, were made in 1926–1927, just at the time of the development of the quantum mechanical calculations by Heitler and London. Improvements in computed values were made up to 1935, but the accuracy was not high. Two decades later, new techniques in high-resolution infrared, far-ultraviolet, and Raman spectroscopy at the NRC made it possible to determine precise values for the energy levels of the ground and excited states of hydrogen and its isotopes.[17,18] At the same time, the availability of modern computers provided the opportunity to make calculations of these levels from first principles (*ab initio*), and comparisons of experimental and calculated values were extended to such basic quantities as rotational and vibrational energy levels, and dissociation energies and ionization potentials, in order to test quantum theory.

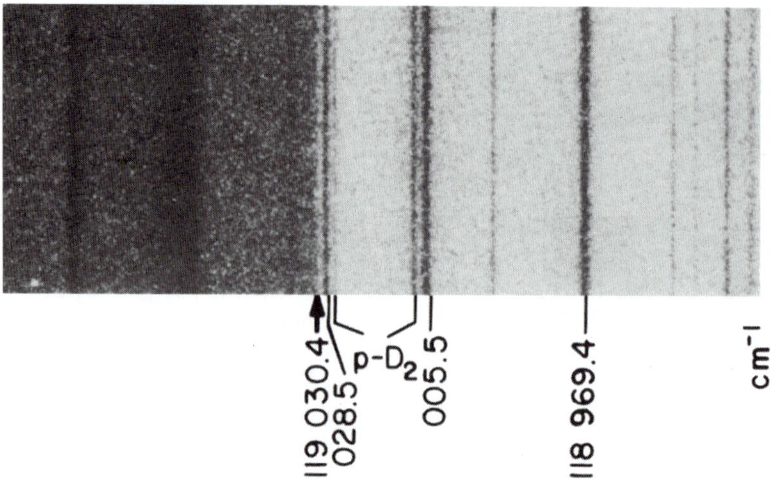

Absorption limit (dissociation energy) of D_2 near 840.1 Å, after Herzberg, 1969.

In 1960, the much-improved experimental and calculated values were in closer agreement, but discrepancies still existed for the dissociation energy and for the vibrational energies of the ground state. Only when the NRC 10-metre ultraviolet spectrograph became available was it possible for Herzberg and colleagues to obtain more accurate experimental values for the dissociation energy and ionization potential, and these were in good agreement with theoretical values.[19,20] Finally, calculations using improved potential functions, including the interaction of the ground state with excited electronic states, gave excellent agreement between *ab initio* and experimental data for the ground state. Herzberg continued his investigations of the electronic spectra of molecular hydrogen and its isotopes into the late 1990s and obtained detailed data of the highly excited states of hydrogen.

From his first publications on hydrogen in 1927, Herzberg's seminal contributions on atomic and molecular hydrogen were reported in over forty papers. In a presidential address given at the end of his term as President of The Royal Society of Canada in 1967, Herzberg chose to review the current knowledge of hydrogen with the topic "The spectra of hydrogen and their role in the development of our understanding of the structure of matter and of the universe".[21] This was perhaps not the proper occasion for such an exhaustive treatment of the subject since the Society was not solely an Academy of Science and its membership included scholars in the humanities and social sciences. He began by quoting Victor Weisskopf that

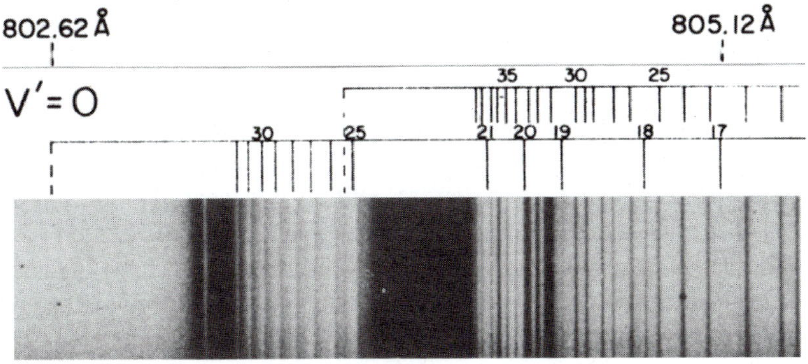

Absorption spectrum of para-H_2 showing two Rydberg series, going to two different limits, after Herzberg and Jungen, 1972.

"if you understand hydrogen, you understand all that can be understood".[22] After listening to an hour-long dissertation illustrated with copious slides, the incoming president of the Society, geologist James Harrison, in thanking Herzberg, added that he believed "if we could understand hydrogen we could understand anything".

Spectra of Free Radicals

Free radicals are chemically unstable diatomic and polyatomic molecules that are short-lived (transient) in the gas phase. They had long been postulated by chemists as intermediates in chemical reactions, and the building blocks of larger molecules, but had not been isolated or characterized by the usual chemical methods. Herzberg argued that as a spectroscopist he would naturally want to observe the spectrum of a free radical before he could feel entirely convinced of its presence in a chemical reaction, a flame, an explosion, or a discharge. Moreover, once the spectrum of a free radical was obtained it would be possible to derive much useful information about its electronic and geometrical structure and its behaviour.

Herzberg first became interested in polyatomic free radicals in 1942, when he had reproduced in the laboratory in Saskatchewan a spectrum at 4050 Å found in comets.[23] He had used a discharge in methane (CH_4) and thought he had produced the spectrum of the free radical CH_2. Only seven years later at the NRC did he have the opportunity to carry out further experiments to confirm this result. That year, a paper appeared describing the results of an experiment similar to his in 1942 but using heavy methane (CD_4) instead of CH_4. The 4050 Å feature was reproduced and had exactly the same appearance and wavelength as that of CH_4, whereas if the feature belonged to CH_2 it should certainly have changed or shifted in going to CD_2. This result was a shock for Herzberg who thought he had found the spectrum of CH_2 seven years before. Within two years Douglas proved conclusively that the 4050 Å spectrum was due to triatomic carbon (C_3).[24]

These results posed a supreme challenge for Herzberg: what in fact was the true spectrum of CH_2? His pursuit of this question culminated in what undoubtedly became one of his most notable and satisfying achievements, the first observation of the spectra of the free methyl (CH_3) and methylene (CH_2) radicals. Seventeen years after Herzberg's first involvement with CH_2, his persistence and determination finally solved this puzzle. Such tenacity was to be repeated on several other occasions and was illustrated by Luise in an amusing incident about life at home:

> Gerhard being a vegetarian and not accustomed to gourmet dishes was quite happy with being served omelettes and potatoes for dinner, day after day. One evening, Luise cooked spaghetti for dinner, and while Gerhard liked it he reminded her, "Now Luise, when you have found a good thing and like it, you stick with it!"

With Shoosmith's help, Herzberg tried several different experimental approaches in an effort to obtain the spectrum of CH_2, all in vain. Finally he settled on the technique of flash photolysis, which he and Ramsay were

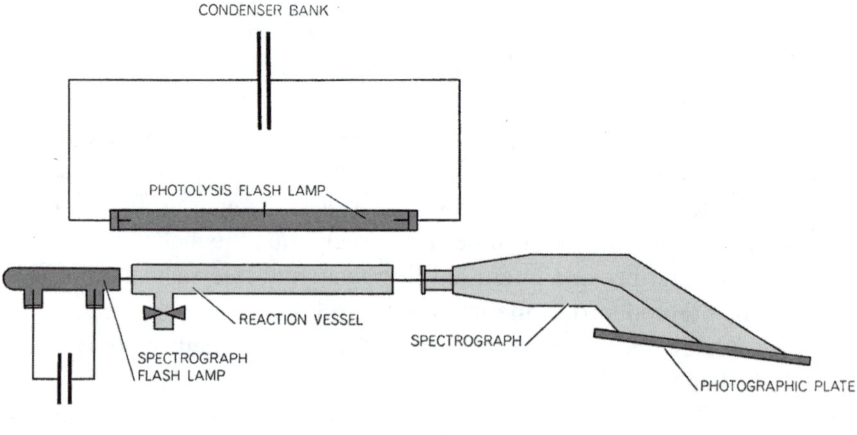

Diagram of a flash-photolysis apparatus.

pioneering. In this technique, a long reaction vessel containing the parent compound serves as the absorption tube. It is irradiated along its length by a powerful pulsed flash lamp through which a condenser of high capacity is discharged. The extremely bright flash of short duration (10–500 microseconds) provides the energy to break up the parent molecules to momentarily produce a concentration of fragments, that is, short-lived free radicals, in the absorption tube. A very short time afterward, and this interval can be controlled, the light from a second flash lamp (providing a continuum spectrum) is sent through the absorption tube and into the spectrograph to obtain the absorption spectrum. By varying the time interval between flashes from the two lamps while taking absorption spectra, the life of free radicals can be determined, usually in the range of microseconds. In this way, Herzberg and Shoosmith first succeeded in obtaining spectra of CH_3 from the parent molecules $Hg(CH_3)_2$ and $(CH_3)_2CO$ in 1956. Proof that in fact the spectrum observed at 2160 Å was that of CH_3 was established by using partially deuterated samples which produced four slightly shifted spectra arising from the isotopic species CH_3, CH_2D, CHD_2, and CD_3.[25] Accolades for this work came from many colleagues, including competitors such as Norrish in Cambridge, who wrote: "I greatly envy your spectroscopic techniques and wish that we could match them".[26] In the following year, Herzberg presented his results on CH_3 and his attempts to find the

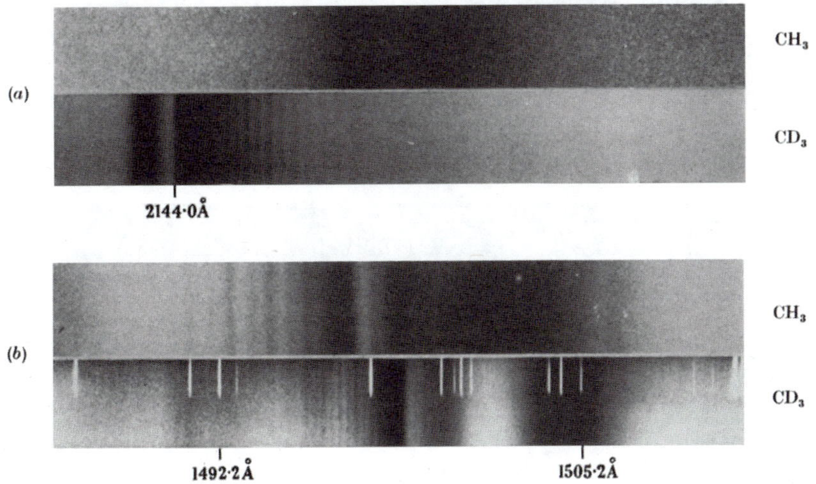

Rotational structure of CH_3 and CD_3 absorption bands: (*a*) at 2150 Å and (*b*) at 1500 Å, after Herzberg and Shoosmith, 1956.

spectrum of CH_2 when invited to give the Centenary Lecture of The Chemical Society in London, Southampton, Dundee, Sheffield, and Liverpool.

Two years later, Herzberg's continuing efforts to produce a spectrum of CH_2 were finally rewarded. In this case, the parent molecule was CH_2N_2, an explosive compound, and the spectrum was found in the extreme ultraviolet region, which also posed several difficulties. Shoosmith carried out many experiments and, on developing the photographic plate, one day found that a prominent new feature was present at about 1415 Å. He imme-

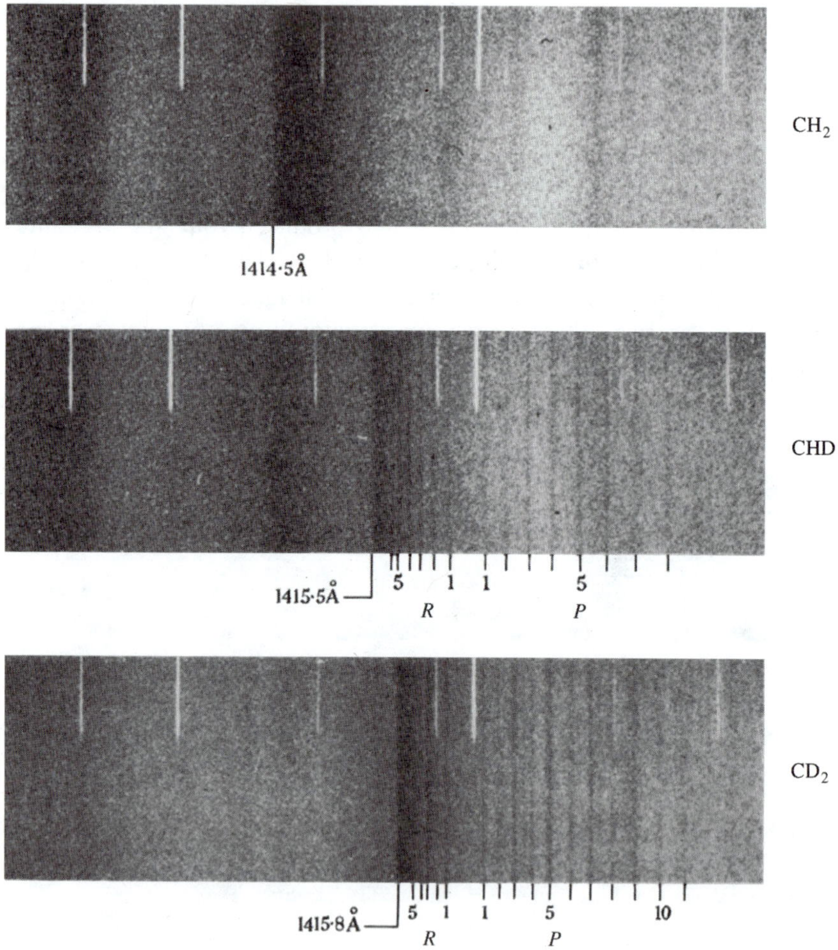

Rotational structure of CH_2, CHD, and CD_2 absorption bands near 1415 Å under high resolution, after Herzberg and Shoosmith, 1959.

Herzberg, Jack Shoosmith, and M. Horani examining a spectrum, 1969.

diately bounded up to Herzberg's office with the news. Herzberg was very busy at the time, but Shoosmith insisted that he had to come to the laboratory now to see this plate. By the time they had raced down the two flights of stairs to the lab, a group had gathered to see what all the excitement was about. With one look at the spectrum and realizing this was what they were looking for, an elated Herzberg exclaimed "Oh boy! Oh boy!" It was an inspiring moment.

Further experiments with the partially and fully deuterated compounds ($CHDN_2$ and CD_2N_2) showed three, slightly shifted spectra (due to CH_2, CHD, and CD_2), proving that the free radical had two H atoms, and finally the spectrum with $^{13}CH_2N_2$ established the presence of a carbon atom.[27] Detailed analyses of the spectra led to a non-linear symmetrical structure with C–H distances of 1.071 Å and an H–C–H angle of 140 degrees.[28] Almost four decades later, CH_2 was detected in the interstellar medium, and CH_3 in the atmospheres of Saturn and Neptune and in the interstellar medium.[29–31]

The proof that he had finally discovered the spectrum and structure of CH_2 was one of the most exciting milestones in Herzberg's career. He was immediately congratulated by colleagues around the world for this striking achievement and was invited to give the prestigious Bakerian Lecture of The Royal Society. He presented the results of his discovery in London in November 1960, the year in which The Royal Society, the oldest continuing scientific society, was celebrating its 300th anniversary.[32]

Spectra of over thirty free radicals were discovered and studied by Herzberg, Ramsay, and other members of the laboratory during the 1950s and 1960s.[33] Their method of flash photolysis coupled with the superb spectrographs built at the NRC changed in a dramatic manner the field of free radicals from unobservable chemical intermediates to well-known molecules and provided a gold mine of new molecules for study.

This long-standing problem of the spectra and structures of CH_2 and CH_3 and Herzberg's many attempts to solve it perhaps best exemplify the manner in which much of science is actually done. Rather than the direct methods described in published papers on a project, which usually read as though the ideas and procedures are straightforward and lead directly to the desired result, the actual path is often one step forward and one or two steps back, in reality a zigzag pattern, either because of somewhat incorrect preconceived ideas or for the lack of suitable equipment and techniques. But persistence and attempts with a variety of different methods as they become available may finally lead to success, as occurred with Herzberg and his discovery of the spectra of CH_2 and CH_3 after almost two decades of thinking about the problem.

Molecules of Astrophysical Interest and the Diffuse Interstellar Bands

The research of Herzberg and Douglas was often stimulated by astrophysical problems and particularly by the question of what species could give rise to the many diffuse interstellar bands found in the visible and near-infrared regions of the spectrum. Thus, in addition to his continuing investigations of absorption spectra of free radicals, and of hydrogen, oxygen, and carbon monoxide in the extreme ultraviolet, Herzberg studied emission and absorption spectra obtained by a variety of sources, including hot-cathode tubes, ordinary and flash discharges, and flash radiolysis. By these means, he and his group found the spectra of many molecular ions, diatomic as well as polyatomic. Such spectra are important for an understanding of the electronic structure of molecules, for the study of ion molecule reactions, and for the chemistry of the interstellar medium. They observed and analyzed spectra of C_2^+, CO_2^+, N_2O^+, $C_4H_2^+$, and H_2S^+ and discovered the spectrum of C_2^-, the first discrete spectrum of a gaseous negative molecular ion. Douglas and colleagues investigated spectra of CO^+ and N_2^+, which along with CO_2^+ and CH^+ occur fairly strongly in the spectra of comets and especially in comet tails.[34] However, none of the laboratory ion spectra coincided with the observed diffuse interstellar bands. Much of Herzberg's future research was motivated by his continuing interest in molecular astrophysics, especially in the quest for the elusive molecular ion H_3^+ and the carriers of the diffuse interstellar bands.

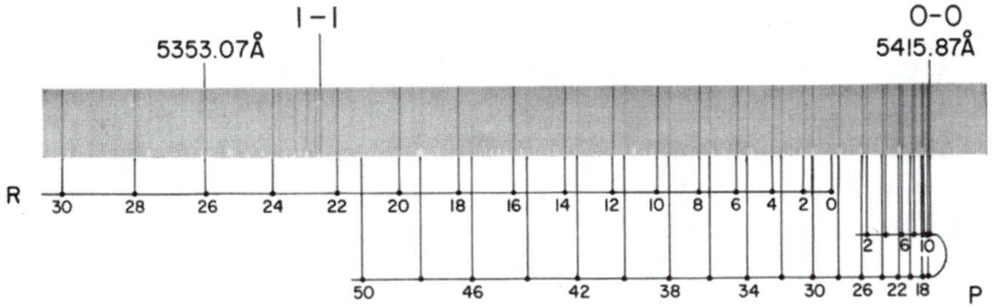

Absorption spectrum of the ion C_2^-, after Herzberg and Lagerqvist, 1968.[35]

It is not to have climbed Everest that matters:
it is to have seen the Everest in oneself.

Robertson Davies

17. AMBASSADOR OF CANADIAN SCIENCE

With the constant stream of visitors to the NRC and such an active research program on a variety of topics, and with progress reported in an ever-increasing number of publications from his laboratory, it was inevitable that Herzberg and the Spectroscopy Laboratory would quickly gain international attention. He was invited to participate in essentially every conference on molecular spectroscopy, usually as a keynote speaker. These numerous invitations to give lectures took him to many countries and research institutes around the world. He attended as many national and international meetings dealing with molecular spectra and structures as his NRC duties permitted, and he encouraged members of the laboratory to do likewise. He knew that in order to keep abreast of worldwide progress and to remain in the forefront in this rapidly expanding field, personal interaction with colleagues was of the utmost importance, and conferences provided the necessary forum for discussion and exchange of ideas.

North American Conferences

The International Symposium on Molecular Spectroscopy at Ohio State University in Columbus, Ohio, was the main meeting in North America for all active scientists in this field. This annual meeting, held for a week in June, was organized immediately after the war by Harald H. Nielsen, an eminent theorist at the university. The pattern of these meetings reminded Herzberg of those arranged by Mulliken and Struve that he had attended at The University of Chicago in the late 1930s and early 1940s. Members of the Spectroscopy Laboratory attended the Columbus meetings on a regular basis and presented invited and contributed papers on their most recent research. These were exciting meetings, and many of the giants in the field (David M. Dennison, John H. Van Vleck, Walter Gordy, Charles H. Townes, Peter Debye, E. Bright Wilson, Robert S. Mulliken, Harald H. Nielsen, Bryce L. Crawford, Earle K. Plyler, Richard C. Lord, Gordon B.B.M. Sutherland, Harold W. Thompson, and Gerhard Herzberg) were present. For the younger researchers and graduate students, the Columbus meetings were the highlight of the year; there were discussions of many innovations in theory and experimental techniques and especially the chance to mingle and get acquainted with the movers in the field. Another important set of molecular spectroscopy meetings were part of the Gordon Research Conferences, held annually in New Hampshire in the summers. Meetings on infrared and Raman spectroscopy and electronic spectroscopy were held in alternate years, with technical programs organized by different groups and attendance limited to about one hundred scientists. By the mid-1950s, at the end of the infamous McCarthy era (the beginnings of which had helped to persuade the Herzbergs to leave Yerkes Observatory), many eminent European and Japanese spectroscopists were eventually granted visas to the United States and were able to participate at these meetings.

A special two-week symposium was held in Ottawa in June 1955 in honour of Paul Dirac, Lucasian Professor of Mathematics in Cambridge University and Nobel Laureate in 1933 along with Erwin Schrödinger for the discovery of new productive forms of atomic theory. The idea for this meeting came about because Dirac was refused a visa to the United States. He had originally planned to spend two weeks with Ta-You Wu's theoretical group in Ottawa following a proposed visit to Princeton University in 1954. However, Dirac wrote to Herzberg that he had been denied a U.S.

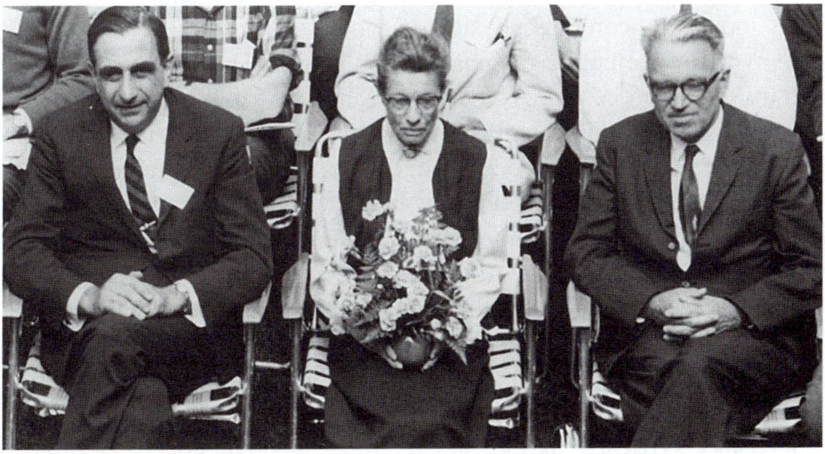

Göttingen colleagues Edward Teller, Hertha Sponer, and Gerhard Herzberg at a Gordon Conference on Molecular Electronic Spectroscopy, 1964.

visa.[1] Herzberg immediately began to organize a colloquium in theoretical physics to be held at the NRC to give Dirac's American friends the opportunity to meet with him. Friends and colleagues in the U.S.A. were stunned to learn of Dirac's denial of entry and felt humiliated by the inability to be proper hosts to foreign colleagues. One even suggested that "We should really have our universities and institutes on Ellis Island".

Herzberg invited senior theorists from the United States and Canada to participate in the Dirac Colloquium, and the large attendance of theorists and experimentalists signalled its huge success.[2] Among the principal speakers were H.A. Bethe, G. Breit, R.J. Eden, S. Chandrasekhar, V.F. Weisskopf, G.M. Volkoff, W.H. Watson, and G. Wentzel. Some who were not able to come because of prior commitments to be in Europe or because of illness included Eugene Wigner, Abraham Pais, J. Robert Oppenheimer, and Enrico Fermi, who died a month after receiving the invitation. Unfortunately, Dirac himself was not able to attend the Colloquium because of extended illness after a long sojourn in India. He and his wife arrived in Ottawa a few weeks later and stayed for two months to rest and recover, and he was able to give a series of lectures. Dirac again visited the NRC for a month in 1959. A further outcome of the Dirac Colloquium, and a tribute to the far-sighted Herzberg, was that it brought together for the first time over a hundred Canadian theoretical physicists and so helped to promote the formation of a theoretical section of the Canadian Association of Physicists, which began to hold annual colloquia and summer schools on timely topics in theoretical physics.

A two-day memorial symposium was held at The University of Chicago in May 1966 in honour of James Franck (1882–1964), who had died two years earlier while visiting friends in Germany. Herzberg's opinion about invited speakers had been sought by the organizers, and during the planning stages he mentioned his worry that possibly among the invitees from Germany might be some whose behaviour during the Nazi regime Franck found especially objectionable. He suggested that the list of names should be sent to Mrs. Hertha Sponer-Franck for her opinion.[3] The Symposium, with an attendance of two hundred, was a welcome celebration of Franck's achievements. Some thought of it as a "Göttingen reunion" of colleagues, as much German was spoken and many messages arrived from Franck's friends of the happier days in Germany. Herzberg was invited to give the opening talk and chose to discuss Franck's earliest molecular research and the importance of the Franck–Condon principle to molecular spectroscopy. Edward Teller recalled Franck's remarkable personal qualities, as did Franck's colleague Robert Pohl in a talk given by his son, and Eugene Rabinowitch spoke of Franck's political contributions, especially the "Franck Report".[4]

Visits to Europe and Germany

Herzberg's first trip to Europe and return to Germany in 1950 was much anticipated, with the opportunity to meet colleagues at conferences and to see his brother and friends in Hamburg and Darmstadt. Yet he had some qualms about his visit to Germany, particularly with the possibility of meeting ex-Nazi science colleagues. He discussed his plans with President Mackenzie, who immediately approved of his travel and visits to laboratories in England and the Continent. The Department of External Affairs saw no reason why Herzberg should not make these visits and obtained Military Permits for him to visit Bonn and Hamburg in the British Zone and Darmstadt in the American Zone of West Germany. Herzberg had been invited to visit and give a lecture at the University of Bonn by Professor W. Weizel, whom he considered to be one of the few academics to hold high democratic ideals and was worthy of support by visits from scientists in the Allied countries.

After having made all of the necessary arrangements with colleagues he planned to visit, Herzberg cancelled the trip on learning that Luise had to have an operation in June, only two years after surgery in Chicago. This was another trying period for the whole family, particularly for Paul and Agnes, since this was the end of the school year with its many examinations. With Luise's surprisingly rapid recovery, Herzberg was able to resume plans for a part of his overseas trip, after delaying his departure by almost two months. He spent a much shorter time away from home yet managed to attend the Faraday Society Meeting in London and spectroscopy meetings in Liège and Amsterdam and to visit over twenty laboratories. He met many of his scientific friends in Oxford, Cambridge, and Bristol, as well as in Liège, Amsterdam, and Paris, and some of his former colleagues in Darmstadt. On the whole, his brief visit to Germany was more agreeable than he had expected, although he had to put up with the fact that he could not avoid shaking hands with a number of known former Nazis, who somehow had managed to remain in high academic positions. He was especially pleased to see his mentor Rau in Darmstadt and his brother Walter and boyhood friends Alfred and Hans-Werner in Hamburg. Wherever he turned, he saw evidence of the wartime devastation of Darmstadt and Hamburg, yet he found that the revival of German universities was proceeding at an accelerated pace. In particular, the Technische Hochschule in Darmstadt, which had been almost completely destroyed, was making very good progress; the new Physics Institute was greatly enlarged, the equipment available was adequate, and the workshop facilities were as good as anywhere.

It was during his visit to the University of Oxford that Herzberg met the dynamic D.K.C. MacDonald and made him an offer to come to the NRC to establish a low-temperature and solid-state physics laboratory, which he duly accepted, arriving in Ottawa a year later. Herzberg also visited Norrish and Porter at the University of Cambridge; here they had developed the technique of flash photolysis and were to receive the 1967 Nobel Prize in Chemistry for this achievement. Herzberg told the story of how Norrish met him at the railway station and took him to the nearby tavern. Norrish was enjoying his pint and Herzberg was having tea, when Mrs. Norrish arrived and was furious that lunch was being ruined because they were a half-hour late, "... but Herzberg needed a drink," Norrish explained. Towards the end of his brief stay in Cambridge, Herzberg received a note from Prof. H. Fröhlich about Emil Wolf, a young Czechoslovakian refugee who was his assistant at the time, asking for advice and help in finding employment for him in Canada.[5] At Fröhlich's suggestion, Wolf went to see Herzberg, who was just at the point of leaving Cambridge, but Herzberg was sensitive to this request and invited Wolf to ride with him in the taxi to the railway station to discuss the matter. On his return to Canada, Herzberg made inquiries to several colleges and universities as to whether there were openings for this "pleasant and serious young scientist", and Wolf was later contacted by them. Wolf thanked Herzberg for his efforts and informed him that he was still interested in coming to Canada but in the meantime had accepted an invitation from Max Born in Edinburgh to write a new book on optics. In due course, their volume *Principles of Optics*, based on Born's 1933 treatise *Optik*, became the celebrated classic reference book on optics, and over time, seven updated and expanded editions were published.

Herzberg's next overseas trip came almost a year later and was occasioned by his induction to Fellowship in The Royal Society of London on 31 January 1952. He again gave lectures at many universities and laboratories in England, Ireland, and Europe and visited his brother and friends in Hamburg and Rau in Darmstadt, as well as Heitler in Zurich. Two years later, Herzberg was again in England and on the Continent in June, and this time Luise joined him for her first return to Europe and a holiday in Switzerland. Following this trip, Herzberg was in Europe on almost an annual basis, attending meetings, giving lectures at universities and institutes, and receiving honorary degrees and awards. On one of his visits to Oxford University, he was urged by Francis Simon (later Sir Francis), formerly a research professor in Berlin, to make a claim for restitution in Germany. But Herzberg never did. He maintained that he was better off in Canada and was thankful to Hitler for forcing him to emigrate because he then had much luck and everything in Canada had gone in his favour. In 1948, his father-in-law, Paul Oettinger, began attempts to obtain restitution for the loss of his company in Nürnberg, but without success, and he died in 1957 while in Germany pressing his claim.

With each succeeding visit to Germany, Herzberg felt psychologically more comfortable as the scene slowly changed after the enmity and devastation of the war years. Whenever possible, he squeezed in a holiday in the Alps to enjoy his favourite outdoor activity of hiking and climbing, often with his friends Walter Heitler or Ernst Miescher. Miescher also introduced Herzberg to his friend the nuclear physicist Konrad Bleuler, who invited the Herzbergs to his chalet in Saas-Fee. A close friendship developed, and Gerhard and Luise spent many holidays with the Bleulers in the midst of the glorious Alps and in sight of the Dom, the highest peak in Switzerland.

Herzberg was appointed to the Francqui Chair at the University of Liège in Belgium, and he enjoyed a four-month sojourn in 1960 with colleagues in spectroscopy and astrophysics. His stay in Belgium also gave him the opportunity to visit institutes in Hungary, Sweden, and Denmark and to participate in a meeting commemorating the centenary of Kirchhoff's and Bunsen's discovery of spectral analysis, which was held in Heidelberg, Germany. Besides giving lectures on the work of the Spectroscopy Laboratory, he encouraged young scientists in these countries to apply for postdoctoral positions at the NRC.

Global Travel

Herzberg's first visit to India, at the invitation of the Government of India, occurred in 1957 with his participation in the 44th session of the Indian

Science Congress held in Calcutta.[6] A day after his arrival in mid-January, he gave a lecture to a convention of spectroscopists, and the following day he addressed the Congress. Herzberg was invited to visit the principal scientific institutes in all parts of India and during his five week visit was pressed to give twenty-five talks on his research and on the work of the Spectroscopy Laboratory. His host and companion for much of his stay was his friend R. Krishna Asundi, who took good care that Herzberg was given time to rest between travel and the many lectures and saw to his needs for simple vegetarian meals without the many spices normally used in Indian dishes. Among the many scientists whom Herzberg met were the physicist Homi J. Bhabha in Bombay, the spectroscopist S. Bhagavantam in Hyderabad, and Nobel Laureate Sir C.V. Raman in Bangalore. Along with visits to scientific institutes, Herzberg explored the Ellora and Ajanta caves, marveled at the sublime Taj Mahal, and spent four days in Darjeeling hiking in the foothills of the Himalayas, where he met the Dalai Lama, who was still in power in Tibet and was on a state visit to India.

Herzberg had met Raman in 1929 at the Faraday Meeting in Bristol, when Raman gave a fascinating lecture on his new discovery in light scattering, which came to be known as the Raman effect. During Herzberg's three days in Bangalore, he visited Raman at his institute, where there was much activity on the fluorescence of crystals and spectra of diamonds. Raman made it a habit to come to see him at the hotel each evening for a chat and they had a good time together. It was at this time that Herzberg learned from Raman that he was the uncle of his friend Chandra (who had often talked about Raman with Herzberg at Yerkes but had never mentioned this family relationship). Herzberg also heard from Raman the story of his Nobel Prize. When Raman was elected a Fellow of The Royal Society in 1924 for his research on the acoustics of violin strings, the University of Calcutta had arranged a dinner in his honour. Raman was seated next to the Vice-Chancellor, who complimented him on this wonderful honour, and Raman replied: "Mr. Vice-Chancellor, it's really nothing. The only honour worth having in science is the Nobel Prize, and mark my words, Mr. Vice-Chancellor, in five years I will have it." Raman told Herzberg, "I should have had it in 1928, but I only got it in 1930 because Rutherford wanted Richardson to have it first".[7] This remark surprised Herzberg, "One can wish for the Nobel Prize in one's heart, but one doesn't have to tell other people about it!"

One evening, Raman asked him "Have you ever seen the zodiacal light?" and when Herzberg said that he had not, Raman took him in his chauffeur-driven car out into the country, where it was exceedingly dark, and there overhead was the zodiacal light, a broad band of sunlight reflected by the dust from meteors. Herzberg was much impressed with Raman's personality and with his broad knowledge and interest in all aspects of light. As a parting gift Raman gave Herzberg a signed photograph of himself, but to Herzberg's disappointment Raman did not show him his famous diamond collection, perhaps because he thought that Herzberg was only interested in gases.

His next visit to India in 1962 was a business meeting of the Executive Committee of the International Union of Pure and Applied Physics, on which he served as a Vice-President from 1957 to 1963. This meeting was hosted by Homi Bhabha, President of the International Union. During a recess, Bhabha showed the group a selection of his paintings and drawings of famous scientists and personalities. Five years later, Herzberg and Luise attended the Indian Science Congress as guests of the spectroscopist S. `Bhagavantam and were delighted to have the opportunity to spend a few days in Kathmandu, the capital of Nepal, surrounded by the Himalayas and in sight of Mount Everest.

Another of Herzberg's memorable visits was to Israel to take part in a four-day symposium on the occasion of the opening of the Nuclear Science Institute of the Weizmann Institute in Tel Aviv in May 1958.[8] The list of participants was most impressive, including Niels Bohr, after whom the new institute was named, F. Bloch, S. Chandrasekhar, Herzberg, J.E. Mayer, L. Neel, J.R. Oppenheimer, G.T. Seaborg, H.C. Urey, and V.F. Weisskopf. All were invited with their wives, and all expenses were paid with travel in luxury class. The opening ceremony was attended by the President of Israel and Prime Minister Ben-Gurion, whom they had the opportunity to meet. Bohr gave the primary talk, speaking for over one and a half hours to an audience of about five hundred in an auditorium that seated only three hundred. Bohr was known to have a rambling way of speaking, and this time it was even impossible to know the language in which he was speaking, he was so hard to understand. Chandrasekhar, who was chairing the session, asked the audience, "Are there any questions?" There was only one, and Bohr carried on for another half hour. In a discussion with friends afterward, Chandrasekhar commented about this occasion with a famous epigram: "That's the sign of a really great man—people stay for two hours to listen to something they don't understand!"[9] On the return trip, Gerhard and Luise stopped for brief visits with friends and some sightseeing in Athens, Rome, Madrid, Paris, and London.

A meeting of the International Astronomical Union in Moscow in August 1958 provided the opportunity for a visit to the Soviet Union. Herzberg was most impressed with the caliber of the scientific work in the institutes and observatories he visited in Moscow and Leningrad and with the elaborate hospitality shown throughout his stay. He noted that the capital was serious and glum, without much laughter or conversation in the streets, while Leningrad seemed to be more relaxed and more western than Moscow. Within a year, he was again in the U.S.S.R. (July 1959) for a business meeting of the Executive Committee of the Union of Pure and Applied Physics. On this occasion Herzberg visited S. L. Mandelstam and his Institute of Spectroscopy. They had corresponded a year earlier when Mandelstam sent him a copy of the Russian translation of *Atomic Spectra and Atomic Structures*, and he in turn sent Mandelstam a copy of the English version along with a copy of *Diatomic Molecules*. While in Moscow, Herzberg took the opportunity to visit the Publishing House for Foreign Literature. He had learned of the 1949 Russian translations of his atomic book and Volumes I and II from External Affairs in Ottawa and had written to the publisher inquiring about royalties but had never received a reply. With the help of an interpreter from the Canadian Embassy in Moscow, an appointment was arranged with P. Chuvikov, the Editor , who was very cordial and immediately deposited 40,000 rubles in a Soviet bank for Herzberg. Since these funds could not be taken out of the country, Herzberg purchased a fine Persian fur hat for himself and, at the Editor's suggestion, an airline ticket from Moscow to Montreal and two return tickets from Montreal to Zurich, all of which he returned to the Canadian office of Aeroflot for cash. Further funds from royalties were deposited in the Soviet bank over the years, but with the devaluation of the ruble by a factor of ten in 1961, the balance was only sufficient for purchasing music records and other small items on future visits.[10]

In 1962, Herzberg went to Japan, where he participated as plenary speaker along with S. Mizushima, H.W. Thompson, and E. Bright Wilson, Jr., in the International Congress on Molecular Spectroscopy in Tokyo. In a talk titled "Recent Work on Spectra of Free Radicals", he reviewed the results obtained in Ottawa on spectra of polyatomic free radicals over the past decade and discussed the spectra and structures of the free methyl (CH_3) and methylene (CH_2) radicals.[11] He visited universities in Tokyo and Kyoto and through his lectures encouraged several young Japanese scientists to come to the Spectroscopy Laboratory as postdoctoral fellows, the first being Takeshi Oka, who came in 1963, became a staff member two years later, and quickly established himself as a leading worker in the field of molecular spectroscopy and astrophysics. Herzberg was to make several more visits to Japan, the next being in 1967 when he lectured at many universities.

Herzberg's travel was curtailed somewhat because of a kidney operation in July 1965, but he recovered quickly and continued on his global journeys. He enjoyed visiting and meeting scientific colleagues for discussion and giving lectures on work of the Spectroscopy Laboratory. Wherever he travelled in Australia, India, Europe, the U.S.A., and U.K., he gave major lectures on the work of the Spectroscopy Laboratory and managed to excite candidates who applied for NRC fellowships in spectroscopy and in other branches of the Physics Division.

In August 1971, Herzberg attended the Symposium on Fundamental and Applied Laser Physics in Esfahan, Iran, a city resplendent with its many colorful mosques and the motto "Esfahan is half the world". This small conference was organized by Ali Javan, Professor at the Massachusetts Institute of Technology, who had been born in Iran and was the principal figure in the development of the helium–neon laser at the Bell Telephone Laboratories in New Jersey a decade earlier. The symposium was held just a few weeks before the main celebrations of the 2,500th Anniversary of the Persian Empire. Herzberg's presentation "Experimental Tests of the Quantum Theory of Molecular Hydrogen" and Willis Lamb's "Highly Excited States of the Helium Atom", while not dealing directly with laser work, set the tone for future, precise frequency measurements of atomic and molecular spectra, which had just become possible with lasers.[12] During this conference, Herzberg and several senior scientists were invited to tea with His Majesty Shahanshah Arya-Mehr Pahlavi and His Excellency Prime Minister A. Abbas Hoveida.

With his many overseas journeys to numerous countries, Herzberg had become Canada's unofficial "Ambassador of Science" and in essence one of the world's elder statesmen for science. He also continually travelled across Canada giving lectures and participating in opening ceremonies for several new institutes in physics and chemistry. In 1970, the Canadian

Meeting the Shah of Iran in 1971. Left to right: Pierre Jacquinot, Nicholaas Bloembergen, Herzberg, Rem Khokhlov, and Alexander Prokhorov.

Opening ceremony for the new McLennan Physical Laboratories, University of Toronto, in 1966. Left to right: Omond Solandt, Chancellor, Harry Welsh, Chairman Department of Physics, Jack Sword, Acting President, and Herzberg, unlocking the doors.

Association of Physicists, as part of its twenty-fifth anniversary celebrations, accorded Herzberg a special honour by establishing the Herzberg Medal to be awarded annually "for outstanding achievement in any field of research by a physicist who in the year of the award is not more than thirty-eight years of age". He was genuinely touched by this tribute. On being shown the medal at the Spectroscopy Lab Christmas party that year, Herzberg approved of the vibrational level diagram of the hydrogen molecule on the one side and, on seeing a likeness of himself on the other side exclaimed, "But that doesn't look like me!" At this point Luise, remembering Picasso's reply to Gertrude Stein, who had made a similar comment on seeing the artist's painting of her, smiled and with a twinkle in her eye, calmly remarked, "Just wait".

When travelling or attending conferences, Herzberg would bring sheet music of Mozart, Schubert, Schumann, Brahms, and Verdi and get together with friends to make music. Many of his scientific friends were able musicians, with the piano being the favourite instrument, so there were always opportunities for him to sing, no matter where he was. In Toronto, his accompanist on the piano was Harry Welsh; in Cambridge, then Edinburgh, and later Sussex, it was Christopher Longuet-Higgins; in Southampton, Alan Carrington played the piano while his wife and Herzberg sang duets; in Saas-Fee, Konrad Bleuler accompanied him on the piano; and in France, he sang duets with Gilbert Amat.

In full voice in Columbus, Ohio, with Gilbert Amat and colleagues.

Herzberg's wide-ranging program of research and travel to conferences all over the world, the preparing of papers and technical talks, along with his administrative responsibilities and conscientious attention to answering letters, obviously took its toll on family life. While growing up, Paul and Agnes missed their frequently absent father; they did not realize that he was famous and often had to be away. When he was home, he was up early and so by habit was the rest of the family; breakfast was usually hurried. Gerhard did not like variety in his meals, and Paul and Agnes naturally complained about it. Luise tried to vary their dinner meals from the regular omelettes and potatoes by adding some meats and other vegetables but countered their complaints by reminding them that she was not running a cafeteria. On Sundays, Paul and Agnes helped their father with the many chores around the house, planting shrubs and flowers, and mowing the lawn. They often joined their parents in entertaining visitors at home and in the countryside. On one occasion, Agnes remembers the family walking for hours with Professor Dirac in the Gatineau Hills without anyone saying a word. Then back at home with Dirac for dinner, again no one said a word, and she thought perhaps this was how science was done.

Paul and Agnes completed their elementary and high school education in Ottawa, and both entered Queen's University in Kingston. Paul was awarded a Woodrow Wilson Scholarship to Princeton University, where he

The Doctors Herzberg.

obtained a Master's degree in physics in 1961. While enjoying his studies, Paul realized that in taking physics, he was inadvertantly following his parents' careers. He changed to psychology and obtained a Ph.D. in 1967 at the University of Illinois. There, in the meantime, he had met Louise Frankel, an Australian, and they married in 1964. Agnes continued her interest in mathematics by returning to her favourite city, Saskatoon, and its university. She received a Master's degree and in 1966 a Ph.D. in mathematics and statistics. Both Paul and Agnes pursued academic careers, Paul at York University in Toronto, and Agnes at Imperial College, London, followed by Queen's University in Kingston.

Luise continued her active interest in spectroscopy, yet she somehow managed to take care of home and all of the family needs, even finding time to accompany Gerhard on some trips to Saskatoon and Europe. Originally, she served as a Voluntary Research Assistant at the NRC, then joined the Dominion Observatory in 1952, first as a Summer Assistant then as a Scientific Officer, with her own office and program of research and the opportunity to attend and participate in conferences. In spite of such busy lives, the Herzbergs were regular hosts for groups of visitors and staff,

Luise, Lalitha, and Chandra at the wedding of Paul and Louise, 1964.

The happy bride and groom, 1964.

Luise, Paul, and Agnes at Waterton Lake, 1947.

Herzberg at Lake O'Hara, 1952.

often at luncheons or dinners, and they took the time to attend the NRC parties and the many formal functions to which they were invited by the Government and various embassies in Ottawa.

While holidays were few, the Herzbergs preferred spending these precious days in the mountains; the Lake O'Hara region in the Canadian Rockies was a favourite of the family. In Europe, Gerhard and Luise would often spend a week or two at Saas-Fee in the Swiss Alps. Hiking in the mountains was the main form of exercise rather than rigorous climbing, and at least in the early days Luise managed to keep up with him. While he would have liked to climb the Matterhorn he never attempted it, but with a guide, Herzberg did reach the top of the nearby Nadelhorn, only 200 metres lower and not as difficult a climb.

By 1971, Herzberg had been awarded eighteen honorary degrees, his first being from the University of Saskatchewan in 1953, the others mainly from Canadian universities, as well as from Dublin, Oxford, Stockholm, Chicago, and Göttingen. In Göttingen, he gave a lecture in the same hall where he had attended the seminars of many distinguished visitors in 1929. Herzberg received many other honours, awards, and medals. In particular, he was appointed Academician of the Pontifical Academy of Sciences in 1964 and Companion of the Order of Canada in 1968, the highest honour accorded by his adopted country.

The first honorary Doctorate degree, LLD,
University of Saskatchewan, 1953.

Appointed Companion of the Order of Canada
by Governor General Roland Michener, 1968.

The debt which all spectroscopists and physical chemists owe to Gerhard Herzberg is enormous. None of the younger generation can realize the impact which each of his books has had in the development of our knowledge of atomic and molecular structure.

G.B.B.M. Sutherland

18. THE CLASSIC VOLUMES

Herzberg's talent for lecturing was recognized very early by his colleagues. In 1929, while a postdoctoral fellow in Göttingen, he was invited by students to informally review for them the theory of atomic and molecular spectra and to bring them up-to-date on the topics being discussed in colloquia by the many distinguished visiting speakers.[1] He accepted this extra task, his purpose being to learn as well as to teach. He enjoyed the experience and early in his career gave introductory courses on spectroscopy in Bristol, Erlangen, and Darmstadt. When encouraged to publish these lectures, he again accepted the challenge in the belief that by writing for publication he would ensure that he understood the topic under discussion.

What started out to be a book of about 160 pages, finally blossomed into four volumes, one on atomic spectra and three on molecular spectra, totalling more than 2,200 pages. Later, when books of molecular constants and on spectra of free radicals were added, the total reached over 3,200 pages. These six volumes were conceived, written, and brought to fruition in five decades, while at the same time Herzberg carried out an enormous amount of fundamental research, much of which helped to develop and clarify the concepts of the many topics treated in these volumes.[2] As his colleague Robert Mulliken perceived, "Herzberg's books are an expression of his joy (and hard work) in teaching others what he had learned".[3]

Atomic Spectra and Atomic Structure

In 1929, Herzberg entered into an agreement with Theodor Steinkopff, a Dresden publisher, to prepare a manuscript of his course "An Introduction to Spectroscopy". This was to be an elementary introduction for the beginner in the field of atomic and molecular spectra. Herzberg began to write and revise as he gave more courses on the topic, but he was also deeply involved in research, and as "privatdozent" he had the unique opportunity to set up a new laboratory in Darmstadt. Thus, he was long overdue on his commitment and was regularly reminded by Steinkopff about the book. As

The classic texts of *Atomic Spectra and Atomic Structure* and *Molecular Spectra and Molecular Structure.*

Herzberg developed his presentation, he realized that the topic was far too extensive to treat in a single volume and decided to write one on atomic spectra and another on molecular spectra. This division into two volumes was approved by the publisher, although even the one volume on atomic spectra was eventually longer than two hundred pages. Herzberg submitted the completed manuscript in 1935 and hoped that he would not be asked to reduce or revise it since he was on the point of leaving the Third Reich and on his way to Canada as a guest professor.

The Herzbergs were hardly settled in their new home in Saskatoon in September 1935, and he was just beginning to feel comfortable with his teaching assignments at the university, when galley proofs for *Atomspektren und Atomstruktur* arrived from Germany to be read and corrected and any changes made as soon as possible. He immediately took up this onerous task, working far into the nights, long after preparing lectures, and the book was published in 1936.

Edward Condon, editor of a new physics series for the Prentice-Hall Company, immediately reminded Herzberg of the promise he had made in 1935 to translate the book into English. Condon thought that Herzberg's book was an excellent introduction to the detailed theoretical treatise on line spectra titled *The Theory of Atomic Spectra*, which he and George H. Shortley had written and published in 1935.[4] In fact, at least a dozen new books on atomic spectra had appeared in the past decade. Yet with spectroscopy being a key contributor to the development of quantum mechanics and with its many applications in physics, chemistry, and astronomy, there was a great demand for elementary texts on this subject.

Herzberg felt uneasy about doing the translation himself, mainly because he was still not confident in English and was concerned about the time it would take from research. He managed to involve his friend John Spinks in this task. Spinks was anxious to help and was very quick in translating the book. Their colleague Newman Haslam then read the proofs of the entire book and helped with improvements in the presentation. The English version, *Atomic Spectra and Atomic Structure*, was published in 1937.

With World War II in progress soon afterwards and fewer students in universities, the sale of texts, including Herzberg's, decreased dramatically. Nevertheless, by 1944 Prentice-Hall had sold its original printing of 1,500 copies at approximately 200 books per year. However, the publisher was not interested in reprinting or in a revised edition, "We cannot reprint because we need our quota of paper for more profitable books". The original type had been destroyed and the copyright was returned to Herzberg by the publisher.

Herzberg felt that at war's end there would be a demand for books on spectroscopy, and he sought out other possible publishers. He inquired of Edwards Bros. Incorporated of Ann Arbor, Michigan, the G.E. Stechert & Company, New York, and Dover Publishers, New York, whether there was any interest in producing and distributing a litho-printed edition. Edwards replied that it only produced at cost to the customer, who would then have to take care of distribution. Stechert wrote that it would print 1,000 copies and give the same royalty as Prentice-Hall, but it would be impossible to include any corrections in a photo-offset reprint. On the other hand, Dover, a relatively new company, was definitely interested and would include corrections and up-dates of tables of data and start with a printing of 2,000 copies. The only problem was the limited paper quota allotted to Dover, not the unquestionable merit of the book.[5] Herzberg signed a contract to receive 5 percent royalty on all paper copies sold, with 7.5 percent for the first 5,000 cloth copies and 10 percent on all cloth copies thereafter. For

John Spinks' assistance in translating the original German version, Herzberg chose to pay him 60 percent of the royalty received, as with the Prentice-Hall edition. The publication date of this second edition was 1944, with 3,000 copies printed in each of 1945 and 1946.

Sales boomed just after the end of World War II and amounted to about 11,000 cloth and 3,400 paper copies sold in the first decade with the printing of six editions. Later copies were all paper. In 1959–1960, the book was adopted for university courses in England and India, and sales soared to over 10,000 per year. In 1987, Hayward Cirker, President of Dover Publications, wrote to Herzberg, " It's been many years since we entered into agreement and I'm glad we are around and active.... We are delighted to keep your fine book alive."[8] By then over 100,000 copies of *Atomic Spectra and Atomic Structure* had been sold by Dover. Today, this small volume is still in print in its original version, serving as an important introduction to atomic spectroscopy after five decades.

Molecular Spectra and Molecular Structure: I. Spectra of Diatomic Molecules

Herzberg's contract with Steinkopff in Germany was for the above book on atomic spectra and one on molecular spectra. Before leaving Germany he had made a good start on the molecular manuscript in about seven hundred handwritten pages and realized that a proper treatment of molecular spectra was not possible in a single volume. His writing thus far had only dealt with diatomic molecules: it became clear that polyatomic molecules would require another volume. The thought even crossed his mind that to explain what was already known about polyatomic molecules might best be presented in two volumes, one dealing with rotational and vibrational spectra and another with electronic spectra.

The 1935 contract with the Prentice-Hall Company included three volumes: one on atomic spectra, a second on diatomic molecules, and a third on polyatomic molecules. On completion of the volume on atomic spectra in German and in English by 1937, Herzberg immediately resumed his writing of *Diatomic Spectra*. While awaiting the construction of his major spectrograph in Saskatoon, he devoted any time free from his regular duties to writing. Over the years, he had made brief notes on index cards of published papers he had read and of results he had heard at conferences, and this information was of enormous help. Now he spent much time in catching up on the latest research findings, checking references, and preparing long tables of useful data to be included in the new volume. He wrote the book in German, by hand, and the university was very supportive by providing a secretary to type the manuscript. Luise prepared the many drawings for the book, which were then drafted by Lorne Gray, an engineering student at the University of Saskatchewan. (Gray served as President of Atomic Energy Canada Limited from 1954 to 1965 and on meeting Herzberg in Ottawa told him, "I'm still proud of having done those figures for you".) While the writing was going on in German, John Spinks was busily translating it into English, and Newman Haslam was helping with stylistic improvements. Herzberg decided that this volume was to be the beginning of a series on molecules and chose the title *Molecular Spectra and Molecular Structure: I. Diatomic Molecules*. Both the German and English editions were published in 1939, just before World War II erupted. Understandably, this volume was dedicated to the memory of Walter Charles Murray, the first President of the University of Saskatchewan, who had done so much for the Herzbergs. Murray was genuinely touched by this gesture.

Herzberg was commended by numerous friends for this volume. Robert S. Mulliken of Chicago wrote:

> It is a very fine book. It will hardly be possible for anyone to write a better one serving the same purposes—at least for a long time to come. I am looking forward to cutting down on lectures for my band spectra course, referring the students to your book.[7]

In addition to The University of Chicago, several other universities quickly adopted the book for graduate classes, including Berkeley, Los Angeles, Ohio, and Wisconsin.

Reviews of the book were all favourable. W. Jevons, an eminent English spectroscopist who had written a book on diatomic molecules, was asked by Steinkopff for comments:

> I wish to thank you very cordially for your kindness in sending me a copy of Professor Herzberg's new book on *Molekülspektren* etc. It is a magnificent piece of work and a most fitting sequel to his Atomspektren etc. which you presented to me about two years ago and which I had the pleasure of reviewing later in its English edition.[8]

Excerpts from two lengthy reviews follow:

> Herzberg's powers of exposition have been shown in his previous book *Atomic Spectra and Atomic Structure*. Here, ... characteristics of the earlier book show to even greater advantage, the orderliness of the treatment, the avoidance of irrelevant complication, the good choice of illustrative material, and the care taken with such accessories as indexes and captions of figures and tables.... An excellent final chapter summarizes some of the main results—and gives an account of applications to a wide variety of fields in physics, chemistry and astrophysics. It is a masterly exposition, which should meet the needs and stimulate the interest of a wide variety of readers.[9]

The second reviewer began with a lengthy description of progress in experimental study and theoretical interpretation of molecular spectra and of what is contained in the text:

> All this is so much in the spirit of modern physical chemistry, and yet so difficult a field for the novice to enter, that the appearance of a comprehensive text-book in English on the subject by Prof. Herzberg is an event of considerable importance. It will undoubtedly accelerate the future development of physical chemistry.... In the earlier book *Atomic Spectra and Atomic Structure*, ... we became familiar with that singular clarity of style which makes learning a pastime and renders a comparatively short text both suitable to beginners and sufficiently comprehensive to assist the research worker. The new book has all the simplicity and crisp directness of the old; and it goes definitely further in the direction of comprehensiveness.[10]

The book also raised attention and comment in Nazi Germany as early as 1940. Ludwig Glaser, a former student of Johannes Stark and along with him a Nazi and a leading proponent of the anti-Einstein and Aryan-science movements, wrote:

> This book is by an author of the Jewish clan who emigrated to a hostile foreign country. This mental attitude is also reflected by him in the book. It represents, as Philipp Lenard maintains, the Jewish physics of Born's *Optik* and of modern physics. An extremely unpleasant book that is to be rejected as a German physics publication.[11]

Nevertheless, along with the earlier volume on atomic spectra, *Molekülspektren und Molekülstruktur: I. Zweiatomige Moleküle* apparently sold reasonably well in Germany since some royalties accumulated. At the end of the war, Herzberg asked Steinkopff to send these royalties to a cousin in Langensalza.

Herzberg, now thirty-five years of age, had just begun to take voice lessons for relaxation, but neither this extra activity nor family obligations stopped him from pursuing his ambition of completing the series of books on molecular spectra. On finishing *Diatomic Molecules*, he simply continued with writing about what was known concerning polyatomic molecules.

Molecular Spectra and Molecular Structure: II. Infrared and Raman Spectra of Polyatomic Molecules

World War II quickly brought Herzberg's research at the University of Saskatchewan to a standstill. Few students pursued graduate studies and no papers were published in 1943–1944. Moreover, being legally an enemy alien, he was not permitted to contribute to major wartime research until in 1943 he was invited to carry out spectroscopic work on new explosives. He therefore turned to the writing of his second volume, *Infrared and Raman Spectra of Polyatomic Molecules*. The next three years, including almost every weekend, were largely devoted to its completion. Although Luise had given up any idea of active research while raising her children, she was an indispensable contributor to this volume, having produced all of the drawings and many of the tables of molecular data. Paul and Agnes remember that on many Sundays they would go to the lab to visit their dad. They would knock on the basement window and he would give them a piece of chocolate kept in his desk for just such occasions. As a special treat, he would sometimes take them to the sod hut behind the physics building where explosives were tested. Then they would walk home for lunch and work together in the "victory" garden.

Although the original contract with the Prentice-Hall Company also included this second volume in the series, the publisher cancelled the contract because of the rationing of paper and the desire to use the limited supply for more profitable books; the publisher had declined to reprint *Atomic Spectra and Atomic Structure* for the same reason. This news was a serious predicament for Herzberg since he had just finished the manuscript, all handwritten in English. At the time, Charles Dollard, Assistant to the President of the Carnegie Corporation, happened to be visiting the University of Saskatchewan and, on discussing with Herzberg his activities and experiences in Canada, learned of this latest problem. Dollard promised to raise the matter with several publishers he knew, including the Van Nostrand Company.[12]

Herzberg wrote a long letter to the editor of Van Nostrand asking whether there was any interest in publishing this companion to *Diatomic Molecules*. He included a table of contents, an outline of the book, gave several reasons for the need of such a book, and sent along reviews of volume I. He also mentioned that the manuscript of about 750 written pages (not all typed yet) was complete and that there would be 157 line drawings and 13 halftones. Moreover, he indicated that a first version of the third volume in the series on electronic spectra of polyatomic molecules was essentially finished.

Within two weeks, Herzberg received an answer from Edward M. Crane, President of Van Nostrand. "Send me the manuscript."[13] A month later Herzberg informed Crane that he was sending the work in four batches to reduce the risk of a loss and that the typing was being done by six typists. All sections of the manuscript, except for an index, were received in the following two weeks. Two months later, Herzberg received copies of two reviews: one favourable, the other overly critical. Crane wanted to publish the book and suggested revisions of certain sections. He also included a statement on the royalty to be paid: 10 percent on the first thousand, 12.5 on the second thousand, and 15 percent thereafter. Herzberg approved the royalty basis and agreed to improve the clarity and style with Newman Haslam's help and to accept further suggestions. But he would not countenance another review after this revision, since he felt that with reviewers as critical as the second one (who asked that group theoretical methods should be included), there would be no end of revisions. As Herzberg noted: "There are only very few brilliant theorists, of which your reviewer is one of the most prominent (if I guess his identity correctly), who think that avoiding group theory makes things less understandable. Well, for them my book is not written."[14] Finally, Crane agreed to no further reviews and felt that they understood each other, adding: "There will be restrictions on books of fiction and other non-technical subjects, but I cannot conceive how restrictions can be made to apply to books that are useful in the war effort, and any branch of physics is in this category."

Haslam read the entire manuscript and proofs and K.J. MacCallum of Chemistry also read the proofs, and both helped with suggestions. After considerable rewriting and abbreviation of certain sections, Herzberg received a letter of congratulations from Crane on the splendid manner in which the manuscript was completed. Crane hoped Herzberg would agree that the book had benefitted tremendously from this additional labor. In the meantime, Crane appeared to have qualms about Herzberg's suggested title of the book, but he finally accepted the series title *Molecular Spectra and Molecular Structure: II. Infrared and Raman Spectra of Polyatomic Molecules*. In spite of the good will on both sides and regular friendly correspondence, there were long delays in printing the book. As time passed and in order to keep the book up-to-date, Herzberg requested changes and deletions, leading to further delays and higher costs. The book was eventually published in May 1945. When he received his first copies of the book, he was very pleased with its general appearance.

Gerhard dedicated the volume to Luise. He gratefully acknowledged her help in the preface: "I am particularly indebted to my wife who prepared all the figures, calculated many of the tables and contributed many improvements to the text. Without her help many a figure and table that I believe has greatly increased the usefulness of the book, would not have been included." On receiving a copy of this volume, Harrington, the Head of the Department of Physics in Saskatoon, wrote: "It is a wonderful book. Whenever I look at it, I shall see you and Mrs. Herzberg giving long hours in the effort to make it a perfect job".

Once volumes I and II were published, they were recognized as standards for the field of molecular spectra, and Herzberg was much in demand by the science community to assist in developing standards of notation, nomenclature, and units for molecular states and spectra. Thus, he served on several committees involved with setting standards in physics, chemistry, and astrophysics, including the relevant commissions of the Institute of Astrophysics, the Inter-Union Committee on Spectroscopy, the International Union of Pure and Applied Physics, and the International Union of Pure and Applied Chemistry. He served for many years, becoming chairman of several committees, all of which required considerable travel and much time in attending meetings and writing reports. Such commitments took valuable time away from his own research, but he felt it his duty to contribute in this way and gave unstintingly of his time and energy to these various tasks, all for the sake of science.

Diatomic Molecules, Second Edition

With the end of World War II, Herzberg was anxious to move to the Yerkes Observatory to begin his research in astrophysical spectroscopy. The prospect of setting up a completely new laboratory at Yerkes, carrying out research with students and visitors, and giving lectures did not curtail his enthusiasm for completing the series of books on molecular spectra. A few months after arriving at Yerkes, he personally received many requests for the English edition of *Diatomic Molecules*, which he learned was sold out. Since the original publisher (Prentice-Hall Company) was reluctant to continue printing the book, Dover Publishing asked for Herzberg's permission to reprint it photographically. However, he noted that while there was much activity and progress in spectroscopy, no new books on the spectra of diatomic molecules had appeared, and he decided it was time to revise the 1939 edition of volume I. He arranged for its publication by Van Nostrand.

It seems unbelievable that after writing three books and nursing them through the publication stage, while carrying out original research and publishing many papers, Herzberg would not say "enough is enough". But as noted above, he had already launched into the third volume of the series on molecular spectra. Moreover, with the field of molecular spectroscopy developing so rapidly, he realized that revisions of volumes I and II would be necessary. In fact, he obviously had every intention of revising these books, because he had requested from the publishers specially bound copies of these volumes with blank pages inserted between the printed pages. As he kept up to date on the latest developments by personal contacts, attending conferences, and reading current issues of many technical journals, he would make notes of new results on these blank pages (instead of on index cards as he had done earlier). In this way he had at hand the most recent results on molecular spectra, and these references would make revisions of the texts much more efficient.

In early 1946, Herzberg and Crane of Van Nostrand agreed on a revised edition of *Diatomic Molecules*, with Crane expecting the manuscript to be ready within a year because of the demand for the book. By January 1947, Herzberg had rewritten about 40 percent of the old version and added many new results, especially from microwave spectroscopy, so that more than half of the "revised" book was new. A major feature was an extensive table (eighty printed pages) of molecular constants of the ground and excited states of all known diatomic molecules, which took considerable time and care to compose. With Herzberg's preparations to leave Yerkes Observatory for the NRC in Ottawa, while carrying out his most important experiment at Yerkes, there was some further delay. Nevertheless, he managed to send the first three chapters to the publisher just before departing from Williams Bay in August 1948, and the remainder of the manuscript was sent a month later from Canada.

At Yerkes, Chandra, who was himself an extraordinary worker, was continually impressed with Gerhard's boundless energy and productivity in the laboratory, not to mention his astonishing appetite for writing books:

> Besides building up of the laboratory and the experimental studies, a major task which Herzberg completed during those years was the revision, towards the second edition of his already standard book on *Diatomic Molecules*.... I recall the incredible discipline with which he used to set apart the larger part of each weekend to this task. His office was across the corridor from mine; and often on Sunday mornings, I used to interrupt him in his work with an invitation to go for a walk along the lake. He always acceded, though after some initial hesitation. During those walks, he infected me with his own enthusiasm for the study of molecules; enough for me to volunteer to read the proofs of his book: and I am still proud of his acknowledgement to my having done so in the preface to his book. Indeed, after Herzberg left for Ottawa in 1948, I continued to give his course on Atomic and Molecular Spectra for some two or three years. But alas, without his constant presence the pressure of other interests gradually drifted me away from "Atoms and Molecules".[15]

On reading the proofs of this second edition, Chandra wrote to Herzberg:

> I have found your book one of the best I have ever read and I do want to congratulate you on making an admittedly complex subject so transparent. It is so well written, that I find I can learn the subject very much more easily than I thought I could: life would be so much simpler if there were equally well written books on other subjects.

By the end of the year, printing of the book had not been started, much to Herzberg's disappointment, because of the length of time a reviewer took to read the manuscript. On receipt of the report Herzberg quickly accepted some of the suggestions of the reviewer and rebutted others. He made revisions and added illustrations because of new spectroscopic results, and then made many corrections in the proofs, so that final printing was not completed until the end of 1949. The revised edition of *Molecular*

Spectra and Molecular Structure: I. Diatomic Molecules was finally available in May 1950. The book was immediately adopted by twenty-six universities and colleges for graduate courses in physics and chemistry.

Herzberg sent copies of this second edition to many friends in Europe and one to W.P. Thompson, President of the University of Saskatchewan, along with a letter stating:

> The first edition of my book on *Diatomic Molecules* was dedicated to Dr. Murray while he was still living. In the new second edition, which has just appeared, I have renewed this dedication to the memory of one to whom personally I owe more than I can express in words. Since, alas, Dr. Murray is no longer with us, it is perhaps fitting that I should send a copy of my book to you, his successor, as a token of my devotion to the University of Saskatchewan and of my admiration and unfailing remembrance of its first president. At the same time I recall with great pleasure the many kindnesses that you have extended to me and the support that you have always given to my work.[16]

Herzberg also wished to acknowledge his friend John Spinks, who had helped with the translation of the 1939 edition, and he arranged with the publisher that the words "With the co-operation, in the first edition, of J.W.T. Spinks" should appear on the title page and that Spinks should receive 25 percent of royalty payments.

Molecular Spectra and Molecular Structure: III. Electronic Spectra and Electronic Structure of Polyatomic Molecules

This final volume of Herzberg's trilogy had been incubating for at least a decade, and he had even suggested a 1955 completion date to Crane at Van Nostrand, but the book finally made its appearance in 1966. Such a delay was to be expected; not only was Herzberg extremely busy with his many responsibilities at the NRC, but he also felt that he should await the results of the rapid progress being made in electronic spectroscopy during the 1950s. The developments in his own laboratory and elsewhere, including improvements in vacuum ultraviolet techniques and studies of free radical spectra, made possible enormous strides in the understanding of electronic spectra of polyatomic molecules, and he continued his methodical writing and rewriting of this volume for another decade.

Herzberg devoted Saturdays for fifteen years to the writing of this book, no matter whether he was in Ottawa or on travels to conferences or on other business. At the NRC we all understood that we would not see him on Saturdays. He would arrive as early as 7 A.M., go directly to his office, have lunch there, and return home at about 6 P.M. He would not appear in the laboratory for tea, nor did we trouble him with any of our problems. During my first years at the NRC I was allotted an office immediately below his. Every now and then, I would hear him pacing back and forth, no doubt trying to work out the proper wording to best express and explain a particularly complex idea.

This third volume was undoubtedly the most difficult to write, and it turned out to be by far the longest, exceeding the earlier volumes by approximately one hundred pages. Understandably, the electronic spectra of polyatomic molecules are more numerous and more complicated than those of diatomic molecules because of the larger number of atoms. Polyatomic molecules have more excited states, and changes in structure of some molecules occur as different electrons are excited to higher energies. Thus, while Herzberg took great pains to show a variety of observed spectra and to explain their meaning and analysis, this volume was meant for the serious student of molecular spectra and structure. Herzberg acknowledged the assistance and suggestions of Jon Hougen and Alex Douglas, who read the entire manuscript, Christopher Longuet-Higgins, who had helped with theoretical problems, and John Callomon, John Johns, and Klaus Huber, who proofread large sections of this enormous volume.

On reading this volume, Christopher Longuet-Higgins, one of the few who could understand every aspect of this enormous subject, wrote to Herzberg:

> Part III is quite obviously a work of no less classic quality than Parts I and II. Your books, like the great masterpieces of music and architecture, are among the finest monuments of our civilization. They are outstanding among the records of modern science for the hard thought, scholarship and attention to detail, which are evident on every page. You ought to be very proud of your scientific achievements: would that the rest of us could live up to such high standards.[17]

Herzberg sent a copy of volume III to Günter Scheibe, whom he had met in 1929 in Göttingen:

> On this occasion I remember with pleasure the first stimulus to write these volumes which was given by you about forty years ago. Originally, of course, you had suggested that I write one small volume on both atomic and molecular spectra. In the course of these forty years the plan has degenerated into four rather substantial volumes, and has taken a lot longer than it should have.[18]

Over the years, Herzberg was amused to learn that several of his musical friends had noted an analogy of his first four books with "Der Ring des Nibelungen" by Richard Wagner (1813–1883), which he began with the thought of composing a single opera, but finally expanded into a tetralogy. Herzberg's four works evolved over a period of more than thirty years, the last being completed in his Spectroscopy Laboratory, while Wagner's were finished in twenty years, with "Die Götterdämmerung", the last in the series being performed in Das Festspielhaus, the theatre Wagner built in Bayreuth.

The Spectra and Structures of Simple Free Radicals

In 1968, Herzberg was invited to present the prestigious George Fisher Baker Lectures in Chemistry at Cornell University, which were followed by a publication of the lectures. He chose to discuss the spectra and structures of free radicals, since much had been learned of these short-lived species during the preceding two decades. However, for a general audience of chemists to understand his topic, he felt it would be necessary to give an introductory lecture on molecular spectroscopy, and this was the substance of his first lecture. This also gave him the opportunity to fulfill his dream of forty years earlier, when he began to write his first book, namely, to produce a small book on an introduction to the field of atomic and molecular spectroscopy. Thus a highly abbreviated version of the material in the trilogy *Molecular Spectra and Molecular Structure* formed the basic introduction to *The Spectra and Structures of Simple Free Radicals: An Introduction to Molecular Spectroscopy*. This small volume was published in 1970 by Cornell University Press.

By 1986 the book was out of print, and Herzberg was informed by Cornell University Press that he would be free to explore other means of keeping it in print. Since his first book *Atomic Spectra and Atomic*

Structure was still being produced by Dover Publications after forty years of good sales, he approached Dover and was pleased with the agreement to reprint *The Spectra and Structures of Simple Free Radicals*.

Molecular Spectra and Molecular Structure: IV. Constants of Diatomic Molecules

In 1978, a fourth volume was added to the trilogy on molecular spectra comprising an extensive series of tables of data on electronic states and molecular constants for over nine hundred diatomic molecules and ions. This compilation took eleven years to complete. It became a volume of seven hundred pages, and its size is a measure of the myriad spectroscopic studies that were carried out after the original eighty page table (and thirty pages of bibliography) was produced for the second edition of *Diatomic Molecules* in 1950. Herzberg offered to hire Klaus Huber, who was in the last year of his fellowship in the Spectroscopy Laboratory, provided he would spend half his time on the book. Huber began in 1965 and in later years worked full-time on this project, preparing the final manuscript for the photo-offset production of the volume. In this way, typographical errors were avoided, although much time was spent carefully checking numbers and references in the manuscript by Izabel Dabrowski, Herzberg's assistant, and Marjorie Thompson, his secretary. The volume was published by the Van Nostrand Reinhold Company in New York in 1978. Royalty payments were split 50:50 with Huber. By 1985 the small number of copies of the original printing had been sold, and the publisher agreed to print another 500 copies if the authors would waive payment of royalty. Also, in order to keep the price of the volume below $40 a subsidy of $2,500 was requested.[19] Huber and Herzberg consented to both of these conditions in order to keep volume IV in print.

On receiving an inscribed copy of this latest volume, Chandra wrote:

> Coming after your three magnificent treatises, this volume represents the completion of a total effort that passes imagination—one cannot believe it except for the fact that the fruits of that effort are here for all to enjoy. I do not doubt that you have a feeling on completing this work, similar to what you must feel after climbing to the top of one of the Swiss peaks you love.[20]

Translations, Reprint Editions, and Sales

Herzberg's first two texts, the first on atomic spectra and the second on diatomic molecules, were written in German and translated into English with the help of John Spinks. All other texts were written in English. Every one of Herzberg's six books was translated into Russian, and some appeared in Italian, Hungarian, Chinese, Japanese, German, and Yugoslavian. All of the books in English have had good sales and are still available, having been reprinted by the Krieger Publishing Co. Inc., Florida, in 1989 and 1991. *Atomic Spectra and Atomic Structure* has sold over 100,000 copies, while volumes I, II, and III have sold about 30,000, 25,000, and 15,000, respectively.[21] As expected, volume IV, being a set of tabular data, has sold a smaller number, only about 4,000 copies, mainly to libraries and scientific institutions, and sales of *The Spectra and Structures of Simple Free Radicals* have also been low, perhaps because of the book's specialized topic.

The three volumes on *Molecular Spectra and Molecular Structure* form an authoritative and comprehensive review of the vast literature on molecular spectra, with countless examples presented in a style adequate for the beginning student as well as for active research scientists. It would be difficult to find a comparable and as thorough a compilation of such an extensive field of science by a single individual. Many who are familiar with the trilogy have said that these volumes are in essence "the Bible" for this field of knowledge. Thus, it is not at all surprising to see this series on the desks of all active molecular scientists and to hear the cry "Look it up in Herzberg!"

One doesn't tear the house down because the chimney smokes.

Galileo Galilei

19. CHALLENGING THE NEW POLITICS OF SCIENCE

The importance of the sciences to governments in industrial countries led to tremendous growth in research worldwide during the 1950s and 1960s, forcing issues of priorities and fiscal accountability into the public arena. All countries, and Canada was no exception, were confronted with such problems, and there were calls for a "national science policy" in Canada. Numerous commissions and committees began studying new mandates of funding, organization, and management, and of directing the sciences towards solving economic and social problems of the country. Given its prominence, the NRC with its wide-ranging powers and historic responsibilities for the natural sciences and engineering, was vulnerable to the closest scrutiny, raising the spectre of bureaucratic political controls, which were anathema to Steacie, Herzberg, and many others.[1]

Growth of NRC Science and Its Problems

As Canada's needs for basic and applied research kept increasing in complexity and costs, President Steacie became specially concerned about the growth of the NRC and some direct government intrusion. In an address to the Montreal Canadian Club in 1958, he outlined his incisive views of the crucial problem for the future of science in Canada:

> With the increasing importance of science to technology, and incidentally to defence, science has relatively recently and suddenly begun to impinge on government policy. Under these circumstances the need for government facilities and permanent advisers has arisen, and there has been an enormous increase in government science. The fact that science has become a matter of government policy and interest has brought with it the customary advantages and disadvantages. Public interest always means increased support, but also means increased control and diminished freedom. The reconciliation of these two opposing factors in government, in industry, and even in universities, is the most important problem facing science in the next decade or two.[2]

Steacie's main worry for the NRC was that any changes in the Research Council Act could lead to reduced freedom for the NRC through "the very dangerous activities of government planning and co-ordination, which are usually carried out by a management that knows nothing about science, and is controlled by accountants whose emphasis is on efficiency".[3] His apprehension was fuelled by a recommendation of the Heeney Report of 1958 that in the interests of uniformity and equity, all scientists, whether in government departments or in outside agencies such as the NRC, should be treated alike. Steacie felt that this advice was an attempt to bring the NRC into the Civil Service Commission, to which he was "implacably opposed".[4]

A variety of studies of government research and of the need for a national science policy were initiated in the 1960s, but Steacie did not live to see their damaging criticisms of the NRC. After a brief terminal illness Steacie died on 28 August 1962. He had served the NRC for twenty-two years, the last ten as its indomitable President.[5] With his untimely death, the euphoria that had pervaded the NRC and science in Canada after World War II came to an end. Most of the staff at the NRC knew nothing of Steacie's illness. Nor did they suspect any problem as they saw him walking down the hallway to the east end of the building on almost daily visits with Keith MacDonald, who was then in a wheelchair because of his progressive fatal paralysis.

Colleagues and friends at the NRC, in Canada, and around the world were stunned by Steacie's sudden death. One who had worked closely with him summed up his attributes: "Steacie was a rare combination of dedicated research scientist and hard-headed, no-nonsense administrator, with a clear analytical mind, which rapidly cut through to the core of the numerous problems he faced".[6] A chemical colleague, on first meeting Steacie, had immediately recognized his humanity: "Apart from his shrewd common sense, his greatest assets were his patent honesty, integrity and unselfishness, coupled with a total lack of pomposity".[7]

For Herzberg, Steacie's death was one of the biggest shocks in his life:

> In him, Canada has lost one of its most outstanding citizens; the scientific community of this country and of the world has lost a colleague renowned both for his original contributions to physical chemistry and for his deep influence on the organization of national and international scientific organizations.... It was he who persuaded the Government to increase more and more the support of universities by research grants

> (almost by a factor of ten during his presidency). It was he who conceived and initiated the post-doctorate fellowship scheme at the NRC and later at universities and in other Government departments. It was he who recognized at an early date the need for encouraging industrial research in Canada.... Steacie's great gifts and his personal charm produced a wonderful spirit at the National Research Council.[8]

Two major programs that Steacie had planned were brought to fruition during his last years. One was an exchange program between the Academy of Sciences of the Soviet Union and the NRC, which he had fostered during his visit to the U.S.S.R. in 1959 when he was inducted as a Foreign Member of the Academy. The other was a grants program for research in industry, analogous to the successful NRC research grants program, which provided financial encouragement to universities. The objective of the Industrial Research Assistance Program (IRAP) was to enable Canadian industry to overcome the branch–plant mentality (which accepts research and development from outside the country) and spend money on research. IRAP grants provided funds for salaries and wages to an amount that matched a company's expanded research. The program began slowly with the Treasury Board's approval of a sum of only $1 million, but in its first year IRAP gave rise to sixty-two new projects involving forty-four Canadian companies, and the following year the government's commitment was tripled.[9]

Just before Steacie's death, a government austerity program was announced with the further caveat that future NRC appointments and projects be referred first to the Treasury Board. Steacie co-operated with the financial urgency and reduced NRC's budget by $1.5 million, but he informed Treasury Board that financial stringency did not make the NRC less competent or the Board more competent to judge the relative merits of people and research projects.[10] He was the guardian of the NRC's autonomy to the very end.

The Short Road Down

Dr. Bristow Guy Ballard, Vice-President Scientific since 1954, served as Acting President until he was appointed President in February 1963, a post he did not covet. A graduate electrical engineer of Queen's University, he had joined the NRC in 1930 and during the Second World War helped to develop magnetic mine-sweeping equipment, for which he was appointed an Officer of the Order of the British Empire. He was instrumental in building up the extensive Division of Radio and Electrical Engineering. His was a difficult task to succeed the dynamic and well-known Steacie. Although Ballard supported the growth and funding of university research, he recommended that industrial research should now become a first priority for the NRC, but this initiative was thwarted by the Advisory Council. Ballard's term in office was a challenging period for the NRC and for the country since it coincided with the election of the new minority Government of Lester B. Pearson that concentrated on national unity but had difficulty in accommodating itself to the political and social temper of the 1960s. On his appointment, Ballard was confronted with the publication of the extensive Report of the Royal Commission on Government Organization (or Glassco Report, so named after its Chairman J. Grant Glassco). Along with its general study of departments and agencies of the Federal Government, the Glassco Report made far-reaching recommendations for accountability and co-ordination of scientific activities of government departments and for new structures to assist in the formulation of a national science policy.[11]

The Commission made several recommendations: appointment of a Minister to be made responsible for policy decisions in scientific research; establishment of a Scientific Secretariat, with a small staff, to operate under the direction of the President of the Treasury Board; and the establishment of a National Scientific Advisory Council. This new structure would assume the role of advising the Government, because the National Research Council was not without a perceived conflict of interest and there was an evident breakdown of the system as originally intended in the Research Council Act. The Glassco Commission also argued that the NRC was no longer broadly representative of the Canadian scientific community and having been "built by scientists for scientists" was involved mainly in pure research. This was an inaccurate assessment by the Commission since their own data clearly showed that more than 80 percent of NRC activities were involved with applied science and engineering.[12] It was also an unfortunate statement since all further studies on science policy made use of this misleading allegation to publicly criticize the NRC for stressing basic rather than applied research and technology.

On Ballard's retirement at age sixty-five, Dr. William George Schneider became the sixth President of the NRC. He was a chemistry graduate from the University of Saskatchewan, having taken some of Herzberg's courses on atomic and molecular spectroscopy. After obtaining his Ph.D. from McGill University in 1941, he was employed by the Woods Hole Oceanographic Institute before joining the NRC in 1946. Schneider served as Director of the Division of Pure Chemistry (1963–1965), Vice-President Scientific (1965–1967), and President from 1967 to 1980. The first years of his term were imbued with the exhilaration of Expo'67 and the Centennial celebrations and by the election of Pierre Trudeau with a majority government. But Schneider's tenure became exceedingly difficult as the new government declared that "for every problem there was a rational solution.... Rational planning seemed, in 1968, like an idea whose time was long overdue.... For four years, rational planning swept through Ottawa ...". According to columnist Richard Gwyn:

> Hand in hand with the idea went all the shiny new tools, artefacts for rational managers: computers, data banks, flow charts, flip charts, new problem-crunching theologies like "Program, Planning and Budgeting Systems", and "Management by Objectives", plus the awesome new jargon: interface, feedback, optimize, priorize, input and output.... Ottawa became a paper world. Out poured an interminable number of studies, interim reports, and "conceptual evaluations" evaluating everything and anything from taxation to urban affairs, to Indian affairs to information itself. Each study treated its subject as if nothing had ever been said about it or done about it before. All studies reached the same conclusion: a new agency, or branch, or unit should be created to deal with the subject, mostly by studying it more.[13]

How could the "rational planning" of Canadian science escape in such a pervasive climate? The NRC and Schneider and his colleagues bore the initial brunt of these bureaucratic excesses, which carried on well into Dr. Larkin Kerwin's term as President of the NRC from 1980 to 1989.

The first to jump on the rational planning bandwagon was Senator Maurice Lamontagne. Lamontagne, an economist and former professor at Université Laval and the University of Ottawa, was a strong believer in planning. He then became a member of Parliament and cabinet minister and was involved in establishing the Economic Council of Canada. In his maiden speech in the Senate in 1967, he outlined his views on a national science policy and within a few months won approval to set up a Senate of Canada Special Committee on Science Policy.[14] The first report, *A Critical Review: Past and Present*, was launched in 1970 with a press conference, where the Senator pronounced that "the NRC has been a complete failure in its fifty years as a guiding force for Canadian science".[15] He claimed that "it was the purpose of the Committee to give Canadian science policy a shock treatment in this first volume of the Report".[16] In discussing science, Senator Lamontagne included the "hard sciences" (physics and chemistry) as well as the life sciences and the social sciences. To many readers of this document, it was surprising that the Senate Committee concentrated about a third of its Report on the history and criticism of the NRC, which was mainly concerned with physics, chemistry, and engineering. The volume ended with the compelling conclusion "We must develop a coherent overall science policy so that we can not only meet our economic objectives more effectively but also more realistically face our mounting social problems". The second volume, *Targets and Strategies for the Seventies*, specifying the essential recommendations for realizing such a policy was to appear in early 1972, to be followed by a third volume a year later.

Herzberg Speaks Out

Herzberg was admired the world over in scientific circles for his integrity, for speaking authoritatively only about subjects in which he was conversant, and for carefully listening to others during a discussion. He was exceedingly reticent about speaking publicly on topics other than his specialty. But once the reputations of Steacie, Mackenzie, and the NRC were impugned and the freedom of scientists was attacked, he reluctantly came forward to air his personal views on the dangerous course that was being taken by the numerous studies of the NRC.

His first sally was a letter to Ballard on the great concern of the scientific staff of the Pure Physics Division on the attempt to introduce collective bargaining at the NRC.[17] Herzberg noted that the inroads of a civil service mentality would surely have an adverse effect on the NRC, particularly with the recommendation of the Glassco Commision that all purchases, large and small, should be handled by one government purchasing department. Members of the permanent staff, on their own, had collected signatures of virtually all of the scientific staff on the question "Why does the government not leave us alone and let us continue to thrive?" However, the Hon. C.M. Drury, the President of Treasury Board, was adamant about a centralized purchasing department, and eventually the NRC's own Purchasing Branch was dissolved in December 1969.

Herzberg's first public speech "Pure Science and Government" took place in May 1965 at a symposium at Queen's University on the occasion of the opening of a new physics building.[18] He noted that he agreed somewhat reluctantly to participate in the symposium and came only because "recently there have been some developments in Canada which, if not closely watched and guided with great wisdom, may destroy the congenial climate and the loose but effective organization of science in this country". He also emphasized that he was expressing his own personal views and was not speaking on behalf of the NRC in any official capacity.

He was impressed not only with the sound way in which scientific activities had been built up, but also by the compactness and flexibility of scientific organization in Canada as represented by the Research Council Act. So he was shocked that the Glassco Commission had suddenly discovered that there was "a lack of a science policy in Canada and an evident breakdown in the system as designed, ... and that the NRC was built by scientists for scientists". In his opinion, these statements were absolutely incorrect. The NRC had a clear conception of what a science policy can and cannot do. The first requirement for building up scientific research in Canada was to develop first-rate research at the universities in order to provide the skilled and educated manpower that would be needed for research in industry. This was what the NRC policy had achieved. Now that the number of highly educated graduates per year appeared to be sufficient for the country, it was time to encourage more industries to get involved in research, and this too was happening with the grants program for industrial research (IRAP). He reminded the audience that three of the first five presidents of the NRC (McNaughton, Mackenzie, and Ballard) were all engineers, and many of the early employees, such as J.H. Parkin, who headed aeronautical research, J.T. Henderson, radio and electrical research, and R.F. Legget, building research, were engineers. Moreover, President Steacie had received a Bachelor's degree in chemical engineering, and R.W. Boyle, the founding director of the Physics Division, had received a degree in electrical engineering.

Herzberg stressed that what had made the NRC one of the best research organizations in the world was its flexibility and capacity to depart from the rigid lines of departmental organization, and particularly the overriding philosophy that it is the working scientist in the basic and applied fields who should determine what is to be done. The Glassco Commission and before it the Heeney Commission were only interested in uniformity and conformity, believing this would provide more efficiency in government organizations. This was the theme of the efficiency experts for a national science policy. Herzberg then quoted the conclusions of several administrators and scientists who had been involved in attempts to institute science policy in their countries. One of his favorites was a recent statement of Lord Hailsham, the former Minister for Science of the British Government:

> No country in the world has ever successfully set up a Department of Science in the sense of a Ministry directly controlling the pace, the scope and the methods of scientific research. This is due to two considerations. The first is that the strategic planning of science cannot be undertaken without the full participation of the scientists themselves—and by this I mean, not just a staff of administrators with scientific degrees, but also men and women who actually carry on scientific work, whether in universities, government research stations, or industry.

Another quotation was from a speech by the administrator and scientist Warren Weaver, Vice-President of the Rockefeller Foundation:

> The crucial word diversify is at the heart of the dependence of science upon the government. There are those who think that the National Science Foundation ought to sit like an infinitely wise spider, at the centre of a web which reaches into every governmental activity in science and presumably into every other science activity in our whole nation, planning just how science should advance, tightening up here, slackening off there.... There is no person, and certainly no committee, which is wise enough to do this. We should, I think, be glad that this is so. For what keeps the total scientific effort from being chaotic and meaningless is not central planning or any attempt to achieve it, but a kind of grand homeostasis, under which a multitude of influences interact in a natural way. What science needs is not a lot of planning, but a lot of convenient communication, so that controls may arise naturally from feedback.

The Council of the NRC had provided a system of convenient communication by the early and effective use of its many Associate Committees, one of the best examples being its joint initiative with the Department of Agriculture to stimulate the research on the successful prevention of grain rust. Herzberg's final message, which he was to repeat on many occasions, contained the principal reasons for the support of pure science in Canada and elsewhere. "One was strictly mercenary, since experience has shown that pure science helps applied science and technology in their development", which he illustrated with examples of the discovery of electromagnetic induction, which is the basis of all modern electric power production, the semi-conductor chip, the laser, and nuclear physics, all leading to major modern applications. "The other reason was that scientific research of the purest kind is an intellectual activity, which like art, music, literature, archaeology, and many other fields helps us to understand who we are, and what is the nature of the world in which we live."

At a convocation address at York University in 1969, Herzberg chose to speak on "The Dangers of Science Policy", where he elaborated on the above themes and added a few barbs about the Glassco Commission and its recommendations:

> Even the Glassco Commission, entrusted with the task of recommending improvements in government organization, had reluctantly to admit that the National Research Council had been very successful. However, the Glassco Commission was really not interested in good science. It was interested in good accounting. Mr. Glassco, after all, was an accountant. There is nothing wrong with good accounting, except that it does not necessarily lead to good science.... What it should have done was to enquire what particular organizational features were the reason for the high international standing of the NRC and how this standing could be further improved. Instead, the Glassco Commission recommended reorganization aimed at making the set-up tidier and more amenable to accounting.
>
> Prime Minister Trudeau recently quoted in Parliament, a Roman official, Petronius Arbiter, who lived at the time of Emperor Nero almost two thousand years ago, and who said "We tend to meet any new situation by reorganizing. And a wonderful method it can be for creating the illusion of progress while producing confusion, inefficiency and demoralization." I believe that the opinion expressed by Petronius Arbiter is still valid today, particularly when attempts are made from outside to reorganize and centralize flourishing research laboratories.[19]

Herzberg ended his convocation address with the following words:

> May I suggest to the new graduates that they ponder the problem of our national goals in Canada.... The countries in past history that we admire most are not necessarily the economically prosperous ones but those that have made major contributions to our cultural heritage. Our aim should be to make Canada a country that is recognized throughout the world, and throughout history, as a country that has advanced in a significant way the progress of science, art, and literature.

He also took exception to the recommendations of the OECD report (1969), namely that the work in fundamental research at the NRC (the quality of which it acknowledged and praised) should be stopped because the Canadian universities were now sufficiently well developed to carry on with this work, also that a new central granting agency, replacing the NRC, the Canada Council, and the Medical Research Council, should direct the efforts of Canadian scientists at universities into predetermined fields that were likely to advance Canadian technology.

Herzberg's point was that all such recommendations are made by people who have not worked in the laboratory on actual research for many years and who think that some administrator will be able to mastermind the direction in which research should go in the laboratories.[20] Moreover, he was against the proposal of Omond Solandt, Chairman of the Science Council, that "there should be a continuing technical audit of all science programs", since this would only lead to more reports—and to what purpose, except to waste the time of scientists involved in research?

He was astounded by the first Report of the Senate Special Committee on Science Policy and by its extensive publicity through an unfair and biased press conference, especially with its focus on the NRC and past presidents as the villains of presumed "failures of Canadian science". He rose to the challenge with his address "Remarks on the Report of the Senate Special Committee on Science Policy" at the symposium "Formulation and Implementation of a Science Policy for Canada", held at Queen's University in March 1971:

> My first venture into the discussions on science policy occurred six years ago here at Queen's University and my opinions on the subject have not changed much since that time. But during this period a remarkable change has come over Canadian science. The work of scientists has been surveyed and reviewed by our scientific societies, by our universities, by the National Research Council, by a Cabinet task force, by the Science Council, by the OECD, and by the Senate.[21]

Clearly he was mystified that a Committee of the Senate of Canada could "publish such a biased report without declaring forcefully and unambiguously that it intended to do so, ... and to lead the general public and all the news media to believe that it represents a fair and objective assessment of Canadian science". Successes of the NRC were scarcely mentioned in the Report, only its presumed failures. That anyone, let alone a Senate

Committee, should use "such dishonesty in the presentation of the historical review of Canadian science" in order to create attention to themselves and their opinions was completely foreign to Herzberg. This surely was not the way to befriend scientists in a cooperative venture for the good of the country. It was also clear that parts of the twelve thousand pages of evidence collected during three years of public hearings and written briefs were selected and printed to substantiate Senator Lamontagne's point of view as presented in his maiden speech to the Senate in 1967, before the study by the Special Committee was even approved.[22]

Herzberg went on to question whether the Senators were sure of what they meant by science policy. Even Sir Solly Zuckerman, who for some ten years was Scientific Adviser to the British Cabinet, had remarked in a lecture in 1967:

> Most of us think we understand what is meant by the phrase "foreign policy", "housing policy" or "educational policy". On the other hand, many of us—and I among them—find it difficult to use the term "Scientific Policy" with any precision.

The only thing a science policy can do, in Herzberg's view, was clearly stated by the British Council for Scientific Policy:

> Science policy does not direct the advance of scientific knowledge, though it may well be concerned to encourage or to direct the application of the results of scientific advances. The tasks of science policy are of another kind: to maintain the environment necessary for scientific discovery; to ensure the provision of a sufficient share of the total national resources; to ensure that there is a balance between fields and that others are not avoidably neglected; to provide opportunities for inter-fertilization between fields, and between the scientific programmes of nations.

Herzberg had read with utter disbelief a statement included in the Senate Report, which he quoted to the audience: "it is evident to any historian of technology that almost all innovations are produced from previous innovations rather than from any injection of any new scientific knowledge".[23]

> Are we to believe that the development of the modern nuclear reactor did not depend on the discovery of nuclear fission made by research scientists in the search for knowledge, or that the development of modern communication and the computer industry did not depend on basic discoveries in solid state physics, or that the discovery of antibiotics, now the basis of

> much of our pharmaceutical industry, came about by industrial innovation rather than pure research?

He stressed the obvious fact that the Senators did not appreciate at all the relation between basic research and modern technology. Herzberg stated his conclusions clearly and repeated them on several occasions: "The Senators perhaps do not understand science or scientists and they certainly do not understand how scientists work or how science is organized". His careful study of *A Critical Review: Past and Present*, the first Report of the Senate Committee, provoked these strong vocal criticisms, which came as a surprise to many who knew the mild-mannered Herzberg.

Herzberg sent a copy of his address to Senator Lamontagne, noting that Senator Allister Grosart had been present at the Symposium and had expressed satisfaction at having the point of view of a working scientist with regard to the Report.[24] While awaiting the second volume with the specific recommendations of the Senators, Herzberg was unwilling to spend the time in further public discussion about the Report or the methods of the Senate Committee. But in numerous convocation addresses, he continued to express his opinion about the importance of recognizing science as part of our culture, as is art, music, and literature. His only face-to-face encounter with Senator Lamontagne was to occur at a symposium on science policy in 1974.

Distinguished Research Scientist

At the time of these many reviews of the NRC and discussions on science policy, Herzberg was fast approaching the age of official retirement. Whether or not the NRC administrators knew of the earlier agreement made with President C.J. Mackenzie that Herzberg would be permitted to continue in research after the normal retirement age of sixty-five, a request was made to Treasury Board that he be retained by the NRC. Approval for continuation of his employment was readily given for an initial five-year period to age seventy. President Schneider informed Herzberg of this decision in February 1968, a year and a half before Herzberg reached retirement age, noting that he would continue to have secretarial, computational, and technical assistance. Moreover, the appointment was to carry the new title of Distinguished Research Scientist.[25] The official announcement was made at the conference "Free Radical Spectroscopy" in honour of

Herzberg's sixty-fifth birthday, held in the resort town of Banff, Alberta, in June 1969. The meeting was a great success, with over two hundred of Herzberg's friends and colleagues from all over the world in attendance. This meeting proved to be the inauguration of a series of scientific conferences in his honour to be held every five years in different locales in Canada.[26]

As planned, Herzberg offered his resignation as Director of the Division of Pure Physics to take effect on 1 October 1969, with Alex Douglas becoming the Director of the new Division of Physics, combining the Divisions of Pure and Applied Physics as of old, but now operating in two buildings about ten kilometres apart. In his usual thoughtful manner, Herzberg added in his letter to Schneider:

> In leaving my administrative position, I should like to express a sincere feeling of appreciation towards you, your predecessors and associates in the Executive of the NRC, who have made the administrative part of my work at all times as easy and as little time-consuming as possible, so that I had adequate time available for my scientific work. It has been a great privilege to be one of the directors of the NRC. I hope that in my new position I shall be able to justify by my work the confidence that the Council has placed in me.[27]

This new position gave Herzberg the opportunity to continue his research within the Spectroscopy Section with essentially the same financial and technical support, although he missed the daily interaction with his long-time assistant Shoosmith, who retired in August 1969 after twenty years of devoted service. As a parting gift to Shoosmith, Herzberg had presented him with a leather-bound collection of reprints of the papers in which he was a co-author or was thanked for his contribution to the success of the research.

An Acute Personal Loss

Herzberg's concerns about the repeated investigations of the NRC, the annual reductions in budgets, and the long-awaited outcome of the Senate Committee recommendations were seemingly minor in comparison with his traumatic experience of the sudden death of Luise in the summer of 1971. He had reduced his travel commitments that year. Yet, having accepted an honorary degree from Cambridge University, which was to be conferred 10 June, he had also agreed to participate at a meeting of the French Physical Society in Evian the week before. Just as the meeting in Evian ended, he was called home because Luise had had a severe heart attack while at work. He arrived the following day, in time to talk with her before she died on 3 June 1971. Gerhard was devastated. At the NRC he remained in his office with the door closed, without seeing anyone, not even his secretary. He was completely lost to his colleagues and his assistants in the Spectroscopy Section for at least two weeks, venturing out of his office only to attend to pressing NRC business.

Luise's friends were deeply saddened to learn of her death. Many had come to know her quiet manner and appreciate her warm humour. They remembered that she had admirably managed a busy household and yet had had the energy and enthusiasm to be active in research. In her first four years in Ottawa, she had spent time at the NRC as a Voluntary Research Associate whenever family and home could spare her. There, she analyzed spectra taken at Yerkes Observatory and wrote papers with Gerhard on this work. She then joined the Dominion Observatory where she had her own program of research on solar spectra for seven years. In 1959, she moved to the Radio Physics Laboratory at Shirley's Bay in Ottawa. Her twelve years there were scientifically her happiest and most productive. Her main interests and contributions were in solar spectroscopy and photochemical processes in the upper atmosphere caused by solar activity. She was especially proud to have participated in the development of the Alouette satellite. She published twenty-three papers while in Ottawa, thirty-three in total, and presented her work at conferences in Canada, the U.S.A., and Europe. With her death, Canada lost one of its few accomplished women physicists.

Your extraordinary achievement has won you the praise and admiration of Canadians and citizens throughout the world....Canada is richer and greater because of your contribution. It is with great pleasure that I offer my congratulations and best wishes.

Pierre Elliott Trudeau

20. NOBEL LAUREATE

There is no award in science that can match the high honour and esteem bestowed on recipients by their peers than the Nobel Prize. World fame is immediate. In 1971, the name of Gerhard Herzberg was propelled from being virtually unknown, even in Canada, to one of world renown. Of course, Herzberg was well known to the science communities in Canada and abroad, but there was little reason for his name to be known by the citizenry. Only recently had his name appeared in Canadian newspapers as he voiced his strong objections to the Senate Report *A Science Policy for Canada*. Now he was celebrated in many households in Canada as well as in science laboratories as the first Canadian Nobel Laureate in the natural sciences. Only two earlier Nobel Prizes had been awarded to Canadians: to Frederic G. Banting and John J.R. MacLeod in medicine in 1923 for the discovery of insulin and the Peace Prize to Lester Bowles Pearson in 1957 for his role in the Suez Canal crisis of 1956.

In later years, three more Canadians were to receive Nobel Prizes in the natural sciences: John C. Polanyi and Michael Smith in Chemistry in 1986 and 1993, respectively, and Bertram N. Brockhouse in Physics in 1994. It is not so well known that other Canadians have received Nobel Medals. One recipient was Adelaide Sinclair, a neighbour of the Herzbergs in Rockliffe Park, who as Deputy Executive-Director of the United Nations International Children's Emergency Fund (UNICEF) had accepted the Nobel Peace Prize on behalf of UNICEF in 1965.[1] A more recent recipient was Dr. James Orbinski, President of Médicins Sans Frontières (MSF), who along with Dr. Marie-Eves Raguenaud of France, accepted the 1999 Nobel Peace Prize on behalf of the organization.[2]

Announcement in Ottawa

The official announcement of Nobel Prizes is often made during October, and for Physics and Chemistry usually on 15 October. In 1971, a delay of two weeks occurred because of the sudden illness and death on 29 October of Arne W.K. Tiselius, the chairman of the Nobel Committee. Tiselius was himself a Nobel Laureate, having received the Prize in Chemistry in 1948.[3]

While nominations and the ensuing investigations, opinions, and recommendations concerning the award of a Nobel Prize may not be disclosed, and access to such material may be granted only fifty years after an award has been made, it is not unusual to find that the Swedish TV and radio media, and the local media of a prospective recipient, are aware of an impending award a day or two before the official announcement by the Swedish Academy. This happened in Ottawa in Herzberg's case.

Early Monday morning on November 1st, his secretary Marjorie Thompson and his assistant Izabel Dabrowski entered the office to ringing telephones: reporters were asking for interviews with Herzberg to discuss the Nobel Prize he was to receive. This took both of them completely by surprise. Many more calls came from the media that morning to Herzberg's office and to Alex Douglas and the President's office. TV crews from Sweden arrived at 100 Sussex Drive to film and interview Herzberg, only to learn that he was half the world away in the Soviet Union. However, no official word had been received at the NRC from Sweden. There was great jubilation in the Spectroscopy Laboratory as the group had anticipated for more than a decade that Herzberg would be named, and finally it seemed to be happening. Nevertheless, it was decided not to spread the recent rumour but to wait for the Swedish Academy to make its official announcement.

That evening, a reception and dinner of Fellows of the Royal Society of Canada living in the Ottawa area was held at Le Circle Universitaire on Laurier Street in Ottawa. This annual event was always a popular and well-attended affair. Senator Lamontagne, as a duly elected Fellow for his earlier contributions to economics, was also present. During the reception he took the opportunity to corner one of the senior administrators of the NRC to expound his ideas of replacing the NRC by a central bureau dealing with all of the government's endeavors in basic science. After listening quietly to this lengthy account of the newest proposal of the Senator's Committee on Science Policy, the officer could no longer contain his dismay. He informed the Senator that since he was so interested in Canada's scientific well being, he would no doubt be delighted to know that the next day an announcement would be made of the award of the Nobel Prize to Gerhard Herzberg of the NRC. On hearing this astonishing news Lamontagne turned on his heel and without another word walked out of the reception and dinner. The Senator immediately realized that with this blow any further criticism of the NRC and recommendations for its downfall by his Committee would lose its punch.

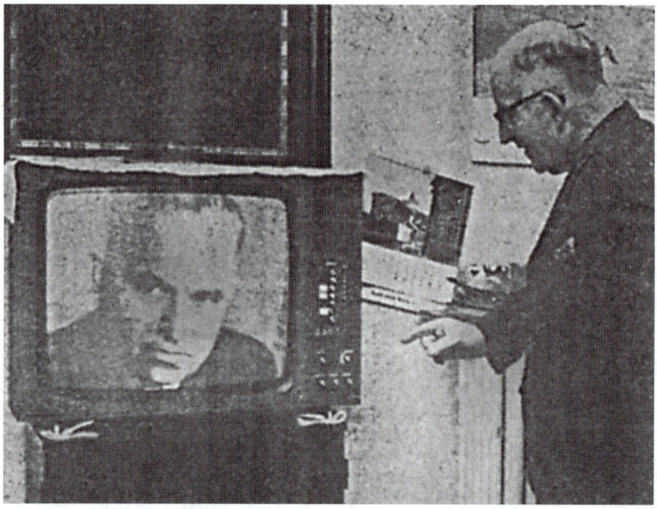

Walter Herzberg in Hamburg, watching his brother on television, on announcement of the Nobel Prize, 3 November 1971.

Canada awoke the next day to the news that a Canadian had been awarded a Nobel Prize in science, after a hiatus of five decades. No doubt the phone rang off the hook in Herzberg's home, since even the Swedish Academy did not know of his whereabouts until later in the day. Herzberg's office was inundated with congratulatory telegrams, phone calls, and letters from friends, colleagues, and admirers from all over the world.[4] Telegrams arrived from the Governor General, the Prime Minister, the Premier of Ontario, the Mayor of Ottawa, and many other Canadian politicians, as well as from the Mayor of Hamburg, Herzberg's birthplace. In Hamburg, Walter Herzberg and his wife Erika were deluged with calls from friends congratulating the family, and reporters interviewed Walter about his distinguished brother.[5] The Johanneum Gymnasium proudly added the name of alumnus Gerhard Herzberg to that of Gustav Hertz as a Nobel Laureate on its honours list.

Notably absent were any greetings that day or later from Senators Lamontagne or Grosart, and only one arrived from the remaining twenty members of the Senate Special Committee on Science Policy. Senator Joseph A. Sullivan, the one dissenting member of the Senate Report, graciously congratulated Herzberg on his outstanding achievement.[6] Miss Thompson and Miss Dabrowski posted telegrams all around office walls and on billboards, awaiting Herzberg's return from the Soviet Union.

Celebrations, Greetings, and the Governor General's Dinner

For Herzberg, the first hint of the Nobel Prize award had come just after his seminar "Spectra of Free Radicals" at the University of Leningrad. During discussion at the informal lunch that followed the talk, his host Professor Sergei Frish was called to the telephone for an urgent message. He quickly returned to the table and excitedly announced that Herzberg had been selected for the 1971 Nobel Prize in Physics. Herzberg sat momentarily stunned. Could this be possible? Could he accept such a rumour? Why in physics? Never mind, his hosts popped open bottles of champagne and filled glasses, serving first their unbelieving, teetotal guest.

After a lengthy train ride from Leningrad to Moscow, Herzberg was met at the railway station by Soviet colleagues Drs. S.L. Mandelstam and Igor I. Sobel'man and by Mr. and Mrs. P.L. Trottier, Counsellor in the Canadian Embassy, who relayed two telegrams, one from the Nobel Foundation:

> The Royal Academy of Sciences today awarded you the 1971 Nobel Prize in Chemistry for your contributions to the knowledge of electronic structure and geometry of molecules, especially free radicals. Our sincere congratulations.[7]

and one from NRC President Schneider:

> The President and Members of the National Research Council meeting in Ottawa, together with the entire staff, extend their heartfelt congratulations on your award of the Nobel Prize in Chemistry.[8]

These welcome messages confirmed that Herzberg had indeed been selected as a 1971 Nobel Laureate, but in Chemistry, not Physics, and he could finally put any doubt to rest. Although this had been a long day for him, Herzberg knew he wouldn't be able to sleep after such excitement. After being interviewed by Soviet TV and radio crews, he accepted Mandelstam's kind invitation to relax in his apartment. Together with his colleagues and Mrs. Mandelstam, he quietly celebrated the day's extraordinary news well into the night, a quite unforgettable occasion for Herzberg.[9]

Mr. and Mrs. Trottier invited Herzberg to their home the next afternoon, and a telephone interview was held with the famed Peter Gzowski of the Canadian Broadcasting Corporation in Toronto. The program, which included conversations with friends in Canada, was aired across the country. Herzberg then cancelled his original schedule of visits to Paris and Basel in order to return home as soon as possible. He flew to Stockholm for interviews with Swedish TV and radio media, since they had missed him in Ottawa. He also managed a brief visit with his friend Albin Lagerqvist at the university before boarding the plane for his return home.

At his office next morning, Herzberg was overwhelmed by the billboards covered with telegrams from all over the world and friendly greetings from the spectroscopy group and the piles of telegrams and letters on his desk. He read some of the messages and realized it would take days to go through all of them, and weeks if not months to answer them, even with the efficient help of Miss Thompson. One of the most heartwarming greetings came from Jack Shoosmith:

> It was with a great deal of pleasure and pride that I read of the Nobel award. Few people know better than I how great has been your dedication, patience and perseverance through many years of research which have culminated in this great honour. I am delighted to have had the opportunity to associate with so distinguished a scientist and occasionally to discuss gardening and the art of living.[10]

Herzberg at the entrance of the NRC on arrival from the U.S.S.R.

Telegram greetings from around the world.

A welcoming office on Herzberg's return from the U.S.S.R.

The spectroscopy group had not seen such a jubilant Herzberg since late spring, before Luise's unexpected death. He had regained his usual composure and vitality and now took the time to catch up on the progress and research plans with each member of the group.

Much to his surprise, Herzberg was invited to a special luncheon of the Science Council by the President of the Treasury Board, the Hon. Charles M. Drury, and there he met with Omond Solandt, the Chairman of the Council, Allistair Gillespie, the Minister of Science, and other members of Government. Drury also arranged for Herzberg to attend a sitting of the House of Commons, the Parliament Chamber of elected members, on 17 November, where the Speaker, the Hon. Lucien Lamoureux, said it was "a rare occasion when anyone other than a member of parliament was welcomed to the Commons, but he was proud to introduce Dr. Herzberg, an oustanding scientist who had brought great honour to himself, the National Research Council, and all Canadians". Herzberg stood up to acknowledge a rousing welcome of cheers and desk thumping—the parliamentary form of applause. This accolade from the Government of his adopted country was an historic moment for him and for Canada.[11]

The Right Honourable Roland Michener, Governor General of Canada, then hosted a festive dinner in Herzberg's honour at Government House on Tuesday, 30 November 1971. The eighty-five guests included Prime Minister Pierre Elliott Trudeau, the Hon. C.M. Drury, Herzberg's collaborators past and present at the National Research Council, and Canada's science elite from across the country.

After the dinner, the Governor General addressed his guests:

> The serious purposes of this gathering are about to be revealed. They are: to give enjoyment to Dr. Gerhard Herzberg and to ourselves in his company, and to rejoice with him in the recognition which has just been given by the Nobel Foundation to his great scientific achievements. Under such conditions he would not forgive me, nor would you be happy, if I were to embark on the eulogy he so well deserves. However, I hope that I may be allowed to say, for my wife and myself, how happy we are to welcome our distinguished guest to Rideau Hall.
>
> We are equally delighted that so many of his friends and admirers have come together, some from quite long distances, to join with us in honouring Dr. Herzberg. What impresses me most is the preponderance of brain power … never have the Philistines been so completely routed from Government House.
>
> À tous, nous exprimons notre plus chaleureux accueil. Je sais que j'exprime non seulement votre pensée, mais celle de tous les Canadiens, quand je dis à Docteur Herzberg qu'en lui nous rendons honneur à un grand Canadien. Nous sommes fier qu'en 1935, alors que le climat de son pais natal lui devenait intolérable, il ait arrêté son choix sur le Canada, comme patrie d'adoption. Nous sommes également fiers de l'habilité, de l'industrie, et de la détermination dont il a fait preuve dans son exploration des molécules et atomes.
>
> Son expertise dans l'enseignement et dans l'étude de la physique est l'objet de notre profonde reconnaissance. Nous lui savons un gré infini des services rendus à la collectivité, et, en dernier lieu, nous l'aimons en ami.
>
> Dr. Herzberg, to say that you have brought honour to Canada in winning the Nobel Prize in Chemistry for 1971 is no mere form of words. No other Canadian has received this coveted recognition since 1957, when the Right Hon. Lester B. Pearson, who regretted that he could not be here

tonight, was awarded the Nobel Peace Prize. There was only one before him, another great scientist, Sir Frederick Banting, whose Nobel Prize in Medicine in 1923 was for his work with insulin. As we all know, the discoveries made by Banting, Best, and Collip and others of the famous team have been a great boon to humanity since they were announced fifty years ago, and we know that Dr. Herzberg's discoveries are of great use both in industry and in science.

Dr. Herzberg, I do not profess the knowledge to appreciate fully the work which you have pursued to such good effect inside the molecule and the atom, or as the Swedish Academy of Science put it in its citation, 'for your contribution to the knowledge of electronic structure and geometry of molecules, particularly free radicals'. I am sure that free radicals and other activists deserve our closest scrutiny. But diatoms and polyatoms have so far escaped my observation.

Like most other mortals, my knowledge of matter has been limited to what is disclosed by our five senses. It is fortunate that some amongst us have been able to peer beneath the surface of things and to discover the secrets of our infinitely small and infinitely large environment.

As for "molecular spectroscopy" I sympathize with your daughter Agnes. Although she desired, as good children do, to follow in their father's footsteps, she said at an early age that she would be a nurse, and gave as a reason that she could not even spell "molecular spectroscopy". But she holds one of the four Ph.D.'s which have been earned within the family circle.

Dr. Herzberg's other awards, honorary degrees, medals, fellowships, and the offices which he has discharged so well in scientific societies, are numerous beyond recollection and put him up in the stratosphere. But his hobbies and avocations keep him a very human and engaging person. His love of Italian opera and a fine bass voice commend him to other music lovers. But in mountain climbing for exercise and relaxation, one would have difficulty in keeping up with him—he loves the heights.

In all his varied activities he has our good wishes. Will you join me in expressing them in a toast to the health and continued happiness and success of Dr. Herzberg, C.C., D.Sc., LL.D., F.R.S., F.R.S.C., Canadian physicist.[12]

Dr. Herzberg replied:

Your Excellencies, Mr. Prime Minister, Ladies and Gentlemen.

I am deeply touched by the honour that you, Your Excellencies, have done me in having this delightful dinner for me, and that you, Sir, have done me in addressing me in such generous terms. On a few previous occasions I have had the privilege of being invited to these beautiful surroundings and being entertained by Your Excellencies, who know so well how to make your guests feel comfortable and relaxed and enjoy your hospitality. When I came to this country with my wife thirty-six years ago as a refugee (incidentally with exactly $2.50 in my pocket), I could not have dreamed that one day I would be honoured in such an extraordinary way by the Government of Canada.

It is obvious that the work that has earned me the Nobel Prize was not done without a great deal of help. First of all, while at the University of Saskatchewan I had the full and understanding support of successive Presidents and of the Faculty of the University who, under very stringent conditions, did their utmost to make it possible for me to proceed with my scientific work. It was the first President of the University of Saskatchewan, Dr. Walter C. Murray, who was stimulated by a then junior staff member, John Spinks, now President of the University of Saskatchewan, to invite me to come to Saskatchewan. Indeed this was the only firm offer of a position that I had at the time.

Since I came to the National Research Council twenty-three years ago, I have had the support of the Presidents of the NRC, from C.J. Mackenzie, E.W.R. Steacie, and Guy Ballard to the present President, Dr. Schneider. I would like particularly to pay tribute to the late Ned Steacie. As soon as he heard that I was not entirely happy in the United States, he suggested that we have a discussion about the possibility of my coming here; later he persuaded me to take on the Directorship of the Physics Division. He also taught me how to direct a Division, namely not to tell people what to do but mainly to find bright people. Last, but by no means least, I must mention my indebtedness to all my collaborators during all these years. I shall not name them all individually but shall mention only one name. I was extraordinarily lucky when the most brilliant student I had during my university career agreed to join me at the NRC right from the beginning and help me to set up a laboratory in spectroscopy. I am not exaggerating when I say that without Alex Douglas's constant help, his critical judgment and his experimental skill, I would not be standing here now. Another person to whom I owe a great deal is my technical assistant for twenty years, Mr. Jack Shoosmith, who helped me in all the experimental work with great efficiency and devotion. I am glad that both he and Alex Douglas and many of my other collaborators, past and present, as well as former Presidents and the present President of NRC, are here tonight. I appreciate, Your Excellency, the implication of your invitation to them that this honour, the Nobel Prize, is an honour to the members of our spectroscopy laboratory and to the National Research Council.

There has been a tendency on the part of the public and the press to think that with the award of a Nobel Prize the international status of Canadian science has suddenly changed. I believe that the respect for Canadian science and Canadian scientists throughout the scientific world has not changed one iota. What has changed is the public knowledge of this respect. There are today just as many internationally recognized Canadian scientists as there were five weeks ago, and among them are quite definitely several of Nobel Prize calibre.

By building the National Arts Center and by other actions, the Government of Canada has shown that the people of this country are not interested in mere survival as a national goal, that they want to support the performing arts, as well as the fine arts and literature. What I would like to emphasize is that pure science is another of the activities that lifts us above a purely mercenary status and that the support of science for cultural reasons alone should not be neglected. In this connection it is interesting to record that the Nobel medal which I shall be receiving next week has a Latin inscription from Virgil, the same for all four prizes (even though otherwise the medals are different), which is

"Inventas vitam juvat excoluisse per artes",

for which, in the book which was sent to me, only a French translation is given, Qu'il est doux de voir la vie humaine s'embellir par l'invention des arts", or in English,

"It is wonderful to see life enriched by the invention of the arts".

Clearly the Nobel Foundation considers the Prizes in the Sciences to have the same purpose as the Prize in Literature, namely to reward contributions to the human spirit, i.e., to the cultural benefits of mankind.

In science, of course, such contributions often lead to material benefits to mankind. Since one cannot predict discovery these material benefits are usually quite unexpected and not forseen by the scientists involved (nor of course by anyone else). The motivation of many scientists working in pure science is striving for knowledge for its own sake. Applications can rarely be forseen and are up to the technologist to find on the basis of the work of the pure scientist.

In a speech last March, I compared the present situation in science with the situation in the Army. I said: "Recent reports indicate that for every private in the Army there are four of higher rank. Now it appears to me that for every working scientist there are four persons spending their time deciding how and where and when he should work". Some of my friends have warned me that after receiving the Nobel Prize I would now belong to this higher rank. May I say that I have every intention of returning to the rank of private in the army of Canadian scientists, once the first flurry connected with the Prize is over. Indeed, my future happiness will depend on how successful I shall be in this effort.

Thank you again, Your Excellencies, for this memorable occasion with which you have so greatly honoured me, the National Research Council and the many brilliant collaborators who have made our laboratory known throughout the world.[13]

The guests then mingled, talking with Herzberg and Their Excellencies. This also turned out to be a very special occasion to meet Prime Minister Pierre Trudeau, who asked President Schneider to introduce him to members of the Spectroscopy Laboratory, past and present. He met each in turn, spent a few minutes discussing their roles and interests, and then thanked them for their contributions in bringing fame to the NRC and Canada. This grand event at Rideau Hall on 30th November 1971, with its magnificent tribute by the Government of Canada to Herzberg and the Spectroscopy Laboratory, will never be forgotten by members of the NRC.

Next day, Herzberg sent a very moving letter to the Right Honourable Roland Michener:

Your Excellency: The dinner last night was such an extraordinary occasion for me that I find it difficult to put into words my deep gratitude to you and Mrs. Michener for having tendered it to me. The warmth of your reception and the very kind words you said about me will remain in my memory for the rest of my life. The inclusion among the guests of so many of my collaborators, past and present, on this festive occasion was a particularly fine gesture on your part, since I owe so much to them and am anxious to share with them the recognition that has come to our joint efforts....[14]

Herzberg also dispatched a letter to Esmond Butler at Rideau Hall thanking him and his staff for the thoughtful arrangements at the dinner.

On to Stockholm

A day later, Herzberg was on his way to Stockholm by a circuitous route, for he had a previous obligation to attend to in Seattle. He had been awarded the Linus Pauling Medal of the American Chemical Society months earlier and wished to honour his commitment to attend the presentation. He was especially delighted that Linus Pauling was there and that they had time to discuss their favourite topics of molecular structure and molecules in medicine. In the past, it had been the custom for the medal recipient to give an award address at the banquet, but Herzberg felt that it would be a hardship for a captive audience, some of whom were not scientists, to have to listen to a technical talk. So he presented the technical paper "Spectra of Simple Free Radicals in the Gaseous Phase" at a symposium in the afternoon and a more general talk at the banquet. He chose to address the audience with "Some Remarks on Science and Culture" and began with an introduction to C.P. Snow's *The Two Cultures and the Scientific Revolution* on the lack of understanding between scientists and humanists. Herzberg's theme was that now a third group, politicians, recognizing the importance of the sciences for their economies, believe that this is all science is good for—so scientists should to be told what to do. Politicians do not realize that science, at its best, is a creative or cultural pursuit, that its prime motivation is the desire to understand nature. Another group, some student activists, don't understand science either, because they think of technology when they speak of science, just as politicians do. They are concerned, and rightly so, about the consequences of technological developments of our time, but they are fighting science when their goal is the same as that of the sciences, namely to emphasize the cultural aspects of life, to understand our place in the world, and to make human life worthwhile.[15]

Herzberg arrived in Stockholm on 6 December and to his surprise was met at the airport by Her Excellency Margaret Meagher, the Canadian Ambassador to Sweden, and by Professor Erik Rudberg, the Permanent Secretary of the Royal Academy of Sciences. He was introduced to Tom Engdahl, a secretary in the Royal Ministry for Foreign Affairs, who would serve as Herzberg's attendant along with a chauffer and car during Nobel week. Herzberg was driven to the Grand Hotel, settled in a splendid suite overlooking the harbour, and welcomed with a huge basket of fruit and vases full of flowers. He carefully unpacked his formal attire, which was to be worn at the main functions during Nobel week. As was his custom when travelling, he reviewed his busy schedule of receptions, lunches, and dinners before relaxing with a hot bath and retiring after his long flight from Seattle.[16] He was to go over his Nobel lecture and his address to His Majesty at every opportunity in the following days.

The week of activities began the next afternoon with a press conference at the Chancellory of the Canadian Embassy. On the morning of 8 December, he met his daughter Agnes at Arlanda Airport, on arrival from London. She was to join him in the formal events to which Laureates and families were invited. Unfortunately, his son Paul was not able to go to Sweden on this very special occasion. Later that morning, Herzberg visited his friend Albin Lagerqvist at the Physical Institute of Stockholm University. That evening, Herzberg and Agnes joined the Laureates and spouses at a dinner in the home of Professor and Mrs. Erik Rudberg on the grounds of the Royal Academy of Sciences. Next day, they both went to the airport to meet Monika Tenthoff, the niece of Herzberg's gymnasium friend Alfred Schulz, whom Herzberg had invited as his guest to the Nobel Festival. All three attended a reception in the afternoon in the Nobel Library of the Swedish Academy, hosted by the Directors of the Nobel Foundation.

Nobel Festival, 10 December 1971

Finally, the ceremonial day, Friday December 10th, arrived and began with a morning rehearsal for the Laureates. The Nobel Festival began at four in the afternoon with the city in darkness as the sun had set two hours earlier. A stream of black limousines escorted by police left the Grand Hotel at 3:30 P.M. with the Nobel Laureates and dignitaries headed for the Filadelfiakyrkan (Philadelphia Church) where this year's ceremony was to take place, instead of the usual Concert Hall which was closed for repairs. The drive to the church was a spectacle as the streets were lit up with Lucia candles in every window and the twinkling lights of Christmas trees. At 4:15 P.M. the audience, in formal attire, filed into the immense hall to music by the Stockholm Philharmonic Orchestra. The hall was decorated with garlands of flowers, an annual gift from the town of San Remo in Italy where Alfred Nobel had spent his last years. At 4:30 the King of Sweden entered the hall and the audience rose to honour him, the Royal Prince and his wife, and the Royal Highnesses of Denmark and Holland. The Laureates and presenters followed and stepped onto the stage to take their places in front of red padded armchairs. They were followed by members of the Royal Academy and the audience. It was a glittering setting of grandeur and pageantry.[17]

After the opening music, the President of the Nobel Foundation, Professor U.S. von Euler, recalled that this was the seventy-fifth anniversary of Alfred Nobel's death. He welcomed His Majesty King Gustav VI,

Nobel Festival, 10 December 1971, with Nobel Laureates and presenters on the stage of the Philadelphia Church and his Majesty and Royal Families in the front row, right.

observing that as a young prince he had been present when the Prizes were first awarded in 1901.[18] The participation in 1971 turned out to be his last.

The Laureates were then presented to the King, following the overture of Mozart's "The Marriage of Figaro". In his will endowing the Prizes, Alfred Nobel had put physics at the top of the list, and so the Physics Prize was presented first.[19] Dennis Gabor, a Hungarian-born British scientist, received it for his invention and development of the holographic method.

Then came chemistry, and Herzberg was introduced by Professor Stig Claesson of the Royal Academy of Sciences, who began:

> Your Majesty, Your Royal Highnesses, Ladies and Gentlemen,
>
> This year's Nobel Prize winner in Chemistry, Dr. Gerhard Herzberg, is generally considered to be the world's foremost molecular spectroscopist and his large institute in Ottawa is the undisputed centre for such research. It is quite exceptional, in the field of science, that a single individual, however distinguished, in this way can be the leader of a whole area of research of general importance. A noted English chemist has also said that the only institutions which have previously played such

> a role were the Cavendish Laboratory in Cambridge and Bohr's institute in Copenhagen....
>
> One may now ask why Herzberg—originally a physicist and even famous as an astrophysicist—finally was awarded the Nobel Prize in chemistry.
>
> The explanation is that around 1950 molecular spectroscopy had progressed so far that one could begin to study even complicated systems of great chemical interest. This is brilliantly demonstrated by Herzberg's pioneering investigations of free radicals. Knowledge of their properties is of fundamental importance to our understanding of how chemical reactions proceed.... Many of the most important results were only achieved after several year's work and some of the most exciting as late as the end of the 1960s. One can therefore note that this year's Prize is truly an award for contributions of great current interest.[20]

Professor Claesson then turned to Herzberg.

> Dr. Herzberg: I have tried to explain your great contributions to molecular spectroscopy and particularly your pioneering work on free radicals. The ideas and results presented by you—not least regarding the quantum mechanical aspects of the interpretation of molecular properties—have influenced scientific progress in almost all branches of chemistry.
>
> On behalf of the Royal Academy of Sciences I beg you to accept our congratulations and ask you to receive your Nobel Prize from the hands of His Majesty the King.

A fanfare of trumpets sounded as Herzberg stood up, descended the steps, and approached the King. Herzberg bowed and received the blue leather-bound diploma and the 23-karat gold medal. There was thunderous applause as he bowed again to the King, to members of the Royal Academy and dignitaries, and to the audience.

This procedure was followed by all of the Laureates. The next was Earl W. Sutherland, an American scientist awarded the Prize in Physiology and Medicine, followed by Pablo Neruda, the Chilean poet with the Literature Prize. After a musical interlude—Rossini's Overture to "The Magpie"—Simon Kuznets, a Russian-born, American economist, received the Memorial Prize in Economic Science. Willy Brandt, the Chancellor of West Germany, was presented with the Nobel Peace Prize at the University of Oslo in Norway on the same day. That year, the Nobel Prizes in all six categories were awarded to single individuals. The last time this had happened was in 1948; each Prize is often shared by two and up to three persons.

Congratulations from His Majesty King Gustav VI, 10 December 1971.

The 1971 Nobel Laureates: from left, Simon Kuznets, Pablo Neruda, Earl W. Sutherland, Gerhard Herzberg, and Dennis Gabor.

On examining the medal, Herzberg noted the profile of Alfred Nobel on the front and the Goddess of Nature on the reverse, holding in her arms the horn of plenty as the Genius of Science lifts the veil from her eyes. Along the rim there is the Latin inscription from Virgil's *Aeneid* that Herzberg had mentioned in his address in Rideau Hall. His name and the year of the award were on the bottom. The colourful diploma included a large landscape of mountains, no doubt a suggestion by his Swedish friends who knew of his love of heights. A continuous spectrum was added along the base of the mountains. On the opposite side was Herzberg's name and the Prize citation in Swedish: "For his contributions to the knowledge of electronic structure and geometry of molecules, particularly free radicals".

After the ceremony, all departed by car for the magnificent City Hall, where the new Laureates and their families gathered in the Prince's Gallery to be introduced to His Majesty and to members of the Royal Families of Sweden, Denmark, and Holland. In this way, Herzberg and Agnes had a few personal moments with them. The Banquet then followed in the glorious "Golden Hall", dazzling with its myriad gold-leaf mosaics and filled with hundreds of guests seated at tables covered in fine linen, flowers, and glowing candles. Accompanied by choral music, the Laureates and immediate families followed the King along the hallway and aisle to their designated places. Herzberg escorted Princess Margareth of Denmark to the head table: she sat on his right and Mrs. Simon Kuznets sat on his left. A fanfare of trumpets, horns, organ, and singing heralded a stream of waiters each carrying a tray aloft as they paraded along the aisles, preceded by pages carrying torches, banners, and gigantic baskets of flowers. Course after course was served in this manner, while wine and water goblets were refilled after each sip. Choral and instrumental music entertained the revellers throughout the evening.

At the Banquet, the President of the Nobel Foundation presented a toast in honour of the King, followed by a fanfare and the Swedish National Anthem. The Royal Prince presented a silent toast in memory of Alfred Nobel. After the dinner a brief speech and toast to the year's Laureates was offered by Dr. Sture Petrén of the Swedish Academy, and the Laureates were given the opportunity to briefly address the King and guests. When it was Herzberg's turn to speak, he walked to the podium accompanied by a flurry of trumpets:

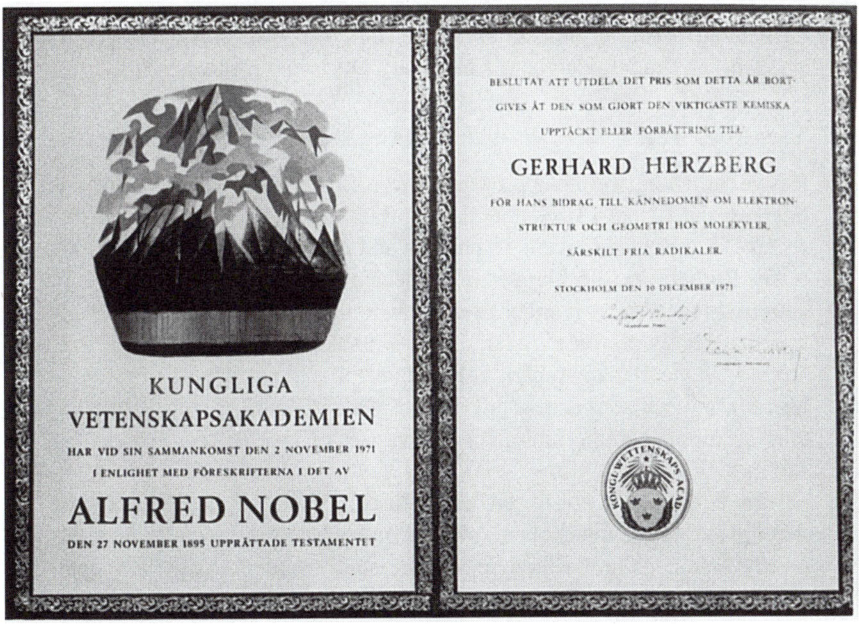

KUNGLIGA
VETENSKAPSAKADEMIEN
HAR VID SIN SAMMANKOMST DEN 2 NOVEMBER 1971
I ENLIGHET MED FÖRESKRIFTERNA I DET AV
ALFRED NOBEL
DEN 27 NOVEMBER 1895 UPPRÄTTADE TESTAMENTET

BESLUTAT ATT UTDELA DET PRIS SOM DETTA ÅR BORT-
GIVES ÅT DEN SOM GJORT DEN VIKTIGASTE KEMISKA
UPPTÄCKT ELLER FÖRBÄTTRING TILL
GERHARD HERZBERG
FÖR HANS BIDRAG TILL KÄNNEDOMEN OM ELEKTRON-
STRUKTUR OCH GEOMETRI HOS MOLEKYLER,
SÄRSKILT FRIA RADIKALER.
STOCKHOLM DEN 10 DECEMBER 1971

The Nobel Medal and Diploma.

The Golden Hall of Stockholm's City Hall. This occasion is a banquet at the time of Herzberg's Honorary Doctorate Degree, 1966.

Your Royal Highnesses, Distinguished Guests, Ladies and Gentlemen,

It is very difficult to find appropriate words to say "thank you" for an honour like the Nobel Prize. It is the supreme honour that a scientist can receive. Some of the giants in physics and chemistry have received this prize. Rutherford, the founder of nuclear physics, received the prize in chemistry in 1908. A number of those who have taught me either directly or indirectly are on that list: James Franck, Max Born, Peter Debye, Harold Urey and many others. I should also like to pay tribute to two pioneers in molecular spectroscopy from Sweden, Heurlinger and Hulthén, who accomplished the first difficult analyses of molecular spectra in the 1920s.

In receiving the award this year, I think not only of these giants from whom I learned so much but also of my first teacher, Hans Rau, who guided my first steps in research, and to the many collaborators who helped me in my later work. Of them, I should like to single out A.E. Douglas, whose quick and critical mind was always ready to help. I also think of my adopted country Canada, which gave a haven to me and my wife when we arrived as refugees. I think of the University of Saskatchewan

> which supported my work in its early stages and the National Research Council of Canada which provided an atmosphere so conducive to research.
>
> Five years ago I received the great honour of an Honorary Degree from the University of Stockholm here in this building. It was at the same ceremony that His Majesty the King received an Honorary Degree from the Royal Caroline Medico-Chirurgical Insitute. I felt doubly honoured that His Majesty was present throughout this ceremony. I could hardly have expected at that time that five years later I would stand here again in this building having received the great and supreme honour of the Nobel Prize from His Majesty's hands. I shall be forever grateful. *Tak så mycket.*[21]

A ball was held in the enchanting "Blue Hall". Herzberg, Agnes, and Monika met briefly with the Laureates, spouses, and members of the Academy in the adjacent Prince's Gallery and then made an early exit as the long night of partying was known to be carried on well past midnight.

This had been an unforgettable day—breathtaking in grandeur, and highly emotional, yet full of charm and grace—and thoroughly enjoyable!

Further Nobel Activities

Dennis Gabor and Herzberg were greeted at the Royal Institute of Technology by a packed auditorium of scientists, students, and the general public who had come to hear their Nobel Lectures on Saturday afternoon. Herzberg chose for his title "Spectroscopic Studies of Molecular Structures", and he talked about some of the more significant results of his studies extending over the forty-four years of his scientific life.[22]

That evening, the King hosted a dinner at the Palace. Again a procession of limousines brought the Laureates and families into a torch-lit courtyard. A flight of ninety marble steps led into a stately drawing room (some had to stop and catch their breath on the way up, but Herzberg took it all in stride) where they were received by His Majesty, the Royal Prince and Family, Academy Officers, and other notables. Dinner was a quieter affair than the Nobel Banquet but full of congenial discussion.

Sunday turned out to be a day of rest, except for an informal and impromptu TV discussion in the afternoon between the Laureates of Physics, Chemistry, and Medicine, organized by Bengt Feldreich, the Science Editor of Sveriges Radio/TV. In the evening, Albin and Brita

Lagerqvist hosted a dinner at home for their friend Gerhard Herzberg, who was joined by Agnes, Monika, Stig Claesson, and Bengt Feldreich.

On Monday morning, 13 December, Herzberg was awakened by an unannounced invasion of his bedroom by the "Lucia" singers, young damsels dressed in long white gowns and crowned with laurels of lights, escorted by young men also in white, all singing "Santa Lucia". They brought a tray of pastries, ginger cookies, and hot coffee while singing carols, all of which was being filmed by a TV crew. This was an initial shock for Herzberg, and no doubt for all of the Laureates who had not been forewarned, followed by much amusement. Later, the Laureates had tall tales to tell of their encounters with this annual Nobel prank. A visit to the offices of the Nobel Foundation that morning added to the day's enjoyment, as arrangements were made to pick up the monetary awards or to transfer the prize amounts to respective banks. That year each award was 447,000 Swedish kroner or about $91,000 Canadian for Herzberg.

In the afternoon, Her Excellency Ambassador Meagher hosted a luncheon at her residence and invited Professors Lagerqvist and Claesson as well as Monika to join the Herzbergs. The evening was another white-tie affair, the annual Lucia Dinner given by the Students of Science Union of the University of Stockholm. St. Lucia is a "patron" of Swedish winter, and her feast falls on 13 December when the nights are darkest and longest, at a time when the days are about to grow brighter with the promise of spring. Lucia is a symbol of this light and the Lucia Dinner marks the beginning of the Christmas season in Sweden. A traditional dinner was served in a candle-lit hall, accompanied by music, singing, and hilarious skits, followed by the Lucia singers descending the stairs singing "Santa Lucia" and Swedish carols. Shortly after, the Laureates were called to the stage. Each was eulogized mercilessly and dubbed a "Knight of The Supreme Order of the Ever Jumping and Smiling Green Frog" and then were decorated with a green porcelain frog hanging on a ribbon, all amidst much laughter and cheering. So ended Nobel Week, with good fun and the high jinks of students.

Herzberg completed his ten days in Sweden by visiting his friend Stig Claesson at the University of Uppsala and on the next day Bengt Edlén at Lund University, giving lectures at both institutes. He then spent a few days with Alfred Kastler in Paris and with Ernst Miescher and Konrad Bleuler in Switzerland before flying to London to be with Agnes during Christmas.

PART FOUR

LATER YEARS (1972–1999)

Posterity, in time, will give us all our true measure and assign to each of us our due and humble place; and in the end it is the judgement of posterity that really matters.

Edward Arthur Milne

21. WEATHERING THE AFTERMATH

Along with the glamour and esteem, many other consequences accrue to recipients of Nobel Prizes. In the first year or two, they are overwhelmed with invitations to speak at universities and conferences, to address young students and local clubs, and to participate in charitable funding appeals. Moreover, their opinion is requested on all sorts of matters public and private, whether or not they have any expertise on the topic. While some Laureates bask in this new found glory, it has often taken its toll on others, and some have stopped doing research altogether.

Herzberg was well aware of the added responsibilities as well as opportunities for speaking to the young about the importance and pleasures of doing science. He was also being urged by colleagues to use his newly recognized prestige to defend Canadian science and the NRC from the attacks by the Senate Special Committee on Science Policy. However, he was worried about the time away from his beloved research. Friends who were Nobel Laureates tried to forewarn him. Along with his congratulations Isidor Rabi wrote: "The Nobel Prize brings with it many problems and you may as well enjoy it before the avalanche descends on you and interferes with your proper work." Alfred Kastler pointed out "the only way to survive is to learn to say no!"

Myriad of Invitations

As expected, Herzberg was swamped with invitations; they arrived two each day in the first year and slackened off to one per day, then slowly to one every two or three days in the following years. He couldn't say "no" to many of these requests since he felt he owed Canada a debt for the long-time support of his research. In 1972, he travelled widely giving lectures, accepting honorary degrees and awards, and participating in the ceremonial openings of new laboratories. His time for research work was cut to half, as the decrease in publications for the years after 1972 reveal, and his scientific productivity resumed its normal level only near the end of the 1970s through his dogged determination. After the first year he set aside three months, December to February, for which he did not accept engagements, and with his disciplined approach to research, he managed to achieve an enormous amount. The first celebratory occasions took place in Ottawa, Saskatoon, and Toronto, with special lectures at the Universities of British Columbia, Toronto, and Harvard, followed by a visit to England. All of these activities had to be fitted in with a new lifestyle following his marriage to Monika Tenthoff in 1972.

But first things first. Herzberg personally answered many of the telegrams and letters of congratulation from close friends and colleagues, and others were thanked with a formal card signed by him. The letter of congratulations from his devoted technical assistant Jack Shoosmith elicited this reply:

> Many thanks for your letter which reached me while in London celebrating Christmas with Agnes. I had intended to write to you for some time but life has been very hectic indeed and still is. However, I must no longer postpone sending you a small token, taken from the Nobel Prize, to acknowledge in a little more tangible way my indebtedness to you for all your efforts in those twenty years, which proved to be an important contribution towards the award. Without your enthusiastic support at all times much less would have been accomplished and it is more than a little doubtful whether the prize would have been awarded to me. I shall be forever in your debt and I realize that this small token cannot begin to repay that debt. I hope that both you and Mrs. Shoosmith are in good health. With all good wishes to you both.[1]

Along with the many invitations to speak at schools in Ottawa and at universities across the country and in the United States, there were constant requests to be interviewed for newspapers, magazines, radio, and TV. Herzberg agreed to most of them. For interviews that were to appear in print he asked to see proofs before publication and in one instance noted to the writer: "You compare me with Rutherford, Thomson, Planck, and Bohr—they are of such a different order of magnitude that I would feel rather embarassed if such a comparison were included in your article." Often when asked "What research are you doing now?", he would not hesitate to remind the questioner, adding his little chuckle, that he had very little time for work since much of his time was spent in just such interviews. Even so, Herzberg seemed to enjoy the attention and was pleased that science was getting more coverage in the media.

There was one interview he especially welcomed, since it dealt with his love of music, opera, and singing.[2] He and the interviewer carried on a light-hearted exchange, with Herzberg confessing (but not with conviction): "Yes, after all is said and done, opera is my true love not science. And now that I have won the big prize, … maybe now is the time to look at my singing." The interviewer then went to the trouble of contacting David Galbraith, Herzberg's private voice teacher in Ottawa, and two of the world's leading opera singers, Richard Tucker in Florence, Italy, who was performing in Verdi's *Masked Ball*, and the bass-baritone Jerome Hines in New York. Galbraith told him that Herzberg has tremendous potential: "I only take advanced pupils, so there you are. He's one of my best, a fine student." Tucker noted: "I think it's wonderful, marvellous. But he might be too old for many roles. Of course there's the father in 'La Traviata' and that's even a bass-baritone like him. I'd like to give him some pointers. Have him call me at my private number". Hines, too, wanted to talk to Herzberg and gave his number: "I am a chemist myself, Master's degree in

Serenaded by student band on a visit to the University of Saskatchewan, with his friend President John Spinks, 1972.

organic chemistry from UCLA, but I knew I would be an opera singer from the time I was sixteen. I find that science and opera satisfy contrary things in my nature. If I had a choice I would be a chemist."

The first celebratory occasion on Herzberg's return to Ottawa was to be greeted by his colleagues at a special reception to which all NRC personnel were invited. He was overwhelmed by this thoughtful gesture and the warmth of the gathering. He was also delighted to receive an invitation from his "home town" Saskatoon, with the Mayor, the President of the University of Saskatchewan, and the Lieutenant Governor of Saskatchewan honouring him at a festive dinner to be held in Saskatoon in February 1972. There he was presented with the City Award of Merit, and Herzberg Park was named in his honour.[3] Later, the University inaugurated the Gerhard Herzberg Fellowships of $5,000 each in the basic physical sciences, one for the Saskatchewan campus and one for the Regina campus.

Marriage

Gerhard and Monika were married on 21 March 1972 at the Provincial Court in Ottawa. His son and Monika's mother served as witnesses, and a few friends attended the civil ceremony followed by a reception at the

Monika and Gerhard at their wedding reception.

Herzberg home on Lakeway Drive. Monika Elisabeth Tenthoff was born in 1941 in Germany, the daughter of Carl Tenthoff and Hertha Schulz (the sister of Herzberg's gymnasium friend Alfred). Monika grew up in Hamburg living with her mother, grandmother, and Uncle Alfred. She never knew her father: he had gone off to war, then her parents divorced shortly after the war. After elementary and high school, Monika spent nine months in London as an "au pair" in order to improve her English and while there earned a "Lower Cambridge Certificate". Back in Hamburg, she attended a College of Commerce and then worked as a secretary for a shipping company there and later for a weekly magazine in Munich. During her childhood and adolescent years, Uncle Alfred was a very important person in her life. Through this family connection, Monika had often met Gerhard while on his visits with Alfred and had also met Luise on similar occasions.

As some of his letters reveal, Gerhard was concerned as to what his close friends thought of his second marriage and to one so young. In a letter to Harry Welsh in Toronto he wrote: "I will marry soon. I hope this will not shock you too much." And to his longtime friends Chandra and Lalitha with their traditional Indian upbringing, he wrote: "All of my friends and even Luise's friends and relatives (in particular her favourite nephew Peter Thurnauer, who with his wife was present at the wedding) have been very understanding of the situation. I can only hope that you will give a friend of such long standing the benefit of the doubt."

Understandably, some friends and colleagues questioned this marriage and took their time in accepting Monika within their circle. This could have been a lonely period for her in Ottawa, but she was immediately caught up in the busy life of travel with Gerhard, as he felt obliged to accept many of the invitations to give lectures, especially to young students. In time, his friends realized this was a good marriage, enriching the lives of both over the twenty-seven years of their life together.

Further Tributes

At the meeting of Council of the NRC in March 1972, members began to consider how best to honour Herzberg in a permanent way.[4] Suggestions were made to name an NRC building after him and to ensure the preservation of some of the apparatus connected with his research. However, Carleton University had pre-empted the NRC in naming its physics building, the Herzberg Laboratories for Physics. This marked a triumvirate of

The Gerhard Herzberg Laboratories for Physics
at Carleton University, Ottawa.

NRC leaders for Carleton University with its C.J. Mackenzie Engineering Building and E.W.R. Steacie Chemistry Building. Another suggestion was to have a portrait painted to hang in the rotunda of the Sussex Drive Laboratories, along with portraits of the NRC Presidents. It was finally decided to commission a life-size bronze bust of Herzberg for display in the rotunda. Since the expenses for such a project could not be covered by official funds, friends, colleagues, and NRC staff contributed towards this lasting tribute.[5] The selected sculptor was John Miecznikowski of the Fine Arts Department of McMaster University in Hamilton, Ontario. Herzberg marvelled at the speed with which he worked and admired his persistence until he was satisfied with the result. Herzberg found Miecznikowski to be an extremely likeable person and the experience of working with him was a very pleasant one.[6] Two bronze busts were completed, one for the NRC and one for Herzberg. The formal unveiling of the sculpture by C. Jack Mackenzie took place in the NRC Auditorium on 7 August 1973.

William C. Price of King's College, London, an eminent spectroscopist and friend, organized an exhibit on the scientific work of Herzberg and of Dennis Gabor at the Institute of Physics Exhibition held 13–16 March 1972, in London. Photographs of the two Nobel Laureates were shown, along with

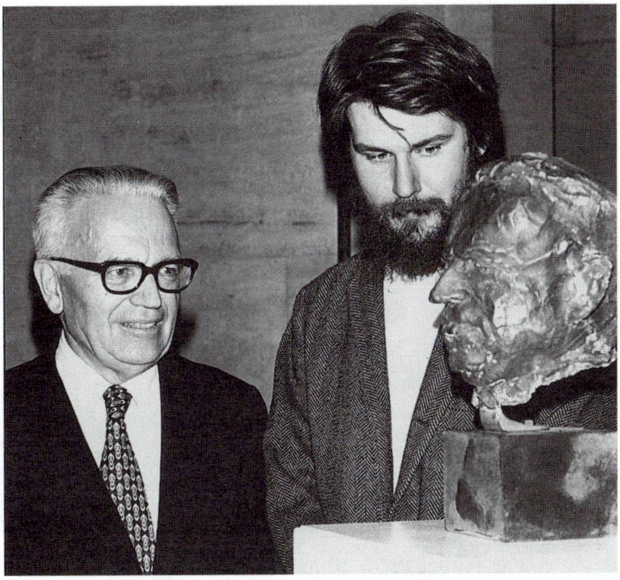

Sculptor John Miecznikowski and Herzberg at
the unveiling of the bust at NRC, August 1973.

their medals and diplomas, their laboratories, their publication lists, and many letters from colleagues and friends extolling their achievements.[7]

> There is a sort of purity and perfection in his work and writing which has an irresistable appeal to the idealism of young scientists. This has enabled him to build in Ottawa a superb school of spectroscopy which serves as a standard of excellence by which other spectroscopists can judge their achievements. [William C. Price of King's College, London]

> The respect and affection which Dr. Gerhard Herzberg commands are unique. They are based on a genius for friendship and an enthusiasm and excitement about spectroscopy which he communicates in person. [Richard Barrow of Oxford University]

> Gerhard Herzberg has always been characterized, not only by scientific skill, but also by integrity of purpose, which has been an inspiration to younger workers and to his colleagues everywhere. [Harold W. Thompson, also of Oxford]

> I find the greatest achievement has been the writing of his three books on molecular spectra. These, besides giving a clear account of the basic

The Nobel Prize commemoration by the
Institute of Physics in London, England, 1972.

> theory, have served largely to fix spectroscopic notation and include, most valuable of all, detailed tabulation of spectroscopic data. [A.G. Gaydon of Imperial College, London]

> To work in the Spectroscopy Laboratory after the years spent on one's doctoral thesis was to enter a new world. Here was a group of men devoted to the pursuit of science in a spirit of the highest ideals.... One learned so much: but perhaps three things above all. Firstly, hard facts are what count. Secondly, humility in the face of one's own ignorance. And thirdly, perhaps the most enduring, that a thing of beauty is a joy forever. [John Callomon of University College, London, and former NRC postdoctoral fellow]

The Honourable William G. Davis, Premier of Ontario, entertained many friends of Herzberg at a special dinner in his honour at the Ontario Science Centre in Toronto on 17 May 1972.[8] Davis presented Monika with a gold brooch featuring Ontario's flower, the trillium, and Herzberg with a complete set of the recorded works of Beethoven. A special gift was the mask worn by Renato in the *Masked Ball*, this being suggested by Robert Herman, the Assistant General Manager of the Metropolitan Opera in New York. Herzberg began his speech in a light-hearted vein, mentioning that in the last five months he had gone through the experience of listening to quite a number of speeches about himself and as a result had developed a split personality. On the one hand, he very much appreciated and enjoyed the remarks, and on the other, he was beginning to wonder more and more whether they referred to him or to an idealized Herzberg. He was thrilled with the Premier's splendid gifts, especially noting that the aria "Eri tu" from the *Masked Ball* was one of his very own favourites.

The month of June found the Herzbergs in England, first in Cambridge, where he received an honorary degree (postponed because of his bereavement the year before), and then in London, where he attended the Lord Mayor's Midsummer Banquet in honour of those eminent in the arts, sciences, and learning.

In an effort to relax from his busy schedule of research and travel, the Herzbergs purchased a small cottage on Lynch Lake in Quebec, about an hour's drive north of Ottawa. They spent many a weekend enjoying the silence of the area, with swimming and canoeing on their own lake. The Spectroscopy Group joined them for picnics and visitors and colleagues were invited. In the first few years, Paul and Louise came from Toronto and stayed for a few weeks during summer vacations. Gerhard and Monika soon found that with their frequent travels, they were not able to spend as much time at the cottage as they would have wished, and visits there became a rare treat.

Maintenance at the cottage on Lynch Lake in Quebec.

Renewed Challenge on Science Policy

Among the stacks of letters and telegrams covering his desk in the new year, Herzberg noted a pre-publication copy of the long-awaited second volume of the Senate Committee. As much as he procrastinated in studying the report during this extremely busy period, he finally succumbed to scanning its forty-five recommendations, especially those of concern for the NRC. He was astounded to read about the suggested partitioning of the NRC's remaining roles (the role of advising the government had already been taken over by the Science Council).

> The granting function should be separated from operation of the laboratories. This had been a recommendation of the OECD and Macdonald Reports of 1969, commissioned by the Science Council and co-sponsored by the Canada Council.
>
> Basic research by government should be carried out by a National Research Academy with three institutes, namely, physical, life, and social sciences, resulting in the separation of all basic research from the applied laboratories.[9]

In effect, these recommendations meant the end of the NRC as the scientific institution known and acclaimed worldwide. On thanking Senator Joseph A. Sullivan, one of the Senate Committee members, for his kind letter on the award of the Nobel Prize, Herzberg mentioned that he was a little surprised to see that the Senate Committee recommended the dismemberment of the NRC at the very time when the work of the NRC had been acknowledged internationally.[10] He also noted that Senator Sullivan's name was still listed among the members of the Senate Committee in the pre-publication copy of the Report. "Of course it is not for me to make such a suggestion, but I am wondering whether a renewed statement that you disassociate yourself from the Report, and in particular from its recommendation of dismembering NRC, might not be useful." To which Senator Sullivan replied:

> I am fully cognizant of what you stated in your letter and both Lamontagne and the others know that I disagree with them completely. When I saw this final report come out, [I was flabbergasted: it was] not the dismemberment of the NRC but the disemboweling of the NRC. I propose on a question of privilege in the House, to disassociate myself from it completely. Again, with warmest regards and my sincere congratulations.[11]

As happened a year before with the first Report of the Senate Committee, journalists across the country had a field day with the second Report. To quote one of them:

> Lester B. Pearson once said that the only thing worse than a dormant Senate would be an active one, and now that the Senate is active, we are beginning to see what Pearson was getting at. Through its committees, a rejuvenated Senate has been sticking its nose into almost every aspect of public business and bringing down reports that contain many table-thumping recommendations. The trouble is that regardless of their quality, the Senate reports tend to contribute more to public confusion than to public enlightenment....
>
> So it is with the (second) report and recommendations of the Senate Special Committee on Science Policy, which made such a splash this week. It was grandly titled Targets and Strategies for the Seventies. It should have been labelled "Targets and Strategies of Some Senators". It bristled with urgent recommendations and dire warnings, including a critique of the National Research Council which caused that body to spring to its own defence, contributing to the quite erroneous impression that something of importance had happened in high places, with grave import for the future.[12]

In February, Herzberg was invited by the Science Undergraduate Society of the University of British Columbia to a debate with Senator Lamontagne. Herzberg thought it unwise and declined, noting: "I have just been reading some of the Senate Debates on the report of Senator Lamontagne and I have come to the conclusion that scientists and senators live in different worlds, and for that reason also a discussion in open confrontation would not be useful".[13] In fact, he avoided any public discussion of the two Reports except to comment briefly during addresses at university convocations.

Only when the opportunity came to express his opinions at a symposium in the presence of Senator Lamontagne did he accept to give a formal presentation. This occurred at a SCITEC Forum in Ottawa on 2 May 1974.[14] The third volume, *A Government Organization for the Seventies*, had also appeared by this time. Herzberg did not hold back his fundamental criticisms of the Senate Committee Reports. He began with:

> I believe that all of us, that is the senators and the scientists, agree (more or less) about the aim before us, namely, the improvement of science and its contributions to technology in Canada. The difference arises in the

> means suggested to arrive at this aim. The Senate Committee believes that if we only apply the right strategy, the right bureaucratic set-up, we will reach our aim and reach it sooner than if we do not change our strategy in accordance with their views.

He noted that the right strategy may win a war or an election but that the use of strategy becomes difficult or impossible when one is dealing with a subject that depends essentially on discovery and creative thought. While many countries envied Canada for development of the NRC, both with regard to its in-house research and its function as a granting agency for university research, the Senate Committee insisted on reorganization instead of trying to support what was excellent in Canada's scientific set-up. In fact, Senator Grosart had said in Herzberg's presence that "one of the greatest impediments to establishing a coherent science policy in Canada was the excellence of the NRC". Herzberg emphasized that the trouble with the Senate Committee had been all along, and quite naturally, that they did not and could not understand how science works and how scientists work. They could have had a simple lesson on the subject by visiting the laboratories of the NRC in Ottawa, but they did not. Rather, they preferred to look at all sorts of organizations in other countries, following the Canadian habit of belittling our own accomplishments. Had they visited the NRC, they would also have found that there is no sharp limit between basic and applied research: often the same person can be involved at one time in one and at another time in the other. Close contact between basic and applied scientists can be most important in the development of applied science and technology, simply because it is not possible at the time of a scientific discovery to predict whether or not it may be of use for practical purposes. He illustrated this point with the laser, which was developed in studies of the basic field of light and spectroscopy, and its importance to present communication systems was not foreseen. A further misleading pronouncement by the Senate Committee was that basic research was over-supported by the Canadian government. This was not so according to the OECD Report (often quoted by the Senators, but not in this case), which noted that Canada was only spending per capita about one-half of what the U.S.A. was spending on fundamental research.

Having directed these remarks as forcefully as he could to the Senator, Herzberg was surprised on speaking with him afterwards to find Senator Lamontagne to be a charming and intelligent man. So, he was completely bewildered that the Senator could have spent so much time and effort in attempting to formulate "Utopian" procedures for government science policy and, in the process, had deprecated the NRC and the sincerity of its Presidents, who all had had the good of the country in mind. If Lamontagne had visited the NRC he could have seen for himself the accomplishments of the NRC Presidents: they had built up graduate schools in Canadian universities, created one of the strongest government laboratories in the world, and supported scientific activities to the point where Canadian science had a high international reputation. As Herzberg's colleague John D. Babbitt, who had made a careful study of the Reports of the Senate Committee and had written a number of articles defending the NRC, concluded:

> It seems to me that the great benefit to be gained from the studies by the Senators … is the realization that a policy for science in the sense of a formulated plan is a visionary ideal that bears little relation to the realities either of science or of national life. If the studies of the Senators could only succeed in impressing this lesson, once and for all, on those responsible for Canadian policy and could induce them to return to an examination of those fundamental principles which enabled the NRC to become an outstanding example of a national scientific organization, the debt that the country owes to Senator Lamontagne and his Committee would be immeasurably increased.[15]

This was a vain hope, since this viewpoint had not registered with the Senators. Both Babbitt and Herzberg realized that their arguments were not being heard nor would they be: as scientists they placed far too much faith on the power of common sense and reason. Besides, they did not command press conferences as politicians were accustomed to doing. The *Zeitgeist* of the era of quantum mechanics, the high point of science in the twentieth century, had no place in the Senators' zeal for a centralized science policy. Its currently strong appeal was so pervasive that it would take many more studies and reports, as well as trials at reorganization of existing departments, before scientific activities in Canada could resume the stimulating pace and advances of the sixties.

A Changing Role for the NRC

Over the years of these various studies (Heeney, Glassco, MacDonald, OECD, Science Council, and Lamontagne), and partly as a result of their recommendations, the NRC was evolving with five year programs and more focus of laboratory research and engineering (R and D) on industrial needs for the economic and social benefit of Canada. NRC's traditional role of advising the federal government on matters relating to science was terminated with the revision of the NRC Act in 1966 and taken over by the Science Secretariat established in 1964 and the Science Council of Canada created two years later. A Ministry of State for Science and Technology (MOSST) was created in 1971 and superseded the Science Secretariat. As stated in the Senate Committee's fourth volume in 1977, "we had anticipated that MOSST would become a dynamic agent and that action on our other recommendations would soon follow. However, our expectations were not realized".[16] This result was not surprising since the Ministry had no budget and therefore little power. MOSST was eventually (1990) absorbed into the Department of Industry, Science and Technology. The Science Council was abolished in 1992, along with the Economics Council.

What affected the NRC most was the transfer of its university grants and scholarships function to the newly created Natural Sciences and Engineering Research Council (NSERC) in 1978. Yet, this transfer was inevitable, not simply because there was a perceived conflict of interest in the NRC's role as both an operator of research laboratories and a granting agency for university research. The rapid growth of the university research community from a few hundred in the 1940s to tens of thousands in the 1970s necessitated this change. At the same time, the Social Sciences and Humanities Research Council (SSHRC) was formed to fund the liberal arts in the universities.

The NRC had never been intent on building an empire of science, contrary to the views of politicians and even some scientists. Just after the Second World War, when the NRC was urged to assume the administration of all government activities in the sciences, Mackenzie and Steacie chose to divest the NRC of military research, work in atomic energy, and medical research. Succeeding Presidents Ballard, Schneider, and Kerwin would not have wished to enlarge its mandate even if given the opportunity.

Dr. Larkin Kerwin was appointed President of the NRC by Prime Minister Pierre Trudeau on the retirement of Schneider in June 1980. Kerwin had been an active research scientist at Université Laval. His talents for administration became recognized at an early age, with his election as President of the Canadian Association of Physicists and later as Rector of Université Laval. He then served as President of The Royal Society of Canada and of the International Union for Pure and Applied Physics. His leadership and organizational skills at the NRC helped to maintain morale during a very difficult period of external pressure, severely reduced budgets, and depletion of scientific and technical staff. At the end of his second and final presidential term, Kerwin wrote to Herzberg that he felt very little had been accomplished: "In spite of decades of effort in collaboration with so many distinguished Canadian scientists, our Nation's commitment is really no greater than when we started. Islands of excellence are surrounded by seas of indifference and neglect."[17]

Despite these problems, the scientific and engineering communities in Canada had matured by 1990, thanks in large measure to the foresight and policies of all of the NRC Presidents and the Advisory Council. "The Canadian centre of intellectual gravity in industrial technology was now in industry, and of academic sciences in the universities—precisely what the NRC had set out to create."[18] It was time for the NRC to emphasize research and development in new fields of science and engineering and to work with universities and industry as equal partners in promoting such enterprises. It was understood that basic scientific research was of crucial importance for contributing to any progress in new fields of technology, and fortunately Presidents Schneider and Kerwin had insisted on sustaining basic research at the NRC during the difficult 1970s and 1980s. Herzberg's continuing contributions, prestige, and leadership in stimulating new areas of scientific research were instrumental in this endeavour.

So the lively force of his mind won through, and he has reached out far beyond the flaming walls of the world and ranged with his imaginative intelligence throughout space, whence he triumphantly reports to us what can and cannot arise.

Lucretius

22. THE HERZBERG INSTITUTE OF ASTROPHYSICS

Think of the irony! As a youth, Herzberg had set his heart on becoming an astronomer and was then advised not to study astronomy in university unless he had private means. Five decades later, the Herzberg Institute of Astrophysics, with optical and radio observatories and extensive laboratory facilities, was named after him.

In 1974, at the opening ceremonies of the conference "Perspectives in Spectroscopy" held in honour of Herzberg's seventieth birthday, President Schneider announced the intention of Council to set up an Institute of Astrophysics within the NRC.[1] "In recognition of Herzberg's outstanding scientific contributions, his interest in and contributions to astrophysics, and his distinguished role as a scientist and scientific leader at the NRC, the new Institute is to bear his name. It is Council's fervent wish that Dr. Herzberg will continue as an active research scientist in the Institute." Herzberg had every intention of doing so. At seventy years of age, when most men are happy to retire from day-to-day activities, Herzberg was as driven to do research as in the days when he first entered a science laboratory fifty years before. The Nobel Prize was fine, but discovery to him was by far the most satisfying and important thing in the world. That was what Herzberg lived for!

A New NRC Institute for Basic Research

The Herzberg Institute of Astrophysics (HIA) was established formally on 1 April 1975. On being congratulated for this unique honour Herzberg would reply: "I feel very flattered to have this institute named after me", and then with a resounding laugh, "but I am just a worker there". The aim of the HIA was to develop in Canada a centre of scientific excellence in the field of astrophysics. In this way, the NRC planned to consolidate its various activities in optical astronomy and radioastronomy (which had been transferred to the NRC in 1969), along with cosmic-ray research, spectroscopy, and laboratory astrophysics, and thus bring about increased interaction among scientists, as well as more visibility for Canadian activity in this field. An added stimulus for creating the Institute was the possible availability of an important new telescope. Four years later the Canada– France–Hawaii Telescope came into operation. It was built on the extinct volcano Mauna Kea in Hawaii, found by Herzberg's friend Gerard Kuiper to be the best observation site in the world. The telescope has operated as an international partnership of the NRC, the Centre Nationale de la Recherche Scientifique of France, and the University of Hawaii.

With its many interests in molecular astrophysics, particularly with its studies of spectra of free radicals and molecular ions, the Spectroscopy Laboratory was an integral part of the HIA. Added to the earlier techniques of microwave, infrared, visible, and ultraviolet spectroscopy was the use of a variety of lasers and Fourier-transform interferometers. New vistas in molecular astrophysics were being opened by recent observations of diatomic and polyatomic molecules in the interstellar medium by radio-astronomers. The HIA was prepared to play its part in this burgeoning field of science.

New Fields to Explore

The spectroscopy program for the study of molecular ions provided an important confirmation of some early ideas that comets consisted mainly of ices, including water (H_2O). Since the water molecule does not exhibit a spectrum in emission, several attempts had been made by various groups to obtain the spectrum of the ion H_2O^+ as a means of proving that water was present in comets and in other astrophysical bodies, but without success. Herzberg suggested to Hin Lew that he try to look for this spectrum because of his expertise with electron filament discharges, an important technique that is required to sustain a discharge at extremely low gas pressures. Lew succeeded in obtaining a rich and complex emission spectrum in the visible region, just as astronomers were awaiting the reappearance of Comet Kohoutek.[2] When spectra of the tail of the comet were sent to Herzberg by colleagues in Italy and Israel, he and Lew immediately identified parts of the spectrum to be the same as the laboratory spectrum of H_2O^+, thus demonstrating that Comet Kohoutek was partly composed of ice.[3] Later H_2O^+ was also detected in the upper atmosphere from spectra of the twilight glow.

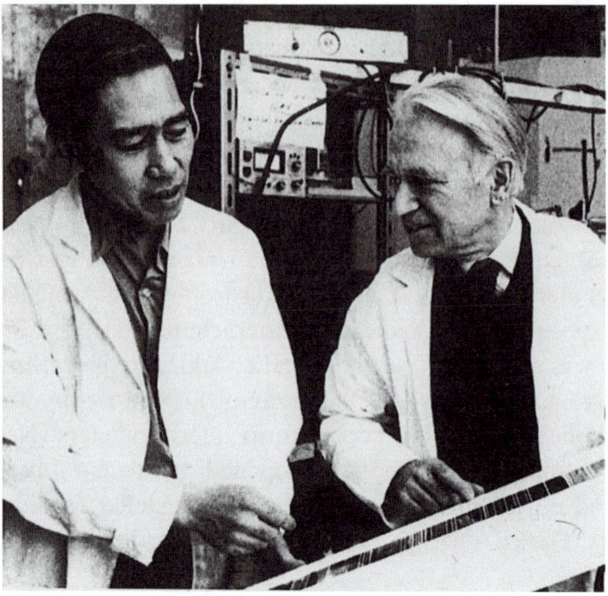

Discussing the spectrum of H_2O^+ with Hin Lew.

A major discovery of the HIA was the detection of spectra of long carbon-chain molecules in the interstellar medium. The study began with the measurement in 1975 of the microwave rotation spectrum of the molecule HC_5N (H–C–C–C–C–C–N) by Harry Kroto and his colleagues at the University of Sussex.[4] Kroto was an alumnus of the Spectroscopy Laboratory, having spent 1964–1966 as a postdoctoral fellow working with Cec Costain and Takeshi Oka (who had begun to work on astrophysical problems at that time). Kroto contacted Oka with the HC_5N results and asked "Is this any good as far as interstellar experiments are concerned, and would you be interested in collaborating in such a search?" The immediate reply was "Yes, very, very, very much interested!" The prospects seemed encouraging since another member of this family of molecules, HC_3N, had been found to be abundant in the interstellar medium. Oka initiated a search for HC_5N in space using the HIA Algonquin radio telescope. Within a few months, the group was successful in detecting HC_5N in space.[5] Two years later, the HIA group, including Kroto who had come to Canada for the interstellar search, discovered spectra of the molecules HC_7N (based on Kroto's laboratory data), and HC_9N (based on a predicted rotational constant

Celebrating the award of the 1972 Steacie Prize to Takeshi Oka. From left: Oka, President Bill Schneider, Mrs. Oka, and Past-President C. Jack Mackenzie.

by Oka[6]).[7] These carbon-chain species are all linear molecules that appear in the atmospheres of cool carbon stars, but the formation of such complex molecules remained to be explained. In the meantime, Douglas had proposed that the long carbon-chain molecules could be the cause of the diffuse interstellar bands, but this had yet to be proven.[8]

Both puzzles fascinated Kroto, whose pursuit of the role of carbon in space, eventually (1985) led to the discovery of "buckminsterfullerene", the molecule C_{60}, consisting of 60 carbon atoms with the structure of a geodesic dome (or soccer ball). Kroto and colleagues Robert F. Curl and Richard E. Smalley of Rice University, where the experiments were carried out, were awarded the Nobel Prize in Chemistry in 1996 for their discovery of the fullerenes. At the 75th Anniversary Celebrations of the NRC in 1991, Kroto gave the plenary HIA lecture in which he noted: "It could be said that NRC's fundamental science is particularly responsible for the discovery of C_{60}".[9]

After having studied many aspects of the spectra of atomic (H) and molecular hydrogen (H_2) over the years, Herzberg turned his attention to the next member in the series, the molecule H_3 and its related ion H_3^+. He concentrated on a search for the spectrum of the ion because it is the

Harold Kroto (later Sir Harold) and the buckeyball C_{60}, 1991.

simplest polyatomic molecule, consisting of three protons and two electrons, and this ion was predicted to be the starting point for the creation of most of the molecules found in interstellar space. The existence and stability of H_3^+ in an electrical discharge had been discovered by J.J. Thomson in 1911. Its great stability and the simple reaction forming H_3^+ from collisions of hydrogen (H_2) and hydrogen ion H_2^+ suggested to Herzberg that H_3^+ must be present in interstellar space, where hydrogen is by far the most abundant element. However, the spectrum of H_3^+ was not known; it had not been observed in the laboratory or in space. Could H_3^+ explain some of the diffuse interstellar bands that were constantly on Herzberg's mind?

There was no question that in order to probe for H_3^+ in the interstellar medium, its spectrum had to be found in the laboratory. This challenge was another of Herzberg's long-lived trials. He had first learned of the ion when Heinrich Peters, a close colleague during student days in Darmstadt, was trying in vain to observe the spectrum of H_3 or H_3^+ in a hydrogen discharge tube. Herzberg himself had made a brief first attempt to look for an emission infrared spectrum of H_3^+ during his visit to the University of Michigan in the summer of 1940, but was unsuccessful. Twenty years later at the NRC, he had searched for an absorption spectrum in the far-ultraviolet region using an electrical discharge under conditions favouring a high concentration of H_3^+. Later, with the help of John Johns, he tried several different discharges while looking for an absorption spectrum in the infrared, but again without success.[10] Then he began a search for its infrared emission spectrum.

Herzberg's discussions during the weekly group meetings of his search for the spectrum of H_3^+ and the importance of finding it intrigued Oka, who was working in molecular astrophysics. In 1975, he came up with the idea of looking for an infrared absorption spectrum using laser techniques. Douglas, who was Head of the Spectroscopy Section at the time, encouraged him to try, and a friendly competition developed in the search for this elusive species, with Oka looking for an absorption spectrum and Herzberg an emission spectrum.[11] It was predicted from quantum theory that H_3^+ has the structure of an equilateral triangle, with H atoms separated by 0.88 Å, and that its vibrational spectrum should occur at about 2522 cm^{-1} in the infrared region. Thus, they had an inkling of the wavelength region to look for the spectrum and what the spacing of the rotation–vibration lines would be.

On scanning this spectral region of the emission from a discharge conducive to formation of H_3^+, Herzberg found some interesting features, which turned out to be new spectra of H_2, but there was no evidence of H_3^+. While he was to be away on a lecture tour in the Soviet Union in 1978, he asked Brian Hurley, his new assistant and the successor to Shoosmith, to photograph emission spectra of the discharge in the visible region in order to check on the behaviour of the particular discharge they were using. Upon his return, Herzberg was presented with a number of spectra taken with hydrogen and deuterium in the discharge. A spectrum at 5600 Å with very broad lines for hydrogen and sharper lines for deuterium caught his attention. He concentrated on the spectrum taken with deuterium, but he was baffled. It was neither a spectrum of D_2 nor of D_3^+. He kept the plate on a viewer at his desk, and every now and then over the next two months he examined the spectrum, wondering what molecular species could have caused it.

Finally, one morning in January 1979, Herzberg realized what it was. The idea came out of the blue, "It was a bright flash, something you can't explain", he said later. He had discovered the molecule D_3 (and H_3), the neutral molecule of three hydrogen atoms (three protons and three electrons). He was searching for H_3^+ and had unexpectedly found H_3. Earlier, he and many others had thought that H_3 was unstable, because it was known that when H and H_2 are brought together, they do not attract each other. But he was able to explain that the molecule is stable in its excited states, that is, when energy is added to either H or H_2, they attract one another to form H_3.[12] The structure was an equilateral triangle, as predicted for H_3^+, but with the third electron in an orbit far from the three protons. This he called a "Rydberg molecule". Other bands of a similar nature but with sharper lines were found in the visible region at 6025 Å, and Herzberg continued to question why these spectra had not been observed or reported by earlier workers. Jim Watson of the HIA and Jon Hougen, a former member of the Spectroscopy Laboratory, collaborated in the evaluation of the spectra of H_3 and D_3. Herzberg encouraged the group at the Max-Planck Institute for Quantum Optics in Garching to examine these and other excited-state spectra using their advanced laser techniques, and they also studied spectra of H_2D and HD_2.[13] With the discovery of H_3 and D_3, Herzberg opened up a whole new field of molecular spectroscopy, yet he couldn't help but wonder why this spectrum had not been observed much earlier. The concept of Rydberg molecules also helped him to unravel a spectrum that had lain unexplained in the scientific literature for 110 years. He showed it to be due to NH_4, another Rydberg molecule (that is, the ion NH_4^+ plus an electron).[14] The serendipitous discovery of these Rydberg molecules was sheer joy. In 1984, the American Physical Society awarded Herz-

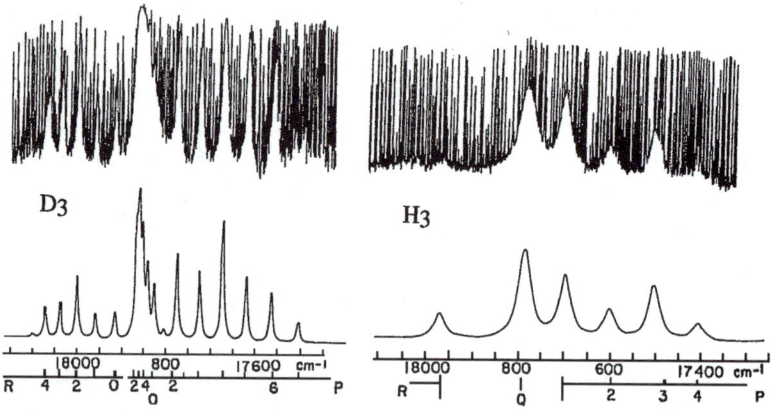

The 5600 Å bands of D_3 and H_3. The photometer curves at the top (showing the broad lines of D_3 and H_3 among the many sharp lines of D_2 and H_2) are compared with simulated spectra at the bottom.

Discussing the spectrum of H_3 with Wolfgang Ketterle at the Max-Planck Institute in Garching, 1983.

berg, at eighty years of age, the Earle K. Plyler Prize citing: "With his analysis of the Rydberg States of H_3 and NH_4 he has served as a role model for all spectroscopists, an inspiration to us all".

While H_3 and NH_4 were the first two polyatomic Rydberg molecules to be discovered, diatomic Rydberg molecules were well known. These included dimers and hydrides of the rare gases and their respective ions, some of whose spectra were being investigated by Herzberg and his colleagues at the HIA and the Quantum Optics group in Garching. In view of the known fairly high abundance of H, He, Ne, and Ar, he kept in mind the possibility that these molecules and ions could be detected in space and might even be the cause of the diffuse interstellar bands. He was particularly interested in HeH^+, $HeNe^+$, $HeAr^+$, KrH, KrD, XeH, XeD, ArH, and ArD.[15]

Meanwhile, Oka searched for the absorption spectrum of H_3^+ and, after four years of concentrated effort, succeeded in detecting and measuring fifteen absorption lines of its infrared spectrum in 1980.[16] This accomplishment was a fundamental discovery for interstellar spectroscopy and chemistry. While Herzberg was not directly involved in these experiments, he was delighted that the first observation of the long-sought H_3^+ spectrum had been made in the Spectroscopy Laboratory of the HIA. The discoveries of H_3^+, Rydberg molecules, long carbon-chain molecules, and H_2O^+ during the 1970s were the high points in the NRC search for molecular species in extraterrestrial bodies and in the interstellar medium.

Oka immediately began the search for H_3^+ in space but was unsuccessful in the short term. With the dramatic improvement in sensitivity of infrared detector arrays, Oka and Geballe finally obtained spectroscopic evidence for the presence of H_3^+ in interstellar space in 1996. Subsequent studies confirmed its existence in many dense and diffuse molecular clouds in the interstellar medium.[17] Much to the surprise of astronomers and spectroscopists, the first detection of H_3^+ outside the laboratory was made in 1987 by the serendipitous observation of a strong emission spectrum in the polar auroral regions of Jupiter, which was identified by Jim Watson to be the overtone band of H_3^+.[18] The fundamental infrared band was later observed and the emission was used to monitor variations in the dynamic Jovian plasmas. Emission spectra of H_3^+ have also been observed in Uranus and Saturn.[18]

A welcome meeting with long-time friend Ernst Miescher, 1979.

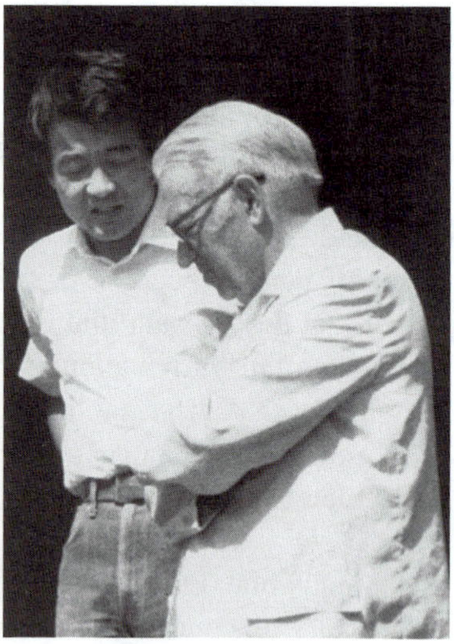

In rapt discussion with Takeshi Oka.

Herzberg continued his attempts to explain the diffuse interstellar bands, which he felt very strongly must be due to some molecular ion or free radical. There seemed to be no question in Herzberg's mind that if the spectra were due to neutral molecules they would have been found long before, since it was easy to produce spectra of all conceivable molecules in the laboratory. On the other hand, ions and radicals would be favoured in the interstellar medium, where they would be much more stable than under laboratory conditions. So he was more inclined to look for spectra of ions and radicals. He searched for spectra of several ions including CH_4^+, since CH_4 was fairly abundant in the outer planets, and NH_4^+ and $HCOOH^+$, since their spectra were expected to be in the region of the diffuse interstellar bands, but found nothing.

Astronomers had originally suggested that the diffuse interstellar bands had something to do with interstellar dust or grains, and more recently others proposed large molecules of polycyclic aromatic hydrocarbons. While Herzberg thought that these could be interesting possibilities, there was no conclusive proof. Since no one had yet succeeded in reproducing any of the spectra in the laboratory, he continued his pursuit of this puzzle.

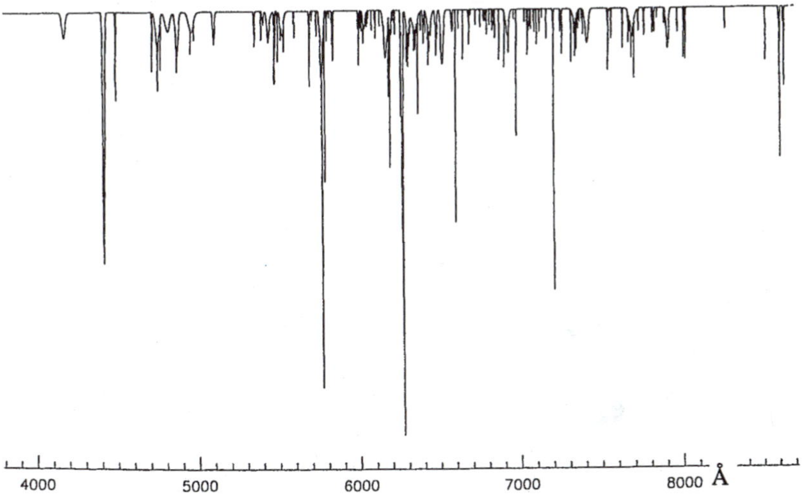

A composite spectrum of the diffuse interstellar bands (DIBS), the enigma of spectroscopists and astrophysicists since the 1930s, after Jenniskens and Désert.[19]

There is a time for all things, and a time to end all things.

Subrahmanyan Chandrasekhar

23. CONTINUING ACTIVITIES

There seemed to be no letup in invitations to give research lectures at national and international conferences or to speak on general topics at anniversary celebrations of friends and research institutes. Herzberg chose carefully because of the time away from research and the rigors of travel in his advancing years. And he would not accept some invitations to speak if a manuscript was also requested for publication.

Requests to Lecture and Advise

In 1975 the Ministry of Education, Science and Culture of the Government of Japan invited him to be the Honorary Advisory Councillor for a new institute for basic research to be established in Okazaki. A year later, on a visit to the site on which this Institute for Molecular Science was to be built, he was asked to give his opinion on the best way to run such a laboratory. Recalling the advice he had received from Steacie when he joined the NRC, Herzberg emphasized that good researchers should be hired and

A sure sign of research activity, 1991.

given the freedom to choose their own problems. He also gave a talk on "Recent Spectroscopic Studies of Interstellar Molecules". He visited again in 1979 and in 1985 when the Institute was in full operation and was being recognized internationally for its basic contributions.[1]

In 1976, the president of the Max-Planck Institute invited Herzberg to participate on the Advisory Board (*Beirat*) for a project on laser research and in 1982 to be a Member of the Board for the Max-Planck Institute for Quantum Optics in Garching.[2] This he welcomed since there was much interest in spectroscopic research at this Institute, and collaboration developed quickly on problems in H_3, D_3, and the ions of noble gas dimers. To his surprise, he was invited to present a Heisenberg Lecture in Munich in 1980 (but was only able to accept for 1982), and he reported to Chandra: "I have no idea how I was selected to do that since my contacts with Heisenberg were few, but a talk on hydrogen has a nice connection with Heisenberg since the topic ortho- and para-hydrogen is specifically mentioned in his Nobel citation".[3] Herzberg gave his lecture "Molekularer Wasserstoff in Laboratorium und im Weltraum" in German, even though his German was less fluent than his English.

A tradition of German Universities is to honour alumni who have made fundamental contributions to knowledge on the fifieth anniversary of their Habilitation. The Institute of Physics of the Technische Hochschule Darmstadt commemorated this event for Herzberg with a special celebration on

Monika and audience amused at the running start of a lecture at the Technische Hochschule in Darmstadt, 1979.

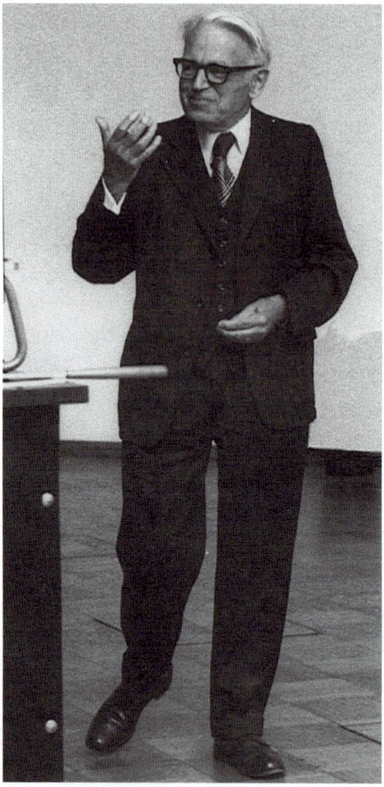

A vital lecturer at the age of seventy-five,
on the fiftieth anniversary of his Habilitation.

2 November 1979. He gave a lecture titled "Erinnerungen an Meine Darmstadter Zeit" (Reminiscences of My Time in Darmstadt) and had the opportunity to meet with former colleagues and to visit the beautifully restored city.

He accepted two invitations that proved to be rather arduous visits with travel almost halfway around the world: one was the Frew Fellowship of the Australian Academy of Science in 1982, the other was the first R.K. Asundi Memorial Lecture in India in 1984. Herzberg had met Asundi in 1930 on a visit to King's College, London, where Asundi was working on a spectrum of CO for his Ph.D. Their scientific interests developed into a lifelong friendship, with Asundi working at the NRC on several occasions. Asundi accompanied Herzberg on his travels in India, introducing him to Indian food (which Herzberg found to be too spicy), Hindu ethics, religion, and philosophy, and the Indian political scene. In spectroscopy, they had similar interests in diatomic molecules and astrophysical applications, and several of Asundi's students joined the NRC as postdoctoral fellows. In memory of Asundi, Herzberg provided a comprehensive review of "The Spectra of Molecular Ions".[4]

He was invited to a medical meeting in Washington, D.C., titled "Cancer Causation and Prevention: Biochemical Mechanisms" to give a talk on oxygen and the electronic state found to be an important carrier of energy in cancer cells. He attended the meeting but claimed no knowledge of cancer. "If anyone had suggested fifty years ago that my spectroscopic studies of oxygen would be important I would have dismissed the idea. But this shows that no one can foresee the applications of basic research." On another occasion, he decided to forego a meeting on atmospheric pollution but was pleased to learn that his work on free radicals seemed to be of importance in evaluating the danger of fluorocarbons from spray cans entering the upper atmosphere and destroying the ozone layer that protects us from the sun's harmful ultraviolet radiation. In Ottawa, he accepted membership in the President's Council of the Civic Hospital and served as Honorary Chairman of the Loeb Institute Advisory Committee. Herzberg was a member of the Editorial Board of the *Canadian Journal of Physics* for several decades and also participated on the Monograph Advisory Committee of the NRC Research Press.

Following the award of the Nobel Prize, Herzberg was honoured in many different ways with fellowships and appointments as a member and honorary member in academies and societies all over the world. He received another nineteen honorary degrees, most of them from Canada but some from the Universities of Drexel, Toledo, Cambridge, Hamburg, Bristol, Frankfurt, Andhra, Osmania, and Delhi and the Weizmann Institute of Science. A park in Saskatoon and a road in Kanata (a technology suburb of Ottawa known as "Silicon Valley North") were named after him, as were scholarships and a lecture series at Carleton University, in addition to laboratories there and at John Abbott College in Ste. Anne de Bellevue, Quebec. His name was given to an award of the Spectroscopy Society of Canada, to a spectrograph for the Canada–France–Hawaii Telescope on Mauna Kea, and to an asteroid (the minor planet 3316) having an orbit of 5.5 years.

Two honorary posts in Canada deserve special mention. Herzberg served as Chancellor of Carleton University in Ottawa from 1973 to 1980.

Appointed a member of the Queen's Privy Council of Canada
by Her Majesty Queen Elizabeth II with Governor General
Ramon Hnatyshyn on her right and Prime Minister
Brian Mulroney on her left, Ottawa 1992.

As titular head of the university he presided over all graduation ceremonies, usually held in the fall and summer, and assisted the President on request. On Canada's 125th Birthday, 1 July 1992, he was appointed a member of the Queen's Privy Council for Canada. He had to cancel his attendance at a meeting of Nobel Laureates in Lindau, Germany, when he received a telephone call from the Prime Minister of Canada, the Right Honourable Brian Mulroney, informing him of this appointment.[5] The swearing-in ceremony was held in Rideau Hall with presentation of new members to Her Majesty Queen Elizabeth II by Governor General Ramon John Hnatyshyn. The Privy Council is an advisory body to the Crown, to aid and advise the Government of Canada. Privy Councillors include all

Cabinet Ministers, all former Ministers, and distinguished individuals appointed as a mark of honour. The exceptional appointment of the latter group is in recognition of outstanding contribution to Canada and its people. Privy Councillors carry the title "Honourable" for life and the initials P.C. after their names, but meetings of the full Council are rare.

Freedom For All

Herzberg's appeals for freedom were not confined to scientists and the NRC, but embraced humanitarian rights for all. He participated in activities of many humanitarian organizations including the Academy of Peace, Science for Peace, International League of Human Rights, World Citizens Assembly, Food and Disarmament International, Committee of Concerned Scientists, Canadian Committee of Scientists and Scholars, Canadian Professors for Peace in the Middle East, and Congress of Nobel Laureates for World Peace, among others. He lent his name to petitions, movements, and projects for the liberation of unjustly detained scientists and did not hesitate to write personal letters on their behalf to Heads of State of countries that had signed the Universal Declaration of Human Rights.[6]

As a strong advocate of nuclear disarmament, he signed Linus Pauling's 1957 petition for stopping tests of nuclear bombs. Herzberg wrote to the President of Syria and requested that he give each member of the Jewish Community in Syria the right to leave the country; he signed with Nobel Laureates many petitions for the release of U.S.S.R. refusniks such as Viktor Brailovsky, Vladimir Kislik, Yuri Orlov, and others; he wrote to the Ambassador of Bulgaria about the detention of a scientist and the treatment of another scientist's family after he had left the country; and he urged Leningrad authorities to give an exit visa to Andrei Petelin, who had asked for Herzberg's support when they met at Leningrad University on the day the Nobel Prize was rumoured. Herzberg was surprised and delighted to receive a letter, seven years later, from Petelin, living in Silver Spring, Maryland, thanking him for interceding on his behalf.[7]

Herzberg's most persistent appeals concerned the release of Academician Andrei Sakharov, Nobel Laureate, from jail and internal exile and did not cease until Sakharov was able to come to Canada for a brief visit. In 1973, when Soviet intellectuals Andrei Sakharov and Alexander Solzhenitsyn were incarcerated, Herzberg initiated an appeal for their release signed by ninety Nobel Laureates and sent it to President Nikolay

Podgorny, Chairman of the Presidium of the U.S.S.R.[8] For openly criticizing the policies of the Soviet authorities, Sakharov was banished by Leonid Brezhnev to the closed city of Gorky in 1980. Several appeals on behalf of Sakharov were sent to Brezhnev by Herzberg, also with Linus Pauling, via Yakovlev, the U.S.S.R. Ambassador to Canada. In a telegram to Flora MacDonald (Secretary of State for External Affairs for Canada), Herzberg indicated his shock and dismay at the detention and internal exiling of Sakharov and recommended suspension of the Canada–U.S.S.R. technical and scientific exchange program.[9] (The Government approved a one year suspension 1980–1981, but this was adopted because of U.S.S.R. intervention in Afghanistan.) These appeals for the release of Sakharov were followed up with letters and telegrams to Konstantin Chernenko and to Mikhail Gorbachev by the Canadian Committee of Scientists and Scholars with Herzberg as its president.[10]

In 1983 and 1984, Herzberg participated in demonstrations in front of the Soviet Embassy in Ottawa. He spoke to the demonstrators about the medical needs of the Sakharovs:

> You are all aware of the serious situation that has arisen with regard to Andrei Sakharov and his wife, Yelena Bonner. We are not here to judge the actions of the Soviet Government, but rather to appeal to it on humanitarian grounds to release the Sakharovs.
>
> The Soviet Government is a member of the United Nations and as such adheres to the Declaration of Human Rights. These human rights include freedom of movement and freedom of thought, that is freedom to express unpopular opinions. We appeal to the Soviet Government to apply these freedoms to the Sakharovs....
>
> Scientific cooperation between Canadian and Soviet scientists has been active and has led to many advances in their respective fields. It has not only been useful from a scientific point of view but has also given us many opportunities to learn about the Soviet Union, and for our Soviet colleagues to learn about our country. It would be a great pity if a serious shadow would be thrown over these personal and scientific relations by the Sakharovs not obtaining the freedom which they are seeking.

In 1986, Gorbachev invited Sakharov to return to Moscow and to his "patriotic activities". The following year, Sakharov was selected as the recipient of the "1987 International Award" of the St. Boniface General Hospital Research Foundation in Winnipeg for his brilliant work as a nuclear physicist and for his dedication to world peace.[11] Previous winners of this prestigious award, inaugurated in 1976, included Dr. Jonas Salk for discovery of the vaccine against poliomyelitis, Dr. Christian Barnard for the first successful transplanting of a human heart, and Mother Teresa for her work among the poorest of the poor. Herzberg wrote to Gorbachev noting:

> The release of Academician Sakharov from internal exile a year ago was greeted by the international scientific community with great satisfaction and hope for the future. This hope and satisfaction would be immeasurably increased if you should find it possible to arrange for Academician Sakharov to leave your country for a short visit to Winnipeg. As a Canadian, I would be especially happy if Academician Sakharov could take his first steps outside the Soviet Union in Canada.[12]

Sakharov and his wife finally came to "the beautiful, hospitable country of Canada" in February 1989 when Sakharov thanked Canadians: "I look back fondly on the efforts that ordinary Canadians made on our behalf".[13] Herzberg was delighted to meet Sakharov and to introduce him at the NRC, where Sakharov gave a brief talk on his work:

> Our guest of honour, Professor Andrei Dmitrievich Sakharov is known to everybody as the foremost fighter for human rights. His remarkable and fearless actions in this field have been justly recognized by the Nobel Peace Prize in 1975. He has taught us that real peace can only be achieved if human rights are established everywhere.

Demonstration in front of the Soviet Embassy in Ottawa, 1983.

Meeting Sakharov at the NRC, 1989.

> I would however like to introduce Professor Sakharov to this group of Canadian physicists, chemical physicists, astrophysicists, as a fellow physicist. He is surely one of the leading theoretical physicists in the world today. He has contributed to some of the most difficult subjects of our field....
>
> I am not qualified to give a balanced review of his work but do know that he contributed to the solution of the puzzle of the preponderance of matter over anti-matter. He has also made basic contributions to high energy physics, to black holes and to cosmology and its relation to high energy physics. It is my great pleasure to introduce Professor Andrei Sakharov.[14]

Herzberg ventured into a decidedly different topic of freedom when he was invited to Rome along with all Nobel Laureates "to meet Pope John Paul II and to bring to his attention the problems which the Nobel Prize winners, in their respective fields of study, consider to be the most urgent for contemporary man". While he could not attend because of his health and other commitments he wrote to Cardinal König, the host of the gathering:

> As a Nobel Laureate, I do not feel particularly qualified to speak on human values and development. The Prize was given to me on the basis of my specialized work in one small section of science. If I may, however, contribute one item to the discussion it would be the problem of overpopulation: I feel very strongly that this is one of humanity's biggest problems from which many others are derived.... I believe that the Catholic Church could greatly contribute to the solution of this problem, if it would take a less rigid attitude towards the question of birth control. I need not expound further on this problem...but if it were possible at your meeting with the Pope to bring this concern to his attention, I believe it would be a great step forward.[15]

There was no reply to his letter or suggestion and a discussion on the topic did not take place on this occasion.

One group that Herzberg declined to support was the War Resisters International: "I would not at the present moment serve in any weapons laboratory, but there are circumstances such as happened during the Nazi regime where one's pacifist ideals must be deferred. We cannot by unilateral disarmament run the risk of terrorists taking over the world".[16]

Keeping in Touch with Family, Mentors, and Colleagues

As much as Herzberg had adapted to the Canadian way of life, there was a traditional German custom that he upheld assiduously, namely to commemorate important birthdays and anniversaries of family, friends, and colleagues worldwide. In addition to the monthly cheques to his mother and sister in Seattle, he sent gifts on birthdays and at Christmas. He particularly remembered the birthdays of his mentors Professors Hans Rau, James Franck, and Max Born and sent them letters expressing his deep indebtedness for their friendly guidance in his early years, not only in physics, but particularly in the proper attitude of a scientist to his work. In honour and memory of Hans Rau, he published a paper in German on fine structure in the spectrum of the helium ion, and for the festschrift on Born's eightieth birthday, he submitted a theoretical paper on the energy of helium and helium-like ions.[17] On C.J. Mackenzie's eightieth birthday, he recalled with pleasure when he first met Mackenzie in 1935 at the University of Saskatchewan and the significant effect he had had on Herzberg's career by making it possible for Herzberg to return to Canada and join the NRC.

Tributes to his closest friends were specially recognized. At a testimonial dinner in 1974 honouring John Spinks after fifteen years as President of the University of Saskatchewan, Herzberg recalled the first letter he had received from Spinks in 1933 (inquiring about the possibility of joining him in Darmstadt) with the puzzling return address, since he had never heard of Saskatoon or Saskatchewan. He soon came to admire Spinks's qualities, the speed at which he worked (he could write a letter or scientific paper faster than anyone else Herzberg had ever encountered) and his ability to take quick and appropriate action. Back in Saskatoon in 1935, Spinks realized that Herzberg would lose his job in Darmstadt and had persuaded President Murray to offer him a guest professorship. Years later, when Herzberg intimated he was not completely happy in the United States, Spinks immediately wrote about this to Ned Steacie and so began Herzberg's return to Canada and the NRC. Herzberg went on to praise Spinks' scientific career and his effective presidency, underlining his fight opposing the strong trend among provincial bureaucrats against the pursuit of excellence in the arts and sciences.[18]

John W.T. Spinks (1908–1997). President of the University of Saskatchewan (1959–1974).

On the occasion of Chandra's sixty-fifth birthday in 1975, Herzberg recounted their first meeting in 1941 and his lifelong friendship, noting that the close association with Chandra at Yerkes Observatory was the most rewarding result, scientifically and personally, of the years he had spent there. Chandra's influence on him was immense, both by his example and by his advice and friendship. The two families often visited each other, and Chandra and Herzberg regularly met at science conferences. On Chandra's death in 1995, Herzberg wrote to Lalitha: "It is hard to imagine a world and life without Chandra.... For the rest of my life I shall remember the frequent joint walks that we had during my time at Yerkes and the many discussions on scientific and many other topics. Needless to say I learned immeasurably from him."[19]

In 1966, Herzberg congratulated his colleague Robert S. Mulliken on being awarded the Nobel Prize in Chemistry, and in 1978, he participated in a symposium in honour of Mulliken's fifty years at The University of Chicago, a period during which Herzberg had known him and admired his fundamental contributions to molecular spectroscopy. Herzberg reviewed his own and the many other spectroscopic studies based on Mulliken's pioneering work. Ten years later, Herzberg gave the first in the series of "Mulliken Memorial Lectures" commemorating Mulliken (1896–1986) and his legacy. On this occasion, Friedrich Hund presented brief reminiscences (via videotaped interview) of the early days of molecular spectroscopy and his association with Mulliken. Among his stories he mentioned that he and Mulliken had had difficulty in understanding the quantum chemistry of Heitler and London within the framework of molecular orbitals. He went on to say: "It was Gerhard Herzberg who explained chemical binding in a simple and convincing manner with bonding and antibonding electrons", and Hund gave his special regards and compliments to Herzberg, whom he hoped was present.[20] A few years later, Herzberg sent Hund greetings to celebrate his one-hundredth birthday.

Telegrams and letters were dispatched to recipients of Nobel Prizes. The year 1983 was rather special for Herzberg since the Nobel Prize in Physics was awarded to his friend Chandra and in Chemistry to Henry Taube, a graduate student in Herzberg's first lecture course "Atomic Structure and Molecular Structure" at the University of Saskatchewan. Top honours in the course that year were shared by Henry Taube and George Thiessen. Thiessen joined the NRC and became Head of the Acoustics Section, while Taube became a faculty member of Stanford University. On receiving Herzberg's congratulations, Taube thanked him and added: "I want to take this opportunity also to tell you that I regard your lecture courses at Saskatchewan as the high point in my academic career there. The example you set in clarity in thinking and exposition has been one of the important influences in my life".[21] Herzberg was delighted with Nobel awards to Canadians, and he congratulated John Polanyi and Michael Smith for their Prizes in Chemistry in 1986 and 1993, respectively, and Bertram Brockhouse for his Prize in Physics in 1994. Telegrams with congratulations were also sent to Andrei Sakharov on being awarded the Peace Prize in 1975 and to Pyotr Kapitsa on being awarded the Prize in Physics in 1978.

Herzberg participated in many symposia and testimonial dinners honouring his friends in Canada: Harry Thode, President of McMaster University and an alumnus of the University of Saskatoon; Harry Welsh in Toronto; Larkin Kerwin, NRC President on retirement from Université Laval; and Rudolph Altschul, former colleague at University of Saskatchewan, and the author in Toronto. In the United States, Herzberg gave lectures in honour of Walter Gordy at Duke University, Joe Hirschfelder in Madison, Bryce Crawford, Jr., in Minneapolis, and George Kistiakowski at Harvard, with tributes to Edward Condon and Isidor Rabi recognized with original papers.[22] He attended various functions on the retirements of Polydor Swings and Boris Rosen in Liège and Albin Lagerqvist in Stockholm and on the seventieth birthday of Y. Morino in Tokyo. On Ernst Miescher's eightieth birthday, he submitted an account of Miescher's basic contributions to molecular physics, especially his immense work on the NO molecule.[23]

By a remarkable coincidence, Herzberg had the opportunity to visit China and to meet Dr. Wu, his postdoctorate fellow of 1933 at the Technische Hochschule in Darmstadt. Wu had returned to China, had survived the Japanese invasion and the Cultural Revolution, and was director of a research institute in Changchun, Manchuria. One of Dr. Wu's students came to work with Dr. Henry Mantsch of the NRC Chemistry Division, and having learned that Herzberg was also at the NRC, he contacted Wu. This resulted in an invitation for Herzberg to come to China, and in 1981 the Herzbergs and Mantsch visited Wu and spent three weeks on a brief tour, during which they also met Vice-Premier Fang-Yi in Peking.

Herzberg was also attentive in congratulating recipients of awards and fellowships, not to mention the countless letters of recommendations he sent for promotions, and of nominations for awards to colleagues, postdoctoral fellows, and spectroscopists whose work he had admired. From 1971 onwards, he was punctual in his annual nomination of scientists for the Nobel Prizes in Physics and Chemistry. He always congratulated those

On a visit to Dr. Wu in Changchun, China, 1981.

Monika and Gerhard enjoying tea with
Vice-Premier Fang-Yi in Beijing, 1981.

he knew on election to The Royal Society and complimented Otto Struve and Max Delbrück when they were elected Foreign Members. Delbrück answered in his usual charming way: "How very kind of you to write to me on this bizarre occasion. I must admit that your letter gave me more pleasure than the election. Who would have thought thirty-seven years ago when we started our budding careers in science that one day we would both crown ourselves with the marvelous wig of Sir Isaac Newton?"[24]

Thinking of Retiring

Herzberg suffered a mild heart attack (angina pectoris) in August 1977 and this curtailed his travel somewhat, although the following year he visited Germany and the U.S.S.R., enjoyed a holiday in Saas-Fee, and spent two weeks in Japan, where he climbed part way up Mt. Fuji (3880 metres). On learning of his heart problem, Linus Pauling recommended that Herzberg take vitamin C, a suggestion Herzberg followed faithfully and was pleased with the results. He resumed more extensive journeys in 1979, including the opening of the Canada–France–Hawaii Telescope and a motor trip to the top of Mauna Kea at 4215 metres. By the following year, he began to realize that he could not keep up this pace of travel and even decided to cancel a visit to Rome, where members of the Pontifical Academy were to meet Pope John Paul II.

With Herzberg's close friend and co-founder of the Spectroscopy Laboratory, Alex Douglas, retired and terminally ill, an international "Colloquium on Molecular Spectroscopy" was held in his honour in Ottawa in June 1980. This was a moving tribute attended by Alex's many friends and associates from around the world. Two months later, the death of Herzberg's long-time assistant Jack Shoosmith was announced. These losses caused Herzberg to seriously consider slowing down, and in September 1980 he sent a memo to Jack L. Locke, Director of the HIA, expressing his wish to retire.[25] On learning this, the newly appointed President Larkin Kerwin discussed the situation with Herzberg and convinced him to remain on staff for the good of science and the NRC. A further blow to Herzberg was the retirement of his longtime secretary Marjorie Phyllis Thompson in December 1983. He had depended on her for attending to all matters concerning his office for fifteen years. She was an ideal assistant: in addition to the daily tasks of typing letters, reports, and papers and of receiving and filing letters and documents, she scheduled meetings, made travel arrangements, and reminded him of a multitude of events and responsibilities. He could not hope to find another Miss Thompson, and never did.

After Herzberg's next heart attack in 1984, Kerwin repeated his request that he stay on. Herzberg agreed and chose to reduce his travel commitments to a minimum. Yet he often felt that he could not refuse to participate in celebratory occasions such as retirements and special anniversaries for his close friends and colleagues. After giving the Mulliken Memorial Lecture in 1988, he visited the Fermi Laboratory, where he had a fall and tore a leg tendon. He lost mobility for a brief time but soon managed to walk with the aid of a cane. During this period and afterwards, he was driven to the NRC and home by John Johns and Henry Mantsch. Linus Pauling wrote to suggest that he increase his vitamin C to 4 grams per day and also take 4 grams of lysine per day in order to gain complete control over the angina and benefit the underlying cardiovascular disease.[26] Herzberg complied by slowly increasing the dose of vitamin and medication.

The conferences held every five years in celebration of Herzberg's birthdays were a continuing joy for him. These were special occasions for him to meet with many friends from near and far and to discuss the latest discoveries in science of close interest to him. On Herzberg's eightieth birthday, President Kerwin convened an open lecture series titled "Physical Sciences in the Eighties" that had such a huge response that the venue had to be changed at the last moment from the NRC Auditorium to the Westin

At a banquet for "Physical Sciences in the Eighties", a conference in honour of Gerhard's eightieth birthday, in Ottawa, 1984. Clockwise from Gerhard: the Governor General Madame Jeanne Sauvé, President Larkin Kerwin, Monika, the Minister of State for Science and Technology Mr. Tom Siddon, His Excellency Mr. Maurice Sauvé, and Mrs. Siddon.

Christopher Longuet-Higgins and Monika look on as Gerhard cuts the cake to celebrate his eighty-fifth birthday, 1989.

Hotel in order to accommodate the six hundred attendees. The seven speakers were Charles H. Townes, Werner Israel, Hendrik Casimir, Sir Denys Wilkinson, Henry Taube, Melvin Calvin, and Carlo Rubbia (who had just been awarded the 1984 Nobel Prize in Physics). At the banquet, Cec Costain offered the toast to Herzberg and spoke of Herzberg's time in Saskatoon and the way he inspired his students. Takeshi Oka gave the after-dinner speech and told of Herzberg's scientific accomplishments and his humanity and of how he made newcomers from far away places feel as members of the Spectroscopy Laboratory. In 1989, the drastic cuts in the NRC budget necessitated a more modest colloquium that featured molecular spectroscopy and was held at the NRC. Chandra presented the results of his latest studies "Newton's Principia—the late reaction of one scientist", and Christopher Longuet-Higgins gave a brief speech on his hero Gerhard after the banquet at the National Arts Centre.

Herzberg became very discouraged with the changing atmosphere at the NRC caused by the Government's continuing reduction in the country's science budget. A new administration at the NRC (1989–1994) carried out wholesale changes in its organizational structure and proposed minimal basic research, resulting in resignations and unbelievably low morale.[27] A plan to transfer the HIA to the university sector was also in the wind. Many wondered: "Did the administration have to propose such a move while Herzberg was still active at the Institute?" The Standing Committee on Industry, Science and Technology, Regional and Northern Development, of the Canadian Government called Herzberg as a witness, and the members (all elected members of Parliament) questioned him on the role of government in performing and supporting basic science and of the effects on NRC of the severe cuts in funding.[28] Letters to NRC President Pierre Perron, to the Prime Minister of Canada, and to the Minister of Science from over one hundred international scientists and from presidents of the Chemical Institute of Canada, the Professional Institute of the Public Service of Canada, and the Academy of Sciences of The Royal Society of Canada no doubt helped to save the HIA and let it remain in Ottawa for the time being.[29] Further resignations of senior scientists were finally stemmed by a revised plan to preserve a cluster of basic science laboratories and form the Steacie Institute for Molecular Sciences.

In honour of Herzberg's ninetieth birthday, a wide-ranging international conference was held titled "The Future of Spectroscopy", with invited talks by twenty-six distinguished young scientists. This was a two and a half day conference that included contributed papers in poster sessions. The organizers were Bob McKellar of the NRC, Takeshi Oka, now at The University of Chicago, and Richard Saykally of the University of California, Berkeley. They chose to hold the meeting in Sainte-Adèle, Quebec, from 25 to 28 September during the fall colour season, and two hundred friends and admirers from eighteen countries participated in singing "Happy Birthday, GH". He gave the brief talk "Some Historical Remarks on the Statistics of Atomic Nuclei" in which he discussed his early work with Walter Heitler on the Bose statistics of nitrogen nuclei, three years before the neutron was discovered. Dr. Arthur Carty, the newly appointed President of the NRC, welcomed the gathering at the banquet, and a number of colleagues gave brief comments, followed by a speech on Herzberg's life and accomplishments by Charles Townes.

"Happy Birthday, dear Gerhard."

At the banquet, Monika, Gerhard, Joan Stoicheff, and President Arthur Carty.

Official Retirement at Ninety

Finally, as Herzberg approached his ninetieth birthday, he formally proposed to retire from his position as Distinguished Research Scientist because his health and failing eyesight prevented him from maintaining an active eight-hour work day. He asked that the date of his retirement be as close as administratively convenient to 25 December 1994. There was unfinished work which he wanted to complete and he "wished to have the continuing use of his office along with some secretarial assistance".[30] His wish to retire was granted as of 31 December 1994. A ceremonial gathering took place on 13 December in the auditorium at 100 Sussex Drive, followed by a reception where he was greeted by many friends. On this occasion, Herzberg received laudatory letters with best wishes from Governor General Ramon Hnatyshyn and Prime Minister Jean Chrétien.[31]

As expected, Herzberg continued to work in his office daily, mainly carrying on his voluminous correspondence and reading technical papers, especially on the latest news of the diffuse interstellar bands. He persisted in his search for the rare molecular species or chemical processes that could give rise to such spectra: "It is one of my aims to solve that problem before I quit". But this was not to be. A fall down a short flight of stairs at home

Monika and Gerhard at his retirement reception at NRC.

Gerhard Herzberg at his desk on 13 December 1994.

prevented him from spending more than a few hours each day at the office. In addition, a trip to Saas-Fee and Munich in the summer of 1996 was cut short by a severe heart attack. He recovered after several days in a Munich hospital and endured the flight home, but his health had noticeably failed. He ceased to go to his office and was often in hospital for tests of a day or more. With the progressing effects of Parkinson's disease, increasing medication, and loss of appetite, he weakened rapidly and was confined to his home, where Monika cared for him faithfully for the last three years of his life. He died at home on 3 March 1999. The Canadian flag flew at half-staff on the Peace Tower of the Parliament Buidings in Ottawa in lament and memory of The Honourable Gerhard Herzberg, P.C., C.C., F.R.S., F.R.S.C., one of Canada's national treasures.

Canadian flag at half-staff on the Peace Tower of the Parliament Buildings in Ottawa in memory of Gerhard Herzberg.

EPILOGUE

"The sole aim of science is the glory of the human spirit." This aphorism attributed to the celebrated mathematician Carl Jacobi became Herzberg's cherished tenet. And he lived by it. It could not have been otherwise, for at the time of his university years, the world's greatest thinkers were involved in the exciting discoveries of quantum theory and of the stunning new world of atoms, molecules, the nucleus, and particle physics. These pioneers passed through the halls of academe in Germany and Britain, where Herzberg had the opportunity to meet them and listen to their exploits in the search for truth about the natural universe. They did not mention any practical use of their findings but spoke of the importance of the concept of beauty in their theories and scientific studies. Herzberg often recalled the esthetic aspect of science expressed by the famous French mathematician and philosopher Henri Poincaré:

> The scholar does not study nature because it is useful; he studies it because it gives him pleasure, and it gives him pleasure because it is beautiful. If nature were not beautiful, it would not be worth knowing and life would not be worth living. I am not speaking of the beauty that strikes the senses, the beauty of qualities and appearances; not that I despise it by any means, but it has nothing to do with science. I speak of the more intimate beauty which comes from the harmonious order of the parts and which a pure intelligence can comprehend. It is for this intellectual beauty, perhaps more than for the future welfare of mankind that the scientist condemns himself to long hours of difficult and exhausting work.

As Herzberg often said, he was so fortunate to have started scientific work just at the time quantum theory was being applied to molecular spectroscopy. He could not have had a more understanding mentor than Hans Rau in Darmstadt, who gave him the encouragement and freedom to choose and work on his own research problems. Almost everything to which Herzberg turned his attention was novel. When he joined the institutes of Max Born and James Franck in Göttingen he met the younger group of Walter Heitler, Friedrich Hund, Eugene Wigner, Max Delbrück, Hertha Sponer, Victor Weisskopf, and Edward Teller and collaborated with some of them. In Bristol, London, and Cambridge he met similar keen minds full of the excitement of pushing back the frontiers of knowledge. All shared a childlike wonder and enthusiasm in this new world of discovery, and they all became theoretical and experimental founders of twentieth century science.

When forced to leave his homeland, Herzberg found the same creative spark in some of his colleagues and students in the Canadian prairies, far away from the centres of science in Europe and America. It was his good fortune, while briefly at Yerkes Observatory, to become lifelong friends with the eminent astrophysicist Subrahmanyan Chandrasekhar, whose aims and achievements, in Herzberg's estimation, best epitomized "the glory of the human spirit".

Herzberg began research with the aim of making a real contribution to science. He wanted other scientists to be able to look on his work and build on it. A big moment came when he found something no one had seen before and was able to describe it and present it in such a way to his colleagues that they couldn't doubt it. He especially enjoyed it if what he found was of value to others and they used it to do something interesting and useful.

The high points in his research were many. In physics, it was the work on atomic hydrogen and helium, the knowledge of molecular hydrogen, of forbidden transitions, and of predissociation. In chemistry, his determinations of many molecular structures and the discovery of spectra of free radicals, especially CH_2 and CH_3, and of the Rydberg molecule H_3 were each outstanding contributions. In astrophysics, the reproduction in the laboratory of the spectrum of CH^+, proving its presence in the interstellar medium, and spectra of C_3, and H_2O^+ and their presence in comets, the quadrupole spectrum of H_2, and discovery of hydrogen in the atmospheres of the planets opened up new applications of spectroscopy for our knowledge of the universe. His classic volumes on molecular spectra and molecular structures provided the background for studies in all of the sciences and remain as encyclopedias of molecular knowledge for all time. Finally, his Spectroscopy Laboratory at the National Research Council helped to bring Canada to an important position internationally. His laboratory became the "Temple of Spectroscopy" for the world—a major institution, the likes of which is difficult to imagine ever rising again in Canada.

In the midst of all these activities, he always seemed to find the time to make the way a little easier for fellow scientists, young and old, by writing letters of encouragement, making recommendations about jobs or advancements, and nominating deserving candidates for awards. Such unselfish interest in other people's careers was surely unique.

One may wonder how he could have achieved all that he accomplished? There is no doubt that it took unusual determination, ambition, and hard work, along with an innate ability and a desire to make life meaningful. He developed a sense of purpose as a young student at the Technische Hochschule Darmstadt, and this kept increasing as he listened to and met the scientific giants of the quantum era. Later, as his own accomplishments began to be recognized, it was not surprising that he became personally acquainted with almost all of the active physicists and chemists working in atomic and molecular spectra and structures, and with astrophysicists interested in the interstellar medium. This added to his sense of the importance of his work in expanding scientific knowledge. Yet he insisted that "I don't have all that many problems which are brilliant, but if I have a problem that I think is important, I persist in it—in a sense I am like a beaver".

He carefully selected what he had time for, not only in his scientific research but also in the limited time left for his family and for daily living. He no doubt gave up much but found inner satisfaction in his music, reading, travels, friends, and colleagues. Even after receiving the Nobel Prize, he continued to work on perplexing scientific problems. As he explained, "When you are awarded the prize you get a slight inferiority complex. You have won, but you know that there are a half-dozen other people who equally or better deserved the prize as much as you did. So you want to demonstrate that you can do things and improve on your qualifications."

Above all, Herzberg was a gentle and peaceful man, and while not outwardly sentimental, he could be strongly moved by biographies of civilization's eminent contributors and by poetry and music. A favourite poem of his was the Wanderers Nachtlied II by Johann Wolfgang Goethe:

There is peace o'er all the peaks,	Über allen Gipfeln ist Ruh
In all the treetops	In allen Wipfeln spürest du
You feel scarce a breath,	kaum einen Hauch
The little birds are silent in the forest	Die Vöglein schweigen in Walde
Just wait, soon	Warte nur balde
You too will rest.	Ruhest du auch.

Combined with the music Franz Schubert wrote for it, this became Herzberg's most treasured song. To him it was one of the supreme accomplishments of the human spirit.

One often heard Herzberg speak of his good luck, not about difficulties or concerns, but about his good luck! He was forever thankful for the welcome he and Luise had received in Saskatoon and for the ten happy years spent there. He remembered, too, that during the first year of World War II, Lord Tweedsmuir (John Buchan), the Governor General of Canada, visited the University of Saskatchewan and made a short speech at a luncheon. He did not talk about honour, bravery, and victory in war but reminded his listeners of humanity, humility, and humour, which in his view were the really important things in life. Lord Tweedsmuir said it so simply, so sincerely and earnestly, that Herzberg could not help but be deeply touched thinking of the contrast with Nazi ideology. This brief speech convinced Herzberg that he and Luise had made the right decision in choosing Canada to be their homeland.

His last visit to the University of Saskatchewan was in October 1994. He met with the faculty and students in the Departments of Physics and Chemistry, gave a lecture, and was feted at a banquet. The main purpose of his visit was to meet donors to the Herzberg Fund and to discuss his bequest to the fund. In his will, he left to the University 40 percent of the residue of his estate, "In recognition of what the University of Saskatchewan had done for me when my late wife and I arrived penniless at the university at that time".

At the south end of the Campus Oval, a Nobel Plaza was erected honouring both Gerhard Herzberg and Henry Taube, Nobel Laureates in Chemistry and former scholars of the University of Saskatchewan.

Herzberg's enthusiasm for Canada began with his kind reception at the University of Saskatchewan and later at the National Research Council, both of which he came to know so intimately and affectionately. He was forever grateful to Canada for giving him the opportunity to establish the Spectroscopy Laboratory and the freedom to carry out basic research with a group of young colleagues and to open its doors to gifted young scientists from all over the world. After the many travails of the NRC, he was pleased to learn of improved morale and the return of encouragement for basic research under the new administration of President Arthur J. Carty, himself an active research chemist. Even while bedridden, Herzberg kept up an interest in science and music. He was delighted when Takeshi Oka visited him in March 1997, bringing the news of his discovery of interstellar H_3^+, a prediction Herzberg had made thirty years before. Later, with the advancing Parkinson's disease and its attendant loss of memory, recognition of friends and conversation became possible only with Monika's help. Yet in late 1998, he seemed to follow Oka's discussion of Mozart's "Don Giovanni", which Oka had just heard on a brief visit to Prague. Monika later told us that this was one of Gerhard's happiest days.

Herzberg leaves a legacy of his vast knowledge in molecular science and hundreds of scientists around the world who had been excited in basic science by their hero "GH" during their sojourn in his Spectroscopy Laboratory at the NRC. His search for the unknown species in the interstellar medium, and in particular an explanation of the diffuse interstellar bands, has kept these problems uppermost in the minds of many scientists and remains a supreme challenge to this day. He worked on them to the very end.

At a Memorial Tribute held on 11 May 1999 in the Auditorium of the National Research Council, President Carty announced the creation of a new "Herzberg Memorial Prize and Fellowship" open to applicants in Canada and around the world to work at the NRC for up to a year. In November 2000, the Federal Government also launched the country's premier research award, the annual "Gerhard Herzberg, Canada Gold Medal for Science and Engineering" with a $1 million research award over five years. This millennium project of the Natural Sciences and Engineering Research Council of Canada is intended not only to celebrate Canadian heroes, but also to provide them with a new level of support that Canadian researchers have never before enjoyed. Such awards to applaud and encourage outstanding research would have delighted Herzberg immensely.

Herzberg's office, Room 2057, in the National Research Council Laboratories at 100 Sussex Drive was renovated and named "The Gerhard Herzberg Reading Room", a most fitting memorial to this illustrious scientist.

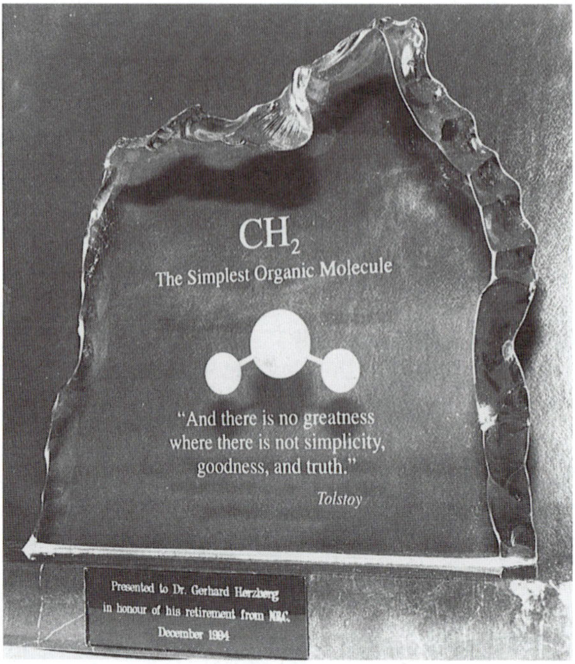

A memento in honour of Herzberg's forty-six years at the NRC.

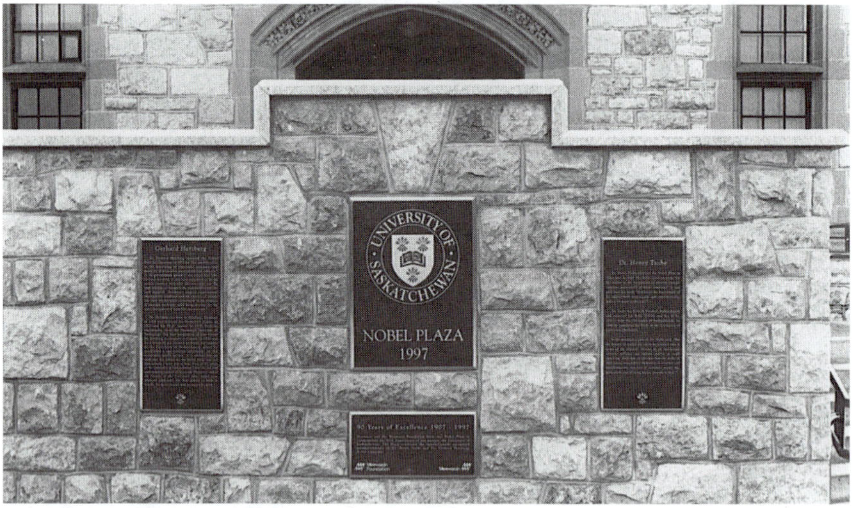

Nobel Plaza at the University of Saskatchewan
honouring Gerhard Herzberg and Henry Taube.

CHRONOLOGY

1904 Dec. 25	Birth of Gerhard Herzberg to Albin and Ella Herzberg in Hamburg.
1911–1915	Student at Vorschule on Hegenstrasse in Hamburg.
1915 Feb. 21	Death of Albin Herzberg after a brief illness.
1915–1924	Student at Realgymnasium of the Johanneum in Hamburg.
1922	Ella Herzberg leaves Germany at the height of the catastrophic inflation and settles in Seattle, Washington, U.S.A.
1924	Graduates from the Johanneum, with the Abiturum and enters the Technische Hochscule in Darmstadt with a scholarship from the Stinnes Company.
1926	Receives a federal scholarship "Studienstiftung des deutchen Volkes".
1927	Graduates with Diplom Ingenieur Degree. Publishes his first three scientific papers on the spectra of hydrogen, as sole author.
1928	Receives Doktor Ingenieur Degree. Publishes nine papers on molecular spectra. Postdoctorate Fellow at the University of Göttingen with Max Born and James Franck. Publishes a paper with Walter Heitler that nitrogen nuclei follow Bose statistics. Research Associate at the H.H. Wills Physics Laboratory, University of Bristol. Completes the Habilitation in Darmstadt with a paper on molecular orbital theory.
1929 Dec. 30	Marries Luise Oettinger in Nürnberg and returns to University of Bristol.
1930–1935	Privatdozent at the Technische Hochschule Darmstadt.
1932	Assistant to Professor Hans Rau at the THD.
1933 Jan. 30	Adolf Hitler appointed Chancellor of Germany.
1933 Oct.	Dr. John W.T. Spinks from the University of Saskatchewan in Saskatoon, Canada, comes to work with Herzberg in Darmstadt.
1933	Begins a book on atomic and molecular spectra but limits it to a volume on *Atomic Spectra and Atomic Structure*. It is published by Th. Steinkopff in 1936.
1933–1934	Seeks a research position outside of Germany and is helped by the Emergency Society of German Scholars Abroad in Zurich and the Academic Assistance Council in London.

1935	Accepts a Guest Professorship offered by Walter C. Murray, President of the University of Saskatchewan in Canada, with the aid of the Carnegie Corporation of New York.
1935 Aug.	Arrives in New York, visits several research institutions in the U.S.A. and Canada, and proceeds to Saskatoon, Saskatchewan.
1936–1945	Research Professor of Physics at the University of Saskatchewan.
1936 Sept. 23	Birth of Paul Albin Herzberg.
1936	J.W.T. Spinks translates *Atomic Spectra and Atomic Structure* into English, and the book is published by Prentice-Hall in 1937.
1938 Dec. 12	Birth of Agnes Margaret Herzberg.
1938	Completes German version of *Spectra of Diatomic Molecules* in 1938, Spinks translates the volume, and it is published in both English and German in 1939.
1939	Elected Fellow of The Royal Society of Canada.
1941	Observes the spectrum of CH^+ with Alex E. Douglas, proving that CH^+ exists in interstellar space.
1944	*Infrared and Raman Spectra of Polyatomic Molecules* is published in 1945.
1945–1948	Assistant Professor, then Professor of Spectroscopy, at Yerkes Observatory of The University of Chicago in Williams Bay, Wisconsin, U.S.A.
1947	Accepts position of Senior Research Officer in the Division of Physics at the National Research Council of Canada (NRC), Ottawa, to begin Aug. 1948.
1948	Observes the quadrupole spectrum of molecular hydrogen in a long-path cell.
1948 Aug. 8	Returns to Canada and the NRC to establish a spectroscopy laboratory.
1949	Appointed Director of the Division of Physics, NRC, a position he holds until 1955.
1950	First return to Europe, visits Darmstadt and Hamburg. Awarded the Médaille de l'Université de Liège, the first of many medals and prizes.
1951	Elected a Fellow of The Royal Society of London.
1953	Awarded the Henry Marshall Tory Medal of The Royal Society of Canada.
1955–1969	Director of the Division of Pure Physics, NRC.

1956	President of The Canadian Association of Physicists.
1956	Observes the spectrum of the free methyl radical (CH_3).
1959	Observes the spectrum of the free methylene radical (CH_2).
1960	Bakerian Lecture, The Royal Society of London.
1964	Academician, Pontifical Academy of Sciences. Awarded Frederic Ives Medal, Optical Society of America.
1966	Publishes *Electronic Spectra of Polyatomic Molecules.*
1966–1967	President of The Royal Society of Canada.
1968	Appointed Companion of the Order of Canada.
1969–1975	Appointed Distinguished Research Scientist, Division of Physics, NRC.
1970	Awarded the Faraday Medal, The Chemical Society of London.
1971	Awarded the Royal Medal, The Royal Society of London.
1971 June 3	Luise Herzberg dies of heart attack.
1971	Receives the Nobel Prize in Chemistry, The Swedish Royal Academy of Sciences.
1972 Mar. 21	Marries Monika Elisabeth Tenthoff, niece of his friend Alfred Schulz.
1973–1980	Chancellor, Carleton University, Ottawa.
1974	Observes spectrum of ion H_2O^+ with Hin Lew and identifies this ion in comet Kohoutek.
1975	Herzberg Institute of Astrophysics established at the NRC.
1975–1994	Distinguished Research Scientist, Herzberg Institute of Astrophysics, NRC.
1979	Observes the spectrum of triatomic hydrogen (H_3).
1985	Awarded the Earle K. Plyler Prize, American Physical Society.
1992	Appointed Member of the Queen's Privy Council of Canada.
1994 Dec. 31	Official retirement from the NRC.
1999 Mar. 3	Death in Ottawa after lengthy illness, cremation and burial in Ottawa.

SELECTED BIBLIOGRAPHY

Abella, I., and H. Troper. *None is Too Many*. Toronto: Lester Publishing, 1983.

Arms, Nancy. *A Prophet in Two Countries: The Life of F.E. Simon*. Oxford: Pergamon Press, 1966.

Bendersky, J.W. *A History of Nazi Germany*. Chicago: Nelson Hall, 1985.

Bentwich, Norman. *The Refugees From Germany*. London: George Allen & Unwin, 1936.

Bentwich, Norman. *The Rescue and Achievement of Refugee Scholars*. The Hague: Martinus Nijhoff, 1953.

Beyerchen, Alan D. *Scientists Under Hitler, Politics and the Physics Community in the Third Reich*. New Haven: Yale University Press, 1977.

Blumberg, Stanley A. and Gwinn Owens. *Energy and Conflict: The Life and Times of Edward Teller*. New York: G.P. Putnam's Sons, 1976.

Böhme, Helmut. *Technische Hochschule Darmstadt*. Darmstadt: Presse und Informationsreferat, 1990.

Born, Max. *The Born-Einstein Letters*. New York: Walker and Company, 1971.

Born, Max. *My Life & My Views*. New York: Charles Scribner's Sons, 1968.

Born, Max. *My Life: Recollections of a Nobel Laureate*. London: Taylor & Francis Ltd., 1978.

Casimir, H.B.G. *Haphazard Reality: Half a Century of Science*, New York: Harper Colophon, 1984.

Cassidy, David C. *Uncertainty: The Life and Science of Werner Heisenberg*. New York: W.H. Freeman and Co., 1991.

Davie, Maurice R. *Refugees in America*. New York: Harper & Brothers Publishers, 1947.

Doern, G. Bruce. *Science and Politics in Canada*. Montreal: McGill-Queen's University Press, 1972.

Dresden, M. *H.A. Kramers: Between Tradition and Revolution*. Berlin: Springer-Verlag, 1987.

Edingshaus, Anne-Lydia. *Heinz Maier-Leibnitz: Ein halbes Jahrhundert experimentelle Physik*. Munich: R. Piper - GmbH & Co. KG, 1986.

Elsasser, Walter M. *Memoirs of a Physicist in the Atomic Age*. Bristol: Adam Hilger Ltd., 1978.

Fermi, Laura. *Illustrious Immigrants: The Intellectual Migration from Europe*. Chicago: The University of Chicago Press, 1968.

Franz, Eckhart G. *Darmstadts Geschichte*. Darmstadt: Eduard Roether Verlag, 1980.

Franz, Eckhart G. *Juden als Darmstädter Bürger*. Darmstadt: Eduard Roether Verlag, 1984.

Frisch, Otto R. *What Little I Remember*. Cambridge: Cambridge University Press, 1979.

Hastings, Max. *Bomber Command*. London: Michael Joseph, 1979.

Hayes, F. Ronald. *The Chaining of Prometheus: evolution of a power structure for Canadian Science*. Toronto: University of Toronto Press, 1973.

Heisenberg, Elisabeth. *Inner Exile*. Cambridge: Birkhaüser Boston Inc., 1984.

Herzberg, Gerhard, interview by Christine M. King on 5 May 1986 in Ottawa, for the Beckman Center for the History of Chemistry.

Herzberg, Gerhard, interview by Brenda P. Winnewisser on 28 February and 2 March 1989 in Ottawa for American Institute of Physics, New York.

Herzberg, Gerhard, "Molecular Spectroscopy: A Personal History," in *Ann. Rev. Phys. Chem.* 36 (1985): 1–30.

Jarrell, Richard A., and Yves Gingras, eds. *Building Canadian Science: The Role of the National Research Council*. Thornhill: The Scientia Press, 1992.

King, M. Christine. *E.W.R. Steacie and Science in Canada.* Toronto: University of Toronto Press, 1989.

Lemmerich, J. *Der Luxus des Gewissens.* Berlin: Staatsbibliotek Preussischer Kulturbesitz, 1982.

McGrayne, S.B. *Nobel Prize Women in Science*. New York: Carol Publ. Group, 1992.

Middleton, W.E.K. *Physics at the National Research Council of Canada 1929–1952*. Waterloo: Wilfrid Laurier University Press, 1979.

Moore, Walter. *Schrödinger: Life and Thought.* Cambridge: Cambridge University Press, 1989.

Mulliken, Robert S. *Life of a Scientist.* ed. Ransil, Bernard J., Berlin: Springer-Verlag, 1989.

Murray, David R. and Robert A. Murray. *The Prairie Builder: Walter Murray of Saskatchewan*. Edmonton: NeWest Press, 1984.

Nachmansohn, David. *German-Jewish Pioneers in Science 1900–1933*. Berlin: Springer-Verlag, 1979.

Osterbrock, Donald E. *Yerkes Observatory, 1892–1950*. Chicago: The University of Chicago Press, 1997.

Peierls, Rudolf. *Birds of Passage*. Princeton: Princeton University Press, 1985.

Reid, Constance. *Hilbert.* New York: Springer-Verlag, 1970.

Reid, Constance. *Courant in Göttingen and New York*. New York: Springer-Verlag, 1976.

Sime, Ruth Lewin. *Lise Meitner, A Life in Physics*. Berkeley: University of California Press, 1996.

Spinks, John. *Two Blades of Grass.* Saskatoon: Western Producer Prairie Books, 1980.

Stokes, Lawrence D. "Canada and an Academic Refugee from Nazi Germany: The Case of Gerhard Herzberg," in *The Canadian Historical Review* 57 (1976): 150.

Wali, K. C., Ed., *S. Chandrasekhar, The Man Behind the Legend*. London: Imperial College Press, 1997

Weisskopf, Victor F. *Physics in the Twentieth Century: Selected Essays.* Cambridge: The MIT Press, 1972.

Wolf, Christa. *Darmstädter Archivschriften 3, Verzeichnis der Hochschullehrer der TH Darmstadt.* Marburg: Symon und Wagner KG, 1977.

NOTES AND REFERENCES

Abbreviations for sources of information used in Notes and References

BSF	B. Stoicheff Files
CCA	Carnegie Corporation Archives
DMM	Deutsche Museum Munich
GH	Gerhard Herzberg
GHA	Gerhard Herzberg Archives (at home)
NAC	National Archives of Canada
THDA	Technische Hochschule Darmstadt Archives
UCA	The University of Chicago Archives
USA	University of Saskatchewan Archives
YOA	Yerkes Observatory Archives

Chapter 1. Family and Early Education

1. Based on interviews of G. Herzberg by B. Stoicheff for the article "GH" in *Physics in Canada,* 28 (1972): 11, and more recent interviews; also "GH—Notes from Conversations 1992–93" by Paul Herzberg, as well as letters in GHA, and discussions with the pastor Matthias Uhlig and archivist Matthius Mergner on a visit by the author to Langensalza in August 1997.
2. Herzberg family tree from 1573, based on a document dated 24 August 1933, and produced by Langensalza state archivist Hermann Gutbier and confirmed in 1940. According to the original document of Gutbier, the family dates further back to Hans Quatmer who changed the family name to Herzberg. While the name Quatmer appears in the records of St. Stephani Church, no further hints could be found of why Gutbier gives a change of name to Herzberg or Hertzbergk; GHA.
3. The Heine sculpture was after a design by Louis Hasselry (Danish) for Empress Elizabeth of Austria in Corfu. Emperor Wilhelm II bought the castle and removed the statue, subsequently purchased by the publisher Julius Campe, Jr., and put up at the Barkhof in Hamburg. In 1939 the Heine statue was a target for political uprisings and was removed and brought to Toulon.
4. Müller, J.P., *Mein System: 15 minuten täglicher arbeit für die gesundheit.* Leipzig und Zurich: Grethlein & Co., 1904.
5. Kuhn, T.S. et al., in *Sources for History of Quantum Physics: An Inventory and Report.* Philadelphia: *Amer. Phil. Soc.* (1967): 2–3.
6. Grimsehl, E., *Lehrbuch der Physik*, eds. W. Hillers and H. Starke; I 4th ed., II 4th revised ed. Leipzig: Teubner, 1922.
7. Bohr, N., "On the Constitution of Atoms and Molecules." *Phil. Mag.* 26 (1913): 1.
8. GH, *Ann. d. Phys.* 84 (1927): 565.
9. This experience turned GH away from turnips for life!

10. GH to Hugo Stinnes, 22 Mar. 1924 (shorthand copy); GHA.
11. Max Warburg to GH, 11 Apr. 1924; GHA.
12. Heinersdorff to GH, 8 Apr. 1924; GHA.
13. GH to Heinersdorff, 11 Apr. 1924 (shorthand copy); GHA.
14. GH to Alfred Schulz, 28 Apr. 1924; GHA.
15. Heinersdorff to GH, 17 Apr. 1924; GHA.

Chapter 2. University Years

1. Based in part on descriptions by Werner Zimmer, in *Darmstadt, Grenzen und Möglichkeiten einer Stadt.* Frankfurt: Verlag Waldemar Kramer, 1954; by Eckhart G. Franz in *Darmstadts Geschichte*. Darmstadt: Eduard Roether Verlag, 1980; by Max Hastings in *Bomber Command.* London: Michael Joseph, 1979; and a visit by the author in January 1995.
2. Böhme Helmut, *Technische Hochschule Darmstadt.* Darmstadt: Presse und Informationsreferat, 1990.
3. During the early 1870s, the prestige of the school had dropped to a low level and threats were made to close the school or move it to Giessen. Otto Wolfskehl (1841–1907), a banker, economic adviser to Ernst Ludwig, and patron of the school, played a major role in saving the school and transforming it to the THD in 1877. His brother Paul (1856–1906) was a mathematician who left in his will 100,000 Gold-Marks to the University of Göttingen as the prize for the mathematician who first solved the 17th century problem known as "Fermat's Last Theorem." In the meantime, the interest was used to finance the annual "Darmstadt Lectures," which brought to Göttingen the most distinguished scientists of the age, such as Bohr, Planck, Nernst, Sommerfeld, Lorentz, and Poincaré, among others. The lectures were discontinued in the early 1920s due to the disastrous inflation. See Paul "Wolfskehl und der Wolfskehlpreis" by Klaus Barner in Mathematische Schriften, Kassel, March 1997; also *A Prophet in Two Countries: the Life of F.E. Simon* by Nancy Arms, Oxford: Pergamon Press, 1966, 17.
4. Marianne Viefhaus to B. Stoicheff, 20 May 1996; BSF.
5. GH to Alfred Schulz, 28 Apr. 1924; GHA.
6. GH to Alfred Schulz, 17 May 1924; GHA.
7. GH to Alfred Schulz, 31 May 1924; GHA. In 1919, the national organization of fraternities had adopted the Nürnberg articles, which stated persons of Jewish descent were inadmissible as members.
8. GH to Alfred Schulz, 16 and 28 June 1924; GHA.
9. GH to Alfred Schulz, 28 June 1924; GHA.
10. GH to Alfred Schulz, 13 July and 9 Aug. 1924; GHA.
11. GH to Alfred Schulz, 31 May 1924; GHA.
12. GH to Alfred Schulz, 13 and 26 July 1924; GHA.
13. Wolf, C. and M. Viefhaus, in *Verzeichnis der Hochschullehrer der TH Darmstadt, Teil 1: Kurzbiographien 1836–1945.* Marburg: Symon und Wagner, 1977.

14. Heinersdorff to GH, 4 Nov. 1924; GHA.
15. Heinersdorff to GH, 25 June 1925; GHA.
16. Heinersdorff to GH, 29 July 1925; GHA.
17. GH to Heinersdorff, 31 July 1925; GHA.
18. Heinersdorff to GH, 5 Aug. 1925; GHA.
19. Schrödinger, E., *Ann. Phys.* 79 (1926): 361.
20. Thomson, J.J., *Phil. Mag.* 21 (1911): 225.
21. Winnewisser, Brenda P., interview of GH, 28 Feb. 1989.
22. GH, *J. Chem. Phys.* 70 (1979): 4806.
23. Herzberg's professors and courses included the following; THDA:

First Year, 1924–1925, Engineering Physics

F. Dingelday	Higher mathematics
H.R. Müller	Descriptive geometry I and II
G. Schlink	Mechanics I and II
H. Rau	Experimental physics and physics laboratory
L. Wöhler	Inorganic chemistry and chemistry laboratory
L. von Roessler	Mechanical drawing
E. Bramesfeld	Machine drawing
J.J. Goldstein	Philosophy

Second Year, 1925–1926, Engineering Physics

J. Horn	Differential equations
H.R. Müller	Descriptive geometry III, kinematics
H. Hohenner	Probability and least-dquares analysis
V. Blaess	Mechanics III
W. Wagenbach	Hydraulics
H. Rau	Physics laboratory
L. Wöhler	Physical chemistry laboratory
K. Wirtz	Electrical engineering
M.L.A. Muss	Economics
P. Luchtenberg	Philosophy

Third Year, 1926–1927, Physics

G. Schlink	Higher mechanics and hydrodynamics
H. Rau	Experimental physics and introduction to independent research
F. Dingelday	Fourier series and integrals; higher algebra
J. Horn	Partial differential equations
H. Baerwald	Statistical mechanics and electrical theory

Fourth Year, 1927, Physics

H. Rau	Independent research; instrumental optics; physical measurements
W. Georgii	Cosmic physics
H. Baerwald	Thermodynamics; electromagnetic theory and optics

24. GH, *Ann. d. Phys.* 84 (1927): 553, 565.
25. GH, *Physik. Z.* 28 (1927): 727.
26. Weisskopf, V.F., "Physics and Physicists the Way I Knew Them," in *History of Twentieth Century Physics*, (Proc. International School of Physics "Enrico Fermi"), ed. C. Weiner. New York: Academic Press, 1977, 435.
27. Sommerfeld, A., *Atombau und Spektralinien*. Braunschweig: F. Vieweg & Sohn, 1920.
28. For a more detailed account see GH in *The Spectra and Structures of Simple Free Radicals: An Introduction to Molecular Spectroscopy*. Ithaca: Cornell University Press, 1971.
29. GH, *Z. Physik*, 49 (1928): 512.
30. GH, *Vistas in Astronomy*, 29 (1986): 201–221.
31. Bonhoeffer, K.F. und G. Kaminsky, *Z. Elektrochem.* 32 (1926): 536; *Z. Phys. Chem.* 127 (1927): 385.
32. GH, "Über das Nachtleuchten von Stickstoff und Sauerstoff und über die Struktur der negativen Stickstoffbanden." Negative bands of nitrogen refers to the bands of N_2^+.
33. GH, report of winter 1928/29 to Studienstiftung des deutschen Volkes; NAC.
34. R. Ladenburg to GH, 24 Apr. 1928; GHA.
35. O. Oldenberg to GH, 10 May 1928; NAC.
36. Wigner, E. and E.E. Witmer, *Z. Physik*, 51(1928): 859.
37. Franck, J., *Trans. Faraday Soc.* 21 (1925): 536.
38. Condon, E.U., *Proc. Nat. Acad. Sci.* 13 (1927): 462; *Phys. Rev.* 32 (1928): 858.
39. Born, M. und R. Oppenheimer, *Ann. Physik*, 84 (1927): 457.
40. Heitler, W. und F. London, *Z. Physik*, 44 (1927): 455.
41. Hund, H., *Z. Physik*, 36 (1926): 657; 37 (1927): 742; 42 (1927): 93; 43 (1927): 805; 51 (1927): 759.
42. Mulliken, R.S., *Phys. Rev.* 32 (1928): 186, 761, 880; 33 (1929): 730.
43. Raman, C.V. and K.S. Krishnan, *Nature*, 121 (1928): 502, 711.
44. Landsberg, G. und L. Mandelstam, *Naturwiss.* 16 (1928): 557, 772.
45. Vonderheid-Ebner, Christine, in *THD Intern*, 6 May 1993.

Chapter 3. A Year in Göttingen

1. Nachmansohn, David, *German–Jewish Pioneers in Science 1900–1933*. Berlin: Springer-Verlag, 1979, 41.
2. GH, "Molecular Spectroscopy: A Personal History." *Ann. Rev. Phys. Chem.* 36 (1985): 1.
3. Born, Max, *My Life and My Views*. New York: Charles Scribner's Sons, 1968; and *My Life: Recollections of a Nobel Laureate*. London: Taylor and Francis Ltd., 1978; N. Kemmer and R. Schlapp, "Max Born," in *Biographical Memoirs*. London: The Royal Society, 17 (1971): 17; David Nahmansohn, *ibid.* 67.
4. Kuhn, H.G., "James Franck," in *Biographical Memoirs*. London: The Royal Society, 11 (1965): 53; David Nahmansohn, *ibid.* 63.
5. Born, Max, *My Life and My Views*. 32.
6. Franck, J. and G. Hertz, Verh. d. Deutsch. *Phys. Ges.* 16 (1914): 12; *Phys. Zeits.* 17 (1916): 409.
7. Sime, Ruth Lewin, *Lise Meitner, A Life in Physics*. Berkeley: University of California Press, 1996, 59; J. Lemmerich, *Der Luxus des Gewissens*. Berlin: Staatsbibliotek Preussischer Kulturbesitz, 1982, 37.
8. Moore, W., *Schrödinger*; *Life and Thought*. Cambridge: Cambridge University Press, 1989, 263.
9. Frisch, Otto R., *What Little I Remember*. Cambridge: Cambridge University Press, 1979, 95.
10. GH to Kurt Lion, 4 Nov. 1928; GHA.
11. Born, Max, *My Life and My Views*, 37.
12. Born, Max, *The Born Einstein Letters*. New York: Walker and Company, 1971, 112.
13. GH, reports of the winter semester 1928/29 and summer semester 1929; GHA.
14. Hayes, William, "Max Ludwig Henning Delbrück," in *Biographical Memoirs*. London: The Royal Society, 28 (1982): 59.
15. GH to Hans-Werner Döring, 9 Nov. 1928; GHA. R.T. Birge, *Nature*, 122 (1928): 842; R.S. Mulliken, *Nature*, 122 (1928): 842.
16. GH, *ZS. f. Physik*, 57 (1929): 601.
17. Rasetti, F., *Proc. Nat. Acad.* 15 (1929): 515.
18. Heitler, W. und GH, *Naturwiss.* 17 (1929): 673.
19. Chadwick, J., *Proc. R. Soc. Lond.* A 142 (1932): 1. He was awarded the Nobel Prize in Physics in 1935 for his discovery of the neutron.
20. GH and G. Scheibe, *Trans. Farad. Soc.* 25 (1929): 716.
21. GH und G. Scheibe, *Z. Phys. Chem. B* 7 (1930): 390.
22. Weisskopf, Victor F., *Physics in the Twentieth Century: Selected Essays*. Cambridge, Massachusetts: The MIT Press, 1972, 3.
23. Franck's home is presently part of the Goethe Institute in Göttingen.
24. Winans, J.G. and E.C.G. Stueckelberg, *Proc. Nat. Acad, Sci.* 4 (1928): 867.
25. Druyvesteyn, M.J., *Nature*, 128 (1931): 1076.

26. Dabrowski, I. and GH, *J. Mol. Spectrosc.* 73 (1978): 185.
27. A.M. Tyndall to GH, 28 May 1929; NAC.

Chapter 4. A Year in Bristol

1. "Molecular Spectra and Molecular Structure," in *Trans. Farad. Soc.* 25 (1929): 611.
2. O.W. Richardson was awarded the 1928 Nobel Prize in 1929.
3. Long, D.A., in *Int. Rev. Phys. Chem.* 7 (1988): 317; "Dr. A.C. Menzies has recalled that Raman, during his stay in Bristol attending the Faraday Meeting, regularly enquired of the hotel porter if there was a cable for him from Stockholm!" In fact Raman was so sure that he would receive this coveted prize that he booked passage for himself and his wife in July so that he would reach Stockholm in time for the Nobel ceremonies on 10 December.
4. Mott, N.F. and C.F. Powell, "Arthur Mannering Tyndall," in *Biographical Memoirs*. London: The Royal Society, 7 (1961): 159.
5. GH, *Leipziger Vortrage*, (1931): 167.
6. P.M.S. Blackett received the Nobel Prize in Physics in 1948 for his development of the Wilson cloud chamber method and his discoveries in the field of nuclear physics and cosmic radiation. J.D. Cockcroft and E.T.S. Walton shared the Nobel Prize in Physics in 1951 for their pioneer work on the transmutation of atomic nuclei by artificially accelerated atomic particles. In 1978 P.L. Kapitsa was awarded the Nobel Prize for his basic inventions and discoveries in the area of low-temperature physics.
7. Naudé, S.M., *Phys. Rev.* 34 (1929): 1498.
8. GH, *Z. Phys. Chem.* B 9 (1930): 43.
9. GH to James Franck, 29 Aug. 1930; NAC.
10. James Franck to GH, 8 Sept. 1930; NAC.
11. Gretel Goldstein to G. and L. Herzberg, 14 Aug. 1930; GHA.

Chapter 5. Privatdozent in Darmstadt

1. Franz, Eckhart G., *Darmstadt Geschichte*. Darmstadt: Eduard Roether Verlag, 1980, 445.
2. Franz, Eckhart G., *ibid.* p. 446.
3. Vonderheid-Ebner, Christine, in *THD Intern*, 6 May 1993, 2.
4. Weisskopf, Victor F., *Physics in the Twentieth Century: Selected Essays*, Cambridge, Massachusetts: The MIT Press, 1972, 6.
5. GH, Annual Report from September 1930 to September 1931, 26 Oct. 1931; NAC.
6. GH, "Molecular Spectroscopy: A Personal History," *Ann. Rev. Chem.* 36 (1985): 1; GH to A.M. Tyndall, 1 June 1932; NAC.
7. F.W. Loomis to GH, 2 May 1932; NAC.
8. Winnewisser, Brenda P., interview of GH, 28 Feb. and 2 Mar. 1989, 12.
9. GH, *Naturwiss.* 10 (1931): 207.

10. GH, *Trans. Farad. Soc.* 27 (1931): 378.
11. P. Debye to GH, 5 June and 22 June 1931; NAC.
12. GH and E. Teller, *Z. phys. Chem. B* 21 (1933): 410.
13. E. Teller to B. Stoicheff, 18 July 1972; BSF.
14. M. Polanyi to GH, 19 May and 5 June 1931; NAC.
15. GH, *Leipziger Vortrage*, (1931): 167.
16. Franz, Eckhart G., *Darmstadt Geschichte*. Darmstadt: Eduard Roether Verlag, 1980, 448.
17. J. Curry to GH, 1931; NAC.
18. S.C. Wu and R.M. Badger to GH, 26 Feb. 1932; NAC.
19. GH to S.C. Wu, 15 Mar. 1932; NAC.
20. GH, *Naturwiss.* 20 (1932): 577.
21. Herzberg, L., *Nature*, 129 (1932): 653.
22. Franz, Eckhart G., *Darmstadt Geschichte*. Darmstadt: Eduard Roether Verlag, 1980, 454.
23. Bendersky, J.W., *A History of Nazi Germany*. Chicago: Nelson Hall, 1985.
24. Nachmansohn, David, *German–Jewish Pioneers in Science* 1900–1933. Berlin: Springer-Verlag 1979; Wolff, Stefan L. "Vertreibung und Emigration in der Physik, *Physikgeschichte* 1933," 1995, 267.
25. Born, M., *My Life and My Views*. New York: Charles Scribner's Sons, 1968; and *My Life: Recollections of a Nobel Laureate*. London: Taylor and Francis Ltd, 1978.
26. Franck, J., in *Der Luxus des Gewissens*; *Max Born, James Franck, Physiker in ihrer Zeit*. Berlin, Staatsbibliothek, 1983, 115.
27. Franck, J., in *Göttinger Zeitung*, 18 April, 1933; reprinted in *Der Luxus des Gewissens; Max Born, James Franck, Physiker in ihrer Zeit*, Berlin, Staatsbibliothek, 1983, 114.
28. GH to James Franck, 19 April, 1933; UCA.
29. McGrayne, S.B., *Nobel Prize Women in Science.* New York: Carol Publ. Group, 1992, 82.
30. Rupp, Susanne, in *THD Intern,* 6 May 1993.
31. Edmund Stiasny, with a Roman Catholic mother and Jewish father emigrated to Sweden with his Swedish wife, and was a director of a research institute for tanning chemistry in Halsingborg from 1933 until his retirement in 1943. Ernst Berl emigrated to the United States of America in September 1933, as Professor at the Carnegie Institute of Technology in Pittsburgh. Erich Aron, Emeritus Professor in 1933 died in Theresienstadt Camp in 1943. Paul Leser of Jewish descent, whose parents had converted to Protestanism before his birth, returned the venia ligendi and emigrated to Sweden in 1936 and to the United States of America in 1942. Michael Evenari obtained his Habilitation in Feb. 1933, was dismissed on 1 April, and emigrated to Palestine where he developed a program for turning the desert green. William Prager emigrated to Turkey, then to the U.S.A. where he joined the Department of Mathematics at Brown University in Rhode Island.
32. GH to Alfred Schulz, 10 May 1933; GHA.

33. Franz, Eckhart G., *Darmstadts Geschichte*. Darmstadt: Eduard Roether Verlag, 1980, 461.

34. GH document, 6 May, 1933; NAC.

35. Oskar Prochnow to GH, 23 April 1933; NAC. Gradstein was employed by the Phillips Co. in Eindhoven, eventually becoming the Editor of the Phillips journal *Review*. During the war he was sheltered by his Dutch wife's parents and survived to resume his position at the Phillips Co. after the war.

36. Gradstein, S., "Fluoreszenz des H_2CO," *Zeits. Phys. Chem.* 22 (1933): 384.

37. Kurt Lion found temporary employment in Turkey, and eventually went to the United States where he joined the Massachusetts Institute of Technology in Cambridge, Massachusetts.

38. "Nationalism and Academic Freedom," *Nature*, 131 (1933): 853.

39. GH to J.E. Lennard-Jones, 7 July, 1933; NAC.

40. GH to J.E. Lennard-Jones, 26 July 1933; NAC.

41. Luise Herzberg, Ph.D. diploma, dated 30 Aug. 1933; GHA.

42. J.W.T. Spinks to GH, 29 Mar. 1933; NAC.

43. Stoicheff, B., "GH," in *Physics in Canada*, 28 (1972): 11.

44. Spinks, J.W.T., *Two Blades of Grass*. Saskatoon: Western Producer Prairie Books, 1980, 35.

45. A.J. Allmand to GH, 24 May 1933; NAC.

46. GH to J.W.T. Spinks, 27 May 1933; NAC.

47. Spinks, J.W.T., *Two Blades of Grass*. Saskatoon: Western Producer Prairie Books, 1980, 36.

48. J.W.T. Spinks to B. Stoicheff, 1972; also in "GH," in *Physics in Canada*, 28 (1972): 11; BSF.

49. Hans Baerwald was placed in the Buchenwald concentration camp in 1936, but being a non-political prisoner, he was released due to Rau's efforts, and permitted to go to England where his daughter lived. He spent the next decade teaching at various schools, but after the war was not given his position at the THD, and died of a heart attack in 1946 in England.

50. Hessian State Ministry document to Rector Hans Busch, 27 Apr. 1934; NAC.

51. Hessian State Ministry to Rector Friedrich Hübener, 27 Nov. 1934; NAC.

52. Bendersky, J.W., *A History of Nazi Germany*. Chicago: Nelson-Hall, 1985, 201.

53. GH's students in the period 1932–1935 were W. Behagel, G. Büttenbender, K. Franz, S. Gradstein, R. Kölsch, and K. Sainisch.

54. GH, Begrundung des Gesuches vom 16 Oct. 1933; NAC.

Chapter 6. Searching the World for an Academic Position

1. GH to Notgemeinschaft Deutscher Wissenschaftler im Ausland, 26 Nov. 1933; NAC.

2. Notice from the Reichsminister fur Wissenschaft, Erziehung, und Volksbildung, Berlin, 28 Nov. 1934; NAC.

3. E. Miescher to GH, 27 Jan. 1934; NAC.
4. Sho-Chow Wu to GH, 20 Sept. 1933; NAC.
5. GH to C.V. Raman, 11 Jan. 1934; NAC.
6. A.M. Tyndall to GH, 29 July 1934; NAC.
7. GH applied to: Indian Institute of Science in Bangalore, India, 26 Jan. 1934; University of Auckland, New Zealand, 17 May 1934; University of Ecuador in Quito, Ecuador, 29 Sept. 1934; University College in Rangoon, Burma, 22 Nov. 1934; NAC.
8. GH to M. Polanyi, 3 June 1934; NAC.
9. M. Polanyi to GH, 5 June 1934; DMM.
10. GH to M. Polanyi, 7 June 1934; NAC.
11. M. Polanyi to W. Heisenberg, 19 June 1934; DMM.
12. W. Heisenberg to M. Polanyi, 9 July 1934; UCA.
13. J. Stark was awarded the Nobel Prize for Physics in 1919 for his discovery of the Doppler effect in canal rays and of the splitting of spectral lines in electric fields. He became a zealous Nazi, who had not kept up with the theoretical physics of his time, and branded relativity and quantum theories as Jewish physics.
14. GH to the Academic Assistance Council, 25 June 1934, and to Emergency Committee of New York, 22 June 1934; NAC.
15. In retrospect, this reply is at odds with the assistance given by the Emergency Committee in Aid of Foreign Displaced Scholars in placing several hundred scholars in positions in the United States of America, including Hertha Sponer at the end of 1934.
16. *Nature*, 131(1933): 793 and 853; Norman Bentwich in *The Refugees from Germany*, London: George Allen & Unwin, 1937, 174; and in *The Rescue and Achievement of Refugee Scholars*, The Hague: Martinus Nijhoff, 1953. During the first two years the Council placed 57 in permanent positions and found temporary appointments for 155 persons. By 1945 the total number of academic refugees registered with the Society was 2541, with over 600 residing permanently in Britain, some returning to their own countries, and others remaining in the countries that offered them refuge.
17. GH to Academic Assistance Council, 29 June 1934; NAC.
18. J. Frenkel to GH, 1 Aug. 1934; NAC.
19. GH applied to: University of Louisville in Kentucky, 23 July 1934; Royal School of Engineering in Giza, Egypt, 2 Aug. 1934; University of Cape Town, South Africa, 4 Sept. 1934; University of Ghent, Belgium, 11 Nov. 1934; NAC.
20. GH was offered a Research Fellowship for two years by J. Verschaffelt, University of Ghent, Belgium, 19 Feb. 1935; NAC.
21. S. Gradstein to GH; NAC.
22. D. Coster to GH, Oct. 1934; NAC.
23. R.A. Mulliken to GH; NAC.
24. H. Sponer to GH, 13 Feb. 1934; NAC.
25. GH to Faculty of Mathematics and Natural Sciences, 19 Feb. 1935; NAC.

Chapter 7. Guest Professorship at the University of Saskatchewan

1. N.D.W. to GH, 14 Jan. 1935; NAC.
2. GH to J.W.T. Spinks, 15 Jan. 1935; NAC.
3. W.C. Murray to H.J. Cody and E.F. Burton, 31 Jan. 1935; USA.
4. Spinks, J.W.T., *Two Blades of Grass*. Saskatoon: Western Producer Prairie Books 1980, 43–44; J.S. Thomson, "Walter Charles Murray," in *Proc. Trans. R. Soc. Can.* 39 (1945): 103; Murray, D.R. and R.A. Murray, *The Prairie Builder*. Edmonton: NeWest Press, 1984.
5. J.W.T. Spinks to GH, 30 Jan. 1935; NAC.
6. H.J. Cody to F.P. Keppel, Carnegie Corporation, 14 Jan. 1935; CCA.
7. H.J. Cody to W.C. Murray, noting McLennan's replacement to be Malcolm F. Crawford, 5 Feb. 1935; USA.
8. F.P. Keppel to H.J. Cody, 8 Mar. 1935; CCA.
9. F.P. Keppel to H.J. Cody, 21 Nov. 1935; CCA.
10. W.C. Murray to H.M. Tory, 8 Feb. 1935, and reply 11 Feb. 1935; USA.
11. J. Franck to GH, 18 Mar. 1935; UCA.
12. J.S. Foster to GH, 1935; NAC.
13. Spinks, J.W.T., *Two Blades of Grass*, 44.
14. J.W.T. Spinks to GH, 21 Nov. 1934; NAC.
15. J.W.T. Spinks to GH, 7 Mar. 1935; NAC.
16. W.C. Murray to R.M. Lester, Carnegie Corporation, 8 Feb. 1935; USA.
17. J. Russell, Carnegie Corporation, to W.C. Murray, 14 Feb. 1935; USA.
18. W.C. Murray to J. Russell, 26 Feb. 1935; USA.
19. R.M. Lester to W.C. Murray, 8 Mar. 1935; USA.
20. S.H. Stackpole, "Carnegie Corporation, Commonwealth Program 1911–1961," 1963; CCA.
21. W.C. Murray to GH, 3 Apr. 1935; USA.
22. GH telegram to J.W.T. Spinks, 15 May 1935; USA.
23. GH to H. Sponer, 14 Mar. 1935; NAC.
24. K. Herzfeld to G. Herzberg, 5 Mar. 1935; NAC.
25. GH to H. Sponer, 15 Mar. 1935; NAC.
26. GH to J. Franck, 17 Mar. 1935; UCA.
27. J. Franck to GH, 18 Mar. 1935; UCA.
28. GH to Alfred Schulz, 5 Apr. 1935; GHA.
29. GH to W.C. Murray, 2 Apr. 1935; USA.
30. GH to W.C. Murray, 19 Apr. 1935; USA.
31. GH to Alfred Schulz, 17 Apr. 1935; GHA.

32. GH to J.E. Verschaffelt, 4 Apr. 1935; NAC.
33. H. Sponer to GH, 8 June 1935; NAC.
34. GH to Academic Assistance Council, 4 Apr. 1935 and to N.D.W., 7 Apr. 1935; NAC.
35. GH to Rector F. Hübener, 4 Apr. 1935; NAC.
36. GH to E.L. Harrington, 19 Apr. 1935; NAC.
37. E.L. Harrington to GH, 20 Apr. 1935; NAC.
38. GH to E.L. Harrington, 6 May 1935; NAC.
39. E.L. Harrington to GH, 28 June 1935; NAC.
40. Abella, I. and H. Troper, *None is Too Many*. Toronto: Lester Publishing, 1983.
41. A.L. Jolliffe to W.C. Murray, 4 July 1935; USA.
42. W.C. Murray to A.L. Jolliffe, 13 July 1935; USA.
43. W.C. Murray to GH, 29 July 1935; GHA.
44. GH to Alfred Schulz, 1 July 1935; GHA.
45. GH to many friends in Germany, early Oct. 1935; GHA.
46. GH, notes of visits to universities and research institutes, Sept. 1935; GHA.
47. GH, "Molecular Spectroscopy: A Personal History," *Ann. Rev. Phys. Chem.* 36 (1985): 14.

Chapter 8. Beginnings in Canada

1. Letters to many friends in Germany, Oct. 1935; GHA.
2. Clubb, Sally P., *Saskatoon: The Serenety and the Surge*. Saskatoon: Midwest Litho Ltd., 1966.
3. Murray, David R. and A. Robert, *The Prairie Builder: Walter Murray of Saskatchewan*. Edmonton: NeWest Press, 1984.
4. Thomson, James S., in *Trans. R. Soc. Can.* 39 (1945): 105.
5. King, Carlyle, *The First Fifty*. Toronto: McClelland and Stewart, 1959, 6.
6. B. Currie to B. Stoicheff, 29 Jan. 1972; BSF.
7. Cameron, Bill, quoted by Michael Taft in *Inside These Greystone Walls*. Saskatoon: University of Saskatchewan, 1984, 169.
8. Spinks, J.W.T., *Two Blades of Grass*. Saskatoon: Western Producer Prairie Books, 1980.
9. A.L. Jolliffe to W.C. Murray, 26 Jan. 1937; USA.
10. W.C. Murray to A.L. Jolliffe, 30 Jan. 1937; USA.
11. A.L. Jolliffe to W.C. Murray 13 Feb. 1937; USA.
12. Rector Karl Lieser notice to GH, 6 Nov. 1937; GHA.
13. GH to E.I. Rabinowitch, 22 Nov. 1936; GHA.
14. H. Sponer to GH, 1936; NAC.
15. GH to H.N. Russell, 8 Feb. 1937; NAC.
16. Osterbrock, Donald E., *Yerkes Observatory 1892–1950*. Chicago: The University of Chicago Press, 1997.

17. GH, "Molecular Spectroscopy: A Personal History," in *Ann. Rev. Phys. Chem.* 36 (1985): 14.
18. GH, F. Patat, and H. Verleger, "On the photographic infrared spectrum of methyl-acetylene (allylene) and the C-C single bond distance," *J. Chem. Phys.* 41 (1937): 123.
19. R.M. Badger as told to GH, in GH, "Molecular Spectroscopy: A Personal History," *Ann. Rev. Chem.* 36 (1985): 1, and M. Christine King, interview of GH, 5 May 1986, 23.
20. E.L. Harrington letter and nomination form to A. Beauchesne, 24 Nov. 1938; USA.
21. E.F. Burton to Members of Section III, Royal Society of Canada, 3 Mar. 1939; USA.
22. W.C. Murray to GH, 1936; NAC.
23. GH to A.L. Jolliffe, 2 and 3 Sept. 1938; GHA.
24. Thomson, James S., in *Trans. R. Soc. Can.* 39 (1945): 108.
25. Heath, Terrence, *Uprooted: The Life of Ernest Lindner*. Saskatoon: Fifth House, 1983.

Chapter 9. The War Years in Canada

1. James S. Thomson to Judge J.F. Bryant, 27 Sept. 1940; USA.
2. E.H. Coleman (Under Secretary of State) to James S. Thomson, 9 Oct. 1940; USA.
3. GH to the Secretary of State, 14 Jan. 1943, and 15 May 1945; GHA.
4. Winnewisser, B.P., interview of GH 1989, 66.
5. E.H. Coleman (Under Secretary of State) to James S. Thomson, 14 July 1941; USA.
6. Dunham, T. Jr. and W.S. Adams, *Pub. Astron. Soc. Pacific*, 49 (1937): 26.
7. Swings, P. and L. Rosenfeld, *Astrophys. J.* 86 (1937): 483; A. McKellar, *Pub. Astron. Soc. Pacific*, 52 (1940): 187.
8. McKellar, A., *Pub. Dom. Astrophys. Obs.* 7 (1941): 251; W.S. Adams, *Astrophys. J.* 93 (1941): 11.
9. The fourth line was later identified by A.E. Douglas and J.R. Morton, *Astrophys. J.* 131 (1960): 1
10. Douglas, A.E. and GH, *Astrophys. J.* 94 (1941): 381; *Can. J. Res. A* 20 (1942): 71.
11. P. Swings to GH, 1941, as described in *Spectrochim. Acta, 50th Ann. Edition*, (1990): 63.
12. GH, *Astrophys. J.* 96 (1942): 314.
13. The Certificate of Identity for G. and L. Herzberg and the two children was received on 4 April 1944, valid for travel to the United States until the end of 1944; GHA.
14. Bill Cameron quoted by Michael Taft, in *Inside These Greystone Walls*. Saskatoon: University of Saskatchewan, 1984, 169.
15. GH and G.R. Walker, *Nature*, 161 (1948): 647; GHA.
16. O. Struve to GH, 30 Aug. 1943; GHA.
17. GH to O. Struve, 4 Sept. 1943; GHA.
18. GH to O. Struve, 10 Dec. 1943; GHA.
19. O. Struve to GH, 20 Dec. 1943; GHA.

20. GH to O. Struve, 29 Dec. 1943; GHA.
21. Weldon Brown to GH, 31 Dec. 1943; GHA.
22. James Franck to GH, 1 Jan. 1944; GHA.
23. R.S. Mulliken to GH, 14 Jan. 1944; GHA.
24. O. Struve to GH, 29 Jan. 1944; GHA.
25. GH to O. Struve, 27 Jan. 1944; GHA.
26. R.E. Gray (National Selective Service) to GH, 21 Mar. 1944; GHA.
27. GH to Mrs. W.C. Murray, 24 Mar. 1945; GHA.

Chapter 10. Interlude at the Yerkes Observatory, The University of Chicago

1. National Selective Service Labour Exit Permit No. 71119, 11 July 1945; GHA.
2. GH to O. Struve, 28 July 1945; YOA.
3. Certificate of Naturalization No. 203958 Series A, dated 22-6-45; GHA.
4. H.C. Daines, Comptroller, to GH, 8 Aug. 1945; GHA.
5. GH to President J.S. Thomson, 29 Aug. 1945; GHA.
6. E. Harrington to J.S. Thomson, 17 July. 1945; USA.
7. Osterbrock, D.E., *Yerkes Observatory 1892–1950*. Chicago: The University of Chicago Press, 1997.
8. Herzberg, Agnes, in *S. Chandrasekhar: The Man Behind the Legend*, ed. K.C. Wali. London: Imperial College Press, 1997, 160.
9. J.G. Philips to B. Stoicheff, 12 July 1998; BSF.
10. B.P. Winnewisser, interview of GH, 28 Feb. 1989, 71; M.C. King interview of G. Herzberg, 5 May 1986, 26.
11. GH, *Science*, 106 (1947): 215.
12. H.J. Bernstein and GH, *J. Chem Phys*. 16 (1948): 30.
13. K.N. Rao to B. Stoicheff, 2 May 1998; BSF.
14. J.G. Philips to B. Stoicheff, 12 July 1998; BSF.
15. O. Struve to W. Bartky, 29 Jan. 1946; YOA.
16. E.L. Harrington to GH, 6 Mar. 1946; GHA.
17. GH to E.L. Harrington, 9 Mar. 1946; GHA.
18. GH to J.E. Duggan, Chief, Naturalization Branch, 1 Sept. 1946; GHA.
19. J.W.T. Spinks to GH, 12 Sept. 1946; GHA.
20. D.E. Osterbrock to B. Stoicheff, 3 Apr. 1996; BSF.
21. GH, speech, 28 May 1975, in honour of S. Chandrasekhar's 65th birthday; GHA.
22. Chandrasekhar, S. in *Nobel Lectures in Physics 1981–1990*, ed. G. Ekspong. Singapore: World Scientific, 1993, 134.

23. I am grateful to Takeshi Oka for telling me that he once asked Chandra about the validity of this statement, and his reply was a definite "yes."
24. Herzberg, Paul, in GH—Notes from Conversations, 1992.
25. Blumberg, S.A. and G. Owens, *Energy and Conflict of Edward Teller*. New York: Punam's Sons, 1976, 258.
26. *Ibid*., 1.
27. Teller, Edward, *Better a Shield Than a Sword*. New York: The Free Press, 1987.
28. "Franck Report," in *Bulletin of Atomic Scientists,* 1946.
29. *Science*, 106 (1947): 5 September.
30. Osterbrock, D.E., *Yerkes Observatory 1892–1950*. Chicago: The University of Chicago Press, 1997, 288.
31. Hynek, J.A. ed., *Astrophysics: A Topical Symposium Commemorating the Fiftieth Anniversary of the Yerkes Observatory and a Half Century of Progress in Astrophysics*. New York: McGraw-Hill, 1951.
32. Kuiper, G., *The Atmospheres of the Earth and the Planets: Papers Presented at the Fiftieth Anniversary Symposium of the Yerkes Observatory, September 1947*. Chicago: The University of Chicago Press, 1949.
33. Wang, Jessica, *American Science in an Age of Anxiety*. Chapel Hill: The University of North Carolina Press, 1999.
34. O. Struve to GH, 30 Jan. 1947; also in *Popular Astronomy*, 55 (1947): 1; GHA.
35. E.W.R.Steacie to GH, 21 January 1947; GHA.
36. GH, *Astrophys. J*. 87 (1938): 428.
37. GH, *Nature*, 163 (1949): 170; *Can. J. Res*. A 28 (1950): 144.
38. Kiess, C.C., C.H. Corliss, and H.K. Kiess, *Astrophys. J*. 132 (1960): 221; L.P. Giver and H. Spinrad, *Icarus*, 5 (1966): 586.
39. Gauthier, T.N., III, U. Fink, R.R. Treffers, and H.P. Larson, *Astrophys. J*. 207 (1976): L129.
40. Babcock, H.D. and L. Herzberg, *Astrophys. J*. 108 (1948): 229.
41. S. Chandrasekhar to B. Stoicheff, 20 Jan 1972; BSF.

Chapter 11. News of Family and Friends in War-Torn Europe

1. S. Gradstein postcard to GH, 13 Aug. 1945; GHA.
2. S. Gradstein to GH, 26 Nov. 1945; GHA.
3. H. Rau to GH, 3 Aug. 1946; GHA.
4. H. Verleger to GH, 27 Mar. and 19 Sept. 1946; GHA.
5. G. Walther to L. Herzberg, 9 Nov. 1946; GHA.
6. Hastings, Max, "A Quiet Trip All Round: Darmstadt, 11/12 September 1944," in *Bomber Command*. London: Michael Joseph, 1979, Chapt XIII, 302.

7. H. Juda to GH, 26 Nov. 1939 and 16 Mar. 1940; GHA.
8. Franz, Eckhart G., *Darmstadts Geschichte*. Darmstadt: Eduard Roether Verlag, 1980, 472.
9. Finkelnburg, Wolfgang to GH, 27 Mar. 1947 and 25 June 1951; GHA.
10. Beyerchen, A.D., *Scientists Under Hitler: Politics and the Physics Community in the Third Reich*. New Haven: Yale University Press, 1977, 176.
11. H.-W. Döring to GH, 3 Aug. 1946, 13 Oct. 1946, and 23 Feb. 1947; GHA.
12. J. Franck to GH, 26 Mar. 1946; GHA.
13. Emmy Langemak to GH, 1 Mar. 1946 and 23 Feb. 1947; GHA.
14. GH to K.-F. Bonhoeffer 20 Oct. 1947; GHA.
15. *The Globe and Mail*, 6 Feb. 1996; *The New York Times*, 11 Feb. 1996.
16. Leibholz-Bonhoeffer, Sabine, *The Bonhoeffers: Portrait of a Family*. London: Sidgwick & Jackson, 1971.
17. Arms, Nancy, in *A Prophet in Two Countries*. Oxford: Pergamon Press, 1966, 127.

Chapter 12. Return to Canada

1. C.J. Mackenzie to B. Stoicheff, 18 February 1972; BSF.
2. D. LeRoy to GH, 8, January 1985; GHA.
3. E.W.R.Steacie to GH, 21 January 1947; GHA.
4. GH to E.W.R. Steacie, January 1947; GHA.
5. C.J. Mackenzie to GH, 13 February 1947; GHA.
6. C.S. Beals to GH, 27 March 1947; GHA.
7. A.H.S. Gillson to GH, 20 April 1947; GHA.
8. W. Bentley to GH, 9 March 1948; GHA.
9. N.S. Gingrich to GH, 24 April 1947; GHA.
10. Der Kultusminister, des Landes Nordhein-Westfalen, to GH 29 August 1948; GHA.
11. C.J. Mackenzie, Diary no. 24, 14 April 1947; NAC.
12. GH to C.J. Mackenzie, 17 June 1947; GHA.
13. C.J. Mackenzie to GH, 23 June 1947; GHA.
14. C.J. Mackenzie Diary no. 24, 24 June 1947; NAC.
15. GH to C.J. Mackenzie, 4 July 1947; GHA.
16. GH to O. Struve, 24 June 1947 and 12 July 1948; GHA.
17. R.S. Mulliken to Chairman Physics Department, Chicago, 1 Dec. 1947; UCA.
18. GH to Mulliken, 14 Dec. 1947; UCA.
19. C.E.S. Smith, Commisioner of Immigration, to GH, 7 November, 1947; GHA.
20. GH to Alex Douglas, 12 Jan., 2 Feb., and 19 Feb. 1948; GHA.
21. L. Herzberg to L. Chandrasekhar, 14 Aug. 1948; UCA.
22. GH to S. Chandrasekhar, 14 Aug. 1948; UCA.

23. S. Chandrasekhar to GH, 13 Sept. 1948; GHA.
24. GH to S. Chandrasekhar, 27 Sept. 1948; UCA.
25. Eggleston, Wilfrid, *The Queen's Choice*. Ottawa: Queen's Printer, 1961; Bond, C.J. Courtney, *City on the Ottawa*. Ottawa: Queen's Printer, 1961.
26. Heinrich Kroeger was a German prisoner of war who spent the war years in Canada, and being a master craftsman was permitted to help in building homes. After the war he was able to return to Canada, by an order-in-council, and became one of Ottawa's best-known home builders. *The Ottawa Citizen*, 6 June 1997.

Chapter 13. National Research Council of Canada: The Temple of Science

1. See the following histories of the NRC: Thistle, Mel, *The Inner Ring*. Toronto: University of Toronto Press 1966; Eggleston, Wilfrid, *National Research in Canada: the NRC 1916–1966*, Toronto: Clarke Irwin 1978; Jarrell, R.A. and Y. Gingras, *Building Canadian Science: the Role of the National Research Council*, *Scientia Canadensis*, 15 (1991).
2. Eggleston, Wilfrid, *National Research in Canada: the NRC 1916–1966*, Toronto: Clarke Irwin 1978. 26; Phillipson, D.J.C., *Associate Committees of the NRCC, 1917–1975*, Ottawa: National Research Council of Canada, 1983.
3. Eggleston, Wilfrid, *ibid.* 79.
4. Mortimer, D.C., *The Temple of Science*. Ottawa: National Research Council Canada Archives 1989. Apocryphal statements from the book of Esdras, forwarded to Tory, 2 March 1931.
5. Mackenzie, C.J., in *The Mackenzie-McNaughton Wartime Letters*, ed. Mel Thistle. Toronto: University of Toronto Press, 1975, 78.
6. Mackenzie, C.J., *ibid.* 130.
7. Mackenzie, C.J., *ibid.* 140.
8. Mackenzie, C.J., *ibid.* 144.
9. Hurst, D.G., *Canada Enters the Nuclear Age*, Montreal: McGill-Queen's University Press 1997; Eggleston, Wilfrid, *Canada's Nuclear Story*, London: Harrap Research Publications, 1966; *Physics in Canada: A Century of Canadian Physics*, 56 (2000): 57.
10. Tickner, A.W., "The NRC Postdoctorate Fellowships," in *Building Canadian Science: the Role of the National Research Council*, eds. R.A. Jarrell and Y. Gingras, *Scientia Canadensis* 15 (1991): 145.
11. Thompson, W.P., *Graduate Education in the Sciences in Canadian Universities*. Toronto: University of Toronto Press 1963.
12. Babbitt, J.D., *Science in Canada; Speeches of E.W.R. Steacie*. Toronto: University of Toronto Press 1965, 122.

Chapter 14. The Spectroscopy Laboratory

1. GH, "Alexander Edgar Douglas, 12 April 1916 – 26 July 1981," July 1981, in *Biographical Memoirs*. London: The Royal Society, 28 (1982): 92; B. Stoicheff, "Alexander Edgar Douglas, 1916–1981," *Trans. R. Soc. Can.* Ser. V 1 (1986): 277.
2. Norrish, R.G.W. and G. Porter, *Nature*, 164 (1949): 658; GH and D.A. Ramsay, *Disc. Faraday Soc.* 9 (1950): 80. Norrish and Porter shared the Nobel Prize in Chemistry in 1967 with Manfred Eigen for their studies of extremely fast chemical reactions.
3. Ramsay, D.A., *Can J. Chem.* 70 (1992): 2511.
4. Costain, Cecil C., *Physics in Canada*, 48 (1992): 186.
5. Douglas, A.E. and GH, "The nuclear spin of ^{3}He," *Phys. Rev.* 76 (1949): 1529.
6. Tickner, A.W., "The NRC Postdoctorate Fellowships 1948–1978," in *Building Canadian Science*, eds. Richard A. Jarrell and Yves Gingras. Thornhill: The Scientia Press, 1992, 145.
7. B. Stoicheff: PDF at the NRC 1951–1953, then Research Officer at the NRC until Aug. 1964, when appointed to professorship in the Department of Physics, University of Toronto, University Professor 1977 and University Professor Emeritus 1989–; served on Council of the NRC 1977–1983.
8. Brief biographies and scientific contributions of members of the Spectroscopy Laboratory can be found in Appendix A.
9. GH, *Astrophys. J.* 115 (1952): 337.
10. Stoicheff, B., *J. Chem. Phys.* 21 (1953): 1410; *Can. J. Phys.* 32 (1954): 339.
11. In addition to those already mentioned: from Australia, A.R.H. Cole, A.D. Walsh; India, K.S. and R.S. Krishnan; Japan, S. Mizushima, Y. Morino, and S. Shimanouchi; USSR, P. Kapitsa, S. Mandelstam, N. Sobolev, and I. Sobel'man; France, G. Amat, L. Brossel, P. Jacquinot, J.P. Mathieu, and B. Vodar; Germany, O. Oldenburg, and R. Mecke; Sweden, B. Edlén; Hungary, I. Kovács; Denmark, B. Bak and A. Langseth; the U.K., R.F. Barrow, A.G. Gaydon, C.K. Ingold, W.C. Price; the U.S.A, S.H. Bauer, N. Bloembergen, B.L. Crawford, G.H. Dieke, H.H. Nielsen, J.R. Nielsen, E.K. Plyler, I.I. Rabi, N.F. Ramsey, D.H. Rank, A.L. Schawlow, C.H. Townes, and J. Van Vleck, among many others.
12. Douglas, A.E., "The NRC Spectroscopy Laboratory," in *Physics in Canada*, 28 (1972): 29; see also Oka, Takeshi, "Reminiscences of Gerhard Herzberg at NRC," *ibid.* 41 (1985): 68.

Chapter 15. Inspiring the Growth of Basic Research

1. GH to S. Chandrasekhar, Sept. 1948; GHA.
2. Middleton, W.E.K., *Physics at the National Research Council of Canada 1929–1952*. Waterloo: Wilfred Laurier University Press, 1979: 68.
3. It was known that R.B. Bennett, who represented Calgary in Parliament, held Tory responsible for the University of Alberta being built in Edmonton rather than in Calgary.

4. Mackenzie, C.J., in *The Mackenzie-McNaughton Wartime Letters*, ed. Mel Thistle. Toronto: University of Toronto Press 1975, 48.
5. GH to C.J. Mackenzie, 3 Dec. 1948; GHA.
6. S. Chandrasekhar to GH, 29 Dec. 1948; GHA.
7. D. Coster to GH, 5 Feb. 1950; NAC. This letter was written in the hospital and not signed by Coster, since he apparently wished to add more to his letter. A handwritten note by his wife told of Coster's death from a stroke on 12 Feb. 1950. Coster was famous for having discovered the element hafnium, and for helping Lise Meitner, who was instrumental in the discovery of fission, to escape from Germany.
8. W. Heitler to GH, 14 Sept. 1948; GHA.
9. Mott, Neville, "Walter Heinrich Heitler," in *Biographical Memoirs*. London: The Royal Society, 28 (1982): 141.
10. I.I. Rabi to GH, 1948; GHA.
11. Ta-You-Wu to GH, 1960; NAC.
12. Mendelssohn, K. "David Keith Chalmers MacDonald," in *Biographical Memoirs*. London: The Royal Society, 10 (1964): 207.
13. Middleton, W.E.K., *Physics at the National Research Council of Canada 1929–1952*. Waterloo: Wilfred Laurier University Press, 1979, 68 and 143; King, M. Christine, interview of GH, 5 May 1986, 27; Winnewisser, Brenda P., interview of GH, 28 Feb. and 2 Mar. 1989, 74.

Chapter 16. Research and Worldwide Acclaim

1. Lamb, W.E. Jr. and R.C. Retherford, *Phys. Rev.* 72 (1947): 241; 79 (1950): 549.
2. S. Chandrasekhar to B. Stoicheff, 20 Jan. 1972; and in *Physics in Canada*, 28 (1972): 11; BSF.
3. Chandrasekhar, S. and GH, *Phys. Rev.* 98 (1955): 1050; Hart J.F. and GH. *ibid.* 106 (1957): 79; *Z. Physik*, 171 (1963): 83.
4. GH to W.E. Lamb Jr., 7 Oct. 1955; NAC.
5. W.E. Lamb Jr., to GH, 12 Nov. 1955; NAC. The footnote to which Lamb referred appears on page 51 of *Atomic Spectra and Atomic Structure*: For H, a transition with $\Delta n = 0$ would correspond to a transition between fine structure terms with equal n; for $n = 2$ the transition has a wavenumber of only 0.3 cm^{-1}, or a wavelength of about 3 cm. Observations of absorption of this wavelength in activated hydrogen are still doubtful [Betz (53); Haas (140)].
6. GH, *Proc. R. Soc. Can.* 248 A (1958): 309.
7. GH, *Astrophys. J.* 87 (1938): 428.
8. GH, *Nature*, 166 (1950): 563; Durie, R.A., and GH, *Can. J. Phys.* 38 (1960): 806.
9. Trauger, J.T., Roesler, F.L., Carleton, N.P., and Traub, W.A., *Astrophys. J.* 184 (1973): L137.
10. Kuiper, G.P., *ibid.* 109 (1949): 540.

11. Welsh, H.L., M.F. Crawford, and J.L. Locke, *Phys. Rev.* 76 (1949): 580.

12. GH, *Astrophys. J.* 115 (1952): 337.

13. Kiess, C.C., C.H. Corliss, and H.K. Kiess, *ibid.* 132 (1960): 221; Giver, L.P. and H. Spinrad, *Icarus*, 5 (1966): 586.

14. Carruthers, G.R., *Astrophys. J.* 161 (1970): L81.

15. Spitzer, L., J.F. Drake, E.B. Jenkins, D.C. Morton, J.B. Rogerson, and D.G. York, *ibid.* 181 (1973): L116.

16. Morton, D.C., *ibid.* 197 (1975): 85.

17. Stoicheff, B., *Can. J. Phys.* 35 (1957): 730.

18. GH and L.L. Howe, *ibid.* 37 (1959): 1293.

19. GH, *Phys. Rev. Lett.* 23 (1969): 1081; *J. Mol. Spectrosc.* 33 (1970): 147.

20. GH and Ch. Jungen, *ibid.* 41 (1972): 425.

21. GH, *Trans. R. Soc. Can.* 5 (1967): 3.

22. GH in letter of 4 Apr. 1967 inquired of Weisskopf whether this attribution was correct, and received a reply 12 Apr.: "I am proud that I am supposed to have made this statement. I do not remember making it, but I do not mind to be quoted since I believe it is a correct statement." NAC.

23. GH, *Astrophys J.* 96 (1942): 314; *Rev. Mod. Phys.* 14 (1942): 195.

24. Douglas, A.E., *Astrophys. J.* 114 (1951): 466.

25. GH and J. Shoosmith, *Can. J. Phys.* 34 (1956): 523.

26. R.G.W. Norrish to GH, 31 May, 1956; NAC.

27. GH and J. Shoosmith, *Nature*, 183 (1959): 1801.

28. GH first reported a linear ground state for CH_2 and this caused considerable controversy since electron spin resonance and *ab initio* theory showed a bent structure. He retracted the linear structure in *J. Chem. Phys.* 54 (1971): 2276.

29. Hollis, J.M., P.R. Jewell, and F.J. Lovas, *Astrophys. J.* 438 (1995): 259.

30. Bézard, B., H. Feuchtgruber, J.I. Moses, and T. Encrenaz, *Astron. Astrophys.* 334 (1998): L41; Bézard, B., P.N. Roman, H. Feuchtgruber, and T. Encrenaz, *Astrophys. J.* 515 (1999): 868.

31. Feuchtgruber, H., F.P. Helmich, van Dishoeck, and C.M. Wright, *ibid.* 535 (2000): L111.

32. GH, *Proc. R. Soc. Can.* A 262 (1961): 291.

33. The free radicals studied included NH_2, HCO, SiH_2, NH_2, BH_2, PH_2, NCO, NCS, C_3, N_3, CCN, CNC, NCN, HNCN, BO_2, HCF, HCCl, CF_2, HSiCl, HSiBr, and HSiI. See GH, *The Spectra and Structures of Simple Free Radicals*, Ithaca, N.Y.: Cornell University Press, 1971.

34. GH, *Quart. Revs.* 25 (1971): 201.

35. GH and A. Laterqvist, *Can. J. Phys.* 46: 2363.

Chapter 17. Ambassador of Canadian Science

1. P.A.M. Dirac to GH, 24 Apr. 1954; NAC.
2. Shanmugadhasan, S., in *Physics in Canada*, 24 (1955); Eden, R.J. in *Science*, 122 (1955): 1278.
3. GH to Nathan Sugarman, 16 Sept. 1965; NAC.
4. Program of "Symposium On Energy Exchange In Molecular Systems," 12 and 13 May, 1966; UCA.
5. Told to the author by Emil Wolf, 2001.
6. Government of India invitation to GH, 21 Sept. 1956; NAC.
7. Winnewisser, B.P., interview of GH, 1989, 27.
8. Weizmann Institute of Science to GH, 15 Oct. 1957.
9. Paul Herzberg in conversations with GH, summer 1993.
10. GH's USSR bankbook, GHA; GH to Harold E. Johns, July 1973, NAC; also told to author by Dudley Herschbach and John Callomon, 1999.
11. Oka, T., "Reminiscences of Gerhard Herzberg at NRC," in *Physics in Canada*, 41 (1985): 68.
12. See: *Fundamental and Applied Physics: Proceedings of the Esfahan Symposium*, eds. M.S. Feld, A. Javan, and N.A. Kurnit. New York: Wiley-Interscience 1973, 491 and 523.

Chapter 18. The Classic Volumes

1. See Chapter 3, p. 52.
2. See Books and Publications.
3. Mulliken, R.S., *Proc. R. Soc. Can.* 49 (1979):
4. Condon, E.U. and G.H. Shortley, *The Theory of Atomic Spectra*. Cambridge: Cambridge University Press, 1935.
5. H. Cirker to GH, 16 May 1944; GHA.
6. H. Cirker to GH, 20 May 1987; GHA.
7. R.S. Mulliken to G. Herzberg, 24 Nov. 1939; NAC.
8. W. Jevons to Steinkopff, 1939; NAC.
9. Stoner, E.C., in *Philosphical Magazine*, 30 (1940): 520.
10. Ingold, C.K., in *Nature*, 147 (1941): 36.
11. Glaser, L., quoted in Nachmansohn, David, *German–Jewish Pioneers in Science 1900–1933*. Berlin: Springer-Verlag, 1979, 137.
12. C. Dollard, record of interview with GH, 23 April 1942; CCA.
13. E.M. Crane to GH, 1 May 1942; NAC.
14. GH to E.M. Crane, 26 Nov. 1942; NAC.
15. S. Chandrasekhar to B. Stoicheff, 20 Jan.1972; BSF.

16. GH to W.P. Thompson, 2 June 1950; USA.
17. H.C. Longuet-Higgins to GH, 21 Dec. 1966; NAC.
18. GH to G. Scheibe, 13 Apr. 1967; NAC.
19. GH to C.S. Hutchison, Jr., 10 Dec. 1985; GHA.
20. S. Chandrasekhar to GH, 9 Apr. 1979; NAC.
21. *Spectra of Diatomic Molecules* was selected by *Current Contents* of 28 March 1983 as "This Week's Citation Classic" having been cited in over 7,905 publications since 1961.

Chapter 19. Challenging the New Politics of Science

1. Doern, G. Bruce, *Science and Politics in Canada*. Montreal: McGill-Queen's University Press, 1972; Hayes, F. Ronald, *The Chaining of Prometheus: evolution of a power structure for Canadian Science*. Toronto: University of Toronto Press, 1973.
2. Babbitt, J.D., *Science in Canada: Speeches of E.W.R. Steacie*. Toronto: University of Toronto Press, 1965, 115.
3. *Ibid.* 37.
4. *Ibid.* 139.
5. Marion, Léo, "Edgar William Richard Steacie," in *Biographical Memoirs*. London: The Royal Society, 10 (1964): 257; Smith, I. Norman, "All Canada Became His 'Lab'," in the *Ottawa Journal*, 29 Aug. 1962.
6. Eggleston, Wilfrid, *National Research in Canada: the NRC 1916–1966*. Toronto: Clarke Irwin, 1978. 352.
7. Dainton, Fred, *New Scientist*, 3 Mar. 1990, in review of *E.W.R. Steacie and Science in Canada*.
8. Herzberg, G., "E.W.R. Steacie, 1900–1962," in *Physics in Canada*, 18 (1962): 42.
9. Eggleston, Wilfrid, *ibid.* 394.
10. King, M. Christine, *E.W.R. Steacie and Science in Canada*. Toronto: University of Toronto Press, 1989, 190.
11. Report, *Royal Commission on Government Organization*. Ottawa: Queen's Printer, 1963.
12. *Ibid.* 212, 213: The figures quoted for operating costs are pure (basic) research divisions $2.7 million, the other divisions including regional laboratories $18.8 million.
13. Gwyn, Richard, *The Northern Magus*. Toronto: McClelland and Stewart Limited, 1980, 95–97.
14. Senate Debates, 29 June 1967, 249; *ibid.* 2 Nov. 1967, 364.
15. Carruthers, Jeff, in *The Ottawa Citizen*, 18 Dec. 1970.
16. Senate Debates, 4 Feb. 1970, 491.
17. GH to B.G. Ballard, 15 Feb. 1965; GHA.
18. GH, "Pure Science and Government," 14 May 1965.
19. GH, "The Dangers of Science Policy," 7 Nov. 1969.

20. GH, "In Defence of Basic Research," in the *NRC Newsletter*, summer 1970.

21. GH, "Remarks on the Report of the Senate Special Committee on Science Policy," 13 Mar. 1971; "Bureaucracy and the republic of science," in *Impact of Science on Society*, No. 1/2, 22 (Jan.–June 1972): 105; and "Notes on Report of the Senate Special Committee on Science Policy"; GHA.

22. The reader may be interested in comparing volume I with Senator Lamontagne's speech, (Ref. 12): an officer of the NRC suggested that the Senator "should be given full marks for not allowing himself to be confused by the facts in arriving at his pre-determined thesis."

23. *A Science Policy for Canada*, Report of Senate Special Committee on Science Policy, Vol. 1, 4.

24. GH to Senator Lamontagne, 15 Mar. 1971; NAC.

25. McKinley D.W.R. to Dr. Hunt (Chairman of Selection Board), 4 Nov. 1968; W.G. Schneider to GH, 24 Feb. 1969; GHA.

26. Symposia in honour of Dr. Herzberg have been held at Mont Tremblant Lodge, Que. in 1974; at Université Laval, Que. in 1979; in Ottawa, in 1984 and 1989; at Sainte Adèle, Que., in 1994; and in Cornwall, Ont., in 1999.

27. GH to W.G. Schneider, 17 Sept. 1969; GHA.

Chapter 20. Nobel Laureate

1. Kingstone, Joan G. of Rockcliffe Park, interview of GH, 8 Apr. 1989; GHA.

2. James Orbinski, brief biography, 2002; BSF.

3. Peter Erman to B. Stoicheff, 12 Aug. 1996; BSF.

4. Some selections from collection of telegrams and letters compiled by J.D. Babbitt, NRC:

   "First of all I want to tell you again how happy I was when I heard that your work had been recognized by award of the Nobel Prize in chemistry. It might equally well have been in physics, of course. Anyway, it is wonderful that the committee has recognized your very great research contributions to our knowledge of molecules and their spectra. Then too, there are the books. I personally felt that to organize and present the results of research in such a way as you have done is itself so major a contribution as to deserve a Nobel Prize. But you have done that in addition to the research for which the prize was given." [Robert S. Mulliken, The University of Chicago.]

   "I cannot tell you how very excited Lalitha and I were when we heard on the TV that you had been awarded the 1971 Nobel Prize for Chemistry. I believe that I had remarked to you once that to give the Prize to Mulliken and to Norrish and not to have given it to you would have been the most flagrant form of injustice. The Nobel Committee can now be commended for their sense of fairness: they have done themselves proud. Soon you must be preparing for the ceremonies in Stockholm; and you will sorely miss Luise - more than ever." [Chandra.]

   "Delighted to hear of your Nobel Prize. We will resist all attempts to make a chemist of you." [Robert E. Bell, McGill University.]

"Nothing since I was a child on Christmas morning has given me as much delight as the Swedes' recognition of the Prince of Spectroscopy as a chemist in disguise. Joyous congratulations." [Bryce S. Crawford, University of Minnesota.]

"We always suspected that deep down you were a chemist. Warmest congratulations." [Jim Morrison, McMaster University.]

"You have created a new field. It was clear for a long time how important this field is, but it is only now that people seem to wake up to its importance. Very much better late than never." [Edward Teller, University of California, Livermore.]

5. Walter Herzberg interview in *Hamburger Abendblatt*, 3 Nov. 1971.
6. Senator Joseph A. Sullivan to GH, 4 Nov. 1971; NAC.

   "Please accept my very warm and hearteous congratulations. This speaks for itself, and probably I did not make any mistake in my attitude that I assumed in regard to a certain committee investigating science and research in this country. I feel I have been vindicated thanks to you.
7. Telegram from the Permanent Secretary Erik Rudberg, Royal Academy of Sciences, Sweden, 2 Nov. 1971; GHA.
8. Telegram from NRC President W.G. Schneider, 2 Nov. 1971; GHA.
9. I.I. Sobel'man to B. Stoicheff, 18 Jan. 1994; BSF.
10. J. Shoosmith letter, see 4 above, compilation by J.D. Babbitt.
11. Herzberg letters of thanks to C.W. Drury, 14 and 19 Nov. 1971; NAC.
12. Governor General's address, in *Physics in Canada*, 28 (1972): 7.
13. GH's address, *ibid.* 8.
14. GH to Governor General, 1 Dec. 1971; NAC.
15. Linus Pauling Award speech in Seattle, 4 Dec. 1971; GHA.
16. Aide-Memoire regarding Nobel Ceremonies, 2 Nov. 1971; NAC and Personal Programme, Nov. 1971; GHA.
17. Based on communications with Agnes Herzberg, Monika Herzberg, and Doris Brockhouse.
18. *Les Prix Nobel, En 1971*, Stockholm: Imprimerie Royale, P.A. Norstedt & Soner, 1972. 29.
19. See Nobel's will and selection of Nobel Laureates in Appendix B.
20. Prof. Stig Claesson, Citation, Ref. 18 (translation), 43. 8The Nobel Foundation 1971.
21. GH, *ibid.* 61. 8The Nobel Foundation 1971.
22. GH, Nobel Lecture, "Spectroscopic Studies of Molecular Structure," *ibid.* 201. 8The Nobel Foundation 1971.

Chapter 21. Weathering the Aftermath

1. GH letter to J. Shoosmith, 26 Jan. 1972. I am indebted to Paul Feldman for a copy of this letter, which he had received from Shoosmith's son.

2. McRae, Earl, *Canada's Nobel-award scientist would sooner be an opera singer*, in *The Toronto Star*, 15 Jan. 1972.
3. GH to His Worship Mayor Herbert S. Sears, Feb. 1972, and similar letters to the Lieutenant-Governor, the Minister of Education, and J.W.T. Spinks; NAC.
4. Proceedings of the 249th Meeting of the Council, NRC Ottawa, 14 Mar. 1972.
5. Proceedings of the 252nd Meeting of the Council, NRC Ottawa, 13 Mar. 1973.
6. GH to McMaster University, 26 Sept. 1973; NAC.
7. GH to W.C. Price, 2 May 1972; NAC.
8. McCabe, Nora, *Province Honors Herzberg at Dinner*, in *The Toronto Star*, 18 May, 1972.
9. A *Science Policy for Canada: Targets and Strategies for the Seventies*, Vol. 2, Ottawa, Information Canada, 1972.
10. GH to Senator J.A. Sullivan, 11 Feb. 1972; NAC.
11. Senator J.A. Sullivan to GH, 18 Feb. 1972; NAC.
12. Lynch, Charles, "Reports Useless," in *The Gazette*, Montreal, 21 Jan. 1972.
13. GH to Science Undergraduate Society, 29 Mar. 1972; NAC.
14. SCITEC, founded in 1970 with the aim of "marshalling the scientific and technical community to provide leadership, and to communicate, co-operate and work within itself, with government and the public in the national interest." National societies which offered founding support included those of chemistry, physics, engineering, agriculture, and biology.
15. Babbitt, J.D., "The Senators and their science policy for Canada," in *Canadian Research & Development*, July–August 1974, 26.
16. *A Science Policy for Canada: Progress and Unfinished Business*, Vol. 4, Ottawa: Supply and Services Canada, 1977.
17. Kerwin, L. to GH, 1 Dec. 1989; GHA. After his two terms as president of the NRC, Kerwin was appointed president of the new Canadian Space Agency.
18. Phillipson, D.J.C., in *Building Canadian Science: The Role of the National Research Council*, eds. Richard A. Jarrell and Yves Gingras. Thornhill: The Scientia Press, 1992.

Chapter 22. The Herzberg Institute of Astrophysics

1. Proceedings of the 257th Meeting of the Council, NRC Ottawa, 23 Sept. 1974.
2. Lew, H and I. Heiber, *J. Chem. Phys*. 58 (1973): 1246: Lew, H. *Can. J. Phys*. 54 (1976): 2028.
3. GH and H. Lew, *Astron. Astrophys*. 31 (1974): 123; Wehinger, P., S. Wykoff, G.H. Herbig, GH, and H. Lew, *Astrophys. J*. 190 (1974): L43.
4. Alexander, A.J., H.W. Kroto, and D.R.M. Walton, *J. Mol. Spectrosc*. 62 (1976): 175.
5. Avery, L.W., N.W. Broten, J.M. MacLeod, T. Oka, and H.W. Kroto, *Astrophys. J*. 205 (1976): L173.
6. Oka, T., *J. Mol. Spectrosc*. 72 (1978): 172.

7. Kroto, H.W., *Astrophys. J.* 219 (1978): L133; Broten, N.W., T. Oka, L.W. Avery, J.M. MacLeod, and H.W. Kroto, *ibid.* 223 (1978): L105.
8. Douglas, A.E., *Nature,* 269 (1977): 130.
9. Kroto. H., *Sphere*, Ottawa: National Research Council of Canada, April 1991, 7.
10. GH, *Trans. R. Soc. Can.* 5 (1967): 3.
11. Oka, T., "Reminiscences of Gerhard Herzberg at NRC," in *Physics in Canada*, 41 (1985): 68.
12. GH, *J. Chem. Phys.* 70 (1979): 4806; Dabrowski, I. and GH, *Can. J. Phys.* 58 (1980): 1238; GH, and J.K.G. Watson, *ibid.* (1980): 1250; GH, J.T. Hougen, and J.K.G. Watson, *ibid.* 60 (1982): 1261.
13. Figger, H., Y. Fukada, W. Ketterle, and H. Walther, *ibid.* 62 (1984): 1274; *Chem. Phys. Lett.* 146 (1988): 180; *Z. Phys. D.* 13 (1989): 129, 139.
14. GH and J.T. Hougen, *J. Mol. Spectrosc.* 97 (1983): 430.
15. GH, *Ann. Rev. Phys. Chem.* 38 (1987): 27.
16. Oka, T., *Phys. Rev. Lett.* 45 (1980): 531.
17. Geballe, T.R. and T. Oka, *Nature*, 384 (1996): 334.
18. For more details see Oka, T., *Rev. Mod. Phys.* 64 (1992): 1141; and in *Spectroscopy: Perspectives and Frontiers*, ed. A.P. Roy. New Delhi: Narosa Publ. House, 1997, 1.
19. Jenniskens, P. and F.-X. Désert, *Astron. Astrophys. Suppl. Ser.* 106 (1994): 39.

Chapter 23. Continuing Activities

1. GH, "Commemorative Talk" in Okazaki, Japan, 9 May 1985; GHA.
2. R. Lüst to G. Herzberg, 20 Aug. 1976; GHA.
3. GH to S. Chandrasekhar, July 1980.
4. GH, *Proc. Indian Natl. Sci. Acad.* 51 (1985): 495.
5. B. Mulroney to GH, 25 June 1992; GHA.
6. Files "Connections with Humanitarian Organizations" and "Appeals"; GHA.
7. A. Petelin to GH, 6 Apr. 1978; GHA.
8. GH to N. Podgorny, Oct. 1973; GHA.
9. GH, telegram to Flora MacDonald, 23 Jan. 1980; GHA.
10. GH, telegram to K. Chernenko, 13 May 1984; GHA.
11. G. Campbell MacLean, Chm. of Board of St. Boniface General Hospital Research, to A. Sakharov, 16 Feb. 1987; GHA.
12. GH to M. Gorbachev, 3 Dec. 1987; GHA.
13. "Sakharov Thanks Canadians," in *The Candle*, Amnesty International, fall 1989.
14. GH introduction of Sakharov to the NRC, 13 Feb. 1989; GHA.
15. GH to Cardinal König, 26 Nov. 1980; GHA.
16. GH to War Resisters International, 28 May 1982; GHA.

17. "Die Feinstruktur der He^+ Linien 1640 Å und 4686 Å" (*Z. Physik*, 146 (1956): 269). Festschrift on Born's 80th birthday: "Twenty-parameter eigenfunctions and energy values of the 2^3S states of He and He-like ions" (*Z. Physik*, 171 (1963): 83).
18. GH, "Testimonial Dinner," University of Saskatchewan, 21 Sept. 1974; GHA.
19. GH to Mrs. S. Chandrasekhar, 24 Oct. 1995; GHA.
20. Ransil, Bernard, J., *Robert S. Mulliken: Life of a Scientist*. Berlin: Springer-Verlag 1989.
21. H. Taube to GH, 4 Nov. 1983; GHA.
22. A tribute to Edward U. Condon: "Beutler-Fano shape in the predissociation of H_2," in *Topics in Modern Physics*. Colorado Associated University Press, 1971, 191. Festschrift for I.I. Rabi: "The predicted infrared spectrum of HeH^+ and its possible astrophysical importance," *Trans. New York Acad. Sci.* 38 (1977): 14.
23. GH, "To Ernst Miescher on His Eightieth Birthday," in *Helvetica Physica Acta*, 58 (1985): 951.
24. M. Delbrück to GH, 24 Apr.1967; GHA.
25. GH to Jack Locke, 4 Sept. 1980; GHA.
26. L. Pauling to GH, 26 Nov. 1993; GHA.
27. Prime Minister Brian Mulroney appointed Dr. Pierre O. Perron, then Associate Deputy Minister of Energy, Mines and Resources as President of the NRC for a five-year term on 25 July 1989.
28. House of Commons, Minutes of Proceedings and Evidence of the Standing Committee on Industry, Science and Technology, Regional and Northern Development, Issue No. 41, 25 April 1990. Ottawa: Queen's Printer.
29. McCulloch, E.A., open letter to President Perron and Members of the NRC, 29 Mar. 1990; Craig, Iris, letter to members of the NRC, 13 Mar. 1990; Dutton, Guy G.S., letter to NRC President, in L'Actualité chimique canadienne, June 1990, 4.; GHA, copies of letters to Prime Minister and Minister of Science; BSF.
30. GH to Vice-President C. Willis, 24 Oct. 1994; GHA.
31. Letters from Governor General Ramon Hnatyshyn and Prime Minister Jean Chrétien to GH, 13 Dec. 1994; GHA.

APPENDICES

A. Staff Members of the Spectroscopy Laboratory

In addition to the founding members, Gerhard Herzberg, Alex Douglas, Don Ramsay, Hin Lew, and Cec Costain, the following were appointed to the research staff of the Laboratory:

Amano, Takayoshi, is presently Chairman of the Department of Materials and Biological Sciences in the Institute of Astrophysics and Planetary Sciences, Ibaraki University in Mito, Japan. His work is in the field of free radicals and ions of astrochemical and atmospheric interest. Amano received his Ph.D. in 1969 from the University of Tokyo working with Professor Y. Morino on studies of microwave spectra of free radicals. He joined the Spectroscopy Laboratory as a visiting Associate Research Officer in 1980 and was appointed as a staff member in 1982. His research included infrared and microwave double resonance spectroscopy and later, laser spectroscopy of free radicals and ions. He returned to Japan in 1993.

Bunker, Philip R., obtained his Ph.D. in 1965 in theoretical chemistry at Cambridge University working with Professor H.C. Longuet-Higgins, and joined the NRC as a postdoctoral fellow with Jon Hougen the same year. He became a staff member of the Spectroscopy Laboratory the following year and after three decades switched to the Steacie Institute for Molecular Sciences where he is a Principal Research Officer. His theoretical interests have spanned the areas of prediction, analysis, and understanding of molecular spectra, the dynamical interactions between the motions of electrons and nuclei, and effects occurring in flexible molecules. He and Per Jensen have produced a highly acclaimed volume on *Molecular Symmetry and Spectroscopy* and edited *Computational Molecular Spectroscopy*.

Chapman, George D. Following his Ph.D. with Prof. Lucjan Krause at the University of Windsor in 1966, Chapman obtained an NRC Postdoctoral Fellowship to work in quantum optics with Prof. George Series at Oxford University. He joined the Spectroscopy Laboratory in 1968 and carried out research on coherence transfer in atomic collisions, the transverse Hanle effect, magnetic predissociation of the iodine molecule, and lifetimes of its rotational levels. In 1972 he transferred to the NRC Mechanics Section and worked in optical physics applied to metrology. Over the years he has served the NRC in various capacities in the Industrial Research Assistance Program, the Mechanical Metrology Group, and Mass Standards Program, among others.

Dabrowski, Izabel, after graduating with a B.Sc. from McGill University, she became Herzberg's technical assistant in 1969, helping to measure plates and doing routine calculations. Her interest in spectroscopy prompted her to obtain a M.Sc. in Chemistry in 1976, when she was promoted to Research Officer. Izabel continued to collaborate with Herzberg until his retirement, and they co-authored many papers on the electronic spectra of hydrogen and the rare gas hydrides.

Hougen, Jon T., attended Oberlin College and the University of Wisconsin, obtaining a B.Sc. in chemistry in 1956. He entered Harvard as a National Science Foundation Predoctoral Fellow and obtained a Ph.D. in 1960 in physical chemistry under the research direction of W. Moffitt and W. Klemperer. Jon joined the NRC that year as a postdoctoral fellow and became a staff member of the Spectroscopy Group in 1962; his early interest being the study of rotational and vibronic energy levels of diatomic, triatomic, and symmetric top molecules. He and Shoba Singh (PDF) were the first to observe electronic Raman spectra of crystals, having studied the ion Pr^{3+} in single crystals of $PrCl_3$. He continued to work with his interests in quantum mechanical and group theoretical calculations of various molecular motions and interactions, and collaborated with Herzberg and other NRC theorists and visitors long after his departure from the NRC. He accepted an appointment to the National Bureau of Standards in Washington in 1964, rose through the ranks to Acting Chief of the Molecular Physics Division, and remains as a Senior Research Fellow following his retirement in 2001. For his outstanding contributions to spectroscopy, Jon has received numerous honours including the Coblentz Award, Plyler Prize, and Lippincot Award.

Howe, Lila L., educated in Prince Edward Island, joined the NRC as Herzberg's technical assistant in 1954. She was soon promoted to Research Officer and collaborated with Herzberg in one of the most extensive analyses of the ground state of molecular hydrogen via the Lyman bands. Lila left the NRC in 1961 and the following year was employed in the editor's office of the Toronto publisher Ginn and Company.

Huber, Klaus-Peter, co-author with Herzberg of *Constants of Diatomic Molecules*, published in 1979, first served as a postdoctoral fellow with the Spectroscopy Group from 1963 to 1965 and was then appointed as a staff member. He obtained his Ph.D. with Prof. Ernst Miescher at the University of Basel with research on the NO molecule, and worked on spectra of NO_2 at the NRC. He helped to develop jet absorption techniques for high-resolution studies of rotationally cold molecules, and has concentrated on spectra of molecules of relevance in astrophysics and in the chemistry of planetary atmospheres. In recent years, he continues with these interests at the NRC and in collaboration with scientists at Université de Paris-Sud, the Observatoire de Paris-Meudon, the Photon Factory in Tsukuba, Japan, and the Institute for Astrophysics and Planetary Sciences at Ibaraki University in Mito, Japan.

Johns, John W.C., studied chemistry at Oxford University, and was supervised by Prof. Richard Barrow in spectroscopy, obtaining his Ph.D. in 1958. He joined the NRC as a postdoctoral fellow that year working with Don Ramsay in developing a large flash photolysis apparatus with which spectra of NH_2 were obtained. On returning to the UK, he attended the Bakerian Lecture by Herzberg, who offered him the job of helping in the analysis of the CH_2 spectrum. He was appointed a Research Officer in 1961, and along with analyses of electronic spectra of free radicals he studied spectra of CH, BH, BH_2, and BO_2. He automated the infrared spectrometer and investigated the complex spectra of N_2H_2, then doubled the resolution of a Bomem FTIR spectrometer and examined line shapes and absolute intensities. In 1988, John served as Section Head of the Spectroscopy Laboratory. He received the Pittsburgh Spectroscopy Award in 1995. John retired in 1996 having been a member of the NRC for thirty-five years.

Marmet, Paul, OC, FRSC, was educated at Université Laval and obtained his Ph.D. in 1960 for studies in the new field of electron spectroscopy. After a postdoctoral year in Australia at the Commonwealth Scientific and Industrial Organization in Melbourne, he returned to Université Laval and rose through the ranks to Professor of Physics in 1970. Paul joined the HIA in 1983 where he continued his research in electron spectroscopy of atoms and molecules until 1991, when he joined the University of Ottawa as a Visiting Professor. His numerous awards for research include the Rutherford Memorial Fellowship, the Herzberg Medal, and the Service Award of the Royal Astronomical Society of Canada.

McKellar, A. Robert W., FRSC, son of Herzberg's friend, the noted astronomer Andrew McKellar, received his Ph.D. at the University of Toronto in 1970 working on infrared spectra of weakly bound van der Waals molecules with Prof. Harry Welsh. McKellar joined the Spectroscopy Group as a Postdoctoral Fellow in 1971, collaborating with Oka and Johns on double-resonance infrared spectroscopy using lasers. He was appointed as a staff member in 1973 and investigated the spectrum of the free radical FO, and the infrared triplet spectrum and singlet-triplet splitting of methylene, CH_2. His research interest has concentrated on studies of infrared spectra of "unusual" molecules (unstable free radicals, ions, and weakly bound complexes) of possible astrophysical importance. He was awarded the Herzberg Medal of the Canadian Association of Physicists in 1982, and served as Spectroscopy Group Leader from 1991 to 1998.

Oka, Takeshi, FRS, FRSC, studied at the University of Tokyo obtaining his Ph.D. in 1960 under the supervision of Professors Koichi Shimoda and Yonezo Morino, and continued research there in infrared spectroscopy as a Fellow of the Japanese Society for Promotion of Science until 1963. He then joined the Spectroscopy Laboratory as a postdoctoral fellow, was appointed a Research Officer in 1965, and rose to the rank of Senior Research Officer. At the NRC his research progressed from studies in the infrared to the microwave region, with major interest in molecular spectra of astrophysical importance. He developed techniques for double-resonance optical and microwave spectroscopy for these studies, and then pursued his search for the illusive spectrum of H_3^+. He succeeded in this important quest, and discovered it in 1980. In 1981 he accepted the position of Professor of Chemistry, Astronomy and Astrophysics at The University of Chicago, where in 1989 he was appointed Robert A. Millikan Distinguished Service Professor. Oka's major interests are concerned with molecular ions in laboratory and astronomical plasmas since such ions play crucial roles in the production of the many molecular species found in interstellar space and star formation. His group and colleagues have discovered H_3^+, H_3O^+, $HCNH^+$, CH_5^+ and other ions in interstellar clouds. For his achievements, Oka has been invited to give many named lectures, and has received the Steacie Prize, Earle K. Plyler Prize, William F. Meggers Award, and E. Bright Wilson Award among others.

Ritter, George, from Stellenbosch, South Africa, with a Ph.D in optical double resonance, joined the NRC and Hin Lew's group as a postdoctoral fellow in 1958 and was appointed as a staff member in 1961. He extended studies of the rare earths initiated by Hin Lew, by investigating the hyperfine structures and nuclear moments of Lutetium and Thulium. He later built an optical double resonance system and examined the hyperfine structures of the lowest excited states of the isotopes of Lithium. In 1964 he returned to South Africa as a research scientist of the Council for Scientific and Industrial Research (CSIR) in Pretoria.

Simard, Benoit, studied chemistry at Université du Québec à Chicoutimi and Université Laval, and obtained his Ph.D. at the University of Saskatchewan in 1986 for research in spectroscopy, photophysics, and *ab initio* calculations of thiocarbonyl compounds, under the supervision of Prof. Ronald Steer. That year Benoit joined the NRC Laser Chemistry and Inorganic Chemical Dynamics Group to work with Dr. Peter Hackett on the spectra of metal-containing molecules and metal clusters. He transferred to the Spectroscopy Group in 1996 and became the Program Leader two years later. His interests include metal–ligand interactions, from nanoparticles to small molecules, to clusters, carbon nanotubes, metal interactions with biological molecules in the gas phase, and spectroscopy of highly reactive ions.

Stoicheff, Boris, OC, FRS, FRSC, after thirteen years at the NRC, he joined the Department of Physics at the University of Toronto where he continued spectroscopic research with lasers. His group carried out studies in Brillouin scattering of liquids and rare-gas solids as well as stimulated Raman and Brillouin scattering. They developed nonlinear techniques for producing tunable extreme ultraviolet radiation to 750 Å, and investigated spectra of rare-gas excimers at high resolution, and determined the dissociation energy of molecular hydrogen to high precision. Electromagnetically induced transparency in atomic hydrogen was studied in great detail. He received numerous awards, among them the William F. Meggers Award, Frederic Ives Award, and the Henry Marshall Tory Medal, and served as president of the Optical Society of America and of the Canadian Association of Physicists.

Vervloet, Michel, curently Directeur de Recherche at the CNRS Laboratoire de Photophysique Moleculaire in Orsay. He received his Ph.D. in Reims investigating the emission spectrum of NH_2 and joined Don Ramsay's Section on Larger Molecules as a Research Officer in 1980. His research concerned studies of the emission spectra of diatomic and triatomic molecules and free radicals using Fourier transform techniques. He returned to France after ten years at the NRC and is involved in spectroscopy with synchrotron radiation in the terahertz region.

Watson, James K.G., FRS, FRSC, studied chemistry at the University of Glasgow and obtained his Ph.D in 1962 under the supervision of Professor John Brand. Jim was a post-doctoral fellow at the NRC from 1963 to 1965, a Lecturer at the University of Reading 1966–1971, a Visiting Associate Professor at The Ohio State University until 1975, and then a Senior Research Fellow at the University of Southampton 1975–1979 and 1980–1982. He served as a Visiting Scientist at the HIA in 1979 and was appointed a Senior and later a Principal Research Officer in 1982. His interests include molecular symmetry properties, analysis of molecular rotation–vibration and electronic spectra, clarifying spectra of Rydberg molecules, and the diffuse interstellar problem. Jim is considered to be one of the most outstanding theoretical spectroscopists of our time, especially for his contributions to the understanding of molecular rotation and vibration. His honours and awards are many, including the Earle K. Plyler Prize, the Marcus Marci Medal, and the Henry Marshall Tory Medal.

B. The Nobel Prizes

On 27 November 1895, Alfred Bernhard Nobel (1833–1996) established the Nobel Foundation and gave the bulk of his vast fortune to endow annual prizes in physics, chemistry, physiology or medicine, literature, and peace to be awarded to those who shall have conferred the greatest benefit on mankind. In 1968 an Alfred Nobel Memorial Prize in Economic Science was instituted by the Sveriges Riksbank (Central Bank of Sweden). All of the awards are made for the most recent achievements in these fields of culture, and for older works only if their significance had not become apparent until recently. Presentations of a diploma and a gold medal are made in Stockholm for five of the Prizes on 10 December, the Festival Day of the Foundation, this being the anniversary of the death of Alfred Nobel in 1896. The Peace Prize is presented on the same day in Oslo, Norway. Sweden and Norway were united when the Nobel Foundation and Prizes were inaugurated, hence this sharing of Nobel Prize presentations.

The regulations for submission of proposals for the awards and for selection of laureates are similar for the different prizes. For each field, about a thousand individuals from all over the world (most of them different from year to year) are invited to nominate candidates. In this way the Nobel Committees get indications of the development in all branches of these fields and obtain a foundation for evaluating which scientists are making the most significant contributions. Proposals received for an award, and the ensuing investigations and opinions concerning the award of a prize, may not be disclosed and access to such material may be granted for purposes of historical research only after at least fifty years have elapsed after a decision for an award has been made.

BOOKS AND PUBLICATIONS

BOOKS

Atomspektren und Atomstruktur

Th. Steinkopff, Dresden & Leipzig, 1936

Atomic Spectra and Atomic Structure

1st edition, Prentice Hall Inc., New York, 1937

2nd edition, Dover Publications, New York, 1944

Russian translation, Moscow, 1948

Italian translation, Torino, 1961

Japanese translation, Tokyo, 1964

Molekülspektren und Molekülstruktur: I. Zweiatomige Moleküle

Th. Steinkopff, Dresden & Leipzig, 1939

Molecular Spectra and Molecular Structure: I. Diatomic Molecules

1st edition, Prentice Hall Inc., New York, 1939

2nd edition, D. Van Nostrand Co. Inc., New York, 1950

3rd edition, Krieger Publishing Co., Florida, 1989

Russian translation, Moscow, 1949

Hungarian translation, Budapest, 1956

Chinese translation, Beijing, 1983

Molecular Spectra and Molecular Structure: II. Infrared and Raman Spectra of Polyatomic Molecules

1st edition, D. Van Nostrand Co. Inc., New York, 1945

2nd edition, Krieger Publishing Co., Florida, 1991

Russian translation, Moscow, 1949

Hungarian translation, Budapest, 1960

Chinese translation, Beijing, 1983

Molecular Spectra and Molecular Structure: III. Electronic Spectra & Electronic Structure of Polyatomic Molecules

1st edition, D. Van Nostrand Co. Inc., New York, 1966

2nd edition, Krieger Publishing Co., Florida, 1991

Russian translation, Moscow, 1969

The Spectra and Structures of Simple Free Radicals: An Introduction to Molecular Spectroscopy.

1st edition, Cornell University Press, Ithaca, 1971

2nd edition, Dover Publications, New York, 1988

German translation, Darmstadt, 1973

Russian translation, Moscow, 1974

Japanese translation, Tokyo, 1975

Yugoslavian translation, Belgrade, 1982

Chinese translation, Beijing, 1983

Molecular Spectra and Molecular Structure: IV. Constants of Diatomic Molecules. (with K.P. Huber)

Van Nostrand Reinhold Co., New York, 1979

Russian translation, Moscow, 1983

PUBLICATIONS

1927

Untersuchungen über die Erscheinungen bei der elektrodenlosen Ringentladung in Wasserstoff. *Ann. Phys.* 84: 553.

Über die Spektren des Wasserstoffs. *Ann. Phys.* 84: 565.

Über die kontinuierlichen Spektren des Wasserstoffs. *Physik Z.* 28: 727.

1928

Über das Nachleuchten von Stickstoff und Sauerstoff und den Einfluss der Wände hierauf. *Z. Physik*, 46: 878.

Cathode rays in the electrodeless ring-discharge. *Phil. Mag.* 5: 7 and 446.

Die neuere Entwicklung der Quantenmechanik I und II. *Z. math. naturw. Unterr.* 59: 97.

Resonanzfluoreszenz des Cyans. *Naturwiss.* 16: 464.

Über die Struktur der negativen Stickstoffbanden. *Ann. Phys.* 86: 189.

Spektroskopisches über das Nachleuchten von Stickstoff. Z. *Physik*, 49: 512.

Über die intensitatsverteilung in Bandenspektren. Z. *Physik*, 49: 761.

The dissociation energy of nitrogen. *Nature*, 122: 505.

Ein neues Bandensystem des CO. *Naturwiss.* 16: 1027.

1929

Über die Bandenspektren von CO, nach Versuchen mit der elektrodenlosen Ringentladung. *Z. Physik*, 52: 815.

(With W. Heitler) Eine spektroskopische Bestätigung der quantenmechanischen Theorie der homöopolaren Bindung. *Z. Physik*, 53: 52.

Die Dissoziationsarbeit von Sauerstoff. *Z. Phys. Chem. B*, 4: 223.

(With W. Heitler) Gehorchen die Stickstoffkerne der Boseschen Statistik? *Naturwiss.* 17: 673.

Zum Aufbau der zweiatomigen Moleküle. *Z. Physik,* 57: 601.

(With G. Scheibe) On the absorption spectra of methyl halides and some other methyl compounds in the ultraviolet and in the Schumann region. *Trans. Farad. Soc.* 25: 12.

1930

Der Elektronendrall. *Z. math. naturw. Unterr.* 61: 49.

(With G. Scheibe) Über die Absorptionsspektra der dampfformigen Methylhalogenide und einiger anderer Methylverbindungen im Ultraviolett und im Schumann-Geibiet. *Z. Phys. Chem. B*, 7: 390.

Zur Deutung der diffusen Molekülspektren (Prädissoziation). *Z. Physik*, 61: 604.

Das Stickstoffisotop der Masse 15. *Z. Phys. Chem. B*, 9: 43.

A new band system probably due to a molecule CP. *Nature*, 126: 131.

Predissociation of the phosphorous (P_2) molecule. *Nature*, 126: 239.

Zur Bestimmung von Dissoziationswärmen aus Pradissoziationsspektren und die Dissoziationswarme von O_2. *Z. Phys. Chem. B*, 10: 189.

1931

Ultraviolet absorption spectra of acetylene and formaldehyde. *Trans. Farad. Soc.* 27: 378.

Die Prädissoziation und verwandte Erscheinungen. *Naturwiss.* 10: 207.

Elektrononstruktur der Moleküle und Valenz. *Leipziger Vortrage*, 167.

1932

Über die Struktur und den monomolekularen Zerfall der Moleküle N_2O und CO_2. *Z. Phys. Chem. B*, 17: 68.

Rotational structure and predissociation of the P_2 molecule. *Phys. Rev.* 40: 313.

(With K. Franz) Fluoreszenz des H_2CO (Anregungsbedingungen und Schwingungsanalyse). *Z. Physik,* 76: 720.

Ein neuartiges, "verbotenes" Absorptionsbandensystem des O_2 Moleküls. *Naturwiss.* 20: 577.

Bandenspektrum, Prädissoziation und Struktur des P_2-moleküls. *Ann. Phys.* 15: 677.

1933

(With E. Teller) Schwingungsstruktur der Elektronenübergange bei mehratomigen Molekülen. *Z. Phys. Chem. B* 21: 410.

(With J. Curry) Extension of the visible absorption system of NO_2 to longer wavelengths. *Nature*, 131: 842.

(With R. Kölsch) Die Ultraviolettabsorption der Aminogruppe (–NH_2) und anderer Gruppen in einfachen Molekülen im Gaszustand. *Z. Elektrochem.* Nr. 76.

(With J. Curry and L. Herzberg) Spectroscopic evidence for the molecule PN. *J. Chem. Phys.* 1: 749.

(With J. Curry and L. Herzberg) Spektroskopischer Nachweis und Struktur des PN-Moleküls. *Z. Physik,* 86: 348.

1934

(With J. Curry) Über die ultravioletten Absorptionsbanden des Sauerstoffs (Schumann-Runge-Banden) *Ann. Phys.*, 19: 800.

Photography of the infrared solar spectrum to wavelength 12 900 Å. *Nature*, 133: 759.

(With F. Patat and J.W.T. Spinks) Bands of 'heavy' acetylene in the near infrared. *Nature,* 133: 951.

(With J.W.T. Spinks) Photgraphie der zweiten Obserschwingung des HCl bei 1.19 μ, mit grosser Dispersion. *Z. Physik,* 89: 474.

(With H. Sponer) Über die Dissoziationswärme des Stickstoffmoleküls. *Z. Phys. Chem. B,* 26: 1.

(With H. Verleger) Das Spektrum des schweren Wassers im photographischen Ultrarot. *Z. Physik,* 35: 622.

(With H. Baerwald and L. Herzberg) Bandenspektrum und Struktur des CP-Moleküls. *Ann. Phys.* 20: 569.

(With J.W.T. Spinks) Über das Rotationsschwingungsspektrum des Acetylens (C_2H_2). *Z. Physik*, 91: 386.

(With F. Patat and J.W.T. Spinks) Rotationsschwingungsspektren im photographischen Ultrarot von Molekülen, die das Wasserstoffistotp der Masse 2 enthalten. I. Das C2HD-Spektrum und der C–C und C–H Abstand im Acetylen. *Z. Physik*, 92: 87.

(With J.W.T. Spinks) Absorption bands of HCN in the photographic infrared. *Proc. R. Soc. A* 147: 434.

1935

(With G. Buttenbender) Über die Struktur der zweiten positiven Stickstoffgruppe und die Prädissoziation des N_2-Moleküls. *Ann. Phys.* 21: 577.

(With F. Patat and H. Verleger) Über die geometrische Struktur des N_3H-Moleküls. *Z. Elektrochem.* 41: 522.

(With F. Patat and H. Verleger) Über das photographische Ultrarotspektrum des Methyl-azetylens und den Kernabstand der C–C -Einfachbindung. Z. Physik, 36: 625.

(With H. Verleger) Two new bands of CO_2 in the photographic infrared. *Phys. Rev.* 48: 706.

1936

(With G.W. Funke) On the rotation–vibration spectrum of acetylene in the photographic infrared. *Phys. Rev.* 49: 100.

Dissociation energies of CO and CN, and heat of sublimation of carbon. *Nature*, 137: 620.

Atomspektren und Atomstruktur. Wissensch. Forschungsberichte. Naturwiss. Reihe Bd. 37, Th. Steinkopff, Dresden & Leipzig.

(With H. Verleger) Über die photographischen Ultrarotspektren einiger einfacher Kohlen-stoffverbindungen im Gaszustand. *Physik Z.* 37: 444.

(With F. Patat and H. Verleger) Rotationsschwingungenspektren im photographischen Ultrarot von Molekülen, die das Wasserstoffisotop der Masse 2 Enthalten. II. Das C_2HD Spektrum und der C–C und C–H Abstand im Acetylen (weitere Ergebnisse). *Z. Physik*, 102: 1.

(With J.W.T. Spinks and W.W. Watson) Pressure broadening of the HCN band lines and intermolecular forces. *Phys. Rev.* 50: 1186.

1937

(With E. Blum) On the ultraviolet absorption spectrum of diborane. *J. Phys. Chem.* 41: 91.

(With F. Patat and H. Verleger) On the photographic infrared spectrum of methyl–acetylene (allylene) and the C–C single bond distance. *J. Phys. Chem.* 41: 123.

The heat of dissociation of the carbon monoxide molecule and the heat of sublimation of carbon. *Chem. Rev.* 20: 145.

(With K.F. Herzfeld and E. Teller) The heat of sublimation of graphite. *J. Phys. Chem.* 41: 325.

(With W.S. Herbert and G.A. Mills) An attempt to detect the presence of metastable atoms in active nitrogen by light absorption. *Can. J. Res. A*, 15: 35.

(With J.W.T. Spinks) *Atomic Spectra and Atomic Structure.* (Translation). Prentice-Hall, Inc. New York.

(With L. Gero and R. Schmid) On the Cameron bands ($^3\Pi$–$^1\Sigma^+$) of carbon monoxide. *Phys. Rev.* 52: 467.

(With J.G. Fox) Analysis of a new band system of the C_2 molecule. *Phys. Rev.* 52: 638.

1938

On the possibility of detecting molecular hydrogen and nitrogen in planetary and stellar atmospheres by their rotation–vibration spectra. *Astrophys. J.* 87: 428.

1939

Molekülspektren und Molekülstruktur. I. Zweiatomige Moleküle. Wissensch. Forschungsberichte Naturwiss. Reihe Bd. 50, Th. Steinkopff, Dresden & Leipzig.

Forbidden transitions in diatomic molecules. *Astrophys. J.* 89: 288.

Dissociation, predissociation, and recombination of diatomic molecules. *Astrophys. J.* 89: 290.

(With J.W.T. Spinks) *Molecular Spectra and Molecular Structure. I. Diatomic Molecules.* Translation of (68), Prentice-Hall, Inc., New York.

1940

(With L.G. Mundie) On the predissociation of several diatomic molecules. *J. Chem. Phys.* 8: 263.

(With A.E. Douglas) Spectroscopic evidence for the B_2 molecule. *Phys. Rev.* 57: 752.

(With R.B. Sutton) Tail bands of the Deslandres-d'Azambuja system of the C_2 molecule. *Can. J. Res. A*, 18: 74.

(With L. Herzberg and G.G. Milne) On the spectrum of the P_2 molecule. *Can. J. Res. A*, 18: 139.

On the presence of HNC in hydrogen cyanide. *J. Chem. Phys.* 8: 847.

(With A.E. Douglas) Spectroscopic evidence of the B_2 molecule and determination of its structure. *Can. J. Res. A*, 18: 165.

(With A.E. Douglas) Band spectrum of the BN molecule. *Can. J. Res. A*, 18: 179.

1941

(With A.E. Douglas) CH^+ in interstellar space and in the laboratory. *Astrophys. J.* 94: 381.

(With W. Hushley) Band spectrum and structure of the BCl molecule. *Can. J. Res. A*, 19: 127.

1942

On the heat of sublimation of carbon. *J. Chem. Phys.* 10: 306.

(With A.E. Douglas) Band spectrum and structure of the CH^+ molecule; identification of three interstellar lines. *Can. J. Res. A*, 20: 71.

Evidence for the presence of CH_2 molecules in comets. *Rev. Mod. Phys.* 14: 195.

l-type doubling in linear polyatomic molecules. *Rev. Mod. Phys.* 14: 219.

Laboratory production of the λ4050 group occurring in cometary spectra; further evidence for the presence of CH_2 molecules in comets. *Astrophys. J.* 96: 314.

1945

Molecular Spectra and Molecular Structure II. Infrared and Raman Spectra of Polyatomic Molecules. D. Van Nostrand Company, Inc., New York.

1946

On the electronic structure of the nitrogen molecule. *Phys. Rev.* 69: 362.

On a critical test for the presence of a lunar atmosphere. *Popular Astronomy*, 54: 414.

On the high pressure bands of carbon and the formation of C_2 molecules. *Phys. Rev.* 70: 762.

1947

(With H.J. Bernstein) Ultraviolet absorption spectrum of nitric oxide. *J. Chem. Phys.* 15: 77.

(With L. Herzberg) Fine structure of the infrared atmospheric oxygen bands. *Astrophys. J.* 105: 353.

The spectroscopic laboratory. *Science*, 106: 215.

1948

(With H.J. Bernstein) Rotation–vibration spectra of diatomic and simple polyatomic molecules with long absorbing paths. I. The spectrum of fluoroform (CHF_3) from 2.4 μ to 0.7 μ. *J. Chem. Phys.* 16: 30.

(With L. Herzberg) Production of nitrogen atoms in the upper atmosphere. *Nature*, 161: 283.

Fe II emission lines in α-Herculis and α-Scorpii. *Astrophys. J.* 107: 94.

(With G.R. Walker) Initiation of high explosives. *Nature,* 161: 647.

Molecular constants from spectroscopic data. *Trans. Am. Soc. Mech. Eng.* 70: 623.

(With J.G. Phillips) Infrared CN bands. *Astrophys. J.* 108: 163.

1949

Quadrupole rotation–vibration spectrum of the hydrogen molecule. *Nature,* 163: 170.

Laboratory absorption spectra obtained with long paths, in *The Atmospheres of the Earth and Planets*, ed. G.P. Kuiper. The University of Chicago Press, Chicago, 346.

(With L. Herzberg) Absorption spectrum of methyl iodide in the near infrared. *Can. J. Res. B*, 27: 332.

(With K.Narahari Rao) Rotation–vibration spectra of diatomic and simple polyatomic molecules with long absorbing paths. II. The spectrum of carbon monoxide below 1.2 μ. *J. Chem. Phys.* 17: 1099.

(With A.E. Douglas) The nuclear spin of ^3He. *Phys. Rev.* 76: 1529.

1950

Forbidden transitions in diatomic molecules. I. The quadrupole rotation–vibration spectrum of H_2. *Can. J. Res. A*, 28: 144.

Molecular Spectra and Molecular Structure. I. Spectra of Diatomic Molecules. D. Van Nostrand Company, New York, 2nd ed.

Rotation–vibration spectrum of the HD molecule. *Nature*, 166: 563.

(With R.D. Cowan and S.P. Sinha) Rotation–vibration spectra of diatomic and simple polyatomic molecules with long absorbing paths. IV. The spectrum of methyl fluoroform (CH_3CF_3) from, 19 μ to 0.7 μ. *J. Chem. Phys.* 18: 1538.

(With L. Herzberg) Rotation–vibration spectra of diatomic and simple polyatomic molecules with long absorbing paths. VI. The spectrum of nitrous oxide (N_2O) below 1.2 μ. *J. Chem. Phys.* 18: 1551.

(With C. Reid) Infrared spectrum and structure of the HNCO molecule. *Disc. Far. Soc.* 9: 92.

1951

(With A.Vallance Jones and L.C. Leitch) Photographic infrared spectrum of CD_3CCH and the structure of methyl acetylene. *J. Chem. Phys.* 19: 136.

The atmospheres of the planets. *J. R. Astron. Soc. Can.* 45: 100.

(With A.E. Douglas) Predissociation and the dissociation of the N_2 molecule. *Can. J. Phys.* 29: 294.

1952

(With D.A. Ramsay) Absorption spectrum of free NH_2 radicals. *J. Chem. Phys.* 20: 347.

Forbidden transitions in diatomic molecules. II. The $^3\Sigma_u^+ - {}^3\Sigma_g^-$ absorption bands of the oxygen molecule. *Can. J. Phys.* 30: 185.

Spectroscopic evidence of molecular hydrogen in the atmospheres of Uranus and Neptune. *Astrophys. J.* 115: 337.

Rotation–vibration spectra and structure of simple polyatomic molecules. *Nature,* 169: 997.

(With H.S. Heaps) Intensity distribution in the rotation–vibration spectrum of the OH molecule. *Z. Physik* (Born-Franck issue), 133: 48.

Forbidden transitions in the spectra of diatomic molecules. *Trans. R. Soc. Can.* 46: 1.

1953

(With D.A. Ramsay) The absorption spectrum of free NH_2 radicals. *Far. Soc. Disc.* 14: 11.

Forbidden transitions in diatomic molecules. III. New $^1\Sigma_u^- - {}^3\Sigma_g^-$ and $^3\Delta_u - {}^3\Sigma_g^-$ absorption bands of the oxygen molecule. *Can. J. Phys.* 31: 657.

(With J. Bardwell) Laboratory experiments on the detectability of silane (SiH_4) and methyl deuteride (CH_3D) in the atmospheres of the outer planets. *Astrophys. J.* 117: 462.

(With S. Chandrasekhar and D. Elbert) Shift of the 1^1S state of helium. *Phys. Rev.* 91: 1172.

(With L. Herzberg) Rotation–vibration spectra of diatomic and simple polyatomic molecules with long absorbing paths. XI. The spectrum of carbon dioxide (CO_2) below 1.25 μ. *J. Opt. Soc. Am.* 43: 1037.

(With P.A. Brix) The dissociation energy of oxygen. *J. Chem. Phys.* 21: 2240.

1954

(With P.A. Brix) Fine structure of the Schumann-Runge bands near the convergence limit and the dissociatin energy of the oxygen molecule. *Can. J. Phys.* 32: 110.

Table 625 and 625A of molecular constants of diatomic molecules, in *Smithsonian Physical Tables*, 9th rev. ed., 586.

1955

(With B.P. Stoicheff) The carbon–carbon and carbon–hydrogen distances in simple polyatomic molecules. *Nature,* 175: 79.

Molecular spectra. Chapter 20 in *Fundamental Formulas of Physics*, ed. Donald H. Menzel. Prentice-Hall, New York, 465.

(With C.P. Courtoy) Effect of Fermi resonance on the centrifugal stretching constants in CO_2. *J. Chem. Phys.* 23: 975.

(With S. Chandrasekhar) The energies of the ground states of He, Li^+ and O^{6+}. *Phys. Rev.* 98: 1050.

Laboratory investigations of spectra of interstellar and cometary molecules. *Mm. Soc. R. Sc. Liège*, 15: 291.

Heinrich Kayser, 1853–1940 (Obituary Notice in *Biographical Memoirs of Fellows of the Royal Society*, 1: 135.

(With T.J. Hugo) Forbidden transitions in diatomic molecules. IV. The $a'^3\Sigma - X^1\Sigma^+$ and $e^3\Sigma^- - X^1\Sigma^+$ absorption bands of carbon monoxide. *Can. J. Phys.* 33: 757.

(With D.A. Ramsay) The 7500–4500 Å absorption system of the free HCO radical. *Proc. R. Soc. A* 233: 34.

1956

Lamb shift of the 1^2S ground state of deuterium. *Proc. R. Soc. A* 234: 516.

(With J. Shoosmith) Absorption spectrum of free CH_3 and CD_3 radicals. *Can. J. Phys.* 34: 523.

(With A. Lagerqvist and E. Miescher) Fine structure analysis and mutual perturbation of the δ and β bands of the NO molecule. *Can. J. Phys.* 34: 622.

Die feinstruktur der He^+ linien 1640 Å und 4686 Å. *Z. Physik,* 146: 269.

(With A.E. Douglas and D.C. Rose) Atmospheric ozone near the North Pole, in *Vistas in Astronomy*, ed. A. Beer. Pergamon Press, London, 2: 874.

1957

(With L. Herzberg) Constants of polyatomic molecules, in *American Institute of Physics Handbook*, McGraw-Hill Inc., New York, 7–145.

Recent laboratory investigations on molecules of astronomical interest. *Mm. Soc. R. Sc. Liège*, 18: 397.

(With J.F. Hart) Twenty-parameter eigenfunctions and energy values of the ground states of He and He-like ions. *Phys. Rev.* 106: 79.

(With A.E. Douglas) Separation of overlapping orders of a concave grating spectrograph in the vacuum ultraviolet region. *J. Opt. Soc.* 47: 625.

(With K.K. Innes) Ultraviolet absorption spectra of HCN and DCN. I. The α–X and β–X systems. *Can. J. Phys.* 35: 842.

Lamb shifts in hydrogen and helium. *Physics in Canada*, 13: 8.

1958

Molecular electronic spectra. *Ann. Rev. Phys. Chem.* 9: 315.

Ionization potentials and Lamb shifts of the ground states of ^4He and ^3He. *Proc. R. Soc. A* 248: 309.

1959

Spectra of free radicals. *Proc. Chem. Soc.* (Centenary Lecture, April, 1959), 116.

(With L.L. Howe) The Lyman bands of molecular hydrogen. *Can. J. Phys.* 37: 636.

(With J. Shoosmith) Spectrum and structure of the free methylene radical. *Nature*, 183: 1801.

(With H.R. Moore) The spectrum of Li^+. *Can. J. Phys.* 37: 1293.

1960

(With R.A. Durie) Forbidden transitions in diatomic molecules. V. The rotation–vibration spectrum of the hydrogen–deuterium (HD) molecule. *Can. J. Phys.* 38: 806.

(With A. Monfils) The dissociation energies of the H_2, HD and D_2 molecules. *J. Mol. Spectrosc.* 5: 482.

1961

L'importance de la spectroscopie dans la science moderne. *Revue Universelle des Mines*, 17: 1.

(With A. Monfils and B. Rosen) Spectras moleculaires dans l'ultraviolet lointain. *Mm. Soc. R. Sc. Liège*, 4: 146.

The spectra and structures of free methyl and free methylene. *Proc. R. Soc. A* 262: 291.

The ionization potential of CH_2. *Can. J. Phys.* 39: 1511.

1962

Molecular spectra in the vacuum ultraviolet. (Bologna paper), in *Advances in Molecular Spectroscopy*. Pergamon Press, London, 29.

Report of Commission 14 of IAU. *Trans. of the IAU A*, 11: 97.

Recent work on spectra of free radicals. *ICSU Rev.* 4: 179.

1963

(With J.F. Hart) Twenty-parameter eigenfunctions and energy values of the 2^3S states of He and He-like ions. *Z. Physik*, 171: 83.

(With P.A. Warsop) Spectrum and structure of the free HNCN radical. *Can. J. Phys.* 41: 286.

Spectroscopic investigations in the vacuum ultraviolet at the National Research Council. *J. Quant. Spectrosc. Radiat. Transfer*, 2: 319.

(With J.W.C. Johns) The red bands of CH_2 and their possible importance in the spectra of the major planets. *Mm. Soc. R. Sc. Liège*, 7: 117.

Electronic spectra of simple polyatomic molecules, in *III Molecular Structure* (Proc. Robert A. Welsh Found. Conf., Nov. 1959), 123.

Determination of the structures of simple polyatomic molecules and radicals in electronically excited states. *Disc. Far. Soc.* (12th Spiers Memorial Lecture, Dundee, Apr. 1963), 35: 7.

(With H.C. Longuet-Higgins) Intersection of potential energy surfaces in polyatomic molecules. *Disc. Far. Soc.* 35: 77.

(With L. Gausset, A. Lagerqvist, and B. Rosen) Spectrum of the C_3 molecule. *Disc. Far. Soc.* 35: 113.

1964

(With R.D. Verma) Spectra and structures of the free HSiCl and HSiBr radicals. *Can. J. Phys.* 42: 395.

(With S.H. Bauer and J.W.C. Johns) The absorption spectrum of BH and BD in the vacuum ultraviolet. *J. Mol. Spectrosc.* 13: 256.

(With D.N. Travis) The spectrum and structure of the free NCN radical. *Can. J. Phys.* 42: 1658.

(With D.N. Travis) Identification of free radicals in flash photolysis. *Nature,* 204: 988.

1965

Molecular spectroscopy and astrophysical problems. *J. Opt. Soc. Am.* (Ives Medal Award Lecture, New York, 1964), 55: 229.

(With L. Gausset, A. Lagerqvist, and B. Rosen) Analysis of the 4050 Å group of the C_3 molecule. *Astrophys. J.* 142: 45.

1966

Spectra and structure of triatomic free radicals. *J. All-Union Chem. Soc. in the name of D.I. Mendeleev*, 11: 146.

Molecular Spectra and Molecular Structure. III. Electronic Spectra and Electronic Structure of Polyatomic Molecules. D. Van Nostrand Co. Inc., Princeton, N.J.

Determination of the structures of simple polyatomic molecules and radicals in electronically excited states. *Uspekhi Phis. Nauk* (Translation into Russian, 12th Spiers Memorial Lecture, Dundee, Apr. 1963), 88: 675.

(With A.M. Bass, J.D. Simmons, and S.G. Tilford) The forbidden $I^1\Sigma^- - X^1\Sigma^+$ absorption bands of carbon monoxide. *Can. J. Phys.* 44: 3039.

(With J.W.C. Johns) The spectrum and structure of singlet CH_2. *Proc. R. Soc. A* 295: 107.

1967

(With J.W.C. Johns) The spectrum and structure of the free BH_2 radical. *Proc. R. Soc. A* 298: 142.

A new predissociation of the H_2 molecule. *Sci. Light*, 16: 14.

(With A.E. Douglas) Apparatus for the observation of optical molecular spectra. *Appl. Opt.* 6: 1593.

Remarks on the diffuse interstellar lines. IAU Symp. No. 31, Academic Press, New York, 91.

(With I. Dubois and R.D. Verma) Spectrum of SiH_2. *J. Chem. Phys.* 47: 4262.

The spectra of hydrogen and their role in the development of our understanding of the structure of matter and of the universe. *Trans. R. Soc. Can.* 5: 3. (Presidential Address)

1968

Spectra and structures of triatomic free radicals, in *Advances in Photochemistry*, eds. W.A. Noyes, Jr., G.S. Hammond, and J.N. Pitts, Jr. Interscience Publ., New York, 5: 1.

Some spectral-analytical problems in astronomy. *XIII Colloquium Spectroscopicum Internationale*, (Keynote Address), Hilger, London, 3.

Spectra and structures of simple free radicals. *Chem. Ind.* 21: 474. (In Japanese, translated by T. Nakagawa.)

Absorption spectra of molecular ions. *Pont. Acad. Sci. Commentarii*, 2: 1.

Molecular absorption spectra in flash discharges. Int. Conf. on Spectroscopy, Bombay, India, Jan. 1967, Dept. of Atomic Energy, Govt. of India, 41.

(With A. Lagerqvist) A new spectrum associated with diatomic carbon. *Can. J. Phys.* 46: 2363.

1969

Forbidden transitions in diatomic molecules. *Mm. Soc. R. Sc. Liège*, 16: 121.

(With A. Lagerqvist and B.J. McKenzie) Absorption spectrum of SiH in the vacuum ultraviolet. *Can. J. Phys.* 47: 1889.

(With J.W.C. Johns) New spectra of the CH molecule. *Astrophys. J.* 158: 399.

(With A. Lagerqvist and C. Malmberg) New electronic transitions of the C_2 molecule in absorption in the vacuum ultraviolet region. *Can. J. Phys.* 47: 2735.

Dissociation energy and ionization potential of molecular hydrogen. *Phys. Rev. Letters,* 23: 1081.

1970

The dissociation energy of the hydrogen molecule. *J. Mol. Spectrosc.* 33: 147.

Predissociation and pre-ionization in diatomic and simple polyatomic molecules. *J. Chem. Phys.* 56.

(With B. Edlén, A. Olme, and J.W.C. Johns) Ionization potential of boron and the isotopic and fine structure of $2s2p^2\ {}^2\Delta$. *J. Opt. Soc. Am.* 60: 889.

(With A. Dalgarno and T.L. Stephens) A new continuous emission spectrum of the hydrogen molecule. *Astrophys. J.* 162: L49.

(With T.J. Hugo, J.D. Simmons, and S.G. Tilford) Rotational analysis of the forbidden $d^3\Delta_i - X^1\Sigma^+$ absorption bands of carbon monoxide. *Can. J. Phys.* 48: 3004.

1971

The Spectra and Structures of Simple Free Radicals: An Introduction to Molecular Spectroscopy. Cornell University Press, Ithaca, N.Y.

(With J.W.C. Johns) On the structure of CH_2 in its triplet ground state. *J. Chem. Phys.* 54: 2276.

Spectra and structures of molecular ions. *Quart. Rev.* 25: 201. (Faraday Lecture)

Beutler-Fano shape in the predissociation of H_2, in *Topics in Modern Physics*—A Tribute to Edward U. Condon, Colorado Associated University Press, Boulder, 191.

Laboratory studies of the spectra of interstellar molecules, in *Highlights of Astronomy*, ed. De Jager. D. Reidel Publishing Co., Dordrecht, 415.

1972

(With Ch. Jungen) Rydberg series and ionization potential of the H_2 molecule. *J Mol. Spectrosc*. 41: 425.

Spectroscopic studies of molecular structure. *Les Prix Nobelen, 1971*, P.A. Norstedt & Soner, Stockholm, 202. (Nobel Lecture).

Spectroscopic studies of molecular structure. *Science*, 177: 123.

Spektroskopische Untersuchung von Molekulstrukturen. *Angew. Chem*. 84: 1126. (Nobel-Vortrag)

(With L. Herzberg) Constants of polyatomic molecules, in *American Institute of Physics Handbook,* 3rd. ed. 7/185–199, McGraw-Hill Inc., New York.

1973

Einführung in die Molekülspektroskopie Die Spektren und Strukturen von einfachen freien Radikalen. Wissensch. Forschungsberichte, Reihe 1A, Bd. 74, Dr. Dietrich Steinkopff Verlag, Darmstadt.

(With H. Bredohl) The Lyman and Werner bands of deuterium. *Can. J. Phys*. 51: 867.

Experimental tests of the quantum theory of molecular hydrogen. *Pont. Acad. Sci. Commentarii*, 2: 1.

Experimental tests of the quantum theory of molecular hydrogen, in *Fundamental and Applied Laser Physics*, eds. M.S. Feld, A. Javan, and N.A. Kurnit. (Proc. Esfahan Symp., 29 Aug. – 5 Sept. 1971) John Wiley & Sons Inc., N.Y., 491.

Spectroscopy and molecular structure, in *Physics 50 Years Later,* Proc. 14 Gen. Assembly, Int. Union of Pure and Applied Phys., Natl. Acad. Sci. Washington, 101.

1974

Introductory Remarks (Vail Conference), in *Laser Spectroscopy*, eds. R.G. Brewer and A. Mooradian. Plenum Press, New York, 7.

(With H. Lew) Tentative identification of the H_2O^+ ion in comet Kohoutek. *Astron. Astrophys*. 31: 123.

(With P.A. Wehinger, S. Wyckoff, G.H. Herbig, and H. Lew) Identification of H_2O^+ in the tail of comet Kohoutek (1973f). *Astrophys. J. Letters*, 190: L43.

(With I. Dabrowski) The absorption spectrum of D_2 from 1100 to 840 Å. *Can. J. Phys*. 52: 1110.

Remarks on the boundaries of knowledge. *Trans. R. Soc. Can*. 12: 21.

1976

Experimental Tests of the Quantum Theory of Molecular Hydrogen. "Precise and Accurate Measurements in Chemistry," *Kagaku Sosetsu*, 10: 254. (Translated into Japanese by K. Ohno).

(With I. Dabrowski) The absorption and emission spectra of HD in the vacuum ultraviolet. *Can. J. Phys.* 54: 525.

Cometary spectra and related topics. *Mm. Soc. R. Sc. Liège*, Ser. 6, 11: 115.

1977

(With I. Dabrowski) The predicted infrared spectrum of HeH^+ and its possible astrophysical importance. *Trans. N.Y. Acad. Sci.* 38: 14. (A Festschrift for I.I. Rabi.)

1978

(With I. Dabrowski) The spectrum of $HeNe^+$. *J. Mol. Spectrosc.* 73: 183.

The importance and needs of Canadian research in science. *Trans. R. Soc. Can.* 16: 311.

1979

A spectrum of triatomic hydrogen. *J. Chem. Phys.* 70: 4806.

Cosmochemistry. *Chem. Ind.* 32: 93. (Translated into Japanese by E. Hirota and S. Hirota.)

(With K.P. Huber) *Molecular Spectra and Molecular Structure. IV. Constants of Diatomic Molecules.*, Van Nostrand Reinhold, New York.

1980

Astronomy and basic science. *J. R. Astron. Soc. Can.* 74: 70.

Spectroscopic studies based on the pioneering work of R.S. Mulliken. *J. Phys. Chem.* 84: 2095.

(With I. Dabrowski) The electronic emission spectrum of triatomic hydrogen. I. Parallel bands of H_3 and D_3 near 5600 and 6025 Å *Can. J. Phys.* 58: 1238.

(With J.K.G. Watson) The electronic emission spectrum of triatomic hydrogen. II. The perpendicular bands near 7100 Å. *Can. J. Phys.* 58: 1250.

The interplay of molecular spectroscopy and astronomy, in *Highlights in Astronomy*, ed. P.A. Wayman. D. Riedel Publ. Co. 5: 3. (Proc. IAU 17th Gen. Assembly).

Recent laboratory work on molecules of possible importance for interstellar studies, in *Interstellar Molecules*, ed. B.H. Andrew. IAU #87, 231.

Introduction. 21st Liège Int. Astrophys. Symp. Laboratory and Astrophysical Spectroscopy of Small Molecular Species, 8.

(With I. Dabrowski) The spectra of HeH^+ and $HeNe^+$. 21st Liège Int. Astrophys. Symp. Laboratory and Astrophysical Spectroscopy of Small Molecular Species, 341.

H_2O^+ ions in the upper atmosphere. *Ann. Geophys.* 36: 605.

1981

(With H. Lew, J.J. Sloan, and J.K.G. Watson) The electronic emission spectrum of triatomic hydrogen. III. Infrared perpendicular bands near 3600 cm^{-1}. *Can. J. Phys.* 59: 428.

Rydberg spectra of triatomic hydrogen and of the ammonium radical. *Far. Soc.* 71: 165.

Carlyle Smith Beals, 29 June 1899 – 2 July 1979, in *Biographical Memoirs of Fellows of the Royal Society,* 27: 28.

(With I. Dabrowski and K. Yoshino) The spectrum of $HeAr^+$. *J. Mol. Spectrosc.* 89: 491.

The interplay of molecular spectroscopy and astronomy. *J. Spect. Soc. Jpn.* 30: 407.

Introductory remarks. *Phil. Trans. R. Soc. Lond. A*, 303: 465.

1982

Alexander Edgar Douglas, 12 April 1916 – 26 July 1981, in *Biographical Memoirs of Fellows of the Royal Society*, 28: 90.

The electronic emission spectrum of triatomic hydrogen. IV. Visible bands near 5800 Å and infrared bands near 3950 cm^{-1}. *Can. J. Phys.* 60: 1261.

(With Ch. Jungen) High orbital angular momentum states in H_2 and D_2. *J. Chem. Phys.* 77: 5876.

Molecular hydrogen in the laboratory and in space. *Trans. R. Soc. Can.* 20: 151.

1983

Introduction to Molecular Ion Spectroscopy, in *Molecular Ions: Spectroscopy, Structure and Chemistry*, eds. T.A. Miller and V.E. Bondybey, 1.

(With J.T. Hougen) Spectra of the ammonium radical. I. The Schuster band of ND_4. *J. Mol. Spectrosc.* 97: 430.

1984

Spectra of triatomic hydrogen and of the ammonium radical. *J. Mol. Struct.* 113: 1.

Spectra of the ammonium radical: The Schuler bands. *J. Astrophys. Astron.* 5: 131.

(With I. Dabrowski) The a $^3\Sigma_g^+ - c^3\Pi_u$ and $c^3\Pi_u$ – a $^3\Sigma_g^+$ systems in the infrared spectrum of H_2 and D_2. *Acta Phys. Hungar.* 55: 219.

1985

(With P. Senn, P. Quadrelli and K. Dressler) Spectroscopic identification of the lowest vbibrational levels of the $(2p\sigma)^2F^1\Sigma_g^+$ state of the H_2 molecule. *J. Chem. Phys.* 83: 962.

R.K. Asundi Memorial Lecture—Spectra of Molecular Ions. *Proc. Indian Natl. Sci. Acad. A* 51: 495.

To Ernst Miescher, on his eightieth birthday. *Helv. Phys. Acta*, 58: 951.

Chalmers Jack Mackenzie, 1888–1984. *Proc. R. Soc. Can.* 23: 137.

Molecular spectroscopy: A personal history. *Ann. Rev. Phys. Chem.* 36: 1.

1986

(With Ch. Jungen) The 4f states of He_2: A new spectrum of He_2 in the near infrared. *J. Chem. Phys.* 84: 1181.

Rowland gratings, molecular hydrogen and space astronomy. *Vistas Astron.* 29: 201.

(With P. Senn, P. Quadrelli and K. Dressler) Spectroscopic identification of the lowest rotation–vibration levels of the $(2p\sigma)^2$ $F^1\Sigma_g^+$ state of the D_2 molecule. *J. Chem. Phys.* 85: 2384.

1987

Rydberg molecules. *Ann. Rev. Phys. Chem.* 38: 27.

1988

(With I. Dabrowski, B.P. Hurley, R.H. Lipson, M. Vervloet, and D.-C. Wang) Spectra of rare gas hydrides. I. $^2\Pi - {}^2\Sigma$ and $^2\Sigma - {}^2\Sigma$ transitions of KrH and KrD. *Mol. Phys.* 63: 269.

(With I. Dabrowski and R.H. Lipson) Spectra of rare gas hydrides. II. $^2\Pi - {}^2\Sigma$ and $^2\Sigma - {}^2\Sigma$ transitions of XeH and XeD. *Mol. Phys.* 63: 289.

Historical remarks on the discovery of interstellar molecules. *J. R. Astron. Soc. Can.* 82: 115.

1989

(With Ch. Jungen, I. Dabrowski, and D.J.W. Kendall) High orbital angular momentum states in H_2 and D_2. II. The 6h–5g and 6g–5f transitions. *J. Chem. Phys.* 91: 3926.

Reminiscences of C.V. Raman. *Prajna J.* 33: 17.

Science and the Humanities. *Chem. Ind.* (*Jpn.*), 42: 2.

1990

Molecular Astrophysics. *Spectrochim. Acta*, (50th Anniversary Edition), 63.

The history of the discovery of the spectra of CH_2 and H_3. *J. Mol. Structure*, 217: 11.

(With Ch. Jungen, I. Dabrowski, and M. Vervloet) High orbital angular momentum states in H_2 and D_2. III. Singlet–triplet splittings, energy levels and ionization potentials. *J. Chem. Phys.* 93: 2289.

1991

Essay Review: A leader of Indian science. *Notes Rec. R. Soc. Lond.* 45: 109.

1992

(With Ch, Jungen, I. Dabrowski, and M. Vervloet) The Ionization Potential of D_2. *J. Mol. Spectrosc.* 153: 11.

(With I. Dabrowski, G. DiLonardo, J.W.C. Johns, D.A. Sadovvskii, and M. Vervloet) Spectra of rare gas hydrides. IV. Three new bands of argon deuteride involving a low-lying "p" Rydberg state. *J. Chem. Phys.* 97: 7093.

1996

(With I. Dabrowski) The electronic emission spectra of triatomic hydrogen: The 6025 bands of H_2D and HD_2, in *Amazing Light: A Festschrift for Charles H. Townes' 80th Birthday*, ed. Raymond Chiao. Springer Verlag, New York, 173.

HONOURS AND AWARDS

Fellowships, Medals, Special Lectures

Mueller-Alewyn-Plakette Medal, Darmstadt	1927
Fellow, The Royal Society of Canada	1939
Médaille de l'Université de Liège	1950
Fellow, The Royal Society of London	1951
Henry Marshall Tory Medal, The Royal Society of Canada	1953
Honorary Fellow, Indian Academy of Sciences	1954
Joy Kissen Mookerjee Gold Medal, Indian Association for the Cultivation of Science	1954
Gold Medal for Achievement in Physics, Canadian Association of Physicists	1957
Honorary Fellow, National Academy of Sciences, India	1957
Medal of the Society for Applied Spectroscopy	1959
Chair Francqui, Université de Liège	1959–1960
Médaille de l'Université de Liège	1960
Médaille de l'Université de Bruxelles	1960
Corresponding Member, Société Royale des Sciences de Liège	1960
Bakerian Lecture, The Royal Society of London	1960
Spectroscopy Award, Spectroscopy Society of Pittsburgh	1962
Twelfth Spiers Memorial Lecture, Faraday Society	1963
Frederic Ives Medal, Optical Society of America	1964
Honorary Member, Hungarian Academy of Sciences	1964
Academician, Pontifical Academy of Sciences	1964
Foreign Honorary Member, American Academy of Arts and Sciences	1965
President, The Royal Society of Canada	1966–1967
Honorary Fellow, Optical Society of America	1968
Honorary Fellow, Chemical Society of London (now Royal Society of Chemistry)	1968
Foreign Associate, National Academy of Sciences, Washington	1968
Companion of the Order of Canada	1968
George Fisher Baker Non-Resident Lecturer in Chemistry, Cornell University	1968
Willard Gibbs Medal, American Chemical Society	1969
Gold Medal, Professional Institute of the Public Service of Canada	1969
Honorary Member, Society for Applied Spectroscopy	1969
Faraday Medal, Chemical Society of London	1970
Honorary Member, Royal Irish Academy	1970
Honorary Fellow, Chemical Institute of Canada	1970
Honorary Member, Spectroscopy Society of Canada	1970

Royal Medal, The Royal Society of London	1971
Linus Pauling Medal, American Chemical Society	1971
Nobel Prize in Chemistry, Swedish Royal Academy of Sciences	1971
Foreign Member, American Philosophical Society	1972
Chemical Institute of Canada Medal	1972
Chancellor, Carleton University	1973–1980
Member, International Academy of Quantum Molecular Science	1973
Honorary Fellow, Indian Chemical Society	1973
Madison Marshall Award, American Chemical Society (North Alabama Section)	1974
Foreign Fellow, Indian National Science Academy	1974
Honorary Member, La Asociacion de Quimicos Farmaceuticos de Colombia	1974
Foreign Associate, Royal Academy of Belgium	1974
Centennial Foreign Fellow, American Chemical Society	1976
Honorary Member, Japan Academy	1976
Honorary Member, Chemical Society of Japan	1978
Honorary Member, Real Sociedad Espanola de Fisica y Quimica	1978
Member, European Academy of Arts, Sciences and Humanities	1980
Foreign Member (Physics), Royal Swedish Academy of Sciences	1981
Earle K. Plyler Prize, American Physical Society	1985
Korrespondierenden Milglied Bayerische Akademie der Wissenschaften	1986
Jan Marcus Marci Memorial Medal, Czechoslovak Spectroscopy Society	1987
Minor Planet 3316=1984 CN1 officially named "Herzberg"	1987
Ohio Engineering Hall of Fame, Dayton	1990
Member of the Queen's Privy Council for Canada	1992

Honorary Degrees

LL.D	University of Saskatchewan	1953
D.Sc.	McMaster University, Hamilton	1954
D.Sc.	National University of Ireland, Dublin	1956
LL.D.	University of Toronto	1958
LL.D.	Dalhousie University	1960
D.Sc.	Oxford University	1960
LL.D.	University of Alberta	1961
D.Sc.	University of British Columbia	1964
D.Sc.	Queen's University, Kingston	1965
D.Sc.	University of New Brunswick	1966
Fil. Hed.-Dr.	University of Stockholm	1966

D.Sc.	University of Chicago	1967
D.Sc.	Carleton University, Ottawa	1967
Dr.rer.nat.	University of Göttingen	1968
D.Sc.	Memorial University, St. John's	1968
D.Sc.	York University, Toronto	1969
D.Sc.	University of Windsor	1970
D.Sc.	Royal Military College of Canada	1971
D.Sc.	Drexel University, Philadelphia	1972
LL.D.	St. Francis Xavier University, Antigonish	1972
D.Sc.	University of Montreal	1972
LL.D.	Simon Fraser University, Burnaby	1972
D.Sc.	Université de Sherbrooke	1972
D.Sc.	Cambridge University	1972
D.Sc.	McGill University, Montreal	1972
D.Sc.	University of Manitoba	1973
Dr.rer.nat.	University of Hamburg	1974
D.Sc.	University of Bristol	1975
D.Sc.	Andhra University	1975
D.Sc.	Osmania University	1976
D.Sc.	University of Delhi	1976
D.Phil.	Weizmann Institute of Science	1976
D.Sc.	University of Western Ontario, London	1976
D.Sc.	Université Laval, Québec	1979
Dr.phil.nat.	University of Frankfurt	1983
Ph.D.	University of Toledo	1984
D.Sc.	St. Mary's University, Halifax	1991

NAME INDEX

A

B

C

H

I

J

K

L

M

N

O

P

R

S

T

U

V

W

Y

Z

SUBJECT INDEX

A

B

C

D

E

F

G

H

I

J

K

L

M

N

ACKNOWLEDGEMENTS

Not surprisingly, my main thanks are reserved for Gerhard Herzberg, my mentor, colleague, and friend. During lunch at his home in December 1992 he mentioned that he liked the biographical memoir that I had written of Harry Welsh for The Royal Society, and asked me to write his. I couldn't help but laugh, saying that we couldn't forsee the future and that he might be writing mine. On my return home to Toronto, I kept thinking that such an outstanding scientist and wonderful man deserved far more than a twenty to thirty page biography, and in fact a full book would barely do him justice. This recurring idea finally convinced me to try to write his story, not only to chronicle the history of his scientific achievements but for the enjoyment of the general reader. Far too few books have been written about scientists and their accomplishments, and the story of science in Canada during the mid-1900s is not well known. After discussing this idea with my wife, I telephoned Gerhard and described my thoughts; he was most receptive, but he cautioned me "You don't know what you are getting into".

I soon learned what he meant as he gave me access to his voluminous correspondence. He had saved copies of his own letters as well as of those he had received from 1924 to 1997, and had filed them alphabetically and by year. A stack of about eight metres of letters were housed in the National Archives in Ottawa covering the period 1928 to 1976 in 56 volumes. At his NRC office, I found another six metres, along with extensive files of scientific data (which I occasionally examined), and about two more metres at his home, mainly letters to and from his close friends from 1924 to 1936 and during the 1940s, as well as diplomas, invitations, and news clippings. These extensive collections provided most of the source material, as indicated in the Notes and References. It took many visits to Ottawa to read all of this correspondence. On these occasions I also had the opportunity to discuss my archival research with Gerhard. The rapid debilitation of his memory caused by Parkinson's disease put an end to his reminiscences by early 1997.

I am most grateful to Monika Herzberg for her kind hospitality, and particularly for her assistance in providing the many files and photograph albums at her home for my study. She was instrumental in translating early letters and documents from German for me. Ursula Scheffler also kindly helped wih translations. Paul and Agnes Herzberg were especially helpful in providing me with family photographs, which I have used throughout the book. Moreover, Paul gave me access to copious notes he had taken of conversations with his father in 1992 and 1993 about the early family history, while Agnes provided anecdotes of the family, relatives, and friends.

While writing this book, I visited all of the cities, schools, and research institutes where GH had lived, studied and worked, and was overwhelmed by the ready and willing assistance of archivists and librarians. Marianne Viefhaus of the

Technische Hochschule Darmstadt Archives and Cheryl Avery of the University of Saskatchewan Archives gave generously of their time. I received much help over the years from the National Archives in Ottawa. The archives of the National Research Council Canada, Yerkes Observatory, the Universities of Bristol, Chicago, Göttingen, and the Carnegie Corporation, as well as the municipal archives of Langensalza and Göttingen, provided a lot of useful information.

I should add that in 1972, I had interviewed Gerhard extensively for a biographical sketch that I was invited to write for the Special Issue of *Physics in Canada* celebrating his receipt of the Nobel Prize. Later, Gerhard gave me copies of many interviews as well as the brief review of his research "Molecular Spectroscopy: A Personal History" published in the *Annual Reviews of Physical Chemistry* in 1985. This history was augmented by more personal touches brought out in the transcripts of taped interviews which he gave me: one by Christine King carried out in 1986 for the Beckman Center for the History of Chemistry, and another by Brenda P. Winnewisser in 1989 for the History Center of the American Institute of Physics. I also had the opportunity to interview most members of the Spectroscopy Laboratory, and many colleagues in the fields of atomic and molecular spectroscopy.

My visits to Germany would not have been as productive without the generous assistance of Herbert Walther, Director of the Max-Planck-Institute for Quantum Optics in Garching, who organized and took me on visits to Göttingen and the towns of Herzberg and Langensalza. Bruno Elschner of the THD and Peter Brix, an early postdoctoral fellow in Herzberg's laboratory and past Director of the Physics Institute at the THD, arranged for my visit to Darmstadt and the THD Archives. Takeshi Oka took me on a visit to Yerkes Observatory and Williams Bay, and prepared the way for my research at the Regenstein Library of The University of Chicago. I am most grateful to NRC President Arthur Carty for the use of Herzberg's office during my visits to Ottawa, arranged by Jim Watson, and for Izabel Dabrowski's help with office files, lists of publications and of postdoctoral fellows, visitors, and staff members of the Spectroscopy Laboratory.

I am indebted to the University of Toronto for the use of office space and facilities, and to Derek York, Pekka Sinervo, and Henry Van Driel, successive chairmen of the Department of Physics, for financial support which helped to defray travel costs to Ottawa. In the early stages, a grant from the Association for Canadian Studies provided assistance for library searches carried out efficiently by Sabina C. Watts, a Junior Fellow of Massey College at the time.

Many friends and colleagues read early drafts of one or more chapters, and their suggestions were of immense help: Gerhard and Monika read many of the early chapters, as did Paul and Agnes Herzberg; Peter Brix the chapter on the THD; and Klaus-Peter Lieb read that on Göttingen. Takeshi Oka read drafts of most of the manuscript and was instrumental in helping to review Herzberg's research. I am especially thankful for his writing of the Foreward. My wife Joan, son Peter, and Vincent M. Tovell provided cogent comments as readers of the life and times of Gerhard Herzberg. I am most grateful to all the readers for their insights and helpful comments.

I was taken by surprise when in July 2001 I received a telephone call from Keith Ingold informing me that the Editorial Board of the NRC Monograph Publishing Program had plans to begin a program on biographies of Canadian scientists. He asked whether I would be interested in submitting my manuscript to launch the program. Within a short time, discussions with Gerald J. Neville, Manager of the Program settled several matters, including co-publication with the McGill-Queen's University Press, and activities proceeded rapidly. I am thankful for the encouragement and support given by B.P. Dancik, Editor-in-Chief of NRC Press, and P.B. Cavers, Editor of the NRC Monograph Publishing Program, and particularly for the editorial assistance of Carol McKinley, Nancy Daly, Jennifer McColl, and Diane Candler.

Finally I wish to recognize and thank all those who have provided me with photographs that help to illustrate the family life and friends and colleagues of Herzberg over his lifetime and seven decades of research activity. The many family photographs were generously given to me by Monika, Agnes, and Paul Herzberg. Most of those depicting activities in the Spectroscopy Laboratory were from Hin Lew's copious collection, and spectra were reprinted from Herzberg's own files. Apart from the family photographs, the photographers and sources, when known, are noted below.

Illustration Credits

Frontispiece: by Ted Grant, NRC, courtesy NRC Archives.

Chapter 1

Hamburg, reprinted from Percy Ernst Schramm, *Neuen Generation 1648–1948 (Zweite Band)* 1964, courtesy Vandenhoeck-Ruprecht: Göttingen (p. 7).

Johanneum, courtesy Prof. Dr. Werner Selber, Hamburg (p. 9).

Chapter 2

Darmstadt, reprinted from Georg Zimmermann, *Zerstörung und Wiederaufbau der historische Mitte*, Eduard Roether Verlag, Darmstadt 1985 (p. 19).

Darmstadt houses, courtesy *Darmstädter Echo* (p. 20).

Mathildenhöhe, by the author (p. 21).

Technische Hochschule, courtesy Darmstadt University of Technology (p. 22).

Chapter 3

Institute of Physics, courtesy Göttingen Photo Museum (p. 42).

Professors (detail), courtesy University of Göttingen Archives (p. 44).

Heitler, by Walter Stoneman 1948, © Godfrey Argent, London (p. 47).

Chapter 4

H.H. Wills Laboratory, courtesy University of Bristol Archives (p. 60).

Faculty, courtesy University of Bristol Archives, with thanks to Sir M.V. Berry and Prof. R.N. Dixon (p. 62).

Chapter 5

German Day, courtesy Hesse State Archives, Darmstadt (p. 74).

Two- and three-metre spectrographs, from Wilhelm Schlink, *Die Technische Hochschule Darmstadt 1836 bis 1936*, courtesy Darmstadt University of Technology (p. 76, 77).

Chapter 8

Campus, courtesy University of Saskatchewan Archives (p. 118).

Physics Club, courtesy University of Saskatchewan Archives, with thanks to Prof. Henry Caplan (p. 122).

Chapter 9

Walter C. Murray, by R. Dill, courtesy University of Saskatchewan Archives (p. 156).

Chapter 10

Yerkes Staff, courtesy Yerkes Observatory Photography (p. 161).

Gerard Kuiper, ibid. (p. 171).

Chapter 11

Remains of THD, reprinted from Georg Zimmermann, *Zerstörung und Wiederaufbau der historische Mitte*, Eduard Roether Verlag, Darmstadt 1985 (p. 181).

Chapter 12

Aerial View of Ottawa (detail), by Alex Onoszko 1968, courtesy Ottawa Municipal Archives (p. 199).

Chapter 13

National Research Laboratories, lobby, and corridor, courtesy NRC Archives (p. 212, 213).

C.J. Mackenzie and E.W.R. Steacie, by Paul Horsdal, courtesy NRC Archives (p. 216).

Chapter 14

Herzberg, by Hans Blohm, courtesy Hans Blohm, Ottawa (p. 222).

Alex Douglas, courtesy NRC Spectroscopy Lab (p. 226).

Don Ramsay, courtesy NRC Archives (p. 228).

Hin Lew, by Hin Lew (p.229).

Costain *et al*, by Prof. Koichi Shimoda 1963 (p. 230).

Lila Howe, by Hin Lew (p. 232).

Izabel Dabrowski, courtesy Izabel Dabrowski (p. 232).

Staff, by Hin Lew (p. 234).

Ottawa River and office, by the author (p. 236).

Afternoon tea (p. 239) , party 1951 (p. 240), tea party, and Christmas party

(p. 241) by Hin Lew.
Jon Hougen, by Hin Lew (p.242).
John Johns by Dr. Dieter Hausamann, courtesy John Johns (p. 242).
Group, courtesy NRC Spectroscopy Lab, with thanks to Izabel Dabrowski and Bob McKellar (p. 243).

Chapter 15
Director (p. 248), L.E. Howlett (p. 249), Ta-You-Wu *et al* (p. 253), Keith MacDonald (p. 254), courtesy NRC Archives.

Chapter 16
Herzberg *et al*, by Hin Lew (p. 271).

Chapter 17
Göttingen colleagues, courtesy Gordon Conference, with thanks to Takeshi Oka (p. 275).
McLennan Physical Labs, courtesy University of Toronto Archives (p. 284).
Honorary Degree, by Len Hillyard, courtesy University of Saskatchewan Archives (p. 289).
Order of Canada, courtesy Canadian Government Photo Centre (p. 289).

Chapter 18
Classic texts, by the author (p. 291).

Chapter 20
Walter Herzberg, courtesy *Hamburger Abendblatt* (p. 322).
Herzberg, by Lorne Bradley, NRC, courtesy Lorne Bradley (p. 324).
Telegram greetings and welcoming office, by Hin Lew (p. 324, 325).
1971 Nobel Laureates, © Pressens Bild, Stockholm (p. 335).

Chapter 21
Student band, by L. Taylor, courtesy University of Saskatchewan Archives (p. 345).
Herzberg Labs at Carleton University, by Hin Lew (p. 348).
Sculptor, courtesy NRC Archives (p. 349).
Nobel Prize commemoration, courtesy Institute of Physics (p. 350).

Chapter 22
Discussing H_2O^+, courtesy NRC Spectroscopy Lab (p. 360).
Celebrating award of Steacie Prize, and Harold Kroto, courtesy NRC Archives (p. 361, 362).
Discussing H_3, courtesy Prof. Wolfgang Ketterle (p. 365).
Oka and Herzberg, by Dr. Michio Takami, courtesy Takeshi Oka (p. 366).
DIBS Spectrum, courtesy Drs. P. Jenniskens and F.-X. Désert (p. 367).

Chapter 23
Herzberg at blackboard, courtesy NRC Archives (p. 368).
Running start of lecture and vital lecturer, courtesy Prof. Bruno Elschner (p. 369, 370).
Queen's Privy Council, courtesy Canadian Government Photo Centre (p. 372).

Demonstration at Embassy and meeting Sakharov, courtesy *The Ottawa Citizen* (p. 375).
J.W.T. Spinks, by Les Saunders, courtesy University of Saskatchewan Archives (p. 378).
Dr. Wu, by Henry Mantsch, NRC (p. 380).
Vice-Premier, courtesy Henry Mantsch (p. 381).
Monika and Gerhard, and Herzberg at desk, by the author (p. 386, 387).
Flag at half-staff, by Agnes Herzberg (p. 388).
Epilogue
Memento and Nobel Plaza, by the author (p. 394).

ARCTIC OCEAN
ALASKA
YUKON TERRITORY
Yukon R.
ROCKY MOUNTAINS
Whitehorse
Great Bear Lake
NORTHWEST TERRITORIES
Yellowknife
Great Slave Lake
CANADA
BAFFIN I.
Davis Strait
ARCTIC CIRCLE
GREENLAND
ATLANTIC OCEAN
Hudson Strait
HUDSON BAY
NEWFOUNDLAND
LABRADOR
St. John's
BRITISH COLUMBIA
ALBERTA
SASKATCHEWAN
Churchill R.
MANITOBA
Saskatchewan R.
Lake Winnipeg
James Bay
QUEBEC
Edmonton
Calgary
Saskatoon
Regina
Winnipeg
Vancouver IS.
Vancouver
Victoria
Seattle
PACIFIC OCEAN
ONTARIO
NEW BRUNSWICK
P.E.I.
Charlottetown
Fredericton
NOVA SCOTIA
Halifax
Quebec
Ottawa R.
Montreal
St. Lawrence R.
OTTAWA
Lake Superior
Lake Huron
Toronto
Lake Ontario
Boston
Minneapolis
Lake Michigan
Buffalo
Milwaukee
Lake Erie
New York
Williams Bay
Chicago
UNITED STATES OF AMERICA